ADMINISTRATIVE ASSISTANT'S

——AND——

SECRETARY'S

HANDBOOK

THIRD EDITION

By

JAMES STROMAN

KEVIN WILSON

JENNIFER WAUSON

AMACOM

AMERICAN MANAGEMENT ASSOCIATION

New York ■ Atlanta ■ Brussels ■ Mexico City ■ San Francisco
Shanghai ■ Tokyo ■ Toronto ■ Washington D.C.

Special discounts on bulk quantities of AMACOM books are available to corporations, professional associations, and other organizations. For details, contact Special Sales Department, AMACOM, a division of American Management Association, 1601 Broadway, New York, NY 10019.
Tel.: 212-903-8316. Fax: 212-903-8083.
E-mail: specialsls@amanet.org
Web site: www.amacombooks.org/go/specialsales
To view all AMACOM titles go to: www.amacombooks.org

This publication is designed to provide accurate and authoritative information in regard to the subject matter covered. It is sold with the understanding that the publisher is not engaged in rendering legal, accounting, or other professional service. If legal advice or other expert assistance is required, the services of a competent professional person should be sought.

Library of Congress Cataloging-in-Publication Data

Stroman, James.
    Administrative assistant's and secretary's handbook / by James Stroman, Kevin Wilson, Jennifer Wauson. -- 3rd ed.
        p. cm.
    Updated ed. of: Administrative assistant's & secretary's handbook. 2nd ed.
    Includes index.
    ISBN-13: 978-0-8144-0913-8
    1. Secretaries--Handbooks, manuals, etc. 2. Office practice--Handbooks, manuals, etc. I. Wilson, K. (Kevin), 1958- II. Wauson, Jennifer. III. Stroman, James. Administrative assistant's & secretary's handbook. IV. Title.

HF5547.5.S8163 2007
651.3—dc22

2007020971

Various names used by companies to distinguish their software and other products can be claimed as trademarks. AMACOM uses such names throughout this book for editorial purposes only, with no intention of trademark violation. All such software or product names are in initial capital letters. Individual companies should be contacted for complete information regarding trademarks and registration. A list of these companies appears on pg. vi of this book.

Printing number

10 9 8 7 6 5 4 3 2 1

Special thanks to Linda Wauson
... a corporate rock star.

Contents

13. Database Management 154

14. Computer Networking 159

15. E-Mail 165

16. Using the Internet 186

17. Web Conferencing 198

18. Spreadsheet Software 206

19. Data Security 212

35. Pronunciation   458

36. Punctuation   463

37. Numerals   478

SECTION FIVE

FINANCIAL ACTIVITIES   489

38. Bookkeeping and Accounting   491

39. Business Taxes   504

40. Banking 508

41. Special Business and Financial Information for the Small Business Administrative Assistant 521

42. Weights and Measures 530

SECTION SIX
CAREER ADVANCEMENT 537

43. Your Future 539

44. Presentation Skills 546

45. Communications Skills 552

46. Office Management and Supervision 558

Index 565

Preface

One of the most important positions in any company is that of administrative assistant, also referred to as executive secretary, private secretary, personal secretary, or office administrator. The job requires versatility, skill, precision, efficiency, and a constant willingness to increase one's knowledge.

Being a top-notch administrative assistant in the business or the professional world is a satisfying and rewarding career in itself. It also provides, for those who want it, an excellent opportunity for advancement.

This handbook covers the many aspects of an administrative assistant's job—from opening the mail to handling bookkeeping, from making travel arrangements to operating computers. It's both an ideal how-to book for newcomers and a handy reminder for veterans: a compact yet comprehensive all-purpose business reference that provides the information you need quickly and concisely.

We hope that the *Administrative Assistant's and Secretary's Handbook* will sharpen your interpretation of this exciting vocation and provide you with everything you need to become a valued, competent, indispensable assistant on your way up the wonderful ladder of success.

GENERAL PROCEDURES

SECTION ONE

A good administrative assistant can be an indispensable part of any business team.

Photo by Jennifer Wauson.

1

Overview for the New Administrative Assistant

◇ WHY ARE YOU NEEDED?

As an administrative assistant, you are hired to relieve your busy employer of a great deal of work, especially the details of office procedure and other matters that do not require your employer's personal involvement. You'll act as a liaison between your boss and the rest of the company. Sometimes you'll act as a buffer. Depending on the size of the company, you may also be called on to perform tasks normally outside the secretarial role in sales, banking, billing, payroll, accounting, advertising, public relations, purchasing, and more. Everything you do for your employer must duplicate as closely as possible what he or she would do if not absorbed in work that couldn't be delegated.

Every businessperson dreams of having the perfect administrative assistant, and every administrative assistant dreams of having the perfect boss. Hopefully, you and your boss will become so well adjusted to each other that you'll work as a team, each trusting the other to carry part of the load in harmony.

◇ WHAT DO EMPLOYERS WANT?

It's helpful to know what an employer expects of a "perfect administrative assistant" so that you can present yourself at your best during both the job interview and those critical first weeks on the job. Here are a few of the most important qualities:

- **Punctuality.** An employer wants an administrative assistant who is consistently punctual and always on hand during office hours. An administrative assistant who continually arrives even a few minutes late or who is ill frequently can cause havoc in a busy office. The employer knows from experience that such an administrative assistant may not be truly interested in the work. This person will be passed over or terminated in favor of someone with greater respect for the job—an administrative assistant who is always punctual and always there when needed.

- **Dependability.** An employer considers the applicant's disposition and personality, trying to judge whether he or she is dependable. For example, would the candidate rush home at precisely 5 p.m. despite an office crisis, or would he or she take enough responsibility to volunteer to remain after hours if an emergency arises?

Figure 1–1. An administrative assistant makes copies.

Photo by Jennifer Wauson.

- **Ability to learn.** An employer wants to know the extent of the applicant's education—not only formal programs and degrees but also self-instruction and single courses. This information indicates the applicant's willingness and capacity for learning. For example, an employer may hope that you know the specific computer software the company already uses, but he or she may not be too concerned if you aren't familiar with it if you show the potential to learn quickly.

- **Willingness to follow instructions.** An employer wants a candidate who follows instructions carefully and willingly. Of course, a good administrative assistant soon takes initiative and performs certain tasks differently to save time or improve results. But the administrative assistant who always demands complete control may ultimately become unwilling to follow instructions, debating or questioning every one of the boss's directives. Though intelligent input from an administrative assistant is prized, an employer usually prefers not to argue points that he or she has already decided. The employer is concerned with more important matters than explaining all the reasons for pursuing a particular policy. Therefore, the employer looks for an administrative assistant who will execute a decision no matter how many alternatives may seem obvious, or no matter what a former boss did in the same situation. In other words, the employer wants someone whose personality will be an asset rather than a handicap.

- **Loyalty and confidentiality.** Although these qualities are impossible to discover during an interview alone, every boss wants his or her administrative assistant to possess them. In an office, there is nothing more unwelcome than the "human sieve" who constantly chatters about every conversation heard, spreads idle rumors like wildfire, and must constantly be screened from confidential projects and information. No matter how efficient, how educated, and how experienced that administrative assistant is, his or her employment will be short-lived.

■ **And something else.** A keen employer wants more in a prospective administrative assistant than these general qualifications. During an extended interview, the employer is looking for quick-wittedness, flexibility, commitment to work, a certain quality and level of conversation, and a sense of courtesy. This last attribute is essential in establishing cordial relations with clients and fellow employees.

INTERVIEW TIPS

During your interview, it is wise to be as relaxed as possible despite a natural tendency to be nervous. Appear on time, of course, and be well groomed and neatly dressed; otherwise, the appointment may be canceled at the receptionist's desk.

If you try too hard to sell yourself, you'll make a poor impression. Allow the employer to form his or her own first impression. After all, he or she knows what kind of administrative assistant is needed and, in addition, may prefer to work with a certain type of person. If you're not what the employer wants, it's better for both of you that another applicant be chosen.

During an interview, the employer may try to see where your attention is focused, asking such questions as how many sick days you used on your previous jobs and how many outside activities you engage in. Previous sick days can and will be checked, so don't lie. If you have many outside interests, mention only those that in some way contribute to your job, such as night courses or professional associations. You don't want to give the impression that you're "too busy" to work.

If you receive a job offer, the salary may be less than what you think you're worth. There's often a discrepancy between what we'd like to make and what we can make. Job applicants fresh from school, in particular, may feel this way until they become more familiar with what the market is actually paying. Before refusing a position on the basis of salary alone, first be sure you know what the salaries are for comparable secretarial and administrative assistant positions in your area and for someone with your education and experience. Then find out whether you'll be eligible for a raise after a short period of probation. Finally, consider whether the position has opportunities for increased responsibility and advancement. While it may not seem true to you right now as a job applicant, a big salary is rarely more important than professional satisfaction.

YOUR APPRENTICESHIP

Even if you are already well experienced, once you have a new position, you must be prepared to serve an apprenticeship with your new employer. Your past experience may be useful only in that it has taught you to learn quickly and to evaluate new situations. At your new office, there may be a different method for almost every daily procedure, even for distributing and opening the mail. No doubt, there will be a filing system you haven't used elsewhere. You may be asked to use letter formats, paragraphing, punctuation, and abbreviations that were vetoed by a previous employer.

You may also discover that your new boss has an extensive vocabulary with many

5

words you'll need to learn, or just the reverse—a poor vocabulary that needs your assistance. Will your new boss wish you to type a letter exactly as dictated, or do you have permission to "add to and take from"? Or will the boss furnish only the essentials of what he or she wishes to convey and request that you put the letter together in proper form yourself?

Your need to be flexible extends to the computer system in the new office. You may find many differences between the hardware and software you used in school or at a past job and what you must use now. Even an updated version of the same software package may have a different user interface and functions. You need to familiarize yourself with the new computer and software, even if it means staying after work to read the manual and to experiment.

Stimulated by your brand new environment and your past experience, you may find yourself coming up with dozens of ideas and suggestions within your first few weeks on the job. When you have a suggestion to offer, remember that it may very well have been made before and rejected for excellent reasons. When one of your ideas is refused, don't take it personally. Soon, after you're more familiar with the company and its operations, you'll be able to make a better suggestion. At the same time, don't be reluctant to give input freely when the boss asks for it.

A new employee's overeagerness to offer advice, recommend changes, and carry over methods from old jobs may just disguise a need to be recognized for his or her capability. In this situation, the best way to prove yourself is to do your best, learn quickly, follow instructions accurately and intelligently, and cooperate with fellow employees. Show consideration for others beyond the call of duty. A little extra giving will cost you absolutely nothing and will bring huge dividends in trust and friendship among your co-workers and with your employer.

Daily Routine

◇ YOUR OFFICE

Office conditions for administrative assistants vary. Your employer may be an entrepreneur working from a small office or even from home. You may find yourself in a law firm, a doctor's office, a sales office, a warehouse front office, a retail business, or a service business. Your company may have branches in several states or even several countries. The general activity of the business—selling, servicing, or perhaps manufacturing—may be located in the same area where you're expected to perform your job, or it may be far removed from where you work. All these conditions may change over time as the company does.

◇ YOUR WORKSTATION

The location and conditions of where you do your day-to-day work can be critical to how effectively you perform. Look first at how your workstation is placed physically within the entire office setup. Is there a reason your desk is where it is? Analyze the traffic patterns around and through your workspace. Do co-workers have to pass through it to get from one operation to another? Study your own work patterns. How often do you go back and forth to the filing cabinets each day? How far away from your desk are they? Do other workers share these files? Is there a more efficient way to organize the office?

You may find it helpful to draw a sketch of your office and try out alternative arrangements on paper before you make suggestions to your employer. Each proposed change must consider two questions: (1) Will you work more effectively in a different office layout? (2) Will your proposed changes affect another worker's effectiveness?

Whether or not you have input on the physical placement of your workstation, your desk and immediate workspace are yours to organize in a way that makes you comfortable and allows you to be as productive as possible. Your immediate workspace may include a desk, chairs, files, bookshelves, a credenza, and portable tables. As you arrange these items, plan a layout that considers your work habits as well as the traffic patterns for yourself, other employees, and clients.

Here are just a few factors to consider:

- **Desk chair.** Your chair should help promote good posture and back support, and it should be adjustable so you do not tire quickly. If possible, try to obtain an ergonomically designed chair.

- **Lighting.** Proper lighting is highly important in any office. Your work area should have sufficient lighting to avoid causing you eyestrain and headaches yet be positioned to minimize glare on your computer monitor.

- **Desk.** Your desk should be large enough to hold the office supplies and equipment you work with most often and to provide a clear area on which to work. Keep your most often used supplies and equipment (such as your telephone, memo pad, in-and-out box, and stapler) within easy reach when you are seated at your desk. Any reference books that you use frequently should also be easy to reach, as well as a desk reference organizer. A desk organizer with slots is useful to store various work-in-progress folders so they can be quickly found when needed.

- **Supplies.** In your own desk, keep enough frequently used supplies to last for a week. At the beginning of each week, restock your supply. Neatly arrange these materials in drawer organizers, small boxes, or other containers. Store ink pads upside down.

- **Computer.** Your computer should be on a surface apart from your desk, preferably its own desk or table. In any case, you should be able to fit your legs under this surface comfortably as you work. Power cords should be kept out of the way so you do not inadvertently disconnect them with your feet. Multiple power cables can be connected together with twist-ties.

Besides a computer, keyboard, monitor, and printer, your computer workstation will most likely also be equipped with a mouse, a good-quality mouse pad for extra traction, a modem or network card for communications and file sharing, a hard disk drive, an external storage drive, diskette or CD-ROM files, a diskette or CD-ROM storage system, and software reference manuals. Other useful accessories to help organize and protect this equipment include plastic dust covers for both the computer and keyboard when they are not in use, a computer fan to prevent overheating, an antiglare monitor cover to reduce eyestrain, and acoustical hoods for printers. All expensive office equipment such as memory typewriters and computers should be equipped with a surge protector.

If you work for a small company, you may have to arrange all these elements so they can also be used by fellow employees without interfering with your other work.

◇ OFFICE SUPPLIES

Depending on the size of the company and your own responsibilities, you may have to order office supplies for yourself, your department, or the entire business. You can purchase supplies at an office supply store in person or by ordering over the phone, by fax, or by mail from an office supply catalog. You can also use office supply websites such as Staples.com, Officemax.com, or OfficeDepot.com to order online. Purchases can be shipped or delivered.

When determining an order, do not overestimate your need. A multiple-item discount is not always useful because certain items (such as beverages and snacks) cannot be stored too long. Keep an inventory of your supplies and when you use them. A logbook is a useful way to keep a record of supply use.

In addition to everyday supplies like pens, pencils, staples, paper clips, and file folders, some items may need special consideration. For example, fax paper, computer printer toner or ink cartridges, computer diskettes, copier replacement cartridges or toner, and copier paper must be ordered with your exact office equipment in mind.

Office supplies should be kept on shelves in a supply cabinet or file cabinet. If co-workers have access to these supplies, consider labeling the shelves to help stay organized. Keep the supply storage area orderly and clean. Items that you use most often should be stored at eye level, where they are easy to see and reach. Those that might spill should be kept on the bottom shelf. Try to keep the label from the original packaging attached to the supplies; the information is helpful when reordering the item. For the same reason, keep opened reams of copier and office paper inside the wrapper, leaving the label on one end. There are many different types and weights of office paper, and some are better suited for certain applications than others. For example, most copiers work best with 20-pound uncoated paper stock. Saving the label helps ensure that you have the right product for the job.

The following is a list of common office supplies listed by type:

Audiovisual Supplies and Equipment

- Audiovisual equipment and accessories
- Binding equipment and supplies
- Business presentation tools and supplies
- Graphic arts and drafting supplies
- Laminating equipment and supplies
- Message boards, signs, and lettering
- Wallboards

Basic Supplies and Labels

- Adhesives and tape dispensers
- Cash boxes, coin handling, and key control items
- Clips, pushpins, fasteners, and rubber bands
- Correction fluid and tape
- Labels
- Mailroom supplies
- Message pads, memo books, and Post-it Notes™
- Name tags and tickets
- Paper punches and trimmers
- Safes and security items
- Stamps and stamp pads
- Staplers and staples

Breakroom and Safety

- Beverage dispensers
- Breakroom Appliances
- Coffee and hot beverages
- Cold beverages
- Cups, plates, and utensils
- First aid supplies

- Safety products
- Snacks

- Time clocks

Business Cases

- Attaché cases
- Backpacks
- Briefcases
- Business card holders and accessories
- Catalog and sample cases

- Computer and multiuse cases
- Portfolios
- Ringfolios and pad holders
- Travel accessories

Calendars and Planners

- Address books
- Appointment books
- Calendars
- Organizer book refills and accessories

- Organizer books
- Telephone books
- Wall planners

Cleaning Supplies

- Air fresheners
- Bathroom cleaners
- Brooms and dustpans
- Brushes and dusters
- Floor and carpet cleaners
- General office cleaners

- Glass cleaners
- Mops and buckets
- Soap and hand cleaners
- Sponges and squeegees
- Trash cans and liners
- Vacuums

Custom Printing

- Business and human resources forms
- Business cards
- Business stationery
- Custom stamps

- Engraved products
- Envelopes
- Labels
- Specialty imprints

Filing, Binding, and Storage

- Binder accessories
- Binders
- Boxes
- Catalog racks
- Dividers for binders
- Files
- Index cards

- Indexes
- Portfolios
- Reference systems
- Report covers
- Sheet protectors
- Tabs

Hardware

- Air purifiers
- Batteries
- Extension cords
- Fans
- Hand trucks
- Heaters
- Key control items
- Ladders and stools
- Light bulbs
- Tools
- Utility cabinets

Organizers and Desk Accessories

- Bookends
- Cord and cable management supplies
- Desk pads and blotters
- Desk trays
- Desktop and drawer organizers
- Desktop collections
- Desktop sorters
- Desktop, wall, and floor literature holders
- Hanging wall files
- Partition organizers
- Surface protectors

Paper, Forms, and Envelopes

- Blank certificates
- Business forms
- Card products
- Clipboards
- Document Covers
- Envelopes
- Notebooks
- Paper
- Paper rolls
- Photo and specialty paper
- Record-keeping materials
- Seals
- Tax forms
- Writing pads

Pens, Pencils, and Markers

- Erasers
- Highlighters
- Markers
- Pencil Sharpeners
- Pencils
- Pens

Printer and Fax Supplies

- Inkjet cartridges and supplies
- Laser toner cartridges and supplies
- Printer Ribbons
- Thermal printer supplies

Restroom Paper Goods

- Bathroom tissue
- Facial tissue
- Napkins and dispensers
- Paper towels and dispensers
- Wipes and towelettes

◇ REFERENCE WORKS

Every office should have a minimum number of reference works and other sources of information. These are invaluable in writing, taking dictation, and transcribing and help you improve your work by enlarging your knowledge of the subjects covered in correspondence or reports. By telephoning a specific question to the reference department of your local public library, you can often obtain the information you need or gather advice on how it may be found, but try to avoid problems by having good reference books in the office.

The book you are likely to consult most often is an abridged dictionary, and it should be on your desk. There are a number of good dictionaries. The one recommended here is *Merriam-Webster's Collegiate Dictionary* because it contains most of the information an administrative assistant requires for daily work: spelling, syllabication, pronunciation, meaning, usage, derivation, and even synonyms in many cases. Occasionally, *Roget's Thesaurus* may also be of value, though in a busy office there is seldom time to consult this work.

If you do most of your work on a computer, you may elect to use a software dictionary. These programs can be installed on your computer and allow you to look up word spellings, definitions, synonyms, and antonyms with the click of a mouse. If you have an Internet connection that is always on, you can use an online dictionary. Dictionary.com is an excellent online resource that allows you to look up words from within a word-processing document by typing a special combination of keys on the keyboard.

Among other reference sources, if your employer has a literary bent and inserts quotations in dictation now and then, a copy of *Bartlett's Familiar Quotations* helps prevent misquotations. You should also have a world atlas. In addition, try to have the latest edition of *The World Almanac and Book of Facts* and a good single-volume encyclopedia. A copy of *Who's Who in America* can simplify your search for the addresses of people with whom your employer might correspond (or again, you could call the reference librarian). It would also be useful to have copies of the *Directory of Directors* and *Kelly's Manufacturers and Merchants Directory* or a similar book, which appear periodically. Ask the reference librarian at your local library to advise you which are best for your purpose.

If you have an Internet connection, you'll find many reference works available online.

◇ WORK PLANNING

The first thing to do when you arrive at the office every day should be to air the rooms and regulate the heat or air conditioning (unless it's set on a permanent basis by building maintenance). Then arrange your desk for maximum efficiency, and replenish your supplies. Prepare your notebook and pencils for taking phone messages or to be ready if your employer gives you a task that requires taking notes.

Consult your desk calendar or your computer's calendar to be sure you're aware of all you must do during the day. Check your list of recurring matters: appointments, meetings, payroll dates, bill payments, and tax or insurance deadlines. Give your employer a reminder list of appointments and other activities, and prepare any material from the files he or she will need.

As part of your normal daily routine, try to order your activities in the most productive way. When you have to leave your desk to run an errand, for example, do other errands at the same time. Whenever possible, use the telephone instead of delivering a message in person (unless, of course, your employer asks you to do so). You may also use e-mail.

If you have tasks that involve mailing or shipping, plan them with pickup and delivery times in mind. Maintain a daily To-Do list on paper or in your computer, and check off each item as it is accomplished. When new projects come in, try to complete them as quickly as possible. Prioritize your work. If you have several ongoing projects and a new one comes in, ask your employer which one has the highest priority.

Each evening before you leave the office, make a list of what you need to do the following workday. Then put away all of your work and work-in-progress files, either in your desk drawers or in a filing cabinet. Work that is especially sensitive, such as client lists or accounting records, should be put away in a locked file cabinet.

Your regular routine includes keeping your work area clean. Clean out your desk drawers periodically. Your computer and other office equipment should be cleaned using a slightly damp towel. Compressed air in a can is useful for blowing dust off your computer keyboard and monitor screen. Disk-drive cleaning kits use a special diskette to clean the internal working parts.

In addition to maintaining your immediate area, schedule regular servicing for all office equipment as part of a preventive maintenance program. You do not want to wait for equipment to break down in the middle of a big project with a firm deadline. Here, the old adage is so important: An ounce of prevention is worth a pound of cure.

Finally, always be thinking of ways you can improve your own performance and the efficiency of the office. Look for problems and try to find ways to solve them. An orderly, smoothly running business has a greater chance for success, and your company's success helps ensure your own.

◇ DICTATION AND TRANSCRIPTION

Besides storing notebooks and pens in your own desk, keep a notebook, pencil, and pen in an inconspicuous place in your boss's office so you are always ready to take dictation, even if you've just looked in to announce a caller or deliver a message. You will save your boss valuable time since you won't have to retreat to your own desk for supplies.

Each day, when you begin dictation, first write the date at the top of the notebook page. When the dictation is over, write the date once more at the end, and draw a line across the page. Though there may be several dictation periods each day, you will find this notation helpful, if only in times of emergency; you will be able to refer to your notes rapidly should questions arise.

If you take dictation from more than one person, keep separate notebooks with the name of each person on the outside in a prominent place. If you are asked a question about one of the letters, you will be able to reply without hesitation, especially if you've remembered to write the date before and after each session of dictation.

During regular dictation, your employer will often include faxes, telegrams, or other communications that should be sent out promptly, though he or she may continue dictating for an hour or more before you can take care of them. In such an event, immediately after taking the dictation of the fax, telegram, or urgent letter, turn down the corner of the page in your notebook so that you can find the material as soon as you reach your desk. Occasionally, your employer may dictate a remark that you cannot hear distinctly. It's imperative that you ask your boss to repeat the statement before continuing. Accuracy is more important than an unwillingness to interrupt, and your employer will respect you the more.

When the dictation contains names of correspondents, companies, and products that are unfamiliar to you, ask if these names are in the files or whether there are explanatory papers you should have. Ask this before you close that bit of dictation, and plan to refer to those papers before transcribing your notes.

Dictation Equipment

In many offices, administrative assistants do not take dictation or use shorthand. Instead, the employer uses a dictation machine. These machines save you the job of taking dictation before transcribing the letter. While your employer is dictating into the machine, you can finish other tasks that would otherwise have to be neglected. In addition, some employers have difficulty dictating to another person but can speak into a machine with ease; therefore, their dictation is actually easier to comprehend this way.

Portable dictating machines fit into an attaché case, a purse, or even a pocket, enabling the boss to get dictation done at home or while traveling. In many cases, a small audio tape recorder is used. The tape is delivered or dropped off with you to transcribe when convenient. Transcription machines are usually larger than the recorder and include earphones and a foot pedal for conveniently pausing the tape.

In addition to tape-based recorders, a variety of digital models are available. The digital versions connect to a computer in order to transfer the audio file for transcription. Specialized software is available that allows an administrative assistant to listen to the audio files on the computer for transcription. Some systems include a foot pedal that connects to the computer for pausing the audio playback. Digital recorders typically include built-in memory for storing several hours of audio.

Voice messages can be attached to an e-mail message and listened to using speakers or headphones connected to your computer. Your boss may leave voice messages or forward voice messages from other callers that need to be transcribed. Integrated messaging allows for telephone voice messages to be forwarded to your e-mail system. To listen to the message, simply open the e-mail and press the play button. Figure 2–2 shows an e-mail containing a voice message.

Transcription

Transcription involves good typing skills, knowledge of grammar and punctuation, mastery of word-processing software, and familiarity with transcription software, as well as good formatting, proofreading, and listening skills.

If you find that you have weakness in any of these areas, work on trying to make improvement. Make sure you have the right equipment that will make the job easier. For example, purchase a foot pedal so you don't have to start and stop the recording by pressing a button or clicking your mouse. This takes your attention away from the transcription document and makes the process more tedious. Organize your work area and have reference books available. Always use effective English and sentence structure, even if the speaker on the recording didn't follow the usage rules. To familiarize yourself with the terminology, learn as much as you can about your company's business.

While transcribing your notes, always allow yourself to doubt a spelling now and then rather than hastily type what may be incorrect. When you have the slightest doubt, refer to the dictionary. If the word is one of those demons that you seemingly first have to know how to spell before you can even look it up, ask for help. Usually, at least one person in the office will welcome your inquiry. Computers, of course, have dictionaries built into them to check for spelling or typographical errors, but not every word is in every spell-check program. Be careful when you are correcting what you think is an error on your employer's part. Check a dictionary or a book on language usage, as it may be you who is mistaken.

An employer who is intelligent, well read, and well traveled will have an extensive vocabulary that he or she naturally uses in dictation. Take every opportunity to improve your own vocabulary, adding to your knowledge of language day by day. When dictation contains a word unfamiliar to you, place a large question mark on the page, and when the particular fax or letter is finished, ask your boss—without embarrassment—to spell the word for you. This shows that you want to learn and make your employer's vocabulary your vocabulary.

To improve your listening skills, remove all distractions. As you listen, focus on voice inflection in order to gain an understanding of the meaning.

Listen to a phrase or a sentence and then stop the recording and type what you've just heard. Then start the recording again and listen to another phrase or sentence. As you repeat this process, you eventually get into a rhythm that best suits your working style.

If your boss has noted on the recording that there are several corrections to make, take the time to listen before you type. You may save yourself a second typing this way, especially if your employer failed to mark the end of the letter, or if you want to estimate its length before you begin. In such a situation, perhaps you'll prefer to do a rough draft instead of merely listening. Using a rough draft is also a good idea when you begin to transcribe for a new dictator, because your ear may have to accustom itself to the new voice. A rough draft is simple to do using a computer with corrections made quickly and effortlessly.

After transcription of your notes, be sure to read over what you've typed. If there is even one error, it's better for you to find it rather than another person. With computers, corrections can be made in a second, and you can produce a perfect, well-spaced, and balanced page.

As you proof your work, check to make sure the transcription makes sense. Are there any inconsistencies to references? Is the grammar, punctuation, and formatting correct?

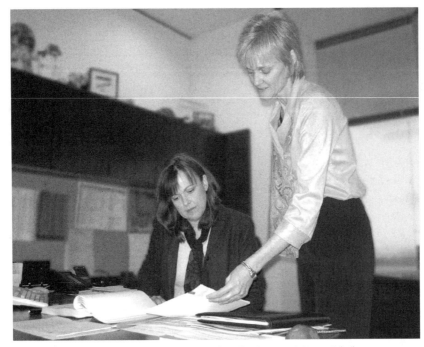

Figure 2–1. An assistant discusses the day's activities with her manager.

Photo by Jennifer Wauson.

Have you used the correct words? And of course, run a spell-checker and proof the document for typos.

◇ YOUR EMPLOYER'S OFFICE

Some employers consider their offices sacred ground that is not to be touched; others appreciate having their assistants dust and straighten up. You'll soon learn your own boss's preferences. If he or she doesn't mind, start by stacking the files being consulted and replacing those already consulted in the cabinet. Ask, however, before removing papers or documents from your boss's desk, especially those you have noticed there for quite some time. Discretion is always necessary. You must not overstep your role by touching or mentioning papers that your employer considers personal or private. In addition, many employers maintain their own unique filing system atop their desks and advise their administrative assistant not to touch those stacks unless absolutely necessary. One such necessity may be if the boss telephones from out of the office and asks you to retrieve a letter or document from atop the desk. If this happens, turn the stack to the side at the point you found the letter, so that you can later replace it exactly where it was.

When you make appointments for your employer, record them on both your boss's calendar and your own. Be sure to remind your boss of these appointments—even though they're clearly on the calendar—so that he or she won't schedule too much work, for example, on the morning of a conference.

Figure 2–2. E-mail message containing a voice message.

Screen shot courtesy of Microsoft Corporation.

◇ THE INTANGIBLES

Besides performing the usual office duties, all administrative assistants encounter many situations that are a test of character, judgment, and memory. The administrative assistant must know exactly what the employer wants kept confidential. In some instances, your employer may frankly explain when something is not for public consumption, but do not assume otherwise if he or she says nothing. When someone asks you about a confidential matter, it should never be necessary to lie. A graceful "I couldn't say," is sufficient, especially in response to those who understand and respect your position.

An administrative assistant must exercise self-control every moment, even when courtesy is strained. While on the job, you are not living your personal life but rather representing your employer. Because of this, you cannot succumb to mood swings or to criticism of those around you. You must always think before speaking and keep yourself open like an impersonal channel for the fulfillment of your role as administrative assistant. Think of how a diplomat must act while representing his or her country in a foreign land.

A great many little matters between an administrative assistant and his or her boss are left unmentioned between them. In a good working relationship, a type of telepathy develops between employer and administrative assistant. Their understanding of each other contributes to their mutual success.

CHAPTER

Telephone Usage

◇ TELEPHONE MANNERS

Administrative assistants must have a pleasing telephone personality and a well-modulated voice that conveys dignity and courtesy. Because you are not seen by the person at the other end of the line, you are judged—and more important, your employer is judged—by your telephone manners. Show interest in what is being said. Reply in clear tones, never raising your voice. Be a good listener, and know what the person at the other end of the line is saying to you.

When the telephone rings, answer it as quickly as possible. At all times, have a memo pad and pen near the telephone. If it's necessary to delay for some reason, make a polite request such as, "Please wait a moment while I check the record for you." If you must spend some time finding the desired information, offer to call back. If the caller prefers to stay on the line, put the line on hold rather than setting the telephone receiver down on your desktop.

For the sake of out-of-town visitors who may call to ask directions, keep a map of the area on a nearby wall or in a desk drawer. You can provide extra courtesy by plotting their trip from the airport or freeway.

◇ TAKING AND TRANSFERRING CALLS

If there is no switchboard, state the name of your company and your own name when answering an incoming call: "The Brown Company, Ms. Robertson speaking." If the business is large enough to have several departments and the operator has already answered the call before ringing your extension, state your department and your name: "Accounting Department, Ms. Robertson speaking." If there is no department and a call is referred to you, give only your name: "Ms. Robertson speaking."

Answering a Colleague's Telephone

When answering a colleague's extension, state the colleague's name and your own: "Ms. Scott's office, Ms. Robertson speaking." If the person called is unavailable, ask if the caller wishes to hold the line, leave a message, or call back. If the preference is to hold, go back on the line at short intervals to explain the delay, asking if the caller wishes to leave a message. (See the next section on taking messages.) If the caller decides to leave a message, be sure that the person called receives the message as soon as he or she returns.

Transferring a Call

If you can take care of the matter yourself, do not transfer the call. If you must transfer the call, first tell the caller: "Mr. Jack Phillips is in charge of insurance, and I am sure he will advise you promptly. I'll transfer you." If the transfer must be made through an operator, always provide full information so that the caller doesn't need to be questioned again: "I have Mr. Black on the line. Please connect him with Mr. Phillips in the insurance department." If the caller has not identified himself, say: "Please transfer this call to Mr. Phillips in the insurance department." If you do not know to whom the call should be directed, advise the caller: "I'll have the proper person call you back in just a few minutes."

Handling Your Boss's Calls

When answering your employer's telephone, you may sometimes discover that the caller's assistant has placed the call. In that case, say: "Thank you. Just a moment, please." Then announce the call. Your boss will pick up the telephone and wait until the person calling is connected. Never ask the administrative assistant who placed the call to put his or her employer on the line first, unless your employer is a high-ranking person requiring special consideration. When one businessperson calls another, both should be treated equally.

When you place a call for your boss, you naturally expect the assistant of the person called to put his or her employer on the line before you connect your own. If you are calling Mr. Fisk and the assistant answers, say: "Is Mr. Fisk there, please, for Ms. Barrett of the Barrett Company?" If Mr. Fisk's assistant knows the proper response, he or she will put Mr. Fisk on the line. Then you say to your employer: "Mr. Fisk is on the line, Ms. Barrett." If Mr. Fisk's assistant is not cooperative, continue to speak courteously. Return to your boss and explain that the other administrative assistant insists that Ms. Barrett go on the line before Mr. Fisk will be connected.

◇ TAKING MESSAGES

Many companies do not have a central switchboard with an operator or a computerized voice mail system. In this case, the administrative assistant is asked to answer incoming calls and place outgoing calls. It's useful for the assistant to keep an accurate written record of both, particularly incoming calls when the employer is not in the office. You should record the caller's name, telephone number, purpose of call, and any message.

When a caller has a message to leave for your employer or another employee, take the message verbatim. Write it exactly as stated, taking time and being patient with the caller. If you don't understand what the caller is saying, ask to have the message repeated. The message may be very important to your employer, and a single word omitted or out of place could make a significant difference in the meaning. If you are unfamiliar with the caller's name, ask for the spelling. Make sure you note whom the message is for.

All office supply stores have telephone message slips to make this record keeping easy (Figure 3–1 shows a typical message slip). Some message slips come in booklets with carbon copies. The original can be placed on the employer's desk. The copy is maintained in the booklet, perhaps for later use or reference if the original has been destroyed.

A major advantage of using printed telephone message slips rather than blank scraps of paper is that you are more likely to take a complete message by filling in the printed form. A telephone message slip has lines for the name of the person being called, the date and time of the incoming call, the name of the person calling, the name of that person's company or organization (if given), the caller's telephone number, and the message (if any). The last line on the slip is for your initials as the taker of the message. By placing your initials at the end, you are assuring yourself as well as your employer that the information is complete and accurate.

```
┌─────────────────────────────────────────────────────┐
│  To: _____  Urgent  [   ]    │
│                                                       │
│  Date: _____ Time: _____                  │
│                                                       │
│              WHILE YOU WERE OUT                       │
│                                                       │
│  From: _____ │
│                                                       │
│  Of: _____ │
│                                                       │
│  Phone: _____ │
│            Area Code       Number          Ext        │
│                                                       │
│      [  ] Telephoned         [  ] Please call         │
│                                                       │
│      [  ] Came to see you    [  ] Wants to see you    │
│                                                       │
│      [  ] Returned your call [  ] Will call again     │
│                                                       │
│  Message: _____ │
│  _____ │
│  _____ │
│  _____ │
│  _____ │
│                                                       │
│  Message taken by: _____ │
│                                                       │
└─────────────────────────────────────────────────────┘
```

Figure 3–1. A telephone message slip.

◇ SCREENING CALLS

Although many employees answer their own telephone, you'll be expected at one time or another to screen your boss's incoming calls. In this case, you become the judge as to whether your boss should be disturbed.

When screening calls, be extremely tactful so the caller is not affronted. You want to be able to meet the caller face-to-face the next day without feeling embarrassed about the way you treated him or her over the telephone. A simple question—"May I tell Mr. Jones who's calling?"—should encourage the caller to give a name without hesitation. If the caller refuses, explain that your employer is unable to accept a call without knowing whom it's from, and suggest that a letter be written.

Many callers ask for your employer by name and tell you the question they need answered. You then need to confer with your boss to know if screening should be done or if you should put the call through immediately.

◇ PROTECTING YOUR EMPLOYER

Don't be overly zealous in trying to "protect" your employer by screening calls when not specifically asked to do so. When a business is just getting under way, for example, many executives welcome all calls and don't want the administrative assistant to screen any potential clients. If that is the case, then simply say to the caller: "Thank you. I will connect you with Mr. Jones." Then, on your intercom telephone, tell Mr. Jones the name of the person calling.

If you answer the telephone for all of the employees in the company and a caller does not request a specific person, inquire as to the nature of the call so you can transfer it to the proper department or employee. When you realize what the caller's needs are, you could say: "Ms. Johnson in our accounting department should be able to assist you with this. I will transfer your call to her."

◇ COURTESY

All callers should be treated with great respect and a patient tone of voice. If another call comes in while you're speaking, ask the first caller to hold the line, answer the second call, ask if the second caller can hold for a moment (saying that you are on another line), and then return to the first caller. Never keep a caller waiting or on hold for any length of time. When you return to the line, thank the caller for holding. Keep in mind that his or her time is valuable.

Never put one line on hold without informing the caller, not even when two or more incoming calls arrive simultaneously and two or more lines are ringing. Many callers hang up when this happens, and your employer could very well miss a much-needed business call. You've no doubt experienced this yourself as a caller and will always retain negative thoughts concerning that company. Always have the courtesy to say, "Hello. Can you hold a moment, please?" Then wait until the caller answers yes or no. It is frustrating for a caller to be asked, "Can you hold a moment, please?" and then be cut off before he or she has had a chance to say no.

◇ TELEPHONE ETIQUETTE TIPS

The following checklist will assist you in practicing good telephone etiquette and performing your telephone answering responsibilities in a professional manner:

1. When you take a call, turn away from your computer, desk, and other work. Don't allow distractions to take your attention away from the caller.

2. Always have something available to write with.

3. Answer calls by the second or third ring.

4. Smile when you answer your calls. Even though the caller can't see it, he or she will hear the smile in your voice.

5. Use a "telephone voice" where you control your volume and speed. Speak clearly.

6. Be enthusiastic and respectful.

7. Greet the caller and identify yourself, your business, and your department.

8. Ask the caller, "To whom am I speaking?"

9. Then ask the caller, "How may I help you?"

10. Avoid unnecessary jargon and acronyms in your conversations.

11. Use the caller's name in your conversation.

12. Practice good listening skills.

13. If there is a problem, be concerned, empathetic, and apologetic.

Figure 3–2. An administrative assistant takes a message from a caller.
Photo by Linda Wauson.

14. Thank the caller for calling. Ask the caller to call again.

15. Never eat, drink, or chew gum while you are on a call.

◇ OFTEN-USED NUMBERS

Your employer no doubt uses certain personal telephone numbers regularly. You will soon memorize many of them without effort, but it's useful to keep a short alphabetical list of these numbers close to the telephone for quick consultation. The list might include numbers for the boss's spouse's workplace, the schools his or her children attend, the stores the boss and his or her family frequent, as well as their country or health clubs and the boss's physician, dentist, mechanic, accountant, and personal friends. Most office telephones can be programmed to dial frequently called numbers automatically, saving you time and effort. Some computers also have this function and can dial frequently used numbers quickly and efficiently.

On any directory that you make up, the telephone numbers opposite each name should contain the area codes. For long-distance numbers, also note the time differences between other cities and your own to avoid disturbing people at awkward times. Some assistants leave their directory fitted beneath the desk blotter or taped to a pull-out shelf of the desk. Others like to keep their desks uncluttered. Still others prefer to keep the boss's personal numbers confidential.

◇ TELEPHONE COMPANIES

Many offices have both a company that provides telephone equipment and a company that provides telephone service. The telephone equipment company is responsible for the functioning of the telephones, fax machines, and computer data lines, as well as voice mail systems. You should contact the telephone equipment company if you are experiencing problems with the telephone hardware.

Your telephone service provider may include a local service provider and a long distance provider. For many telephone users, one of the Regional Bell Operating Companies (RBOCs) provides local service. These companies include Verizon, BellSouth, Ameritech, Qwest, SBC Communications, and Southern New England Telephone. In addition, many traditional long distance companies such as Sprint, MCI, and AT&T are providing local service. Many traditional cable television companies are also providing local service.

The same confusing mixture of companies also provides long distance service. Deregulation of telephone services has opened the local service and long distance markets to anyone and everyone. Normally, your company selects a long distance provider. Any time you make a long distance call, the long distance provider provides the service and charges your account. You can use special dialing codes to have calls billed to particular long distance service providers.

Local calls are those that are made within your local calling area. For some callers, this means within your area code; however, there are limitations in some places where area codes have been divided into zones.

Some offices now rely on cellular telephones that include nationwide long distance and roaming without additional charges.

◇ DOMESTIC LONG DISTANCE CALLS

There are a variety of domestic long distance services available, ranging from direct dialing to calling cards.

Domestic Direct Dialing

When you are willing to speak with anyone who may answer, dial the number yourself. Charges for the call begin as soon as an answer is heard, including an answering machine. Long distance calls within your area code are usually dialed as 1 + seven-digit number; however, many telephone service providers now require dialing the area code as well. In fact, in many places, you must dial the area code to make a local call. Long distance calls outside your area code are dialed as 1 + area code + seven-digit number.

Domestic Operator-Assisted Calls

You need an operator's assistance if you wish to make a person-to-person call or a collect call, or to bill a call to another telephone number. For calls within your area code, dial 0 + seven-digit number. For long distance calls, dial 0 + area code + seven-digit number.

You can make a person-to-person call when you want to speak only to a specific individual. Charges for a person-to-person call do not begin to accrue until the person called answers. This service is more expensive than a direct-dialed call. To make this call, say to the operator: "I wish to make a person-to-person call to Mr. Sullivan at 212-555-7900."

If you expect the person on the other end to pay for the call, say: "This is a collect call. My name is Miss Scott for the Brown Company." If you are willing to speak to a second person if the first person is unavailable, give this information to the operator before he or she places the call. If you have reason to believe that the person called may be at another telephone number or in another city, explain that as well: "If Mr. Greene is not at 555-1860, please try 555-8430."

When billing a call to a third number, the operator usually needs to confirm the billing by calling the third number and speaking with someone authorized to approve the call. Normally, third-party billing is only necessary when you are traveling and do not have access to a calling card.

Calling Cards

Calling cards are credit cards issued by a telephone company for use in making long distance calls. To place a call using a calling card, you usually dial a toll-free access number, wait for a computer tone, then enter your calling card number followed by your password, wait for another computer tone or message, then dial the area code + seven-digit number you wish to call.

Calls made on a calling card are billed to your long distance service provider. Calls are billed by the minute. However, most companies also include a surcharge for each call you place.

◆ DOMESTIC INFORMATION

For telephone number information within your area code, dial 411. For long distance information, dial 1 + area code + 555-1212. See Table 3–1 for a list of domestic area codes.

TABLE 3–1. Domestic Area Codes by Geographic Region

Area Code	Region	Area Code	Region
205	Alabama	661	California
251	Alabama	707	California
256	Alabama	714	California
334	Alabama	760	California
907	Alaska	805	California
403	Alberta	818	California
780	Alberta	831	California
264	Anguilla	858	California
268	Antigua/Barbuda	909	California
480	Arizona	916	California
520	Arizona	925	California
602	Arizona	949	California
623	Arizona	345	Cayman Islands
928	Arizona	670	CNMI (Commonwealth of the
479	Arkansas		Northern Mariana Islands)
501	Arkansas	303	Colorado
870	Arkansas	719	Colorado
242	Bahamas	720	Colorado
246	Barbados	970	Colorado
441	Bermuda	203	Connecticut
250	British Columbia	860	Connecticut
604	British Columbia	302	Delaware
778	British Columbia	202	District of Columbia
284	British Virgin Islands	767	Dominica
209	California	809	Dominican Republic
213	California	239	Florida
310	California	305	Florida
323	California	321	Florida
408	California	352	Florida
415	California	386	Florida
510	California	407	Florida
530	California	561	Florida
559	California	727	Florida
562	California	754	Florida
619	California	772	Florida
626	California	786	Florida
650	California	813	Florida
		850	Florida

Area Code	Region	Area Code	Region
863	Florida	781	Massachusetts
904	Florida	857	Massachusetts
941	Florida	978	Massachusetts
954	Florida	231	Michigan
229	Georgia	248	Michigan
404	Georgia	269	Michigan
478	Georgia	313	Michigan
678	Georgia	517	Michigan
706	Georgia	586	Michigan
770	Georgia	616	Michigan
912	Georgia	734	Michigan
473	Grenada	810	Michigan
671	Guam	906	Michigan
808	Hawaii	947	Michigan
208	Idaho	989	Michigan
217	Illinois	218	Minnesota
224	Illinois	320	Minnesota
309	Illinois	507	Minnesota
312	Illinois	612	Minnesota
618	Illinois	651	Minnesota
630	Illinois	763	Minnesota
708	Illinois	952	Minnesota
773	Illinois	228	Mississippi
815	Illinois	601	Mississippi
847	Illinois	662	Mississippi
219	Indiana	314	Missouri
260	Indiana	417	Missouri
317	Indiana	573	Missouri
574	Indiana	636	Missouri
765	Indiana	660	Missouri
812	Indiana	816	Missouri
319	Iowa	406	Montana
515	Iowa	664	Montserrat
563	Iowa	456	NANP (North American Numbering Plan) area
641	Iowa		
712	Iowa	880	NANP area
876	Jamaica	881	NANP area
316	Kansas	882	NANP area
620	Kansas	308	Nebraska
785	Kansas	402	Nebraska
913	Kansas	702	Nevada
270	Kentucky	775	Nevada
502	Kentucky	06	New Brunswick
606	Kentucky	603	New Hampshire
859	Kentucky	201	New Jersey
225	Louisiana	551	New Jersey
318	Louisiana	609	New Jersey
337	Louisiana	732	New Jersey
504	Louisiana	848	New Jersey
985	Louisiana	856	New Jersey
207	Maine	862	New Jersey
204	Manitoba	908	New Jersey
240	Maryland	973	New Jersey
301	Maryland	505	New Mexico
410	Maryland	212	New York
443	Maryland	315	New York
339	Massachusetts	347	New York
351	Massachusetts	516	New York
413	Massachusetts	518	New York
508	Massachusetts	585	New York
617	Massachusetts	607	New York
774	Massachusetts		

Area Code	Region	Area Code	Region
631	New York	864	South Carolina
646	New York	605	South Dakota
716	New York	869	St. Kitts & Nevis
718	New York	758	St. Lucia
845	New York	784	St. Vincent & Grenadines
914	New York	423	Tennessee
917	New York	615	Tennessee
709	Newfoundland	731	Tennessee
252	North Carolina	865	Tennessee
336	North Carolina	901	Tennessee
704	North Carolina	931	Tennessee
828	North Carolina	210	Texas
910	North Carolina	214	Texas
919	North Carolina	254	Texas
980	North Carolina	281	Texas
701	North Dakota	361	Texas
902	Nova Scotia	409	Texas
216	Ohio	469	Texas
234	Ohio	512	Texas
330	Ohio	682	Texas
419	Ohio	713	Texas
440	Ohio	806	Texas
513	Ohio	817	Texas
567	Ohio	830	Texas
614	Ohio	832	Texas
740	Ohio	903	Texas
937	Ohio	915	Texas
405	Oklahoma	936	Texas
580	Oklahoma	940	Texas
918	Oklahoma	956	Texas
289	Ontario	972	Texas
416	Ontario	979	Texas
519	Ontario	868	Trinidad & Tobago
613	Ontario	649	Turks & Caicos Islands
647	Ontario	340	U.S. Virgin Islands
705	Ontario	435	Utah
807	Ontario	801	Utah
905	Ontario	802	Vermont
503	Oregon	276	Virginia
541	Oregon	434	Virginia
971	Oregon	540	Virginia
215	Pennsylvania	571	Virginia
267	Pennsylvania	703	Virginia
412	Pennsylvania	757	Virginia
484	Pennsylvania	804	Virginia
570	Pennsylvania	206	Washington
610	Pennsylvania	253	Washington
717	Pennsylvania	360	Washington
724	Pennsylvania	425	Washington
814	Pennsylvania	509	Washington
878	Pennsylvania	304	West Virginia
787	Puerto Rico	262	Wisconsin
939	Puerto Rico	414	Wisconsin
418	Quebec	608	Wisconsin
450	Quebec	715	Wisconsin
514	Quebec	920	Wisconsin
819	Quebec	307	Wyoming
401	Rhode Island	867	Yukon, NW Territories
306	Saskatchewan		
803	South Carolina		
843	South Carolina		

◇ **INTERNATIONAL LONG DISTANCE CALLS**

You can place 1 + area code + seven-digit number direct-dial calls to the United States, Canada, Bermuda, Puerto Rico, and most of the Caribbean islands. Other international calls may be dialed directly by dialing the following:

- International call dial prefix 011
- Country code—every country has a two- or three-digit country code (see the list that follows in Table 3–2)
- City code—most major international cities have a one- to five-digit city code
- Local telephone number—local numbers vary in length

TABLE 3–2. International Country Codes

Country Name	Country Code	Country Name	Country Code
Afghanistan	93	Congo	242
Albania	355	Cook Islands	682
Algeria	213	Costa Rica	506
American Samoa	684	Croatia	385
Andorra	376	Cuba	53
Angola	244	Curaçao	599
Antarctica	672	Cyprus	357
Argentina	54	Czech Republic	420
Armenia	374	Denmark	45
Aruba	297	Diego Garcia	246
Ascension Island	247	Djibouti	253
Australia	61	East Timor	670
Austria	43	Easter Island	56
Azerbaijan	994	Ecuador	593
Bahrain	973	Egypt	20
Bangladesh	880	El Salvador	503
Belarus	375	EMSAT (Mobile Satellite Service)	88213
Belgium	32	Equatorial Guinea	240
Belize	501	Eritrea	291
Benin	229	Estonia	372
Bhutan	975	Ethiopia	251
Bolivia	591	Faeroe Islands	298
Bosnia & Herzegovina	387	Falkland Islands	500
Botswana	267	Fiji Islands	679
Brazil	55	Finland	358
Brunei	673	France	33
Bulgaria	359	French Antilles	596
Burkina Faso	226	French Guiana	594
Burundi	257	French Polynesia	689
Cambodia	855	Gabon	241
Cameroon	237	Gambia	220
Cape Verde Islands	238	Georgia	995
Central African Republic	236	Germany	49
Chad	235	Ghana	233
Chatham Island (New Zealand)	64	Gibraltar	350
Chile	56	Global Mobile Satellite System (GMSS)	881
China (People's Republic)	86		
Christmas Island	618	Greece	30
Cocos-Keeling Islands	61	Greenland	299
Colombia	57	Guadeloupe	590
Comoros	269	Guantanamo Bay	5399
		Guatemala	502

Country Name	Country Code	Country Name	Country Code
Guinea-Bissau	245	Nepal	977
Guinea (PRP)	224	Netherlands	31
Guyana	592	Netherlands Antilles	599
Haiti	509	New Caledonia	687
Honduras	504	New Zealand	64
Hong Kong	852	Nicaragua	505
Hungary	36	Niger	227
Iceland	354	Nigeria	234
India	91	Niue	683
Indonesia	62	Norfolk Island	672
Inmarsat (Atlantic Ocean - East)	871	Norway	47
Inmarsat (Atlantic Ocean - West)	874	Oman	968
Inmarsat (Indian Ocean)	873	Pakistan	92
Inmarsat (Pacific Ocean)	872	Palau	680
Inmarsat SNAC	870	Palestine	970
Iran	98	Panama	507
Iraq	964	Papua New Guinea	675
Ireland	353	Paraguay	595
Israel	972	Peru	51
Italy	39	Philippines	63
Ivory Coast (Côte d'Ivoire)	225	Poland	48
Japan	81	Portugal	351
Jordan	962	Qatar	974
Kazakhstan	7	Réunion Island	262
Kenya	254	Romania	40
Kiribati	686	Russia	7
Korea (North)	850	Rwanda	250
Korea (South)	82	St. Helena	290
Kuwait	965	St. Pierre & Miquelon	508
Kyrgyz Republic	996	San Marino	378
Laos	856	São Tomé & Principe	239
Latvia	371	Saudi Arabia	966
Lebanon	961	Senegal	221
Lesotho	266	Serbia	381
Liberia	231	Seychelles Islands	248
Libya	218	Sierra Leone	232
Liechtenstein	423	Singapore	65
Lithuania	370	Slovak Republic	421
Luxembourg	352	Slovenia	386
Macau	853	Solomon Islands	677
Macedonia	389	Somalia	252
(formerly Yugoslav Republic)		South Africa	27
Madagascar	261	Spain	34
Malawi	265	Sri Lanka	94
Malaysia	60	Sudan	249
Maldives	960	Suriname	597
Mali Republic	223	Swaziland	268
Malta	356	Sweden	46
Marshall Islands	692	Switzerland	41
Martinique	596	Syria	963
Mauritania	222	Taiwan	886
Mauritius	230	Tajikistan	992
Mayotte Island	269	Tanzania	255
Mexico	52	Thailand	66
Micronesia, (Federal States of)	691	Thuraya (Mobile Satellite Service)	88216
Moldova	373	Togo	228
Monaco	377	Tokelau	690
Mongolia	976	Tonga Islands	676
Morocco	212	Tunisia	216
Mozambique	258	Turkey	90
Myanmar	95	Turkmenistan	993
Namibia	264	Tuvalu	688
Nauru	674	Uganda	256

Country Name	Country Code	Country Name	Country Code
Ukraine	380	Venezuela	58
United Arab Emirates	971	Vietnam	84
IUnited Kingdom	44	Wake Island	808
United States of America	1	Wallis & Futuna Islands	681
Universal Personal		Western Samoa	685
Telecommunications (UPT)	878	Yemen	967
Uruguay	598	Yugoslavia	381
Uzbekistan	998	Zambia	260
Vanuatu	678	Zanzibar	255
Vatican City	39	Zimbabwe	263

 SPECIAL CALLS

Calls can be made to ships, airplanes, and trains.

Ship-to-Shore Calls

You may call a ship at sea if the ship has facilities for receiving the call. Most ships do. Ask for the ship-to-shore operator.

Air-to-Ground and Ground-to-Air Calls

Some airlines provide air-to-ground and ground-to-air calls while a plane is in flight. Some planes are equipped with telephones that require the use of credit cards when placing a call from air to ground. When placing a call from ground to air, tell the long distance operator the name of the person being called, the airline (e.g., American or Delta), the flight number, the destination of the flight, and the passenger's seat number (if known).

Calls to Trains

For a message to be delivered to someone on a train, give the person's name, number or name of the train, direction the train is traveling, car and reservation number (if known), station, city and state, and arrival date and time. Say also that the message is to be delivered in care of the conductor of the train. For example:

Mr. Philip W. Wade
Care of the Conductor
AMTRAK, Westbound
Car 9, Bedroom 22
Due at LaSalle Station
Chicago, Illinois
December 1, 5:30 p.m.

Telegram Airport Delivery

When calling in a telegram to be sent to an airport for delivery to a plane passenger, provide the person's name, airline, flight number, direction of travel, airport destination, city and state, and arrival date and time. For example:

> Ms. Janet Harrold
> A Passenger
> American Airlines, Flight 88, Northbound
> Due at Chicago, Illinois—O'Hare Airport
> May 5, 1:20 p.m.

◇ VOICE MAIL ETIQUETTE

The goal of voice mail etiquette is to improve communications without being inconsiderate. With voice mail, there are two sides to the communication: the caller and the person being called. Each should follow certain guidelines.

Callers frequently become upset with "bad" voice mail systems; however, they fail to pay attention to the fact that sometimes they are "bad" callers. The following are some things for callers to consider when encountering voice mail:

- Leave a clear, concise message with a phone number.
- Provide a good time for the call to be returned.
- Unless you have indicated it is an emergency or a problem with an extreme time deadline, do not assume the person checks voice mail regularly—you should assume a call back will not be immediate.
- Remember that sometimes voice messages are lost somewhere in the system. A person may accidentally delete a message.
- Use voice mail as a way of informing a person that other communications are waiting or coming, since voice mail users frequently check voice mail more often than e-mail or the fax machine.
- Never leave confidential, inflammatory, or embarrassing messages on a voice mail message.

If your office has voice mail available, you should observe the following guidelines:

- When recording your message, keep your greeting short.
- Tell people how and when they can reach you.
- Update your message frequently to inform people of your schedule, especially if you cannot return messages quickly.
- Keep your message friendly, but don't forget professionalism.
- If you use voice mail to receive messages, check it frequently throughout the day.
- Return calls in a timely manner—don't use voice mail as a way to avoid interaction.

- Encourage your callers to leave detailed messages—you may be able to leave the answer on their voice mail without a two-way conversation.
- Respect the confidentiality of any messages you receive. Treat all voice mail messages the same way you would treat any private conversation.

◆ **ANSWERING SERVICES**

If your company uses an answering service, always let the service know when you come into the office in the morning and when you are leaving in the evening. Many services allow you to forward your telephone calls to the service, or they answer your calls automatically if you do not pick up after a set number of rings. Always leave the answering service a number where your employer can be reached in case of an emergency.

Mail Services and Shipping

Mail is an important method of communication between a company and the outside business world. The administrative assistant usually handles the daily processing of mail. This may include sorting the mail and distributing it to the proper departments or individuals. It may also include opening the employer's mail, prioritizing it, and gathering the necessary preliminary information needed to answer specific requests or solve problems.

Sending out business mail involves much more than a letter and a stamp, even when those letters are sent by the hundreds of thousands. There are larger documents and packages to be mailed, varying timetables to be met, and destinations ranging from next door to around the world. Dozens of work-saving, time-saving, money-saving strategies can help move the mail more efficiently.

A competent assistant should become acquainted with these profit-boosting moves, from the best physical ways to prepare the mail to the advantages of one mail service over another. He or she should also keep abreast of U.S. Postal Service (USPS) rules and regulations and methods of moving the mail. Neither you nor the company may need all this information at present, but companies constantly change and grow. The assistant who can fulfill a company's new mailing needs—or who knows where to get the information quickly—is invaluable.

A company is judged by the way its letters are composed and spaced on the pages, and even by the manner in which its envelopes are addressed. All of this does more than simply create a good impression; it affects whether the mail is delivered in a timely fashion.

The USPS relies on computerized mail processing machines—optical character readers (OCRs) and bar-code sorters (BCSs)—designed to increase the speed, efficiency, and accuracy of processing mail while keeping postal operating costs down. Consistently accurate delivery, faster mail turnaround, and greater profits are just some of the ways your company can benefit from this state-of-the-art system.

This high-speed equipment is programmed to "read" and sort up to thirty-six thousand pieces of mail per hour. That's ten pieces every second. But if your company's mail is not technically compatible, these sophisticated machines are not able to sort it. Your mail has to be sorted by hand, and the company misses the related benefits of the equipment.

Two factors determine whether mail is considered technically compatible: (1) mail that is "machinable" or, in other words, the right size and shape to speed with ease through the equipment, and (2) mail that is electronically "readable," or capable of being read, coded, and sorted by the equipment.

The following is a list of the most common addressing problems:

- Not enough contrast
- Script-type font used
- Address not visible through window
- Address slants
- Serif-type font—not all capital letters
- Characters touch
- Logo behind delivery address line
- Information below delivery address line

◇ How Your Company Can Receive the Benefits

There are a variety of issues related to successful mail delivery such as the size of your letters, address information and location, bar-code area, the use of windowed envelopes, and print quality.

Size

Begin by making sure that your letter mail is the proper size. Table 4–1 lists envelopes and cards with dimensions that fall between the minimums and maximums. Items of the proper size can speed through the machines without a hitch.

TABLE 4–1. Size Requirements for Envelopes and Cards

Dimensions	Minimum (inches)	Maximum (inches)
Height	3½	6⅛
Length	5	11½
Thickness	0.007	3/16 (card stock not to exceed .0095)

Envelopes or cards smaller than the minimums cannot be delivered. Letter mail larger than the maximums may be mailed, but it must bypass the OCR and be processed through slower and less efficient manual or mechanized methods. It may also be subject to a surcharge even though the postage is correct for the weight.

Figure 4–1. Diagram of OCR read area.

Courtesy of the United States Post Office.

Address Location

The OCR looks for the address within an imaginary rectangle on each piece of mail called the OCR read area (Figure 4–1). Make some quick measurements of your company's envelope stationery. The OCR does not have trouble finding the delivery address if it's located within the following boundaries:

SIDES OF THE RECTANGLE:	1/2 inch in from the right and left edges
BOTTOM OF THE RECTANGLE:	5/8 inch up from the bottom edge
TOP OF THE RECTANGLE:	2 3/4 inches up from the bottom edge

To provide the OCR with the information needed for the finest sort, put all the lines of the address within the above area. If that is not possible, it still helps to place as many address lines in the OCR read area as you can. *A WORD OF CAUTION:* Make sure no portion of the return address appears in the read area.

Lines of the Address

The OCR cannot rearrange address information that is out of proper sequence. Make sure addresses are complete, including apartment or suite numbers and proper delivery designations (e.g., street, road, avenue). Often there is, in a single city, streets with the same name—for example, Hanford Street, Hanford Court, Hanford Lane, and Hanford Avenue—so always use the proper designation.

Two-letter state abbreviations (listed in Table 4–2) should always be used because the OCR recognizes them at a glance. Do not place a period after each initial of the abbreviation—that is, use AR instead of A.R.

TABLE 4–2. Two-Letter Postal Abbreviations for States, Territories, and the District of Columbia

Abbr.	Name	Abbr.	Name
AL	Alabama	NE	Nebraska
AK	Alaska	NV	Nevada
AS	American Samoa	NH	New Hampshire
AZ	Arizona	NJ	New Jersey
AR	Arkansas	NM	New Mexico
CA	California	NY	New York
CO	Colorado	NC	North Carolina
CT	Connecticut	ND	North Dakota
DE	Delaware	MP	Northern Mariana Islands
DC	District of Columbia	OH	Ohio
FM	Federated States of Micronesia	OK	Oklahoma
FL	Florida	OR	Oregon
GA	Georgia	PA	Pennsylvania
GU	Guam	PR	Puerto Rico
HI	Hawaii	RI	Rhode Island
ID	Idaho	SC	South Carolina
IL	Illinois	SD	South Dakota
IN	Indiana	TN	Tennessee
IA	Iowa	TX	Texas
KS	Kansas	UT	Utah
KY	Kentucky	VT	Vermont
LA	Louisiana	VA	Virginia
ME	Maine	VI	Virgin Islands, U.S.
MH	Marshall Islands	WA	Washington
MD	Maryland	WV	West Virginia
MA	Massachusetts	WI	Wisconsin
MI	Michigan	WY	Wyoming
MN	Minnesota	AA	Armed Forces, the Americas
MS	Mississippi	AE	Armed Forces, Europe
MO	Missouri	AP	Armed Forces, Pacific
MT	Montana		

Table 4–3 shows common abbreviations that may be used with addresses. Do not use periods at the end of the abbreviation; instead use all uppercase letters.

TABLE 4–3. Common Abbreviations Used with Addresses

Abbr.	Word	Abbr.	Word	Abbr.	Word
AVE	Avenue	MTN	Mountain	WAY	Way
BLVD	Boulevard	PKWY	Parkway	APT	Apartment
CTR	Center	PL	Place	RM	Room
CIR	Circle	PLZ	Plaza	STE	Suite

4 ■ MAIL SERVICES

Abbr.	Word	Abbr.	Word	Abbr.	Word
CT	Court	RDG	Ridge	N	North
DR	Drive	RD	Road	E	East
EXPY	Expressway	SQ	Square	S	South
HTS	Heights	ST	Street	W	West
HWY	Highway	STA	Station	NE	Northeast
IS	Island	TER	Terrace	NW	Northwest
JCT	Junction	TRL	Trail	SE	Southeast
LK	Lake	TPKE	Turnpike	SW	Southwest
LN	Lane	VLY	Valley		

Foreign Addresses

Foreign mailings should have the country name printed in capital letters as the only information on the bottom line. The postal delivery zone, if any, should be included with the city, not after the country. For example:

> Mr. Thomas Clark
> 117 Russell Drive
> London WlP6HQ
> ENGLAND

Non-Address Information

Extraneous (non-address) printing that appears in or near the OCR read area could cause the piece of mail to be rejected. To ensure that the equipment locates and reads only the delivery address, non-address information (advertising copy, company logos, etc.) that must appear in the read area should be positioned above the delivery address line. In other words, the space below and on either side of the delivery address line within the read area should be clear of all printing and other markings not actually part of the address. Positioning such information as far away from the address as possible also helps.

Bar-Code Area

After reading an address, the OCR prints the appropriate bar code on the bottom of the piece of mail. Then, by reading the code, BCSs quickly route each envelope and card to its destination. But BCSs recognize only bar codes and reject mail that has some other type of printing where the bar code goes. Make sure the bar code area (see Figure 4–1) remains free of all markings.

Window Envelopes

If your company uses window envelopes, be certain that the entire address is always visible, even during full movement of the insert. If part of the address is hidden, the OCR rejects the envelope and sends it off for manual or mechanized processing.

Address Characters

The OCR reads most typewritten and other machine-printed addresses (see Figure 4–2). It cannot read type styles such as script, italic, and highly stylized characters. It also has trouble deciphering dot-matrix print if the dots that form each character are not touching each other. Among the best typeface designs to choose from are those known as sans serif.

Figure 4–2. Addressing your mail and packages.

Courtesy of the United States Post Office.

Print Quality and Color

Print quality is of great importance to the OCR. It quickly reads clear, sharp print but may not be able to distinguish characters that are faded, broken, or smudged. Black ink on a white background is best. Although certain color combinations are acceptable, the OCR cannot read the address if there is not enough contrast between the ink and paper. Keep the ink as dark as possible and the background as light as possible.

Spacing

Spacing between characters, words, and address lines is equally important. The OCR must see a clear vertical space between each character and each word, or it does not know where one ends and the next one begins. For similar reasons, it needs a clear horizontal space between each line of the address.

◆ POSTAL AUTOMATION: ENCODING FOR BUSINESS MAILERS

Even if an address is sharply imprinted and speeds through the OCR, the letter itself won't be deliverable if the information in the address is incorrect. If your company maintains its address list on computer, the Postal Service can help you here too. Suppose your company has an in-house list of its best customers. The Business Service Network for your area may be able to help you clean up your list and add valuable ZIP+4 (5-digit zip code plus 4-digit addendum) and carrier route information. This service is available from the USPS website at www.usps.com.

The Postal Service provides this service for your company because the benefits are mutual: for your company, more accurate and readable addresses, which provides faster sorting of mail and fewer undeliverable pieces (undeliverable Third-Class Mail is money thrown away), and for the USPS, more efficient moving of the mail, saving it money, which can then be passed onto customers by holding the line on rates.

To clean up your list, here is what you can do:

1. Standardize your address list, making sure cities match the zip codes on the list.

2. Change all characters to uppercase for increased readability by automation equipment.

3. Correct minor misspellings and add missing directions and suffixes.

4. Validate or correct each five-digit zip code.

5. Add the extra digits of ZIP+4 codes.

6. Give you a report on any address that cannot be coded. For example, you can discover which address needs an apartment or suite number to be complete or which address does not exist as given.

◆ METERING

What's the next step after addressing your company's mail with the most accurate address information? Putting on postage, of course, so you can get the mail on its way. Many small companies stamp their short letters and save longer correspondence and packages for a trip to the post office. Your company can save both time and money by instead investing in its own postage meter.

A postage meter (see Figure 4–3) offers savings for every office, not just larger ones with a heavy flow of outgoing mail. A postage meter ensures that your office does not overpay postage or underestimate it, which results in the embarrassing situation of mail arriving at clients' offices marked "postage due." It takes much less time to put metered postage on mail than it does to apply stamps, helping make more efficient use of staff time. In addition, your business correspondence moves more quickly once it leaves your office since the post office does not have to spend time canceling and post-marking the mail.

A postage meter prints postage directly onto your mail pieces (or onto a meter tape, which you apply to your mail piece). Postage meters are a very convenient way to pay for postage and track postage costs for your business or organization. They are great to have around the office for all of your mailing needs. You can send out any class of mail (except Periodicals) in any quantity at any rate with the same postage meter.

Postage meters come in all sizes. Very large mailers have big, specialized meters that fold, stuff, weigh, and meter postage onto envelopes. Some meters are small and require each mail piece to be hand-fed, which can take time. A meter manufacturer can help you decide which meter is right for your mailing needs.

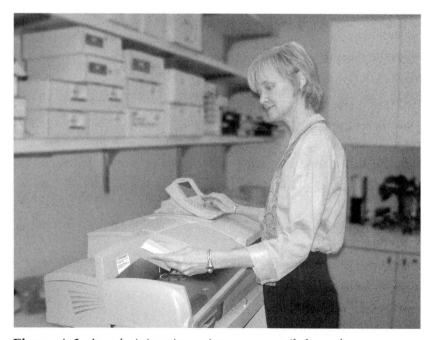

Figure 4–3. An administrative assistant runs mail through a postage meter.
Photo by Jennifer Wauson.

If you already have a postage meter and you're starting to do bulk mailing, using your meter is a smart choice. Although you can use the same postage meter for all of your mail, you must apply for a permit to use the meter for bulk mailings. Also, there are special markings required for bulk mailings that can be applied with your meter stamp. That saves you an extra step.

Postage meters and PC Postage systems generate indicia imprinted on or affixed to a piece of mail as evidence of prepayment of postage. This method of postage payment may be used on any class of mail except Periodicals. PC Postage systems access a personal computer to print postage indicia. Postage meters and PC Postage systems are available only by lease from an authorized provider. The USPS holds the provider responsible for the control, operation, maintenance, and replacement of their products. No one other than the provider may use a postage meter or PC Postage system without a valid USPS postage meter license and a rental agreement with the provider. Table 4–4 gives a list of USPS-authorized postage meter and PC Postage system providers.

TABLE 4–4. USPS-Authorized Postage Meter and PC Postage System Providers

Company	Telephone Number	Web Address
Hasler Inc.	800–995–2035	www.haslerinc.com
Francotyp–Postalia Inc.	800–341–6052	www.fpusa.net
Neopost	800–636–7678	www.neopostinc.com
Pitney Bowes Inc.	800–322–8000	www.pitneybowes.com

Guidelines for Using a Postage Meter

A postage meter can make any business more cost efficient, though using it properly is vital.

Your meter manufacturer will give you instructions on how to operate the meter and how to refill it with postage. Most of the newest systems connect directly to a telephone line and allow you to order postage and charge it to an account.

Until you presort your mail, you may not know how much postage you owe on each piece. Some mailers meter all of their pieces at the lowest rate they qualify for and then pay the difference when they bring their mail to the post office. When using this method, you may meter your mail only at the lowest of the rates you qualify for. You cannot randomly pick a number and meter your mail at that rate. The first time you do a mailing, the business mail entry unit clerk can help you fill out your postage statement to calculate how much postage you still owe.

If you know up front which pieces qualify for which rate, you can go ahead and meter them at the correct postage rate.

There are requirements for what appears in your meter imprint. Your meter manufacturer will help you comply with these requirements: (1) postage amount, (2) meter number, (3) city and state of the post office where you hold your permit, and (4) rate marking (PRSRT STD, NONPROFIT ORG, PRSRT FIRST-CLASS). First-Class Mail (single-piece and presorted) *must* show the date that the mail is deposited with the Postal Service.

If you are using meter tapes, you *must* show the month and year. No date is required for metered bulk mailings if the meter impression is placed directly on the mailing piece (Figure 4–4). If a date is shown, it must be the actual date of the mailing. Meter tape must show the month and year but not the day of the mailing.

Metered presorted and discount-rate mail must be brought to the post office where you hold your permit. Metered presorted and discount-rate mail *cannot* be dropped in a collection box or given to a carrier.

Use special postage meter fluorescent ink. Properly prepared metered mail should bypass the post office's facer/canceler machine. If metered mail inadvertently passes through the machine, fluorescent ink (known as "hot" ink in the trade) will speed the process. Use the ink provided by the meter manufacturer.

As small a thing as facing all metered envelopes up and in the same direction speeds your company's mail on its way. If the post office does not have to turn pieces over to read the address before distributing each to the proper sorting area, a costly step has been saved. In addition, package five or more pieces of metered mail securely with rubber bands, and the pieces will be handled more efficiently. Your post office can provide you with rubber bands for this purpose at no charge.

When preparing large volumes of letter-metered mail, place it in trays secured from the post office. This method creates a cleaner environment for your employees and your mail, and it helps to direct the mail to the appropriate sorting equipment to speed up the process.

If your meter's printing or recording mechanism is faulty, contact your local post office and meter manufacturer for instructions.

Figure 4–4. Examples of metered mail.

Courtesy of the United States Post Office.

◇ PACKAGING

Much of the mail you are asked to send out as an administrative assistant consists of letters and documents. But even with a mailroom on the premises, you may have to prepare and send out the occasional package yourself.

For a package to arrive in good condition at its destination, it's important to observe four basic principles in packaging your shipments:

1. *Use a corrugated container.* These "cardboard boxes" come in a variety of strengths and weights. Primarily, there are three basic types: single-wall, double-wall, and triple-wall containers. You can tell the difference by examining the sides of the box and noticing the number of layers. Single-wall containers have two outside liners and a wavy corrugated medium in the middle. Double-wall containers have two wavy corrugated mediums in the middle separated by a third liner. Triple-wall containers have three corrugated mediums and a total of four liners.

Select a box that is large enough to allow some room around the contents in every direction. This protects the contents from punctures, tears, or rips on the corners or side of the box when turning in transit.

Boxes are available from many shipping supply companies, as well as mailing and packaging chain stores. Make sure that the box can support the weight of your shipment. Every box has a stamp printed on it specifying the maximum weight it will support. Double-wall and triple-wall containers are stronger than most single-wall boxes. It is not a good idea to reuse shipping containers unless they are in good shape and will not be supporting much weight. Moisture and other shipping conditions tend to lessen the strength of corrugated containers.

To see whether a box is strong enough for mailing your item, look for the manufacturer's strength certification on the bottom of the box. The first and last measurements are the most important to you. "BURSTING TEST" shows you (in pounds per square inch) how well the fiberboard can resist rupture or breaking. "GROSS WT LT" shows you (in pounds) how much weight the box can hold. Once you know the load type, weight, and size of your item, you can use Table 4–5 to choose a box by grade if necessary.

TABLE 4–5. Box Grade Requirements

Maximum Weight of Box and Contents

Easy and Average Loads (pounds)	Difficult Loads (pounds)	Maximum Length Plus Girth (inches)	Box Grade
20	–	67	125
40	20	100	175
65	40	108	200
70	65	108	275
–	70	108	350
–	70	130	350

2. *Protect the contents*. Use wadded-up newspaper, crumpled brown grocery bags, air bubble pack, foam peanuts, or shredded paper. Depending on the contents of the package, it may be a good idea to wrap them in plastic as well to keep the packing material from sticking to them or getting inside. The packing material should be placed on the bottom, all four sides, and the top to provide several inches of protection between the contents and the sides of the box.

3. *Close the box securely*. Most shipping companies, including the USPS, do not accept boxes tied with string. Nor should you use masking tape or regular cellophane tape; neither has enough strength to keep the box closed. Instead, use carton sealing tape, pressure-sensitive place tape, water-activated paper tape, or water-activated reinforced tape. In general, you should apply three strips of tape to the top and the bottom. One strip should seal the box, and the other two strips should seal the sides.

4. *Use the proper labeling*. Make sure you include a zip code; as an added precaution, you may want to include the addressee's telephone number. Your company's return address is also important. You never know if the recipient has moved or is out of town and cannot receive your shipment. In some cases, your shipment can be held at the destination, but there are time limits on this. It's also a good idea to pack a copy of the label with all of the identifying information inside the box so if the outside label is damaged or removed, the shipper can determine the destination by opening the box.

When applying your labels to the package, always place them on the top, away from seams or box edges. Then apply several strips of clear carton sealing tape over the label to prevent it from falling off.

You should write both addresses in waterproof ink (or type them on a label), using letters that can be easily read from 30 inches away (arm's length). Ten- to 12-point type is a good size for computer-printed labels.

The address format preferred by the Postal Service uses uppercase letters and has a uniform left margin in the address block. For example:

LUIS ENSOR
23 MAPLE CT APT 4
ANYTOWN, CA 99887-7665

On the outside of your parcel, you should put special markings like those listed below. They let postal employees know the nature of the parcel's contents. But do not assume that the markings in themselves will keep your parcel from getting damaged.

- Mark "Fragile" on parcels that contain breakable items.

- Mark "Perishable" on parcels that contain food or other items that can decay or spoil.

- Mark "Do Not Bend" on parcels that contain photographs, artwork, or similar items, but only if they are protected with a stiffener like fiberboard.

You should put these special markings in three places: above the address, below the postage, and on the back or bottom of your parcel. If you prefer, ask a post office window clerk to rubber stamp your parcel with these markings.

For odd-shaped or extremely fragile objects, it's best to check with the shipping service for advice on how to package the item and the best way to send it.

Hazardous and Illegal Items

Except as permitted by mailing standards, it is illegal to send through the U.S. mail any article, composition, or material that can kill or injure a person, obstruct mail service, or damage property. Harmful matter includes but is not limited to:

- All kinds of poison or matter containing poison
- All snakes, turtles, spiders, poisonous animals (except scorpions), poisonous insects, and poisonous reptiles
- All disease germs or scabs
- All explosives, flammable material, and mechanical, chemical, or other devices or compositions that can catch fire or explode

There are also legal restrictions on who may mail the following items and how they must be prepared for mailing:

- Firearms, knives, and sharp instruments
- Drugs and narcotics
- Other controlled substances as defined by federal law and related federal regulations
- Live scorpions
- Locksmithing devices
- Vehicle master keys

Certain potentially harmful or dangerous articles and substances may be mailed if special packaging and labeling requirements are met. Contact your local postmaster for details and ask for Publication 2, *Packaging for Mailing,* or visit the U.S. Postal Service website at www.usps.com.

◇ U.S. POSTAL SERVICE MAIL SERVICES

Most of your company's mail probably goes out and comes in via the U.S. Postal Service. The following information only touches the high points of the many services it offers so you'll know they are there when needed. A complete and separate brochure is available from the USPS on each subject mentioned. USPS services change from time to time, so it's useful to call or visit a local post office occasionally. In addition, the USPS maintains a Marketing and Communications Office in large metropolitan areas to advise the public of such services and answer questions by telephone or in person.

4 ■ MAIL SERVICES

Express Mail

Express Mail is the U.S. Postal Service's fastest service. It offers guaranteed delivery service 365 days a year, including weekends and holidays. The USPS also offers Global Express Mail to some two hundred countries and territories, and is the only company to offer Express Mail Military Service at domestic prices to select Army Post Office (APO) and Fleet Post Office (FPO) addresses.

Important letters, documents, and merchandise may be sent via Express Mail. A full postage refund is made for all domestic shipments delivered later than the guaranteed commitment for that particular service.

To use Express Mail Next Day Service, you can take your shipment to any designated Express Mail post office, generally by 5 p.m.; deposit it in an Express Mail collection box; call for on-demand pickup; or hand it to your letter carrier. Your local post office can give you specific Express Mail acceptance times for your area. Depending upon the destination, your mailing is delivered to the addressee either by noon or by 3 p.m. the next day. Express Mail post office–to–post office service can also be picked up at the destination post office by 10 a.m. the next day. If you require expedited delivery but are not sure that your correspondents will be physically at the delivery address to accept and sign for the mail, you may exercise the "Waiver of Signature" option at the time of mailing.

The USPS may not be able to reach some destinations overnight and, in this case, they provide guaranteed second-day delivery service. You can get on-demand pickup and information on the delivery status of your mailing by calling 800-222-1811.

Express Mail is convenient to use. The USPS provides you with mailing containers (envelopes, boxes, and tubes) and the necessary mailing labels at no charge. Customers find the two-pound flat rate envelope convenient to use. Any amount of material that fits into it may be mailed in this special flat rate envelope. The rate of postage is the rate charged for a two-pound piece of Express Mail, regardless of the weight of the material in the envelope.

Priority Mail

When the overnight speed of Express Mail is not needed but preferential handling is desired, use Priority Mail. Priority Mail offers expedited delivery at the least expensive rate in the industry. The maximum weight for Priority Mail is 70 pounds, and the maximum size is 108 inches in length and girth combined. You also have the option of sending mail weighing less than 13 ounces as Priority Mail.

For proper handling, Priority Mail should be well identified. Your local post office can provide Priority Mail stickers, labels, envelopes, and boxes at no extra charge. For larger quantities (usually fifty), you can also order over the phone (800-610-8734) or via the Internet (supplies.usps.gov). You will find the post office's special flat rate envelope convenient to use. Any amount of material that fits into the envelope may be mailed at the regular two-pound rate regardless of the weight of the material in the flat-rate envelope.

Priority Mail can be insured, registered, certified, or sent Collect on Delivery (COD) for an additional charge.

First-Class Mail

Use First-Class Mail for sending letters, postcards, stamped cards, greeting cards, personal notes, checks, and money orders. All mail weighing more than 13 ounces sent as First-Class Mail will be handled as Priority Mail.

Additional services such as certificates of mailing and certified, registered, COD, and restricted delivery can be purchased for First-Class Mail. Insurance can also be purchased. However, insured articles mailed at the First-Class Mail rate must contain only merchandise or material not required to be sent as First-Class Mail.

All First-Class Mail receives prompt handling and transportation. If your First-Class Mail is not letter size, make sure to mark it "First-Class." First-Class Mail is generally delivered overnight to locally designated cities and within two days to locally designated states. Delivery by the third day can be expected for remaining outlying areas.

First-Class Mail in mailings of five hundred pieces or more qualifies for a postage rate discount if the mailer presorts and prepares the mail according to specific requirements. There is also a discount rate for properly presorted postcards. Pieces that cannot be presorted and prepared as required are residual mail and are paid at the full first-class letter or postcard rate.

FORWARDING FIRST-CLASS AND OTHER MAIL

First-Class Mail is forwarded at no charge for one year. Second-Class Mail, including magazines and newspapers, is forwarded at no charge for sixty days from the effective date of a change-of-address order. All post offices have information about holding mail, temporary changes of address, and forwarding and return of other classes of mail.

OTHER SPECIAL MAIL SERVICES

In addition to the services already outlined, the USPS offers a wide variety of other options to provide customers maximum convenience and to give individual pieces of mail special handling or protection.

Any piece of mail traveling by one of these special services must be so labeled. The appropriate marking (registered, insured, certified, etc.) should be placed above the delivery address and to the right of the return address.

Post Office Box and Caller Services

Post office box and caller services are available at many post offices for an annual fee. Post office box delivery is a secure and private means of getting your mail any time the post office lobby is open. With post offices conveniently located near most businesses, you can get a jump on your day by picking up your company's mail at a post office box in the morning.

Caller (pickup) service, available when post office retail windows are open, is for customers who receive a large volume of mail or those who need a box number address when no boxes are available. Call your post office for more information.

Passport Applications

You can apply for a passport at more than 1,200 postal facilities nationwide. State Department regulations require that each applicant present two recent photographs (2 inches by 2 inches), valid identification, and a certified copy of his or her birth certificate, along with the appropriate fee when applying for a new passport. The passport fee may be paid in different ways, including in cash, by check, or by money order. For additional information, call the State Department information line nearest you or your local post office.

Money Orders

Because you should *never* send cash through the mail, money orders are a safe way to send money when checks cannot be used. The special color-blend, Benjamin Franklin watermark, metal security thread, and twice imprinting of the dollar amount are incorporated security features. You can buy domestic and international money orders at all post offices in amounts up to $1,000. Military money orders can be purchased on U.S. military ships and foreign bases.

If your money order is lost or stolen, present your customer receipt and the money order can be replaced. For a small fee, you can obtain a copy of a money order for up to two years after the date it is paid.

Address Changes

Before moving from one location to another, each company or individual should obtain a Mover's Guide from the local post office. The guide includes instructions for submitting a change of address using a toll-free telephone number or by accessing the Address Change section of the USPS's website at www.usps.com.

It's best to notify the post office several weeks in advance of the move to keep the mail coming without interruption. Be sure the effective date of the change is on the notification form. Your complete new address on the notification form should include directions (North, East, South, West), the correct suffix (Street, Avenue, Road, Circle), suite number, rural route number, box number, and correct zip code or ZIP+4 code if known—all essential to proper addressing and fast delivery of your mail.

Collect on Delivery (COD) Service

Use COD service when your company wants to collect for merchandise and postage when the merchandise is delivered. COD service may be used for merchandise sent by First-Class Mail, Express Mail, Priority Mail, Third- or Fourth-Class Mail, or registered mail.

The merchandise must have been ordered by the addressee. The fee charged for this service includes insurance protection against loss or damage, although the service is limited to items valued at a maximum of $1,000. COD service is not available for international mail.

Merchandise Return Service

Merchandise return service is available to authorized parties through a special permit. The service enables one of your company's customers to return a parcel and have the postage paid by you. Under this arrangement, the company provides the customer with instructions and a special label to attach to the parcel if it must be returned. The customer applies the label to the parcel and deposits it at a post office or in a mailbox. Unless the label is provided, the customer must pay the required postage charges.

Certified Mail

Certified Mail service provides the mailer with a receipt and a record of the delivery of the item mailed from the post office from which it is delivered. No record is kept at the post office at which the item is mailed. Certified Mail is handled in the ordinary mail and is not covered by insurance. The matter mailed usually has no intrinsic value, with the sender wishing only to be sure that it has been sent to the correct point of receipt. If the item mailed does have intrinsic value, it should be sent via registered mail, *not* certified mail.

Certified Mail may be sent special delivery if additional postage is paid. An additional fee is also charged if delivery is restricted (only to the person named in the address) or if a return receipt is requested by the mailer.

Certificate of Mailing

At a fee somewhat lower than that for certified mail, a certificate of mailing can furnish evidence of mailing only. No receipt is obtained upon delivery of mail to the addressee. The fee does not insure the article against loss or damage to the item mailed.

Return Receipt

When the sender wants evidence that the mail was delivered, he or she should request a return receipt at the time the article is mailed. A return receipt can be purchased for mail that is sent COD or by Express Mail, is insured for more than $50, or is registered or certified. It identifies the article by number, the signer, and date of delivery. For an additional fee, the sender can get the addressee's correct address of delivery or can request restricted delivery service (see below).

Return receipt for merchandise service—another form of return receipt service, which provides a mailing receipt, return receipt, and record of delivery—is available for merchandise sent at First-Class, Priority, Third-Class, and Fourth-Class rates of postage.

Restricted Delivery

Restricted delivery means that the sender's mail is delivered only to the addressee or to someone authorized in writing to receive mail for the addressee. Restricted delivery is offered in connection with return receipt service and is available only for Registered Mail, Certified Mail, COD mail, and mail insured for more than $50.

Restricted delivery mail addressed to officials of government agencies, members of the legislative and judicial branches of federal and state government, members of the diplomatic corps, minors, and individuals under guardianship can be delivered to an agent without written authorization from the addressee.

Insurance

Protection against loss or damage to packages with contents valued in any amount up to $5,000 is available. The fee is based on the amount of insurance desired. Insurance can be purchased for Third- and Fourth-Class Mail, as well as for Third- and Fourth-Class matter that is mailed at the Priority Mail or First-Class Mail rate. Insurance coverage up to $25,000 can be purchased on registered mail, the most secure service offered by the Postal Service. For articles insured for more than $50, a receipt of delivery is signed by the recipient and filed at the delivery post office.

Do not over-insure your packages since the amount of insurance coverage for loss is the actual value, less depreciation. No payments are made for sentimental losses or for any expenses incurred as a result of the loss. For example, if you send a package containing a three-year-old computer that was originally purchased for $2,500, its actual value (due to depreciation) might be only $800. Even if you insured the computer for $2,500, if it were damaged or lost, the insurance would pay only the current value of $800.

Registered Mail

The most secure option offered by the post office is registered mail. Registered articles are placed under tight security from the point of mailing to the delivery office, providing added protection for valuable and important mail. Insurance may be purchased on domestic registered mail up to $25,000 at the option of the mailer. Return receipt and restricted delivery services are available for additional fees. Registered mail to Canada is subject to a $1,000 indemnity limit. For all other foreign countries, the indemnity is currently $40.45. First-Class or Priority Mail postage is required on domestic registered mail.

There are special packaging requirements for registered mail. For example, you can't send a soft-sided package, put tape over the edges, or reinforce an old box with tape. The box must be able to accept a postage ink stamp, and slick tape surfaces do not.

Special Handling

Special handling service is required for parcels whose unusual contents require additional care in transit and handling. Special handling is not required for parcels sent by First-Class Mail, Express Mail, or Priority Mail. Examples of contents requiring additional care—and thus, special handling—include live poultry or bees. Special handling is available for Standard Mail only, including insured and COD mail. This service provides preferential handling to the extent practical in dispatch and transportation.

Special handling service is not necessary for sending ordinary parcels even when they contain fragile items. Breakable items receive adequate protection if they are packed with sufficient cushioning and clearly marked "FRAGILE." Use registered mail for valuable or irreplaceable items.

INFORMATION ON THE INTERNET

A wealth of information is available at your fingertips when you visit the U.S. Postal Service's website at www.usps.com. You can look up ZIP+4 codes, track your Express Mail, get information on the latest postal rates, and find answers to frequently asked questions.

If you keep exploring, you can find postal news releases and learn about the history of the Postal Service. The Inspection Service has included information on consumer fraud and other crimes and information about the history of the Inspection Service. The website is continually changing, so you should visit often for new postal information. You also have an opportunity via the Web to make inquiries and request additional information.

ALTERNATIVES TO THE USPS

Although documents, letters, and advertisements are usually shipped through the USPS, it is likely that your company also uses an alternative form of service—for example, United Parcel Service or air express companies like FedEx or DHL. Many airlines have an air-freight express service that can transport a package from one city to another the same day. In addition, there are trucking freight shippers and even couriers that can deliver packages in town the same day. Here's a quick overview of these delivery options.

United Parcel Service

When it comes to shipping parcels, many businesses turn to United Parcel Service (UPS). UPS specializes in overnight shipping in addition to its regular package shipping service. Its freight charges are comparable to other carriers; prices vary depending on how far your package is being shipped and how much it weighs.

UPS distance charges are based on zones—both ground transportation zones and air freight zones. The ground transportation zones can also tell you approximately how many working days it will take for your package to arrive at its destination. You can determine the zone by looking up the zip code of the package's destination on a UPS zone chart. Use the UPS website (www.ups.com) to find this information and order shipping supplies. You can also print labels for your packages at the website.

There are several ways to ship via UPS:

- Take your packages directly to the nearest UPS office or UPS store. You can find the location by calling UPS at 800-PICK-UPS (800-742-5877) or by checking the website.

- Bring your package to one of the local UPS pickup stations, found at hardware stores, print shops, and office supply stores in addition to chains of mailbox and packaging stores. Because each of these locations has a specific time when the UPS truck arrives to pick up packages, be sure you know when it is before you make the drop-off. You also may want to note that some of these local pickup stations as well as mailbox and packaging stores charge a surcharge on top of the regular shipping costs.

- Call UPS and ask to have your package picked up at your location. Normally, UPS schedules the package pickup for the next day. When calling, you need the weight and dimensions of each package, along with the delivery address. The operator gives you a price for the shipment, which you have to pay by cash or check when the package is picked up. There is a small additional charge for the pickup service.

- If you set up a UPS account for your office, you can schedule shipments for the same day by phone or by using the UPS website. You do not have to provide specific information about your packages, and the cost is charged to your account. There may be a surcharge for pickup.

- Register with UPS for regular weekday pickups. This is the ideal choice for a company that does a lot of shipping. To make the arrangement, meet with a UPS representative, register your company, and pay a small deposit, usually based on the company's normal expected monthly shipping bill. UPS then provides a shipping kit that contains various supplies. With these materials you can prepare your own shipments for a pickup each day. In addition to the shipping charges, there is a small weekly pickup fee, paid whether you have any outgoing packages or not.

UPS Services

The following is a list of UPS services:

- **UPS Next Day Air Early A.M.**—Guaranteed delivery to major U.S. cities by 8 a.m., and most others by 8:30 a.m. on weekdays and 9 a.m. on Saturdays. In addition, 8:30 a.m. delivery is available for most major international cities.

- **UPS Next Day Air**—Overnight money-back guarantee on delivery of letters, documents, and packages to all major U.S. metropolitan areas.

- **UPS Next Day Air Saver**—3 p.m. delivery for commercial destinations and end-of-day for residential locations for packages shipped within the continental United States and from Alaska.

- **UPS 2nd Day Air A.M.**—Guaranteed delivery by noon on the second business day for commercial deliveries in the continental United States. The service is also available from Alaska and Hawaii to the forty-eight states.

- **UPS 2nd Day Air**—Economical, guaranteed second business day delivery of letters and packages.

- **UPS 3 Day Select**—Guaranteed three-day delivery. Developed primarily for longer-distance shippers who need time-definite delivery and higher levels of information, it is priced between traditional ground and air express services. The service is available to any shipper for delivery throughout the contiguous forty-eight states.

- **UPS Ground**—Guaranteed time-definite delivery that applies to commercial ground service throughout the contiguous forty-eight states.

- **UPS Worldwide Express Plus**—Guaranteed delivery of documents and packages to more than 150 cities in Europe by 8:30 a.m. on the second business day. In addition, there is guaranteed overnight delivery by as early as 8 a.m. to thousands of U.S. cities from Europe, Asia, Canada, Mexico, and Puerto Rico.

- **UPS Worldwide Express**—For urgent international shipments, a door-to-door, customs-cleared delivery to more than two hundred countries and territories. There is guaranteed overnight delivery of documents from major U.S. cities to the world's most important business centers. Document and non-document shipments to other destinations worldwide are typically delivered in two business days.

- **UPS Worldwide Saver**—For delivery by the end of the day in more than two hundred countries. There is next day delivery to Canada and Mexico, and second-day delivery to Europe and Latin America.

- **UPS Worldwide Expedited**—For routine shipments that don't require express delivery, a time-definite alternative that is faster than traditional air freight. This is a door-to-door, customs-cleared service available to major trading countries. Shipments to most major destinations in Canada and Mexico are delivered in three business days and to Europe and Asia in four business days.

- **UPS Standard Service**—For routine shipments to and from Canada, this is a prompt, dependable service with low-cost, fully tracked ground delivery. Service is available to every address in all of Canada's provinces.

FedEx

FedEx Express and FedEx Ground offer a wide variety of package shipping services ranging from overnight letters to ground freight. You can set up an account for FedEx by calling 800-GoFedEx (800-463-3339) or by visiting the website at www.fedex.com.

FedEx services include:

- **FedEx Express: U.S.**—For fast, reliable, time-definite delivery.

- **FedEx Express: International**—For shipping to more than 220 countries door-to-door by specific delivery times.

- **FedEx Express Freight**—For time-definite delivery of packages that weigh between 151 and 2,200 pounds.

- **FedEx Express Freight International**—For time-definite delivery of high-volume international shipments in twenty-four to seventy-two hours to major global markets.

- **FedEx Ground–U.S.**—For cost-effective, day-definite delivery for business-to-business packages.

4 ■ MAIL SERVICES

- **FedEx International Ground**—For door-to-door delivery in three to seven days from the United States to Canada and Puerto Rico.

- **FedEx Home Delivery**—For deliveries to residences at extended hours, competitive ground rates, and backed by a money-back guarantee.

To ship a package with FedEx, follow these steps:

1. Pack your shipment in FedEx packaging or your own packaging. Shipping supplies, such as overnight letter envelopes, boxes, and shipping forms, can be ordered or picked up from one of many conveniently located FedEx locations. They can also be ordered from the FedEx website.

2. Log on to the www.fedex.com website and select a service. Then create a shipping label by filling out the same, address, and phone number of the recipient. You can print a shipping label on your laser or ink-jet printer.

3. Drop off your package at the nearest self-service FedEx Drop Box, staffed service center, FedEx Authorized Ship Center, or select post office locations around the country. You can locate one of the more than 48,000 drop-off locations using the www.fedex.com website. You can also schedule a pickup and have FedEx come to your business to get your package. No prequalification is needed for a FedEx pickup; however, there is a small surcharge added to the shipping cost.

DHL

DHL is an overnight document and package shipping service that offers a variety of services. You can call 800-CALL-DHL (800-225-5345) to set up an account or visit their website at www.dhl.com.

On DHL's website, you can save time and money by processing your U.S. and international shipments online. On the website you can:

- Prepare and print shipping labels and international documentation.
- View a cost and service estimate before sending your shipment.
- Send an e-mail to the recipient with the air bill number and a link for tracking.
- Track, view, edit, and void shipments.
- Schedule pickups.
- Store frequently used contacts in your personal address book.
- View reports on shipping history.
- Find drop box locations and shipping centers.

Whether you are shipping across town or across the country, DHL offers a wide array of options including:

- **DHL Same Day Service**—For urgent delivery on the next available flight.
- **DHL Next Day 10:30 am**—For guaranteed delivery by 10:30 a.m.
- **DHL Next Day 12:00 pm**—For overnight delivery by 12 p.m. the next business day.

- **DHL Next Day 3:00 pm**—For overnight delivery by 3 p.m. the next business day.
- **DHL 2nd Day**—For delivery by 5 p.m. on the second business day throughout the United States.
- **DHL Ground**—For delivery throughout the United States in one to six business days.

DHL also offers a wide range of international shipping options, including same day service. Details can be found at the DHL website.

Other Shipping Services

Air Freight

For special situations such as large packages or packages that must be delivered to another city the same day, air freight services are available from many airlines and specialty air freight companies. Some have special offices at the airport for same day shipments. These shipments must usually be dropped off at the freight office and picked up at the destination freight office. The fees are much higher than other next-day air and two-day air shipments.

Trucking Freight

For large shipments and heavy or bulky packages, there are many trucking companies that specialize in hauling freight. These companies load the shipment at your place of business, transport it to the destination, and unload it for a fee that is usually competitive. Depending on what you are shipping and where it is going, coast-to-coast shipping can take anywhere from seven to twenty-one days.

Courier Services

If you need to ship a package across town within a few hours, your best bet is a courier service. These companies operate in most large towns and cities and provide pickup and delivery within a few hours. The prices for these services vary depending on the distance traveled and the weight and size of the package. Most of the time, the charge is paid in advance by the sender. Courier services are bonded against theft or damage.

For documents and other small items, many taxi companies also provide a courier-type service. Check your telephone book for courier services or taxi services.

Travel Arrangements

◇ TODAY'S BUSINESS TRAVELER

In today's competitive market, companies routinely buy and sell products and services both across the country and around the world. Because of this, business-related travel is common to every type and every size of company.

A small business just getting under way may have interest only in local markets; however, as the business grows and expands, a larger domestic market and possibly international markets will be of greater interest. Thus, as a business grows and an owner's needs increase, your administrative duties will include keeping abreast of how to handle your employer's travel needs quickly and efficiently, no matter how far he or she goes.

Even if you work for a larger company that has an in-house travel department, it's useful to know the following procedures to troubleshoot for your boss when needed.

◇ GETTING THE TRIP UNDERWAY

Your main purpose in making travel arrangements is to get your boss to his or her destination and back home again as smoothly as possible. Speed and cost may be other considerations. If you are a new administrative assistant or new to a particular office, see what the policies and precedents for making travel arrangements are. You may find helpful information in the files. There may even be a step-by-step procedures manual to consult, or you may find a special intranet Web page that contains travel information. If such information is not readily available, ask your boss whether to use a travel agency or to make the arrangements without an agent.

Whether you're going to do it yourself or are collecting information for the travel agent, be sure to determine the following basics:

- What is the purpose of the trip?
- What are the desired departure and return times and dates?
- What is the point-by-point itinerary?
- Will the boss be traveling alone, or will other staff members or family members be traveling along?
- What type of transportation does your boss desire? What is the best means of transportation available at that particular destination? If you're not sure, a travel agent

may help you with some of this information even if arrangements are ultimately not made through the agency.

- What is the lodging facility closest to the activities of the trip? If your boss's appointments are scattered throughout the city, perhaps a downtown hotel or an airport hotel or motel would be preferred.

If your employer travels frequently, you should use the Official Airline Guide (OAG), which is available on the Internet at www.oag.com. It includes both domestic and international flight information, hotels, maps, and other useful travel information.

◆ DOING IT YOURSELF

Many employers ask administrative assistants to arrange travel services and not use a travel agent. If this is the case, first have your boss confirm basic departure and return times and dates, and then proceed to make the reservations.

Hotel Reservations

If the meeting is in a major city, make the lodging reservations without delay—by phone or on the Internet—because city hotels are often fully booked weeks in advance. State your employer's name, office or home address, telephone number, type of accommodation preferred (single room, two-bedroom suite, etc.), plus your own name as the contact person. Ask for written confirmation, which your boss should carry when traveling in case he or she arrives only to be told that no such reservation exists.

Some hotels also make airport shuttle or limousine reservations. If your boss needs either of these, make a reservation now. Have the date and the exact time of day the shuttle or limousine is needed, and give that information to the hotel reservation person. Again, ask for written confirmation to be mailed, faxed, or e-mailed to you with the room reservation information.

Hotels hold room reservations only until a specific deadline, typically 6 p.m. You can extend the reservation beyond that time limit by guaranteeing payment whether or not the boss arrives. To do this, you must give the hotel reservation person a credit card number. Remember that if the boss changes his or her mind about making the trip or staying at that hotel, the room charge has to be paid anyway, since you've guaranteed arrival. However, most hotels and motels allow you to cancel a guaranteed reservation without charge if you cancel before 6 p.m. on the day of arrival.

What if you aren't able to make a reservation in the hotel of your boss's choice? You may be able to use a travel agency for this service alone. Large travel agencies often have a number of hotel and motel rooms blocked and held exclusively for them, a practice especially common at conventions. Select an agency that's very large, perhaps choosing on the basis of telephone classified ads if you don't have a personal recommendation. Call and explain your problem. The travel agent will usually be eager to assist you, with the hope you'll eventually become a regular client.

All of this presumes you know which hotel to choose. If your boss is traveling to a city he or she has never visited before or is going to a convention that does not recommend a particular hotel, investigate your choices using the Internet. You may also write to or call the convention bureau or chamber of commerce in that city or secure a local newspaper, both of which can provide much valuable information. If your boss has a favorite hotel chain, you can call the national reservations center for the chain or go to its website and find out if they have a hotel in the city your boss will be visiting. You can then make reservations using the national reservations center or website.

◇ **TRANSPORTATION RESERVATIONS**

Airline

Call the preferred airline's reservation office by consulting your telephone directory for a toll-free 800 number. If you're unable to find one, call 800 telephone information at 800-555-1212.

As soon as you're in touch with the airline, you can instantly make a reservation and usually secure a preferred seat and/or car reservations as well. Advise the reservations agent of the company's or employer's credit card number and whether the ticket and reservations information should be electronic, mailed, or held for pickup.

You can also make reservations with the airline on the Internet by going to its website. Airline reservations made on the website may be less expensive than those made by phone.

The following is a list of major airlines:

- Aer Lingus
- Aeromexico
- Air Canada
- Air China
- Air France
- Air Jamaica
- Air New Zealand
- AirTran Airways
- Alaska Airlines
- Alitalia
- All Nippon Airways
- America West
- American Airlines
- Asiana Airlines
- ATA
- Austrian Airlines
- BMI British Midland
- British Airways
- Cathay Pacific
- China Airlines
- Continental
- Delta
- El Al
- EVA Airways
- Finnair
- Frontier Airlines
- Hawaiian Airlines
- Iberia
- Icelandair
- Japan Airlines
- JetBlue
- KLM
- Korean Air
- Lan Chile
- LOT Polish Airlines
- Lufthansa
- Malaysia Airlines
- Mexicana
- Midwest Express
- Northwest
- Qantas Airways
- SAS
- Southwest Airlines
- Spirit Airlines
- Sun Country Airlines
- Swiss International Air Lines
- Thai Air International
- United
- US Airways
- Virgin Atlantic

Electronic Tickets

Electronic tickets, or e-tickets, allow travel without a paper ticket. An e-ticket confirms your airline ticket purchase without requiring a paper record. The only record of an e-ticket sale is in electronic form in the airline's computer system. Many airlines prefer e-tickets and charge extra for issuing paper tickets.

Airport security and airline check-in locations require you to provide a government-issued photo ID, such as a driver's licence. In addition, when flying on an e-ticket, you must have one of the following documents indicating a flight departure for the current date:

1. An e-ticket receipt (including ticket number)

2. An itinerary (including ticket number)

3. A boarding pass

This information is required in order to enter the secured area beyond the security screening checkpoint. Passengers who do not need to check baggage and already have an approved document (outlined above) may proceed through the security checkpoint directly to the departure gate. The printed documentation you present at the airport must include your airline ticket numbers. Ticket numbers are displayed on your itinerary as well as your e-ticket receipt.

Some employers require paper receipts for business travel expense reports. Some companies accept printouts of confirmation e-mails, but check your company's policy to find out what is acceptable documentation.

Train

In days gone by, rail travel was the way to go, with comfortable Pullman compartments and dining cars with fine food graciously served. But today, with time being money, more and more executives prefer air travel. Still, there are executives who either prefer not to fly or genuinely enjoy leisurely travel such as that provided by Amtrak. Railway travel is usually done when there is adequate time and easy access to rail terminals.

If your employer prefers rail travel, obtain a schedule for Amtrak trains as well as for commuter lines and connecting lines from the nearest rail station or at the Amtrak website at www.amtrak.com. A call to Amtrak at 800-USA-RAIL (800-872-7245) will also answer your questions.

Automobile

Contact the preferred car rental company through its website or by calling its reservation office by consulting your telephone directory for a toll-free 800 number. If you're unable to find one, call 800 telephone information at 800-555-1212. Many car rental companies have frequent renter programs that speed up the rental process both when making reservations and when picking up a car. Check with your employer to find out which car rental company is preferred and whether or not he or she has a frequent renter membership. The following is a list of the major car rental companies:

- Advantage
- Alamo
- Avis
- Budget
- Dollar

- Enterprise
- Hertz
- National
- Payless
- Thrifty

Car rentals are handled much the same way as hotel reservations. You need to provide a credit card in order to guarantee the reservation. You also need to know the following in order to make a car rental reservation:

- City
- Specific rental location in the city
- Car pickup time

- Car drop-off time
- Car class

Check with your employer to determine the car class. A variety of car classes are available for rental including:

- Economy
- Compact
- Midsize
- Standard
- Full size

- Premium
- Luxury
- Convertible
- Mini-van
- Sports utility vehicle (SUV)

USING A WEB-BASED TRAVEL SERVICE

You can book travel yourself using a Web-based travel service such as Priceline, Orbitz, Travelocity, or Expedia.com. These Web-based travel services allow you to make both personal and business travel reservations for airlines, hotels, car rentals, cruises, and other vacation packages.

With a Web-based travel service, you can create a traveler profile for your employer, so that his or her personal preferences regarding airline seats, hotels, car rental agencies, hotel rooms, and so forth are stored for all future trips. You can also instantly create an itinerary that can be printed on your computer's printer. In addition, you can print maps and driving directions.

USING A TRAVEL AGENCY

A good travel agency is invaluable to the busy administrative assistant. Few other outside services provide more time-saving help. A competent agency can provide a host of services. It can recommend hotels and make reservations; make airline, ship, and rail reservations; take advantage of special fares you may not be aware of; issue tickets;

make car rental reservations; assist in securing passports and visas; provide tickets to shows, the theater, sporting events, or a special event occurring in one or more of the cities on the itinerary; and mail all these tickets and reservation information directly to you.

Usually, travel agencies do not charge your company a fee for making these reservations since their commissions are paid directly by the hotels; however, some do add a small surcharge for airline tickets. A charge may also be made for rail reservations, unless the reservation is part of a prearranged package tour. Refunds for any unused tickets can also be obtained by the agency. In addition, a travel agency can often help solve problems that occur during your employer's stay. Even small agencies often have a toll-free 800 number, making it convenient for either you or the boss to call from anywhere.

After you've compiled an itinerary for your boss and know his or her exact travel needs and desires, a telephone call to a travel agency may be all that's needed. This will save you an incredible amount of time from the moment your employer leaves home or the office to the time of return.

Finding a Reputable Agent

To find a reputable travel agent, ask administrative assistants in other companies or your own company for a recommendation, or obtain a list of agencies from the following professional organization:

> American Society of Travel Agents
> 1101 King Street, Ste. 200
> Alexandria, VA 22314
> TEL: 703-739-2782
> FAX: 703-684-8319
> www.astanet.com

Many good and reputable agents do not belong to this society, so do not discount a recommended agency simply because it's not a member. If you need further sources of agencies, consult your classified telephone directory. If you wish, ask if the agency can give you the name of one or more business clients as references.

Once you've found a good travel agent, use that same person whenever possible every time your employer travels. The agent will soon become familiar with your boss's travel habits and travel needs, making it easier to arrange trips. A rapport between you and the agent will be to your employer's advantage and perhaps to your own when your own vacation time comes around.

Making the Arrangements

To establish a good relationship between you, your employer, and your travel agent, always have all the facts ready when you call. If you're not sure what your employer needs, you cannot expect the agent to know. But once you do have complete information, the agent can begin to find the best schedules, the best fares, and the best hotels and hotel rates. The facts you should have ready for the agent include:

- Your name and the traveler's name
- The traveler's office address and office telephone number
- Date and time of departure and of return
- The traveler's preferences: specific carrier, if desired; general time of departure, such as early morning or evening; general time of return; and type of service desired, such as first-class, coach, and smoking or nonsmoking
- The traveler's home telephone number
- The traveler's frequent flyer number(s)
- Your home telephone number (in case an emergency should arise, such as a change in return-flight time or a return-flight cancellation, and the boss needs to be notified while away)

Quickly and efficiently, a good travel agent provides you with confirmation of your reservations, the advised check-in time, the travel time, and estimated time of arrival. These services may be paid for with a credit card. The airline tickets and reservation confirmation forms can be picked up or mailed to you, as you wish.

◇ THE ITINERARY

An itinerary—that is, a written travel agenda—is useful to both the executive and the administrative assistant who remains in the office. Quick reference to it can be made when questions arise. Perhaps the executive has forgotten the address or time for an appointment, or perhaps the administrative assistant, faced with a sudden emergency, needs to know exactly where the employer can be contacted.

Before preparing the written itinerary, confer with your boss, making notes of all activities on the trip. Show your employer a draft of the written schedule so that changes can be made or forgotten items added. Once the itinerary has been completed, it can be typed on small pocket-size cards or on plain paper. Figure 5–1 contains a sample itinerary.

Paul Grome
Itinerary

Monday, June 1 (Dallas to New York)

8:00 AM	Leave Dallas residence by limousine for airport. (Limousine reservation attached.)
9:00 AM	Leave DFW Airport on American Airlines Flight 122, Seat 1B. (Ticket attached.)
12:40 AM	Arrive New York, JFK Airport. Limousine to Americana Hotel. (Limousine reservation attached.)
2:30 PM	Don Daley, president of Bryant Industries, will provide car for trip to his office, Chase Manhattan Plaza, Suite 1000. (Bryant Industries file in briefcase.)

Tuesday, June 2

9:00 AM   Appointment with Henderson, Smith & Jackson, Empire State Building, Suite 8000.

10:30 AM   Appointment with Mary Louise Henderson. (Henderson, Smith & Jackson file in briefcase.)

2:00 PM   Appointment with August Terrell, your hotel; meet in lobby. (Terrell Corporation file in briefcase.)

7:00 PM   Dinner, Don Daley's home (5203 Legendary Lane, New York; Telephone 212-555-6120).

Wednesday, June 3

7:45 AM   Leave hotel by limousine for airport. (Limousine reservation attached.)

9:45 AM   Leave JFK Airport on American Airlines Flight 292, Seat 12A. (Ticket attached.)

11:05 AM   Arrive Dallas. Limousine to office. (Limousine reservation attached.)

◇ BEFORE-THE-TRIP CHECKLIST

Before leaving on a trip, you should confirm the following:

- Airline tickets and frequent flyer number
- Lodging information and confirmation number
- Car rental information and confirmation number
- Money or traveler's checks
- Passport, visa, driver's license, or international driving permit
- Itinerary
- Destination contact names, addresses, and phone numbers
- Meeting agendas
- Speeches, reports, and presentations
- Computer and modem
- Cell phone

◇ INTERNATIONAL TRAVEL

If the boss's trip involves international travel, make plans well in advance because of the many details involved. He or she should be aware of both U.S. requirements regarding foreign travel and the requirements of the country or countries to be visited. There are many conditions imposed on business travelers that are different from those imposed on tourists.

For assistance in arranging an international business trip, you can contact the U.S. Department of State at www.travel.state.gov. You can also visit the U.S. Department of Commerce website at www.commerce.gov.

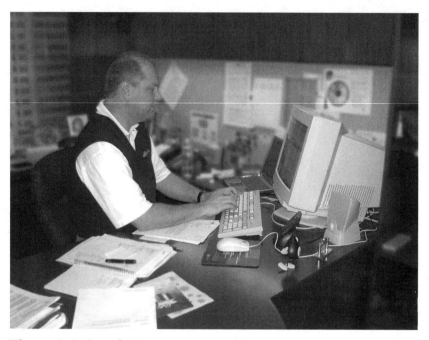

Figure 5–1. Sample itinerary.

Using a Travel Agent for International Travel

Even if you do not use a travel agency to arrange domestic business trips, it's highly recommended that a reliable agency be used for international travel. To select a travel agency, solicit recommendations from co-workers or friends, consult the classified section of your telephone directory, or look for advertisements in the newspaper that indicate an agency is not only well versed in foreign travel rules and regulations but also specializes in individual itineraries rather than package tours.

The agency can handle all of the complicated details involved in foreign travel. Its expertise is invaluable to you, and at little or no cost to your company since the travel agent's fee is paid by the hotels.

The agency can handle all arrangements for transportation, lodging, car rentals, even sight-seeing excursions. It furnishes accurate information about the documents needed for each particular country—passport, health certificates, police certificates, visas, and so forth—and exactly how to obtain each. The agency can handle all checks or arrange for letters of credit, as your employer prefers, and even secure a small amount of currency in the denominations of the country visited so that the boss won't arrive with only U.S. currency.

Visas and Passports

Most U.S. citizens need a passport to leave the United States and to reenter it. As of January 2007, a passport is now required by U.S. law for travel to North America, South America, Central America, the Caribbean, or Bermuda (under previous law, a passport was not required for such travel). Passports are not required for travel to U.S. territories (such as Puerto Rico). All travelers should always carry personal identification, such as a driver's license, which is at the least necessary to board planes.

In addition to a passport, many countries require a visa to enter. Usually, the visa must be obtained in advance and can't be purchased at the border or point of entry. Visas are issued by the individual embassies and consulates of various countries. Some countries charge a small fee, while other countries issue visas for free. Since the requirements can and do change often, even if you have obtained a visa in advance of a trip, double-check before you leave to make sure the visa is still valid.

To find out more about passports and visas, contact the U.S. Department of State at www.travel.state.gov or call 877-487-2778.

Required Immunizations and Vaccinations

Anyone traveling to a foreign country must have up-to-date information concerning required immunizations. The U.S. Department of Health and Human Services has information on required immunizations for travelers available by calling 877-FYI-TRIP (800-394-8747). You can also visit them on the Web at www.cdc.gov/travel.

Customs

When returning from foreign countries, the traveler must declare certain items acquired abroad to determine whether a tax is owed. Travelers returning home to the United States are allowed certain exemptions, which help cover the inevitable souvenirs. Articles totaling $800 (fair retail value in the country where purchased) are duty free, except for cigarettes, cigars, and liquor.

Be aware: Travelers should not try to understate the value of an article or misrepresent the nature of any article. To do so could result in the seizure and forfeiture of the item, and the tax will still be assessed. If a traveler has doubt as to whether to declare an item, he or she should declare it and then ask the customs inspector about it. Complete and detailed information concerning customs regulations are available by visiting www.cbp.gov.

Languages Spoken in Foreign Countries

The average businessperson is sometimes aware of the language spoken in some countries of the world but not in others. Table 5–1 indicates the official language(s) spoken in certain countries.

TABLE 5–1. Countries and Their Official Language(s)

Country	Official Language(s)	Country	Official Language(s)
Afghanistan	Afghan, Persian, Pashto	Argentina	Spanish
		Australia	English
Algeria	Arabic	Bahamas	English
Angola	Portuguese	Bahrain	Arabic

Country	Official Language(s)	Country	Official Language(s)
Barbados	English	Liberia	English
Belgium	Dutch, French, German	Libya	Arabic
		Macedonia	Albanian, Macedonian
Belize	English	Madagascar	French, Malagasy
Bermuda	English	Malawi	English
Bolivia	Spanish	Malaysia	Malay
Bosnia and Herzegovina	Bosnian	Mali	French
		Malta	English, Maltese
Botswana	English	Mauritania	Arabic, French
Brazil	Portuguese	Mexico	Spanish
Bulgaria	Bulgarian	Monaco	French
Canada	English, French	Morocco	Arabic
Chad	French	Mozambique	Portuguese
Chile	Spanish	Myanmar	Burmese
China	Chinese (Mandarin)	Nepal	Nepali
Colombia	Spanish	Netherlands	Dutch
Congo (Democratic Republic of the Congo)	French	New Zealand	English
		Nicaragua	Spanish
		Nigeria	English
		Norway	Norwegian
Congo (Republic of the Congo)	French	Oman	Arabic
		Pakistan	Urdu
Côte d'Ivoire	French	Panama	Spanish
Croatia	Croatian	Paraguay	Spanish
Cuba	Spanish	Peru	Quechua, Spanish
Denmark	Danish	Philippines	English, Filipino, Spanish
Dominica	English		
Dominican Republic	Spanish	Poland	Polish
		Portugal	Portuguese
Ecuador	Spanish	Romania	German, Romanian, Hungarian
Egypt	Arabic		
El Salvador	Spanish	Russia	Russian
Ethiopia	Amharic	Saudi Arabia	Arabic
Fiji	English	Serbia and Montenegro	Albanian, Serbian
Finland	Finnish, Swedish		
France	French	Singapore	Chinese, English, Malay, Tamil
Germany	German		
Ghana	English	Spain	Castilian Spanish
Great Britain	English	Sweden	Swedish
Greece	Greek	Switzerland	French, German, Italian
Grenada	English	Trinidad and Tobago	English
Guatemala	Spanish		
Guyana	English	Tunisia	Arabic
Haiti	French	Turkey	Turkish
Honduras	Spanish	Ukraine	Ukrainian
Iceland	Icelandic		
India	English, Hindi		
Indonesia	Indonesian		
Iran	Persian		
Iraq	Arabic		
Ireland	English, Irish		
Israel	Arabic, Hebrew		
Italy	Italian		
Jamaica	English		
Japan	Japanese		
Jordan	Arabic		
Kenya	English, Swahili		
Korea, North	Korean		
Korea, South	Korean		
Kuwait	Arabic		
Lebanon	Arabic		
Lesotho	English, Sesotho		

◇ TIME ZONES

A variety of useful time zone–related information is available on the Web at www.timeanddate.com. The following is a list of time zone abbreviations:

Standard

- **UTC** Coordinated Universal Time, civil time, the one most often used by "ordinary" people
- **UT** Universal Time, based on the Earth's rotation, often used in astronomy
- **TAI** International Atomic Time, based on atomic clocks

European

- **GMT** Greenwich Mean Time, as UTC
- **BST** British Summer Time, as UTC + 1 hour
- **IST** Irish Summer Time, as UTC + 1 hour
- **WET** Western Europe Time, as UTC
- **WEST** Western Europe Summer Time, as UTC + 1 hour
- **CET** Central Europe Time, as UTC + 1 hour
- **CEST** Central Europe Summer Time, as UTC + 2 hours
- **EET** Eastern Europe Time, as UTC + 2 hours
- **EEST** Eastern Europe Summer Time, as UTC + 3 hours
- **MSK** Moscow Time, as UTC + 3 hours
- **MSD** Moscow Summer Time, as UTC + 4 hours

United States and Canada

- **AST** Atlantic Standard Time, as UTC - 4 hours
- **ADT** Atlantic Daylight Time, as UTC - 3 hours
- **EST** Eastern Standard Time, as UTC - 5 hours
- **EDT** Eastern Daylight Saving Time, as UTC - 4 hours
- **ET** Eastern Time, either as EST or EDT, depending on place and time of year
- **CST** Central Standard Time, as UTC - 6 hours
- **CDT** Central Daylight Saving Time, as UTC - 5 hours
- **CT** Central Time, either as CST or CDT, depending on place and time of year
- **MST** Mountain Standard Time, as UTC - 7 hours
- **MDT** Mountain Daylight Saving Time, as UTC - 6 hours
- **MT** Mountain Time, either as MST or MDT, depending on place and time of year
- **PST** Pacific Standard Time, as UTC - 8 hours
- **PDT** Pacific Daylight Saving Time, as UTC - 7 hours

- **PT** Pacific Time, either as PST or PDT, depending on place and time of year
- **HST** Hawaiian Standard Time, as UTC - 10 hours
- **AKST** Alaska Standard Time, as UTC - 9 hours
- **AKDT** Alaska Standard Daylight Saving Time, as UTC - 8 hours

Australia

- **AEST** Australian Eastern Standard Time, as UTC + 10 hours
- **AEDT** Australian Eastern Daylight Time, as UTC + 11 hours
- **ACST** Australian Central Standard Time, as UTC + 9.5 hours
- **ACDT** Australian Central Daylight Time, as UTC + 10.5 hours
- **AWST** Australian Western Standard Time, as UTC + 8 hours

Time Zone Time Differences

Table 5–2 shows the time differences between countries and various time zones in the United States.

TABLE 5–2. Time Zone Time Differences

Country	GMT	USA Eastern	USA Central	USA Mountain	USA Pacific
A					
Afghanistan	+ 4.5 H	+ 9.5 H	+ 10.5 H	+ 11.5 H	+ 12.5 H
Albania	+ 1.0 H	+ 6.0 H	+ 7.0 H	+ 8.0 H	+ 9.0 H
Algeria	+ 1.0 H	+ 6.0 H	+ 7.0 H	+ 8.0 H	+ 9.0 H
American Samoa	– 11.0 H	– 6.0 H	– 5.0 H	– 4.0 H	– 3.0 H
Andorra	+ 1.0 H	+ 6.0 H	+ 7.0 H	+ 8.0 H	+ 9.0 H
Angola	+ 1.0 H	+ 6.0 H	+ 7.0 H	+ 8.0 H	+ 9.0 H
Antarctica	– 2.0 H	+ 3.0 H	+ 4.0 H	+ 5.0 H	+ 6.0 H
Antigua and Barbuda	– 4.0 H	+ 1.0 H	+ 2.0 H	+ 3.0 H	+ 4.0 H
Argentina	– 3.0 H	+ 2.0 H	+ 3.0 H	+ 4.0 H	+ 5.0 H
Armenia	+ 4.0 H	+ 9.0 H	+ 10.0 H	+ 11.0 H	+ 12.0 H
Aruba	– 4.0 H	+ 1.0 H	+ 2.0 H	+ 3.0 H	+ 4.0 H
Ascension Island	+ 0.0 H	+ 5.0 H	+ 6.0 H	+ 7.0 H	+ 8.0 H
Australia (North)	+ 9.5 H	+ 14.5 H	+ 15.5 H	+ 16.5 H	+ 17.5 H
Australia (South)	+ 10.0 H	+ 15.0 H	+ 16.0 H	+ 17.0 H	+ 18.0 H
Australia (West)	+ 8.0 H	+ 13.0 H	+ 14.0 H	+ 15.0 H	+ 16.0 H
Australia (East)	+ 10.0 H	+ 15.0 H	+ 16.0 H	+ 17.0 H	+ 18.0 H
Austria	+ 1.0 H	+ 6.0 H	+ 7.0 H	+ 8.0 H	+ 9.0 H
Azerbaijan	+ 3.0 H	+ 8.0 H	+ 9.0 H	+ 10.0 H	+ 11.0 H
B					
Bahamas	– 5.0 H	+ 0.0 H	+ 1.0 H	+ 2.0 H	+ 3.0 H
Bahrain	+ 3.0 H	+ 8.0 H	+ 9.0 H	+ 10.0 H	+ 11.0 H

Country	GMT	USA Eastern	USA Central	USA Mountain	USA Pacific
Bangladesh	+ 6.0 H	+ 11.0 H	+ 12.0 H	+ 13.0 H	+ 14.0 H
Barbados	– 4.0 H	+ 1.0 H	+ 2.0 H	+ 3.0 H	+ 4.0 H
Belarus	+ 2.0 H	+ 7.0 H	+ 8.0 H	+ 9.0 H	+ 10.0 H
Belgium	+ 1.0 H	+ 6.0 H	+ 7.0 H	+ 8.0 H	+ 9.0 H
Belize	– 6.0 H	– 1.0 H	+ 0.0 H	+ 1.0 H	+ 2.0 H
Benin	+ 1.0 H	+ 6.0 H	+ 7.0 H	+ 8.0 H	+ 9.0 H
Bermuda	– 4.0 H	+ 1.0 H	+ 2.0 H	+ 3.0 H	+ 4.0 H
Bhutan	+ 6.0 H	+ 11.0 H	+ 12.0 H	+ 13.0 H	+ 14.0 H
Bolivia	– 4.0 H	+ 1.0 H	+ 2.0 H	+ 3.0 H	+ 4.0 H
Bosnia and Herzegovina	+ 1.0 H	+ 6.0 H	+ 7.0 H	+ 8.0 H	+ 9.0 H
Botswana	+ 2.0 H	+ 7.0 H	+ 8.0 H	+ 9.0 H	+ 10.0 H
Brazil (West)	– 4.0 H	+ 1.0 H	+ 2.0 H	+ 3.0 H	+ 4.0 H
Brazil (East)	– 3.0 H	+ 2.0 H	+ 3.0 H	+ 4.0 H	+ 5.0 H
British Virgin Islands	– 4.0 H	+ 1.0 H	+ 2.0 H	+ 3.0 H	+ 4.0 H
Brunei	+ 8.0 H	+ 13.0 H	+ 14.0 H	+ 15.0 H	+ 16.0 H
Bulgaria	+ 2.0 H	+ 7.0 H	+ 8.0 H	+ 9.0 H	+ 10.0 H
Burkina Faso	+ 0.0 H	+ 5.0 H	+ 6.0 H	+ 7.0 H	+ 8.0 H
Burundi	+ 2.0 H	+ 7.0 H	+ 8.0 H	+ 9.0 H	+ 10.0 H
C					
Cambodia	+ 7.0 H	+ 12.0 H	+ 13.0 H	+ 14.0 H	+ 15.0 H
Cameroon	+ 1.0 H	+ 6.0 H	+ 7.0 H	+ 8.0 H	+ 9.0 H
Canada (Central)	– 6.0 H	– 1.0 H	+ 0.0 H	+ 1.0 H	+ 2.0 H
Canada (Eastern)	– 5.0 H	+ 0.0 H	+ 1.0 H	+ 2.0 H	+ 3.0 H
Canada (Mountain)	– 7.0 H	– 2.0 H	– 1.0 H	+ 0.0 H	+ 1.0 H
Canada (Pacific)	– 8.0 H	– 3.0 H	– 2.0 H	– 1.0 H	+ 0.0 H
Canada (Newfoundland)	– 3.5 H	+ 1.5 H	+ 2.5 H	+ 3.5 H	+ 4.5 H
Cape Verde	– 1.0 H	+ 4.0 H	+ 5.0 H	+ 6.0 H	+ 7.0 H
Cayman Islands	– 5.0 H	+ 0.0 H	+ 1.0 H	+ 2.0 H	+ 3.0 H
Central African Republic	+ 1.0 H	+ 6.0 H	+ 7.0 H	+ 8.0 H	+ 9.0 H
Chad	+ 1.0 H	+ 6.0 H	+ 7.0 H	+ 8.0 H	+ 9.0 H
Chile	– 4.0 H	+ 1.0 H	+ 2.0 H	+ 3.0 H	+ 4.0 H
China	+ 8.0 H	+ 13.0 H	+ 14.0 H	+ 15.0 H	+ 16.0 H
Christmas Islands	– 10.0 H	– 5.0 H	– 4.0 H	– 3.0 H	– 2.0 H
Colombia	– 5.0 H	+ 0.0 H	+ 1.0 H	+ 2.0 H	+ 3.0 H
Congo	+ 1.0 H	+ 6.0 H	+ 7.0 H	+ 8.0 H	+ 9.0 H
Cook Islands	– 10.0 H	– 5.0 H	– 4.0 H	– 3.0 H	– 2.0 H
Costa Rica	– 6.0 H	– 1.0 H	+ 0.0 H	+ 1.0 H	+ 2.0 H
Croatia	+ 1.0 H	+ 6.0 H	+ 7.0 H	+ 8.0 H	+ 9.0 H
Cuba	– 5.0 H	+ 0.0 H	+ 1.0 H	+ 2.0 H	+ 3.0 H
Cyprus	+ 2.0 H	+ 7.0 H	+ 8.0 H	+ 9.0 H	+ 10.0 H
Czech Republic	+ 1.0 H	+ 6.0 H	+ 7.0 H	+ 8.0 H	+ 9.0 H
D					
Denmark	+ 1.0 H	+ 6.0 H	+ 7.0 H	+ 8.0 H	+ 9.0 H
Djibouti	+ 3.0 H	+ 8.0 H	+ 9.0 H	+ 10.0 H	+ 11.0 H

Country	GMT	USA Eastern	USA Central	USA Mountain	USA Pacific
Dominica	– 4.0 H	+ 1.0 H	+ 2.0 H	+ 3.0 H	+ 4.0 H
Dominican Republic	– 4.0 H	+ 1.0 H	+ 2.0 H	+ 3.0 H	+ 4.0 H
E					
Ecuador	– 5.0 H	+ 0.0 H	+ 1.0 H	+ 2.0 H	+ 3.0 H
Egypt	+ 2.0 H	+ 7.0 H	+ 8.0 H	+ 9.0 H	+ 10.0 H
El Salvador	– 6.0 H	– 1.0 H	+ 0.0 H	+ 1.0 H	+ 2.0 H
Equatorial Guinea	+ 1.0 H	+ 6.0 H	+ 7.0 H	+ 8.0 H	+ 9.0 H
Eritrea	+ 3.0 H	+ 8.0 H	+ 9.0 H	+ 10.0 H	+ 11.0 H
Estonia	+ 2.0 H	+ 7.0 H	+ 8.0 H	+ 9.0 H	+ 10.0 H
Ethiopia	+ 3.0 H	+ 8.0 H	+ 9.0 H	+ 10.0 H	+ 11.0 H
F					
Faeroe Islands	+ 0.0 H	+ 5.0 H	+ 6.0 H	+ 7.0 H	+ 8.0 H
Falkland Islands	– 4.0 H	+ 1.0 H	+ 2.0 H	+ 3.0 H	+ 4.0 H
Fiji	+ 12.0 H	+ 17.0 H	+ 18.0 H	+ 19.0 H	+ 20.0 H
Finland	+ 2.0 H	+ 7.0 H	+ 8.0 H	+ 9.0 H	+ 10.0 H
France	+ 1.0 H	+ 6.0 H	+ 7.0 H	+ 8.0 H	+ 9.0 H
French Antilles (Martinique)	– 3.0 H	+ 2.0 H	+ 3.0 H	+ 4.0 H	+ 5.0 H
French Guinea	– 3.0 H	+ 2.0 H	+ 3.0 H	+ 4.0 H	+ 5.0 H
French Polynesia	– 10.0 H	– 5.0 H	– 4.0 H	– 3.0 H	– 2.0 H
G					
Gabon Republic	+ 1.0 H	+ 6.0 H	+ 7.0 H	+ 8.0 H	+ 9.0 H
Gambia	+ 0.0 H	+ 5.0 H	+ 6.0 H	+ 7.0 H	+ 8.0 H
Georgia	+ 4.0 H	+ 9.0 H	+ 10.0 H	+ 11.0 H	+ 12.0 H
Germany	+ 1.0 H	+ 6.0 H	+ 7.0 H	+ 8.0 H	+ 9.0 H
Ghana	+ 0.0 H	+ 5.0 H	+ 6.0 H	+ 7.0 H	+ 8.0 H
Gibraltar	+ 1.0 H	+ 6.0 H	+ 7.0 H	+ 8.0 H	+ 9.0 H
Greece	+ 2.0 H	+ 7.0 H	+ 8.0 H	+ 9.0 H	+ 10.0 H
Greenland	– 3.0 H	+ 2.0 H	+ 3.0 H	+ 4.0 H	+ 5.0 H
Grenada	– 4.0 H	+ 1.0 H	+ 2.0 H	+ 3.0 H	+ 4.0 H
Guadeloupe	– 4.0 H	+ 1.0 H	+ 2.0 H	+ 3.0 H	+ 4.0 H
Guam	+ 10.0 H	+ 15.0 H	+ 16.0 H	+ 17.0 H	+ 18.0 H
Guatemala	– 6.0 H	– 1.0 H	+ 0.0 H	+ 1.0 H	+ 2.0 H
Guinea-Bissau	+ 0.0 H	+ 5.0 H	+ 6.0 H	+ 7.0 H	+ 8.0 H
Guinea	+ 0.0 H	+ 5.0 H	+ 6.0 H	+ 7.0 H	+ 8.0 H
Guyana	– 3.0 H	+ 2.0 H	+ 3.0 H	+ 4.0 H	+ 5.0 H
H					
Haiti	– 5.0 H	+ 0.0 H	+ 1.0 H	+ 2.0 H	+ 3.0 H
Honduras	– 6.0 H	– 1.0 H	+ 0.0 H	+ 1.0 H	+ 2.0 H
Hong Kong	+ 8.0 H	+ 13.0 H	+ 14.0 H	+ 15.0 H	+ 16.0 H
Hungary	+ 1.0 H	+ 6.0 H	+ 7.0 H	+ 8.0 H	+ 9.0 H
I					
Iceland	+ 0.0 H	+ 5.0 H	+ 6.0 H	+ 7.0 H	+ 8.0 H
India	+ 5.5 H	+ 10.5 H	+ 11.5 H	+ 12.5 H	+ 13.5 H
Indonesia (Central)	+ 8.0 H	+ 13.0 H	+ 14.0 H	+ 15.0 H	+ 16.0 H

Country	GMT	USA Eastern	USA Central	USA Mountain	USA Pacific
Indonesia (East)	+ 9.0 H	+ 14.0 H	+ 15.0 H	+ 16.0 H	+ 17.0 H
Indonesia (West)	+ 7.0 H	+ 12.0 H	+ 13.0 H	+ 14.0 H	+ 15.0 H
Iran	+ 3.5 H	+ 8.5 H	+ 9.5 H	+ 10.5 H	+ 11.5 H
Iraq	+ 3.0 H	+ 8.0 H	+ 9.0 H	+ 10.0 H	+ 11.0 H
Ireland	+ 0.0 H	+ 5.0 H	+ 6.0 H	+ 7.0 H	+ 8.0 H
Israel	+ 2.0 H	+ 7.0 H	+ 8.0 H	+ 9.0 H	+ 10.0 H
Italy	+ 1.0 H	+ 6.0 H	+ 7.0 H	+ 8.0 H	+ 9.0 H
J					
Jamaica	– 5.0 H	+ 0.0 H	+ 1.0 H	+ 2.0 H	+ 3.0 H
Japan	+ 9.0 H	+ 14.0 H	+ 15.0 H	+ 16.0 H	+ 17.0 H
Jordan	+ 2.0 H	+ 7.0 H	+ 8.0 H	+ 9.0 H	+ 10.0 H
K					
Kazakhstan	+ 6.0 H	+ 11.0 H	+ 12.0 H	+ 13.0 H	+ 14.0 H
Kenya	+ 3.0 H	+ 8.0 H	+ 9.0 H	+ 10.0 H	+ 11.0 H
Kiribati	+ 12.0 H	+ 17.0 H	+ 18.0 H	+ 19.0 H	+ 20.0 H
Korea, North	+ 9.0 H	+ 14.0 H	+ 15.0 H	+ 16.0 H	+ 17.0 H
Korea, South	+ 9.0 H	+ 14.0 H	+ 15.0 H	+ 16.0 H	+ 17.0 H
Kuwait	+ 3.0 H	+ 8.0 H	+ 9.0 H	+ 10.0 H	+ 11.0 H
Kyrgyzstan	+ 5.0 H	+ 10.0 H	+ 11.0 H	+ 12.0 H	+ 13.0 H
L					
Laos	+ 7.0 H	+ 12.0 H	+ 13.0 H	+ 14.0 H	+ 15.0 H
Latvia	+ 2.0 H	+ 7.0 H	+ 8.0 H	+ 9.0 H	+ 10.0 H
Lebanon	+ 2.0 H	+ 7.0 H	+ 8.0 H	+ 9.0 H	+ 10.0 H
Lesotho	+ 2.0 H	+ 7.0 H	+ 8.0 H	+ 9.0 H	+ 10.0 H
Liberia	+ 0.0 H	+ 5.0 H	+ 6.0 H	+ 7.0 H	+ 8.0 H
Libya	+ 2.0 H	+ 7.0 H	+ 8.0 H	+ 9.0 H	+ 10.0 H
Liechtenstein	+ 1.0 H	+ 6.0 H	+ 7.0 H	+ 8.0 H	+ 9.0 H
Lithuania	+ 2.0 H	+ 7.0 H	+ 8.0 H	+ 9.0 H	+ 10.0 H
Luxembourg	+ 1.0 H	+ 6.0 H	+ 7.0 H	+ 8.0 H	+ 9.0 H
M					
Macedonia	+ 1.0 H	+ 6.0 H	+ 7.0 H	+ 8.0 H	+ 9.0 H
Madagascar	+ 3.0 H	+ 8.0 H	+ 9.0 H	+ 10.0 H	+ 11.0 H
Malawi	+ 2.0 H	+ 7.0 H	+ 8.0 H	+ 9.0 H	+ 10.0 H
Malaysia	+ 8.0 H	+ 13.0 H	+ 14.0 H	+ 15.0 H	+ 16.0 H
Maldives	+ 5.0 H	+ 10.0 H	+ 11.0 H	+ 12.0 H	+ 13.0 H
Mali	+ 0.0 H	+ 5.0 H	+ 6.0 H	+ 7.0 H	+ 8.0 H
Malta	+ 1.0 H	+ 6.0 H	+ 7.0 H	+ 8.0 H	+ 9.0 H
Marshall Islands	+ 12.0 H	+ 17.0 H	+ 18.0 H	+ 19.0 H	+ 20.0 H
Mauritania	+ 0.0 H	+ 5.0 H	+ 6.0 H	+ 7.0 H	+ 8.0 H
Mauritius	+ 4.0 H	+ 9.0 H	+ 10.0 H	+ 11.0 H	+ 12.0 H
Mayotte	+ 3.0 H	+ 8.0 H	+ 9.0 H	+ 10.0 H	+ 11.0 H
Mexico (Central)	– 6.0 H	– 1.0 H	+ 0.0 H	+ 1.0 H	+ 2.0 H
Mexico (East)	– 5.0 H	+ 0.0 H	+ 1.0 H	+ 2.0 H	+ 3.0 H
Mexico (West)	– 7.0 H	– 2.0 H	– 1.0 H	+ 0.0 H	+ 1.0 H

Country	GMT	USA Eastern	USA Central	USA Mountain	USA Pacific
Moldova	+ 2.0 H	+ 7.0 H	+ 8.0 H	+ 9.0 H	+ 10.0 H
Monaco	+ 1.0 H	+ 6.0 H	+ 7.0 H	+ 8.0 H	+ 9.0 H
Mongolia	+ 8.0 H	+ 13.0 H	+ 14.0 H	+ 15.0 H	+ 16.0 H
Morocco	+ 0.0 H	+ 5.0 H	+ 6.0 H	+ 7.0 H	+ 8.0 H
Mozambique	+ 2.0 H	+ 7.0 H	+ 8.0 H	+ 9.0 H	+ 10.0 H
Myanmar	+ 6.5 H	+ 11.5 H	+ 12.5 H	+ 13.5 H	+ 14.5 H
N					
Namibia	+ 1.0 H	+ 6.0 H	+ 7.0 H	+ 8.0 H	+ 9.0 H
Nauru	+ 12.0 H	+ 17.0 H	+ 18.0 H	+ 19.0 H	+ 20.0 H
Nepal	+ 5.5 H	+ 10.5 H	+ 11.5 H	+ 12.5 H	+ 13.5 H
Netherlands	+ 1.0 H	+ 6.0 H	+ 7.0 H	+ 8.0 H	+ 9.0 H
Netherlands Antilles	- 4.0 H	+ 1.0 H	+ 2.0 H	+ 3.0 H	+ 4.0 H
New Caledonia	+ 11.0 H	+ 16.0 H	+ 17.0 H	+ 18.0 H	+ 19.0 H
New Zealand	+ 12.0 H	+ 17.0 H	+ 18.0 H	+ 19.0 H	+ 20.0 H
Nicaragua	- 6.0 H	- 1.0 H	+ 0.0 H	+ 1.0 H	+ 2.0 H
Nigeria	+ 1.0 H	+ 6.0 H	+ 7.0 H	+ 8.0 H	+ 9.0 H
Niger	+ 1.0 H	+ 6.0 H	+ 7.0 H	+ 8.0 H	+ 9.0 H
Norfolk Island	+ 11.5 H	+ 16.5 H	+ 17.5 H	+ 18.5 H	+ 19.5 H
Norway	+ 1.0 H	+ 6.0 H	+ 7.0 H	+ 8.0 H	+ 9.0 H
O					
Oman	+ 4.0 H	+ 9.0 H	+ 10.0 H	+ 11.0 H	+ 12.0 H
P					
Pakistan	+ 5.0 H	+ 10.0 H	+ 11.0 H	+ 12.0 H	+ 13.0 H
Palau	+ 9.0 H	+ 14.0 H	+ 15.0 H	+ 16.0 H	+ 17.0 H
Panama	- 5.0 H	+ 0.0 H	+ 1.0 H	+ 2.0 H	+ 3.0 H
Papua New Guinea	+ 10.0 H	+ 15.0 H	+ 16.0 H	+ 17.0 H	+ 18.0 H
Paraguay	- 4.0 H	+ 1.0 H	+ 2.0 H	+ 3.0 H	+ 4.0 H
Peru	- 5.0 H	+ 0.0 H	+ 1.0 H	+ 2.0 H	+ 3.0 H
Philippines	+ 8.0 H	+ 13.0 H	+ 14.0 H	+ 15.0 H	+ 16.0 H
Poland	+ 1.0 H	+ 6.0 H	+ 7.0 H	+ 8.0 H	+ 9.0 H
Portugal	+ 1.0 H	+ 6.0 H	+ 7.0 H	+ 8.0 H	+ 9.0 H
Puerto Rico	- 4.0 H	+ 1.0 H	+ 2.0 H	+ 3.0 H	+ 4.0 H
Q					
Qatar	+ 3.0 H	+ 8.0 H	+ 9.0 H	+ 10.0 H	+ 11.0 H
R					
Reunion Island	+ 4.0 H	+ 9.0 H	+ 10.0 H	+ 11.0 H	+ 12.0 H
Romania	+ 2.0 H	+ 7.0 H	+ 8.0 H	+ 9.0 H	+ 10.0 H
Russia (West)	+ 2.0 H	+ 7.0 H	+ 8.0 H	+ 9.0 H	+ 10.0 H
Russia (Central 1)	+ 4.0 H	+ 9.0 H	+ 10.0 H	+ 11.0 H	+ 12.0 H
Russia (Central 2)	+ 7.0 H	+ 12.0 H	+ 13.0 H	+ 14.0 H	+ 15.0 H
Russia (East)	+ 11.0 H	+ 16.0 H	+ 17.0 H	+ 18.0 H	+ 19.0 H
Rwanda	+ 2.0 H	+ 7.0 H	+ 8.0 H	+ 9.0 H	+ 10.0 H
S					
Saba	- 4.0 H	+ 1.0 H	+ 2.0 H	+ 3.0 H	+ 4.0 H

Country	GMT	USA Eastern	USA Central	USA Mountain	USA Pacific
Samoa	– 11.0 H	– 6.0 H	– 5.0 H	– 4.0 H	– 3.0 H
San Marino	+ 1.0 H	+ 6.0 H	+ 7.0 H	+ 8.0 H	+ 9.0 H
São Tomé	+ 0.0 H	+ 5.0 H	+ 6.0 H	+ 7.0 H	+ 8.0 H
Saudi Arabia	+ 3.0 H	+ 8.0 H	+ 9.0 H	+ 10.0 H	+ 11.0 H
Senegal	+ 0.0 H	+ 5.0 H	+ 6.0 H	+ 7.0 H	+ 8.0 H
Seychelles Islands	+ 4.0 H	+ 9.0 H	+ 10.0 H	+ 11.0 H	+ 12.0 H
Sierra Leone	+ 0.0 H	+ 5.0 H	+ 6.0 H	+ 7.0 H	+ 8.0 H
Singapore	+ 8.0 H	+ 13.0 H	+ 14.0 H	+ 15.0 H	+ 16.0 H
Slovakia	+ 1.0 H	+ 6.0 H	+ 7.0 H	+ 8.0 H	+ 9.0 H
Slovenia	+ 1.0 H	+ 6.0 H	+ 7.0 H	+ 8.0 H	+ 9.0 H
Solomon Islands	+ 11.0 H	+ 16.0 H	+ 17.0 H	+ 18.0 H	+ 19.0 H
Somalia	+ 3.0 H	+ 8.0 H	+ 9.0 H	+ 10.0 H	+ 11.0 H
South Africa	+ 2.0 H	+ 7.0 H	+ 8.0 H	+ 9.0 H	+ 10.0 H
Spain	+ 1.0 H	+ 6.0 H	+ 7.0 H	+ 8.0 H	+ 9.0 H
Sri Lanka	+ 5.5 H	+ 10.5 H	+ 11.5 H	+ 12.5 H	+ 13.5 H
St. Lucia	– 4.0 H	+ 1.0 H	+ 2.0 H	+ 3.0 H	+ 4.0 H
St. Maarten	– 4.0 H	+ 1.0 H	+ 2.0 H	+ 3.0 H	+ 4.0 H
St. Pierre and Miquelon	– 3.0 H	+ 2.0 H	+ 3.0 H	+ 4.0 H	+ 5.0 H
St. Thomas	– 4.0 H	+ 1.0 H	+ 2.0 H	+ 3.0 H	+ 4.0 H
St. Vincent	– 4.0 H	+ 1.0 H	+ 2.0 H	+ 3.0 H	+ 4.0 H
Sudan	+ 2.0 H	+ 7.0 H	+ 8.0 H	+ 9.0 H	+ 10.0 H
Suriname	– 3.0 H	+ 2.0 H	+ 3.0 H	+ 4.0 H	+ 5.0 H
Swaziland	+ 2.0 H	+ 7.0 H	+ 8.0 H	+ 9.0 H	+ 10.0 H
Sweden	+ 1.0 H	+ 6.0 H	+ 7.0 H	+ 8.0 H	+ 9.0 H
Switzerland	+ 1.0 H	+ 6.0 H	+ 7.0 H	+ 8.0 H	+ 9.0 H
Syria	+ 2.0 H	+ 7.0 H	+ 8.0 H	+ 9.0 H	+ 10.0 H
T					
Taiwan	+ 8.0 H	+ 13.0 H	+ 14.0 H	+ 15.0 H	+ 16.0 H
Tajikistan	+ 6.0 H	+ 11.0 H	+ 12.0 H	+ 13.0 H	+ 14.0 H
Tanzania	+ 3.0 H	+ 8.0 H	+ 9.0 H	+ 10.0 H	+ 11.0 H
Thailand	+ 7.0 H	+ 12.0 H	+ 13.0 H	+ 14.0 H	+ 15.0 H
Togo	+ 0.0 H	+ 5.0 H	+ 6.0 H	+ 7.0 H	+ 8.0 H
Tonga	+ 13.0 H	+ 18.0 H	+ 19.0 H	+ 20.0 H	+ 21.0 H
Trinidad and Tobago	– 4.0 H	+ 1.0 H	+ 2.0 H	+ 3.0 H	+ 4.0 H
Tunisia	+ 1.0 H	+ 6.0 H	+ 7.0 H	+ 8.0 H	+ 9.0 H
Turkey	+ 2.0 H	+ 7.0 H	+ 8.0 H	+ 9.0 H	+ 10.0 H
Turkmenistan	+ 5.0 H	+ 10.0 H	+ 11.0 H	+ 12.0 H	+ 13.0 H
Turks and Caicos	– 5.0 H	+ 0.0 H	+ 1.0 H	+ 2.0 H	+ 3.0 H
Tuvalu	+ 12.0 H	+ 17.0 H	+ 18.0 H	+ 19.0 H	+ 20.0 H
U					
Uganda	+ 3.0 H	+ 8.0 H	+ 9.0 H	+ 10.0 H	+ 11.0 H
Ukraine	+ 2.0 H	+ 7.0 H	+ 8.0 H	+ 9.0 H	+ 10.0 H
United Arab Emirates	+ 4.0 H	+ 9.0 H	+ 10.0 H	+ 11.0 H	+ 12.0 H
United Kingdom	+ 0.0 H	+ 5.0 H	+ 6.0 H	+ 7.0 H	+ 8.0 H

Country	GMT	USA Eastern	USA Central	USA Mountain	USA Pacific
Uruguay	– 3.0 H	+ 2.0 H	+ 3.0 H	+ 4.0 H	+ 5.0 H
USA (Central)	– 6.0 H	– 1.0 H	+ 0.0 H	+ 1.0 H	+ 2.0 H
USA (Eastern)	– 5.0 H	+ 0.0 H	+ 1.0 H	+ 2.0 H	+ 3.0 H
USA (Mountain)	– 7.0 H	– 2.0 H	– 1.0 H	+ 0.0 H	+ 1.0 H
USA (Pacific)	– 8.0 H	– 3.0 H	– 2.0 H	– 1.0 H	+ 0.0 H
USA (Alaska)	– 9.0 H	– 4.0 H	– 3.0 H	– 2.0 H	– 1.0 H
USA (Hawaii)	– 10.0 H	– 5.0 H	– 4.0 H	– 3.0 H	– 2.0 H
Uzbekistan	+ 5.0 H	+ 10.0 H	+ 11.0 H	+ 12.0 H	+ 13.0 H
V					
Vanuatu	+ 11.0 H	+ 16.0 H	+ 17.0 H	+ 18.0 H	+ 19.0 H
Vatican City	+ 1.0 H	+ 6.0 H	+ 7.0 H	+ 8.0 H	+ 9.0 H
Venezuela	– 4.0 H	+ 1.0 H	+ 2.0 H	+ 3.0 H	+ 4.0 H
Vietnam	+ 7.0 H	+ 12.0 H	+ 13.0 H	+ 14.0 H	+ 15.0 H
W					
Wallis and Futuna Islands	+ 12.0 H	+ 17.0 H	+ 18.0 H	+ 19.0 H	+ 20.0 H
Y					
Yemen	+ 3.0 H	+ 8.0 H	+ 9.0 H	+ 10.0 H	+ 11.0 H
Yugoslavia	+ 1.0 H	+ 6.0 H	+ 7.0 H	+ 8.0 H	+ 9.0 H
Z					
Zaire	+ 2.0 H	+ 7.0 H	+ 8.0 H	+ 9.0 H	+ 10.0 H
Zambia	+ 2.0 H	+ 7.0 H	+ 8.0 H	+ 9.0 H	+ 10.0 H
Zimbabwe	+ 2.0 H	+ 7.0 H	+ 8.0 H	+ 9.0 H	+ 10.0 H

⬨ INTERNATIONAL CURRENCIES

The following is a list of countries and their currencies. (Note that the euro is the currency of thirteen European Union countries: Austria, Belgium, Finland, France, Germany, Greece, Ireland, Italy, Luxembourg, the Netherlands, Portugal, Slovenia, and Spain.)

- Afghanistan: Afghani
- Albania: Lek
- Algeria: Dinar
- Andorra: French Franc
- Argentina: Peso
- Armenia: Dram
- Australia: Dollar
- Austria: Schilling
- Azerbaijan: Manat
- Azores: Portuguese Escudo
- Bahamas: Dollar
- Bahrain: Dinar
- Bangladesh: Taka
- Barbados: Dollar
- Belarus: Ruble

- Belize: Dollar
- Bermuda: British Pound
- Bhutan: Negultrum
- Bosnia and Herzegovia: Dinar
- Botswana: Pula
- Brazil: Cruzeiro
- Bulgaria: Lev
- Cambodia: Riel
- Cameroon: CFA Franc
- Canada: (Canadian) Dollar
- Chad: CFA Franc
- Chile: Peso
- China: Yuan
- Columbia: Peso
- Congo: CFA Franc

- Costa Rica: Colon
- Croatia: Kuna
- Cuba: Peso
- Czech Republic: Koruna
- Denmark: Krone
- Ecuador: Sucre
- Egypt: Pound
- El Salvador: Colon
- Ethiopia: Birr
- Europe: Euro
- Finland: Markka
- French Guiana: French Franc
- Gabon: CFA Franc
- Gambia: Dalasi
- Georgia: Ruble
- Ghana: Cedi
- Greece: Drachma
- Grenada: East Caribbean Dollar
- Guadaloupe: French Franc
- Guatemala: Quetzal
- Guinea: Franc
- Guyana: Dollar
- Haiti: Gourde
- Honduras: Lempira
- Hong Kong: Dollar
- Hungary: Forint
- Iceland: Krona
- India: Rupee
- Indonesia: Rupaih
- Iran: Rial
- Iraq: Dinar
- Ireland: Pound
- Israel: New Shekel
- Jamaica: Dollar
- Japan: Yen
- Jordan: Dinar
- Kazakhstan: Ruble
- Kenya: Shilling
- Kuwait: Dinar
- Kyrgyzstan: Som
- Laos: Kip
- Latvia: Ruble
- Lebanon: Pound
- Lesotho: Loti
- Liberia: Dollar
- Libya: Dinar

- Liechtenstein: Swiss Franc
- Lithuania: Litas
- Luxembourg: Franc
- Macedonia: Denar
- Madagascar: Franc
- Malaysia: Ringgit
- Maldives: Rufiyaa
- Mexico: Peso
- Mongolia: Tugrik
- Morocco: Dirham
- Mazambique: Metical
- Myanmar: Kyat
- Namibia: Dollar
- Nepal: Rupee
- New Zealand: Dollar
- Nicaragua: Cordoba
- Niger: CFA Franc
- Nigeria: Naira
- North Korea: Won
- Norway: Kroner
- Oman: Rial
- Pakistan: Rupee
- Panama: Balboa
- Paraguay: Guarani
- Peru: Sol
- Philippines: Peso
- Poland: Zloty
- Qatar: Rial
- Romania: Leu
- Russia: Ruble
- Rwanda: Franc
- Saudi Arabia: Riyal
- Senegal: CFA Franc
- Sierra Leone: Leone
- Singapore: Dollar
- Slovenia: Tolar
- Somalia: Shilling
- South Africa: Rand
- South Korea: Won
- Sri Lanka: Rupee
- Sudan: Dinar
- Suriname: Guilder
- Swaziland: Lilangeni
- Sweden: Krona
- Switzerland: Franc
- Syria: Pound

- Taiwan: Dollar
- Tajikistan: Ruble
- Tanzania: Shilling
- Thailand: Baht
- Togo: CFA Franc
- Tonga: Pa'anga
- Trinidad and Tobago: Dollar
- Tunisia: Dinar
- Turkey: Lira
- Turkmenistan: Manat
- Uganda: Shilling

- Ukraine: Hryvnia
- United Arab Emirates: Dirham
- United Kingdom: Pound
- Uruguay: Peso
- Uzbekistan: Ruble
- Venezuela: Bolivar
- Vietnam: Dong
- Yemen: Dinar/Rial
- Zaire: Zaire
- Zambia: Kwacha
- Zimbabwe: Dollar

6

Meetings

◇ ANATOMY OF A MEETING

Whether we like it or not, meetings are a regular and time-consuming part of business life. Because meetings require planning, coordination, and documentation, they are a major job responsibility for most administrative assistants.

The assistant's job includes sending invitations to in-house meetings, finding time in the schedules of meeting attendees, and selecting meeting times and locations. A thoughtful administrative assistant is careful to avoid scheduling meetings for early Monday morning or late Friday afternoon.

Some executive meetings are scheduled weekly. Despite their being routine, the administrative assistant must still schedule the meetings, send invitations, and send reminders. Work on routine meetings also involves creating meeting agendas that include the names of everyone attending the meeting; the date, time, and meeting location; as well as any advanced preparation required of the attendees.

Sometimes a meeting is called with only a moment's notice. When this happens, the assistant needs to coordinate the meeting by calling the attendees on the phone, seeing them in person, or using an e-mail scheduling program such as Microsoft Outlook.

◇ TYPES OF CORPORATE MEETINGS

Every corporation holds an annual meeting of stockholders for the election of directors. During the year, it may also hold other meetings when the stockholders' consent is required for some proposed action, such as an increase or decrease in capital stock, an amendment of the corporate charter, or a merger.

Annual stockholder meetings have special legal requirements for when meeting notices must be sent. Printed notices are sent along with proxy voting forms and a return address, postal paid envelope.

As an administrative assistant, your duties include preparing notices of the meeting as well as a proxy form to be used in case a stockholder cannot attend. This proxy gives another person the right to vote for the stockholder. Notices and proxy forms must be sent to everyone concerned in accordance with the bylaws of the group. In most cases, these must be sent out three to four weeks in advance.

You must arrange for a meeting place and confirm that it will be ready for use at the time specified. You must also type and distribute the agenda. On the day of the meeting, you should place all pertinent papers in a folder with the corporate seal on the conference table at the chairperson's seat.

If you act as the recorder of the meeting, sit beside the chairperson in order to hear every word distinctly. If you have difficulty in hearing, signal the chairperson, who will then ask for a repetition of what has been said. Before the meeting, read all resolutions and reports to be presented so you are familiar with them. In addition, obtain the list of the people attending (which you should have from distributing the agenda) and check the absentees ahead of time rather than write down names while the roll is being called. The greater your knowledge is of the meeting's purpose and the attendees, the easier recording will be.

Corporate director meetings are specified by the corporate bylaws. Most companies have quarterly or yearly director meetings. A written notice of these meetings is not required by law. An administrative assistant may be asked to contact directors via phone, letter, or e-mail to inform them of an upcoming meeting. The assistant is also asked to track who is coming to the meeting and who has declined. A list of those attending the meeting should be created and made available at the meeting.

Other corporate meetings that are not regular events should be scheduled two weeks in advance. You should send out an invitation, agenda, and a follow-up reminder. The date, time, location, and subject should be clear in the invitation.

Outside meetings and conferences usually require printed invitations sent out as a mass mailing. Double-check all the information on a proof of the invitation before it is printed. Confirm the date, week, day, time, room, location, and names of all the speakers. No one should have to telephone the sponsor to get information that was inadvertently omitted from the invitation.

◆ SCHEDULING MEETINGS

Scheduling meetings is one of the most common tasks for administrative assistants. In the past, scheduling a meeting was a time-consuming task that involved hard-copy invitations sent as interoffice memos. The telephone was usually the preferred method of confirming invitations. Today, with computer technology and groupware software such as Microsoft Outlook or IBM Lotus Notes, the task of scheduling a meeting requires only a few mouse clicks.

Despite the advances in technology, scheduling a meeting is not as simple as it looks. There is a lot of judgment involved. Anytime you bring together a group of people, there are many factors to consider. For example, you have to consider pecking order. Some members of the group are more important, so others must change their schedules to accommodate. Decisions about where a meeting is held can be important as well. Is the meeting room large enough and supplied with the right equipment? Can it be reserved for the entire meeting?

Common Problems When Scheduling a Meeting

The following are common problems that occur when scheduling a meeting:

- The meeting is scheduled and after everyone has been invited, you discover that some important participants can't attend. Another date has to be found. This can lead to a cycle of invitations and revisions.

- You ask the participants about their availability for a meeting, but the available dates and times are so limited that no common date and time can be found.

- A meeting location is specified, and then it is later changed in a subsequent meeting notice. Some of the attendees follow the original meeting notice and end up in the wrong room.

- Repeated meeting notices and revisions are sent out, so that everyone is confused about meeting.

- You use an Internet-based meeting scheduling tool, but outside participants don't have the same software.

- A work team uses an Internet system to schedule meetings, but eventually the team members get lazy about updating their schedules and begin to miss meetings.

- A meeting is scheduled and confirmed, but the location is already booked.

- No one sends a meeting reminder, and several attendees forget about the meeting.

- People are invited to a meeting but the meeting organizer didn't say what it is about, so they show up unprepared.

SCHEDULING MEETINGS USING MICROSOFT OUTLOOK'S CALENDAR

Microsoft Outlook is a desktop information management program. It allows you to send and receive e-mails, manage a list of contacts, organize your calendar and scheduling, and maintain a journal. Outlook also allows you to manage files and folders.

Depending on how your company uses Outlook, you may be able to use it to schedule your time. You can schedule appointments that do not involve other people or meeting rooms, and you can assign time blocks. When you are viewing your calendar in Outlook, if you click NEW on the toolbar, the New Appointment window opens. On this window you can enter a subject, location, and start and end times for the appointment, as well as make the appointment an all-day event. If the appointment conflicts with something else in your schedule, a message appears informing you of the conflict. You can also set reminders for the appointment that automatically alert you in advance of the upcoming appointment by an amount of time you choose. The reminder will appear as long as you have Outlook open on your computer. Figure 6–1 shows the New Appointment Window in Microsoft Outlook.

You can also access and view other people's calendars and allow them to access and view yours. This option allows you to see when other team members have time available for meetings.

You can schedule meetings with Outlook very similarly to the way you schedule

Figure 6–1. The New Appointment Window in Microsoft Outlook.

Screen shot reprinted by permission from Microsoft Corporation.

appointments. The main difference is that a meeting is an appointment to which you invite other people and resources. Resources are the things you typically need for a meeting, such as a conference room, overhead projector, whiteboard, and so forth.

Although in many cases not everyone or all resources will be available for a meeting, Outlook allows you to view the availability of the meeting attendees and resources in order to determine a time that best fits everyone's schedule.

To schedule a meeting in Outlook, use the Meeting Planner to create and send meeting invitations and to reserve resources. The Meeting Planner allows you to invite attendees, view their availability, select a meeting location resource, and pick a time. You can enter the names of the people and resources directly into the All Attendees list, or you can use the INVITE OTHERS button. You can select individuals and resources from your Address Book to add to the All Attendees list. You can choose whether each person or resource is required or optional. The All Attendees list displays each person and resource that will be present at the meeting.

When you view the availability of your attendees and resources, the Meeting Planner shows you a time schedule with blue bars designating times when the person or resource is already scheduled for something else. If the time slot is blank, the attendee or resource is available. If you right-click any attendee's or resource's busy time slot in the planner, you can see more details. For example, if a conference room is already booked, you can see who booked it and for what meeting. To avoid scheduling conflicts, you can use the AUTOPICK tool to automatically locate the first time slot available for all specified attendees and resources. Figure 6–2 shows Microsoft Outlook's Meeting Planner with attendee availability data shown.

After you send the meeting notice, meeting responses are delivered to your Inbox

Figure 6–2. Microsoft Outlook's Meeting Planner.
Screen shot reprinted by permission from Microsoft Corporation.

and can be tracked in the Appointment window.

As other users schedule meetings, you receive meeting invitations in your Inbox. You can open the meeting invitation just as you would any e-mail message. You have the option of accepting, declining, or submitting a tentative response. When you click on one of the acceptance buttons, Outlook opens a message box in which you have the option of sending a response. As soon as a meeting invitation is delivered and accepted, it is automatically added to your schedule.

◇ MEETING AGENDAS

The meeting agenda is like a roadmap for the meeting. It tells the participants what the plan is for the meeting, providing a sense of direction and purpose. A meeting agenda should include:

- Meeting start time
- Meeting end time
- Meeting location
- Topic headings
- Topic detail for each heading
- How much time each topic discussion is expected to last
- Which meeting participants will facilitate the discussion of a particular topic

Figure 6–3 shows a sample meeting agenda.

If you use word-processing software such as Microsoft Word, you can use the Agenda Wizard to create an agenda. To access the Agenda Wizard, click on the File Menu, then click NEW. On the NEW dialog, click the OTHER DOCUMENTS tab, then click the AGENDA WIZARD followed by the OK button. Figure 6–4 shows the Agenda Wizard in Microsoft Word.

The Agenda Wizard asks you specific questions about the meeting, and when you are finished it creates an agenda document. You can send the agenda as an attachment to a meeting invitation or print copies and bring them to the meeting.

◇ MEETING MINUTES

Meeting minutes are a record of what took place during a meeting. The minutes allow the meeting attendees to review the meeting later to look for outstanding issues and action items. In some cases, such as stockholder and board of directors meetings, the minutes are required by law and are included in the corporate minute book.

While attending a meeting, you can make handwritten notes, type on a computer if the sound of the typing does not distract the meeting attendees, or use a recording device and transcribe the meeting later. Regardless of which method you use, make sure that all of the essential elements of the meeting are noted: type of meeting, company name, date and time, facilitator, main topics, and time of adjournment.

Make a list of the expected attendees, or review the meeting agenda. As each person enters the room, you can check him or her off the list. Optionally, you can pass around an attendance sheet for everyone to sign as the meeting begins. If necessary, map out a seating arrangement for the meeting and be prepared to introduce any unfamiliar people.

If you prepare an outline in advance based on the agenda, you already have the main topics written down and you can keep your notes organized.

When you transcribe the minutes, you should write them up in formal language according to the following outline:

- Name of organization
- Name of body conducting meeting
- Date, hour, and location of meeting
- List of those present and those absent
- Reading of previous minutes and their approval or amendment
- Unfinished business
- New business
- Date of next meeting
- Time of adjournment
- Signature of recorder

Avoid the mistake of recording every single comment. Instead, concentrate on getting the essence of the discussion by taking enough notes to summarize it later. Remember, minutes are a record of what happened at a meeting, not a record of everything that was said.

Outsourcing Project
Meeting Agenda

Meeting Called By:	Session #:	Date:	Starting Time:
Mark Rivers		1/28/2009	9:30 a.m.

Location:	Dress Code (optional):	Ending Time:
Central Park		12:00 p.m.
Conference Room 11a		

Meeting Objective and Scope:
JAD Session — The Big Picture

Time	Topic	Discussion Leader
9:30–9:35	Welcome and review agenda.	Mark Rivers
9:35–9:55	Basic data flow for enrollments.	Darlene Price
9:55–10:15	Ongoing data requirements including conversion needs.	Darlene Price
10:15–10:35	Basic data flow for pay processing including negatives.	Darlene Price
10:35–10:40	Break.	
10:40–11:00	Basic data flow for 401(k) billing.	Darlene Price
11:00–11:20	Basic data flow for termination processing.	Darlene Price
11:20–11:40	Basic data flow for loans.	Darlene Price
11:40–11:55	Basic data flow for discrimination.	Darlene Price
11:55–12:00	Wrap-up.	Mark Rivers

Facilitator:	Time Keeper:	Scribe:
Darlene Price		Debra Miller

Attendees:			
Anne Fried	Mark Rivers	Donna Morgan	Tonya Smith
Debra Miller	Sally Roberts	Susan Mullins	Ebony Hollings
Tanya Sanchez	Mary McKnight	Daphne Johnson	Mike Harper
Kevin Wilson	Kendall Williams	Rita Zezula	Darlene Price

Figure 6–3. Sample meeting agenda.

Figure 6–4. The Agenda Wizard in Microsoft Word.

Screen shot reprinted by permission from Microsoft Corporation.

Always prepare ahead for meetings where you will take minutes. It's important that you understand the discussion without asking a lot of questions. Following the meeting, don't wait too long to write up the minutes. Always have a draft of the minutes approved by the meeting organizer or facilitator before distributing them to the attendees.

Figure 6–5 is an example of minutes for an organization.

Corporate Minutes

All corporations must document the minutes of shareholder and board of directors meetings. In fact, in many states, the absence of proper meeting minutes may be a liability for the corporation, especially in situations where the shareholders are also on the board of directors, or where there are close relationships among board members. All corporations in the United States are required to hold annual shareholders' meetings to elect directors. In addition, the bylaws of most corporations require the board of directors to have annual meetings. At these corporate meetings, the following actions are normally approved by the board of directors:

- Election of officers of the corporation
- New business policies and plans
- Creation of committees and assignments
- Issuing and selling stock
- Approval of the sale, transfer, lease, or exchange of any corporate property or assets

---

**Minutes of Meeting of
the Historical Society of the University of Texas
Hotel Driscoll, Austin, Texas
May 1, 2009**

At the meeting of the Historical Society of the University of Texas at Austin, some 100 charter members being present, the Society was called to order at 1:05 p.m. by Mr. John R. Combs, Chairperson, who requested Mr. Warren T. Scaggs to serve as Temporary Secretary.

Mr. Combs dispensed with the reading of the minutes of the last meeting because a copy had been previously distributed to all members.

A communication from the National Historical Society, read and accepted by the Society, dealt with the planting of redbud trees throughout America.

A communication from Miss Harriet Allen of New York City asked that the Society refrain from its normal pattern of conducting spring tours throughout the State of Texas. Several members, after the reading, expressed disagreement with the views given by Miss Allen.

There was no unfinished business.

New business was the election of officers for the remaining current year. The following nominations were announced by Mr. Warren T. Scaggs, Chairperson of the Nominating Committee:

President	Mrs. Rutherford Tinsdale
Secretary	Mr. Joseph Mapes
Treasurer	Mrs. Theodore R. Tollivar
Members of the Council	Ms. Louise Allen
	Mrs. Philip W. Crossman
	Mr. John Stobaugh
	Mrs. John C. McCann

After an unanswered call for nominations from the floor, it was moved by Mrs. William R. Metcalfe that the Secretary cast one ballot for officers nominated. The motion was seconded and carried, and the officers were declared elected.

The next meeting of the Historical Society of the University of Texas at Austin will be held on June 11 at the Hotel Driscoll in Austin, Texas, at 1:00 p.m.

After congratulations to the newly elected officers by the Chairperson, the Society adjourned at 3:25 p.m.

Warren T. Scaggs
Temporary Secretary

Figure 6–5. Minutes of a typical meeting.

- Approval of mergers and reorganizations
- Adoption of pension, profit-sharing, or other employee benefit plans and stock-option plans
- Approval of corporate borrowing and loans
- Entering into joint ventures
- Designating corporate bank accounts and authorized signatures
- Changing an officer's compensation
- Entering into major contractual agreements

Small corporations have informal meetings where these matters are discussed. Large corporations have formal meetings. In both cases, the board of directors must pass a resolution to approve the action. Therefore, the meeting minutes are a record of the board's consent and the discussion surrounding the decision.

Resolutions

Formal resolutions may be made in one of these forms:

- WHEREAS it is necessary to . . . ; and
- WHEREAS conditions are such that . . . ; and
- Therefore be it
- RESOLVED, That . . . ; and be it
- RESOLVED further, That . . .

Note that the word *whereas* is in caps with no comma following it; the first word after it is not capitalized unless it is a proper name. The word *resolved* is also set in caps but is followed by a comma and a capital letter.

In formal resolutions, the facts are stated simply:

- . . . and the following resolution was unanimously adopted: RESOLVED, That . . .

Office Meetings

Your boss may ask you to record into written form a meeting of various office personnel, perhaps department heads. Elaborate minutes are not required as long as the group is not a governing body within the company, such as the board of directors. Figure 6–6 is a sample report of an office meeting.

◆ CONFERENCES

Sometimes an administrative assistant is asked to assist in the planning and coordinating of conferences for the company. This involves preparing for the event, carrying out your responsibilities during the conference, and follow-up activities after it's over.

Planning for the Conference

The planning for a conference involves consideration of items related to the conference facilities and the speakers. As you plan for a conference, keep in mind the following:

- Booking the conference site
- Blocking reservations for hotel rooms, selection of room sizes, and price range
- Confirming auditorium sizes and breakout rooms

> **Meeting of the United Way Committee**
> **January 12, 2009**
>
> Attendance:
>
>
> A meeting of the department managers was held in the office of John Smith, Executive Vice President, at 9 a.m. on January 12, 2009. Mr. Smith presided. Present were Martha Johnson, Philip Smith, Martin Allen, Raymond Martinez, Eloise Randolph, Anthony Guerrero, and Patricia Reese. James Augustine was absent.
>
> Items Covered:
> 1. How the company can participate fully in the United Way campaign. Raymond Martinez reviewed last year's company goals and how these goals were reached. Anthony Guerrero suggested our goal for the present year be increased by 10 percent. Recommendations were made by each person present.
> 2. These suggestions and recommendations will be discussed and voted upon at the February 2 meeting of the committee.
>
> Adjournment:
> The meeting was adjourned at 10 a.m.
>
> Martha Johnson, Recorder

Figure 6–6. Sample report of an office meeting.

- Scheduling catering and beverage service
- Confirming smoking locations
- Inspecting facilities you haven't seen before
- Sending letters of invitations to speakers
- Following up with confirmation letters to the speakers and conference site
- Obtaining background information, photos, and resumes of the speakers

Preparing Conference Materials

As the conference time approaches, you need to confirm all necessary supporting materials: table and chair rentals, reports, financial statements, advertisements, meeting agendas, itineraries, and executive travel folders.

If it is your responsibility, you need to make arrangements for printing packets, maps, tickets, and awards. You may also need to make arrangements for local tours and special outside events to entertain the speakers, attendees, and their spouses. Many times family members accompany spouses who are attending a conference, and any thoughtful conference organizer has made arrangements for shopping trips, outside restaurant gatherings, tickets to sporting events, museum tours, and other local attractions.

You also need to coordinate with the conference site to plan meals, refreshments, coffee breaks, and banquets. This should involve evaluating menus in advance and planning what will be served.

You may also be involved in preregistration and registration. This requires organizing a filing system for those attendees who preregister and having badges made. During the registration on the first day of the conference, you may be involved in staffing the registration desk. You should organize registration materials alphabetically. All conference materials should be assembled in packets with programs, brochures, reports, name tags, meal tickets, and so forth.

Confirm with the conference site any audiovisual equipment or meeting supplies you may need. Breakout rooms need chalkboards or whiteboards, easels with large pads of paper, and marker pens or chalk. Conference rooms may need lecterns, microphones, overhead projectors, video players, video projectors, projection screens, television monitors, and a public address system. Usually this involves filling out a reservation request form with the conference facility. Also make sure you order extra projector bulbs and extension cords.

If your conference involves international guests, you may need to make arrangements for a translation service.

Two weeks before the conference, you should mail all pre-work to attendees. You should also ship any supplies and conference materials to the conference site around two weeks in advance.

If it is appropriate, you may need to arrange for press coverage by contacting media outlets, arranging for a photographer to take photos during the conference, and sending out press releases.

Finally, you need to coordinate any security concerns with the conference location or security service. You may also need to coordinate parking with the conference location's parking attendants. You need to provide both groups with a formal agenda with event times, additional security protection needed, and parking requirements.

During the Conference

While the conference is underway, your duties may include checking meeting rooms and making sure all necessary materials are available. Confirm that the lighting and heating are functioning, refreshments are available, audiovisual equipment is available and functioning, and the room is clean.

As conference guests arrive, you should greet and welcome them to the conference. Be a host and introduce people, escort people who need directions, and be helpful where you can.

If you are asked to work the registration desk, you may need to provide statistics on who will attend the various events. Prepare lists of participants with names and addresses.

You may be asked to attend some meetings and take minutes, handle correspondence requests, or route incoming express shipments. You may write and distribute a conference newsletter, coordinate messages among participants, or meet with media representatives and photographers.

After the Conference

Each day after the conference, remove any surplus literature and conference packets from the meeting rooms. Inform the conference site staff regarding any catering items left in the meeting rooms. Make sure any audiovisual equipment is properly secured. Also move and secure any other rental equipment. Any lost and found items should be taken to the conference site receptionist.

When you return to the office, you may need to complete follow-up reports or other conference-related mailings. You may need to send thank you letters to speakers or distribute meeting minutes.

Finally, you need to calculate expenses and fill out expense reports. As a last step, update the meeting file with your notes. With everything fresh in your mind, write down what went well and what challenges you faced. If you have ideas on how to make improvements, put them down on paper in the file.

Conference Notes

If your employer asks you to report on all that is said in a conference, make place cards for the members of the group who are expected to meet. As they enter the room, direct them to sit where they have been assigned. In front of your own seat, arrange tabs showing the names of the members in the same order they are seated around the table so that you know who is speaking at each given moment. This enables you to take your notes in the form of a dramatic dialogue. Preface one remark with "Hansen" if the man whose name is Hansen has spoken; preface the next remark with "Rosen" if the next voice has come from the seat you assigned to Mrs. Rosen; and so forth.

When you transcribe your notes, you can show the discussion in this dialogue form, if that's acceptable to your employer. Alternatively, you can insert a full stage direction such as "Mr. Hansen replied:" or "The next speaker was Mrs. Rosen, who said . . . " In either case, open your transcription with a list of those present, giving the full name or initials and office held, if any, for each.

A recording device is usually used, but you should be ready if it's not available. It may be wise to take notes even when a recording device is used because, unless the meeting is held under strict discipline, there may be a jumble of voices. Your notes will help you decipher the recording.

7

Time Management

◇ OVERVIEW OF TIME MANAGEMENT

Time management is an essential skill for an effective administrative assistant. People who use time management techniques are usually the highest achievers in life and business. If you learn time management techniques, you'll be able to work effectively, even under pressure.

The key aspect of time management involves a change in focus. You must concentrate on the end result, not just on staying busy. Many people find themselves very busy throughout the day, but they don't achieve much because they are not focusing on the right things. The famous Pareto Principle, sometimes called the "80:20 Rule," sums it up nicely: 80 percent of the unfocused effort generates only 20 percent of the results.

By using time management techniques, you can optimize your time and energy by focusing on results that have the greatest payoff. This will ensure that you get the greatest benefit from the time you have available.

◇ CONTROLLING PROCRASTINATION

If you've put off important tasks from time to time, you are like many people. We all sometimes procrastinate to some degree. One of the first keys to effective time management is to not let procrastination stop you from achieving in your career. The key to controlling your urge to procrastinate is to recognize when you are doing it and to take action to better manage your time and effort.

People procrastinate when they put off something they should be doing in order to do something else that is more enjoyable. People who procrastinate may work just as long and hard as everyone else, but they spend their time on the wrong tasks. Sometimes this comes from not being able to prioritize tasks effectively.

If you spend the day being bombarded with one thing after another, you might focus on the most recent task, considering it to be the most urgent even though an earlier project might actually be more important. Similarly, you might decide to tackle the endless list in the order the tasks were assigned, even though that list might not be in priority order.

Feeling overwhelmed by an assignment is another cause of procrastination. You can't figure out how to get started or doubt you have the skills to complete the job, so you put it off in favor of doing other things you feel capable of accomplishing. The problem is that the challenging assignment isn't going away.

Other causes of procrastination include waiting for the right mood to take on an important task, being afraid of failure, being too much of a perfectionist, or not having good decision-making skills.

Whatever the reason you find yourself procrastinating, you must be honest with yourself and take action. The first thing you should do is make sure you understand the priorities of your assignments. Communicate with your boss or the individual making the assignment and find out when it is due. When there is a conflict between two projects, get help to determine which is more important. Many times your boss may make a request early in the day, only to have a more important assignment come up later. By asking your boss which task takes priority, it's easy to focus your effort where it is needed most.

◇ MAINTAINING AN ACTIVITY LIST

To get a better idea of how you are spending your time and what you are actually accomplishing, make a list of your daily activities. After you've recorded several days of activity, analyze the list to see how much time you've spent doing low-priority tasks.

As you examine the list, start by eliminating tasks that are not your responsibility. Are you doing things that someone else in the organization should be doing? Are you doing personal activities at work or sending nonwork-related e-mails?

Try to reduce the number of times you switch between tasks. For example, rather than stopping every half hour to read and reply to e-mail, you could schedule time twice each day to focus solely on e-mail.

Use your activity list to help prioritize your To-Do list. Schedule the most challenging tasks for the time of day when your energy is highest.

◇ CREATING ACTION PLANS

Whenever you find yourself facing a large project that seems overwhelming, it's time to create an action plan. An action plan is a list of all the tasks you need to accomplish in order to complete an entire project. It's different from your To-Do list because it focuses on a single goal.

To create an action plan, first list all the tasks that need to be accomplished to achieve the goal and put them in the order they need to be completed. As you put tasks on the list, try to break each one into smaller subtasks. Listing a few items may cause you to think of others.

Keep the action plan nearby as you begin working through the plan item by item. If additional tasks are needed that were not on the original plan, revise the plan and work from the new version.

After you've completed the project, go back and review the final version of your action plan. Could you have done anything differently? Were you missing some steps? Would a different order of tasks been better? Use your action plan as a learning experience to make improvements in the action plans you create in the future.

◇ KEEPING A TO-DO LIST

If you feel overwhelmed by looming deadlines or sometimes forget to do something important, you badly need to start keeping a To-Do list. A To-Do list is a prioritized list of all of the tasks you need to accomplish. The most important tasks are at the top of the list; the least important are at the bottom.

Many people who become effective at time management say that keeping a To-Do list is one of the main reasons they are successful. If you keep a list in one place of everything you need to do, it's difficult to forget something. If you review the list each morning and reprioritize it, you can easily tell what needs immediate action. Without a To-Do list, you have to juggle everything in your head. When you accidentally forget to do something, people may think you are unreliable. With a To-Do list, you're organized and more responsible. Because of this, keeping a To-Do list can be critical to the success of your career.

To create a To-Do list, start by writing down all the tasks you need to accomplish. Larger projects should be divided into smaller tasks, similar to an action plan. Keep subdividing larger tasks until each item on your To-Do list will take no more than one to two hours to complete. Once you've written everything down, you can prioritize your list by assigning letters or numbers. For example, all items that have a high priority should be assigned the letter A. All items that have extremely low priority should be assigned the letter F. Continue to prioritize your To-Do list using letters B, C, D, and E. After your first pass, review the high-priority items and see if any of them can be demoted. When you are finished prioritizing, sort the list with the high-priority tasks at the top of the list. You may find it easier to use word-processing software to create your To-Do list, since it is simple to revise and sort.

People use their To-Do lists in different ways. Some create a smaller daily version with a list of all the items they plan on completing that day. They then review the master list each morning and create a new daily To-Do list.

You may find that some of the low-priority tasks are carried around from one To-Do list to the next for several weeks or even months. There's no need to worry about this, though you should not forget about such items entirely. If one of the low-priority tasks has an imminent deadline, you need to raise its priority level.

◇ SCHEDULING

So far this chapter has focused on organizing your daily tasks. Scheduling is where your plans become reality. Scheduling is the process where you examine the amount of time you have available each day and plan how you will use it to accomplish the tasks you've identified. By scheduling time to work on each task, you will understand what you can realistically accomplish. You'll be able to make the best use of the time you have available, designating time for those must-do items. You'll be able to schedule time for the unexpected, so you'll be prepared for the twists and turns business life may throw your way. As a result, you'll reduce your stress level by not overcommitting to others. A schedule allows you to take control over your time and your life.

Scheduling is best if you do it regularly, such as at the beginning of each week or month. The first step is to determine the times each day when you will work on your tasks. This depends on the nature of your job and your personal situation. Next, block out the time in your schedule. If you use calendar software or Microsoft Outlook's calendar feature, you can schedule work time in your calendar to keep other people from scheduling meetings for you during these periods.

After scheduling your work time, the next step is to review your To-Do list and schedule the high-priority tasks in your work periods. Make sure you leave time available for the unexpected and schedule contingency time.

The time that is left in your schedule is your discretionary time. This is the time you can use to learn new things, plan, organize yourself, and prioritize. If you find that you have little or no discretionary time, you need to revisit your list of tasks and determine if they are all absolutely necessary or whether they can be accomplished in some abbreviated way.

Keeping Accurate Records

◇ A CRITICAL DUTY

Keeping accurate records and maintaining an up-to-date filing system are important responsibilities for most administrative assistants. Every filing system ever conceived requires that the person maintaining it approaches the duty with a sense of pride. He or she must be confident that any file can be retrieved quickly, perhaps even as the employer is still requesting it on the telephone.

Most companies today, even small businesses, store their letters and documents in their computers or word-processing equipment and automatically maintain them there or on disk (see Chapter 13 on database management). However—as administrative assistants know only too well—even with computers, the amount of paper correspondence and documents to be saved seems to grow daily.

Large companies often have a central file department where all papers are kept by competent file clerks. Other companies maintain files by division, and small companies may have only a few file cabinets for their entire operation. In these cases, it's the administrative assistant who is usually responsible for record keeping and maintenance. But no matter what your usual duties, you should be familiar with the various filing systems used in both small and large offices.

◇ GETTING READY

It's often tempting, especially at the end of the day, simply to throw a file in its own folder. Don't. Filing is an important duty, no matter how tedious it seems. Instead of trying to get rid of that file or piece of paper as quickly as possible, approach it with these questions always in mind: Where could I easily find this tomorrow (or next week, or next year)? What's in this letter or document that would cause me to recall where I'm placing it in the file now?

Follow this checklist before you start to file:

- Prepare the papers by separating personal correspondence from business correspondence and documents.

- Check all stapled papers to be sure that only papers belonging together have been stapled together.

- Remove all paper clips. They not only crowd the file but also can catch papers that should not have been clipped to them.

- Mend any torn papers with tape.

- Underline in bright pencil or with a marking pen the name or subject under which the paper is to be filed.

On the file folders, use staggered tabs or one-position tabs. The straight-line tab, all in the center or in the far right position on the edge of the folder, is often preferred.

When various sets of files are used, it's wise to tab each set with a different color label. For example, use white for correspondence, blue for subject files, and green for case files. Each category then has its own color for quick recognition.

On labels, type the name of the folder on the first line beginning two or three spaces from the left edge. Use initial caps and lowercase letters, and abbreviate freely. Leave two spaces between name and any number.

◇ BASIC FILING SYSTEMS

Common or basic filing systems that might be used in a business office include the following: alphabetical, subject, geographical, numeric, and combination subject (though the office would probably be a very large one with many technical files to utilize the last). About 90 percent of offices use the alphabetical system.

Two less used systems are the decimal filing system and the group name system (sometimes called the phonetic filing system). The decimal system, based on the Dewey decimal classification system, is used primarily in libraries. The material being filed must be organized under ten or fewer main headings numbered 000 to 900. In turn, each main heading is divided into ten or fewer subheadings numbered from 10 to 90 and preceded by the correct hundreds digit. Each subheading may then be subdivided into ten or fewer further headings numbered from 1 to 9, preceded by the correct hundreds and tens digits.

The group name or phonetic system is used when there are a great many names involved, as in census surveys. Names that sound alike but are spelled differently are grouped together according to pronunciation rather than spelling: Allan, Allen, Allyn; Nielsen, Neilson, Nealson; Schneider, Snider, Snyder.

Alphabetical System

The alphabetical system is the most widely used filing method because it's the most efficient and least complicated. Material is filed alphabetically according to name. No cross-indexing is necessary. A label should be typed for each name and applied to the tab on each folder.

Papers are placed in the folder in chronological order with the most current date in front. The folders are filed behind alphabet guides (obtainable in any office supply store). When there is heavy correspondence with one client, several folders may be needed to hold all current material. In this case, it's a good practice to separate the material into time periods: one folder for the year 2007, another for the year 2008, and another for 2009. If several projects have been handled for that customer, one folder may be labeled FLORIDA, another NORTH DAKOTA, another MICHIGAN, and so on.

If only the current year's files are kept handy (with previous years' files stored elsewhere), it's useful, for at least the first few weeks of the new year, to have the old year's files and the new year's files placed back to back or side by side. Of course, a different year is on each file tab, perhaps a different color as well: red for 2008, for example, and yellow for 2009.

Subject System

This classification is used when papers are called for by subject, rather than by a person's or a company's name. Subject classification may be needed when dealing with, say, advertising, brand name products, or materials of all kinds.

You should be thoroughly familiar with the papers flowing through the office and across your desk before attempting to set up this kind of system. The list of subjects must be comprehensive, as simple as possible, and in alphabetical order or by number code. The alphabetical list is usually preferred so that a cross-index is not necessary. Papers in the subject folder are arranged chronologically, always with the latest date in front.

Subject Index

While an index of files is not required for a small filing system, it's imperative for large companies. And since most small businesses hope to grow, it's a good practice to maintain a filing system from the start. The subject index prevents the filing of material under a new heading when a folder has already been set up for that subject, perhaps under a different title. It also permits a person other than the administrative assistant to trace information in the file.

An index card is made for each subject heading or subheading. Each subheading shows the main heading under which it is filed. Cross-reference cards are made if the subject is complex. The employer may indicate on the paper where he or she wants it to be filed, while the administrative assistant may have formerly filed that subject under another heading. A cross-reference enables both to find the paper later. The index cards are filed alphabetically.

How to Alphabetize for Filing and Indexing

Individual or Personal Names

The names of people are alphabetized by their surname. When surnames are the same, the position is naturally determined by the letters that follow:

- Smith, Mary B.
- Smith, Ned
- Smithson, John

When two or more similar names are of unequal length, file the shorter name first:

- Smith, M.
- Smith, Mary
- Smith, Mary C.
- Smith, Mary Charlene

Individual surnames with prefixes are alphabetized as each is written and are considered to be one word, whether or not they are written as one word:

- Mason, Tim
- McFarland, John
- Merrill, Jane
- Vane, K.
- Van Houton, Mae
- Vargas, Louise

A religious title or foreign title is alphabetized when it is followed by a first name only:

- Brother Thomas
- Burton, Francis (Rev.)
- Friar Tuck
- Queen Elizabeth
- Sister Mary Rose
- Tilton, Sarah (S.S.J.)

Company or Business Names

Words joined by a hyphen are treated as one word. However, if the hyphen is used instead of a comma in a business name, the individual parts of the name are treated as separate words, and therefore the name is indexed by the first word alone. The second name of the hyphenate is used only when needed, similar to a given name:

- Johnson, Samuel
- Johnson-Smith & Company
- Johnson, Steven
- Johnson, Victor

Whether a company name is composed of a compound word or is spelled as two words, it is alphabetized as if it were one word:

- New Deal Loan Company of America
- Newdeal Marine Works
- Suncity Shipbuilding Corporation
- Sun City Tannery

The exception is when a company name contains the name of a person. In this case, alphabetize by using the surname, followed by first name, then middle initial or middle name if any. The exception is the names of schools. These are alphabetized as written, as are other organizations, businesses, or institutions. See Table 8–1.

TABLE 8–1. Filing When the Company Name Contains a Person's Name

Name	Filed As
American Petroleum Co.	American Petroleum Co.
Mary Brown Cafe	Brown, Mary Cafe
John Dillard Company	Dillard, John Company
Dillard Stores	Dillard Stores
Joyce Kilmer High School	Joyce Kilmer High School
May's Floral Center	May's Floral Center
John C. Wilson Realty	Wilson, John C. Realty
Wilson Realty Company	Wilson Realty Company

Single letters used as words are treated as words and arranged alphabetically preceding word names:

- BB Shop
- BBB Service Company
- Bakery Heaven
- Brighton Clothes Company

When two or more similar company or business names are of unequal length, file the shorter name first:

- National Bank
- National Bank of Commerce
- Bronson Club
- Bronson Club of New York City

Miscellaneous

Abbreviations are alphabetized as if spelled in full. See Table 8–2.

TABLE 8–2. Filing Abbreviations

Name	Filed As
St. Luke's Church	Saint Luke's Church
Jas. Smith	Smith, James
Chas. Williams	Williams, Charles

Designations following names are alphabetized according to natural order of age:

- Smith, James III
- Smith, James, 2d
- Smith, James, Jr.
- Smith, James, Sr.

Articles, prepositions, conjunctions, and the ampersand are disregarded in alphabetizing:

- Thomas & Anderson, Inc.
- Thomas, Brown R.
- Washington Bank, The
- Workshop for the Blind

When words end in s, the s is considered part of the name:

- Leon Neon and Light
- Leon's Art Supplies

If a name contains a number, do not put it in "numerical order" with other numbered names. Alphabetize it as if the number were spelled out:

- 1020 Building Corporation (one thousand twenty)
- 13 Park Avenue Studio (thirteen)
- 21 Club (twenty-one)

Titles are disregarded:

- Jones, R. L. (Dr.)
- Simms, Carlotta (Countess)
- Smith, Nancy (Miss)

Exception: If a company name starts with a title, the title is considered to be the first word:

- Queen Mary Boat Company
- Sir John Thomas Cigar Company
- Viceroy of India Silk Company

◆ FILE CABINETS

A standard file cabinet has four drawers that accommodate material written on 8½ inch by 11 inch typing or computer paper. An office with many legal-sized papers (8½ inch by 13 or 14 inches) needs a wider cabinet made specifically for these.

Your file cabinet should be near your desk, since you go to it frequently throughout the workday. Label each drawer of the cabinet either horizontally (left to right) or vertically (top to bottom). If an alphabetical system is used, the top drawer might be labeled "A–G," the second drawer "H–M," and so forth.

Many secretarial desks have a built-in file drawer, handy for files used often so you can reach for them quickly without having to leave your desk to go to the larger cabinet.

8 ■ KEEPING RECORDS

OFFICE EQUIPMENT AND COMPUTERS

SECTION TWO

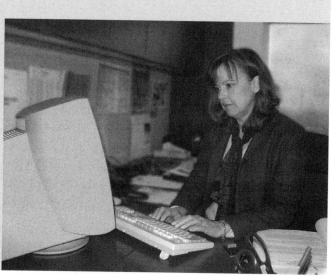

Modern office technology has revolutionized the way we work.

Photo by Jennifer Wauson.

Office Machines

◇ TYPEWRITERS

For years, electric typewriters accomplished much of what is now done with computers and word processors. For some applications, such as typing an address on an envelope or a mailing label, a typewriter is still the simplest office tool available, and now, the merging of electric typewriters with dedicated word processors has produced a machine that does everything a sophisticated computer does, and at much less expense.

Almost all models of electric typewriters have advanced word-processing features built in. At the heart of them is a powerful microprocessor based on the technology found in early personal computers (PCs). Although this technology is outdated for today's PCs, it is perfectly capable of managing a word-processing typewriter, allowing it to do everything from the ordinary to the truly extraordinary.

Here are a few of the many new features of today's electronic typewriters:

- Word erase for simple corrections

- Spell-checkers, comparing every word you type with those in a built-in electronic dictionary

- Display screen

- Advanced revision features combined with an optional capacity for unlimited storage using diskettes

- Capacity to store and merge mail with telephone lists and other documents

- Background print feature to allow you to print documents while you create or revise other documents

- Ability to upgrade, one of the most useful features of all

Whether you're looking at an electronic typewriter as the sole typing tool for a small office or as a supplement to a larger office's PC, consider getting an upgradable machine. Office needs change frequently, and what might not be quite right for you now could be a necessity in the near future. With upgradability, you could move from a one-line display to twenty-five lines on the screen, or you could double your storage memory.

Because much of the correspondence and many of the documents you create tend to be repetitive, having a typewriter with some memory can greatly automate this task. For example, you can store commonly used addresses for typing envelopes or even a

Figure 9–1. Word-processing typewriter.

Photo by Jennifer Wauson.

form letter, such as a thank you letter. These documents can be stored in the typewriter's memory or on a diskette. Later, you can recall and customize it for a particular person or company.

On a word-processing typewriter (see Figure 9–1), you can automatically move to any position on the page and correct characters or whole words at a touch. The type-writer's cursor keys give you the same flexibility of movement on paper that you would have on a computer's display. The Word Tab and Line Find functions can be used in combination with the cursor keys. Whether you want to move across an area of blank space, jump from word to word, or locate your last line of typed text, there is a convenient way to do it.

To make your written letters and documents works of art, there are fast and easy ways to add interest and emphasis to a page: a bold function, automatic underlining, and so on. Both pitch and impression can be set to match ribbon and paper thickness auto-matically. A programmable paper feed function takes you to your customary top writing line and saves you the trouble of positioning the paper. On some advanced models, an adjustable keyboard lets you select from three typing positions the one that suits you best. Automatic correction cleanly removes or covers up typing errors. The Relocate fea-ture automatically puts you back in position to continue typing after you make a correc-tion. Alternate language keyboards allow you to type in many languages, such as French and Spanish.

In selecting the best typewriter for your office, you should consider the following word-processing features:

- CRT display, with or without brightness and contrast adjustment
- Menu display, either text or icons
- PC compatibility, to allow for file data transfer with computers
- Keyboard type and design—number of keys, special keys
- Memory—the amount in kilobytes (KB)
- Online help—the ability to get help via a CRT screen or display
- Double-column printing capability—prints two or more columns on the page
- Hyphenation—automatic insertion of hyphens
- Insert/delete/overwrite—special editing techniques
- Block moves/copy/delete—additional editing techniques
- Global search and replace, allowing replacement of words or phrases throughout the document
- Automatic word wrap—moves words that do not fit in the screen area down to the next line
- Headers and footers—automatic insertion of text at top or bottom of page (e.g., page numbers)
- Automatic page numbering—calculates and inserts page numbers
- Automatic pagination—determines where the page will break before you print
- Paper size adjustment—allows for different sizes of paper
- Save/retrieve documents—storage of documents in memory or on a CD
- Grammar checking—looks for incorrect grammar usage
- Spell-checker—looks for misspelled words
- Word count—automatic counting of the number of words in a document
- Redundancy check—looks for words typed twice in a row (usually part of a spell-checker)
- Thesaurus—an online database of synonyms
- Paragraph/line indent—special function for indentation
- Decimal tab—keeps decimals lined up when printing a column of numbers
- Tab settings—insertion of tabs across the page
- Justification—centering, as well as right, left, and full justification
- Underlining—allows for underlining a word
- Bold typing—makes type darker for emphasis
- Superscript and subscript—allows for typing special characters for formulas
- Line/word/letter correction—will remove typing mistakes

Figure 9–2. Copy machine.

Courtesy of Xerox Corporation.

◇ COPY MACHINES

Another essential office tool is the copy machine. Although the advent of word-processing typewriters and personal computers has reduced reliance on copiers to some extent, because you can make additional paper copies by printing out duplicates, many documents that do not originate from your word processor or PC require copies.

Many small businesses use a local print shop for copies; however, considering the amount of time lost going back and forth to the shop and the convenience and relative cheapness of having your own copier, purchasing or leasing a copier for the business may be a good idea.

Copiers and laser printers function similarly (see Figure 9–2). They are often referred to as "nonimpact printing." Rather than have a hammer strike a ribbon to produce type on the page like a typewriter, copiers use a photographic process involving static electricity.

When you place a document to be copied inside a copy machine, a very strong light is projected on the original. The image of the original is then projected to an electrically sensitive rotating drum. The dark and light areas of the original affect the electric charge on the print drum. After being exposed to the original, the copier drum turns through a powder called toner, which sticks to the electrically charged areas. The drum then comes into contact with a fresh piece of copier paper, transferring the toner to the paper, thus creating a copy.

More advanced copiers magnify the projection of the light from the original to the copier drum, thus enlarging or reducing the size of the reproduction. Many copiers now use microprocessors to store images and to automate many of the functions such as sorting, collating, and making two-sided copies. With the use of multicolor toners, color copies can be produced. Other copiers have automatic document feeders, paper trays, sorters, and even built-in staplers. The choice of features makes for a wide range of prices.

How to Select a Copier

When selecting a new machine for your office, consider these six main factors:

- **Features.** What features do you really need?
- **Reliability.** How much reliability do you demand?
- **Cost.** What is the price of the copier, and are there any hidden costs?
- **Service/maintenance.** Who will maintain or repair your copier?
- **Warranty.** What does the warranty cover, and for how long?
- **Productivity.** Will this copier improve productivity in your office?

For some companies, even copiers stripped of all features are too large. These companies may want to consider the smallest of models, minicopiers, which is the most inexpensive way to acquire the convenience of a copy machine. Minicopiers (Figure 9–3) are so small they don't even have paper trays and just require the insertion of a single sheet of copier paper for each copy made. They use disposable toner cartridges (readily available at office supply stores) and replacement drums. They usually require little to no maintenance, and although it is possible to get paper jams just as in the larger machines, they are easily cleared.

One of the major drawbacks to minicopiers is the cost of the replacement cartridges. While a low-cost minicopier can be purchased for under $300, a replacement cartridge, good for anywhere from one thousand to five thousand copies depending on the model, can cost $75 or more. One alternative to purchasing a replacement cartridge is to have

Figure 9–3. Minicopier.
Courtesy of Xerox Corporation.

the cartridge refilled with toner. This is accomplished by a company that specializes in this service. The cost can be half the price of a new cartridge. You send your empty cartridge to one of these organizations, which evaluates and then refills it. Sometimes a cartridge cannot be refilled as a result of damage such as scratches on the copier drum.

◇ CALCULATORS

Small electronic calculators have been around since the late 1960s and are now required in almost every business, large or small. They are useful for working with budgets, accounting, and other number-intensive business tasks. (For larger projects, a spreadsheet on a personal computer is a better choice.)

Calculators come in a variety of sizes and designs. Some have large LED (light-emitting diode) screens that can be used in dim light situations, and others use LCD (liquid-crystal display) screens that require good lighting to be seen. Some use solar power, while others use batteries or AC power from the wall outlet. Some are very small so they can be carried with you, while others are designed for desktop use. Some also have built-in printers (see Figure 9–4).

Besides being able to add, subtract, multiply, and divide, many calculators also have the ability to use fixed or floating-point decimals and have programmable function keys, memory keys, and special keys to perform square roots. Many calculators are also produced for specific applications. There are scientific calculators, programmable calculators, and graphing calculators.

Figure 9–4. Printing calculator.

Photo by Jennifer Wauson.

◆ OTHER OFFICE EQUIPMENT

Additional office equipment found in today's businesses include:

- Binding systems
- Laminators
- Overhead projectors
- Paper shredders

Binding Systems

Binding systems (see Figure 9–5) are used to create professional-looking bound reports, presentations, and proposals. One of the most common systems is the plastic comb binding system. This is an ideal solution for binding standard letter-size documents in-house. The system includes a punch press that punches up to twenty sheets of 20-pound paper per punch and binds documents sheets with two-inch plastic binding combs. A paper guide and ruler are used to align sheets accurately.

Laminators

Laminators are often used to preserve photographs and to create quick reference cards, place mats, badges, and ID cards. A paper document is placed into a clear plastic lamination pouch

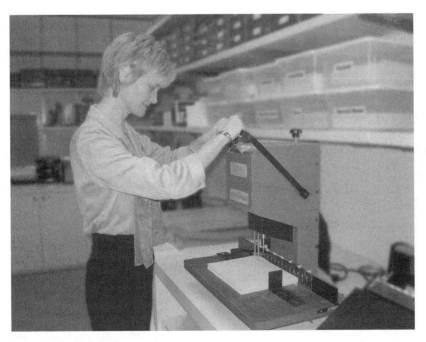

Figure 9–5. Binding system.

Photo by Jennifer Wauson.

and then run through the heated laminator, which seals the document in a protective hard plastic covering.

Overhead Projectors

Overhead projectors and video projectors are often used in meetings and presentations to large groups. With an overhead projector, presentation materials are copied or printed on clear plastic transparency pages called foils or transparencies. The transparencies are then placed on the light table of the overhead projector, and a powerful light passes through the transparency and projects an image on a screen. The transparencies can be written on during a presentation for everyone in the meeting to see.

Video projectors (Figure 9–6) are often used to display videos, television images, or computer data. With a video projector, presentation slides can be created using a program such as Microsoft PowerPoint. The slides are then displayed on a screen by the video projector. When the presenter wants to change slides, the mouse button is clicked or the space bar on the keyboard is pressed.

Paper Shredders

As a security measure to protect sensitive documents, paper shredders are used to destroy draft copies and old documents as an alternative to throwing them in the trash. Paper shredders vary in size from small models that fit on top of a trash can to large freestanding models.

Figure 9–6. Video projector.

Courtesy of Dell Inc.

10

Telecommunications Equipment

New developments in telecommunications equipment are changing the way all businesses, large and small, communicate. The telephone, computer, fax machine, cellular phone, pager, and PDA each now plays a vital role in the success or failure of the company you work for. As a frequent user and a potential purchaser of such equipment for the company, you should be aware of all the latest features and benefits.

◇ TELEPHONES

Telephone service has come a long way since it was invented in the late 1800s. In the early days, telephone service was primitive and selective. Not everyone had a telephone, nor could you call everyone or everywhere. Only towns that put up the poles and ran the wires had service, and even then, many people had to share a telephone line.

Today, telephone service is taken for granted. Businesses use voice mail and computerized answering machines to take messages, to network computers across town or across the country, and to send fax transmissions to offices around the world. Let's start with the basic business services that allow you to call across the street.

PBX

You may have seen in old movies a switchboard operator struggling with a tangle of wires and plugs. Today's larger businesses have replaced the switchboard operator with a PBX (private branch exchange) system. A PBX is a computerized telephone management system that is ideal for a company with many employees and individual phone extensions. It allows a single telephone number for a business to be accessed at the same time by numerous outside callers. As each call is received, it is automatically routed to the appropriate extension via a touchtone phone or with the help of a receptionist or operator.

Multi-Line Telephones

A multi-line telephone system is often the preferred choice in a small business. It allows you to answer an incoming call from anywhere in the office and to route it to another telephone at the touch of a button. If one line is being used, you can access another line to make an outgoing call.

VoIP Telephones

Voice over Internet Protocol (VoIP) is a technology that is rapidly growing in popularity in many businesses today. This technology allows for sending telephone audio over the Internet rather than traditional telephone lines. The advantage is low cost local telephone service and long distance.

IP phones look just like normal phones, but instead of the normal RJ-11 phone connectors, they use an RJ-45 Ethernet connector and are connected to your computer network. IP phones have all the software and hardware to handle IP calls.

Other Business Telephones

A wide variety of other available business telephones combine telephone service with computer operations. Many of these more sophisticated telephones are equipped with special features, such as buttons and lights to designate different lines. More modern telephones use computer-like LED (light-emitting diode) displays to designate and select lines as well as to indicate the number dialed. Others are programmable to store frequently called numbers in the telephone's memory. Some have speaker telephones built in to free up one's hands while talking. Still others have automatic redialing, intercom capabilities, and built-in answering machines.

◈ VOICE MAIL AND ANSWERING MACHINES

When you're away from your desk and no one else can cover your telephone, it's important that you use an answering machine or computerized voice mail system. You don't want to miss critical calls for your boss or yourself. Customers now expect the use of such devices, no matter what size company you work for.

Many different types of answering machines are available. Some use audiotapes to play an outgoing message and to record incoming messages. Others record messages digitally using built-in computer memory. Even the most inexpensive answering machine can automatically record the date and time of the call and allow the person being called to retrieve messages from remote locations. This last is an essential feature to look for, especially if your boss is frequently away from the office. He or she doesn't have to wait to make contact with you to collect messages but can call in any time from home or on the road. By using a code combination from a touchtone telephone, the boss can listen to messages and even record a new outgoing message.

Computerized voice mail systems, often used in larger companies, usually consist of a computer system along with a modem connected to the telephone line. These systems accept incoming calls and route them to various voice mail boxes for each employee. All messages are stored in the computer's memory or on a hard drive. The use of a touchtone telephone is usually required to access voice mail boxes and to leave and retrieve messages.

Integrated Messaging

Integrated messaging is a service that allows voice mail messages to be received as e-mail attachments using e-mail software such as Microsoft Outlook. The message normally includes caller-ID information such as the phone number or e-mail address of the person calling you. You can listen to your messages by opening the e-mail and clicking the attached audio file.

 SPECIAL TELEPHONE SERVICES

Many telephone companies have a variety of special services that enhance the performance of your business telephone system, no matter which model you have. These services may vary from one part of the country to another. Here is a description of some of the more common services available:

- **Call waiting** is useful for individuals and small businesses that have only one incoming telephone line. When you're on one call, you are alerted by a tone that another incoming call is waiting. If you wish, you can put the current call on hold and switch to answer the new incoming call.

- **Select call waiting** permits only the calls the user has programmed into the telephone to beep you in the call-waiting mode.

- **Call forwarding** allows you to redirect calls intended for your telephone to another telephone of your choice—ideal when you or your boss must spend extended time at another location.

- **Select call forwarding** enables you to program your telephone with a list of only those people you want to be able to contact you at the forwarding number.

- **Three-way conferencing** allows you to call more than one person at a time so that three or more people can participate in the same conversation.

- **Caller ID** shows you on a visual display the name and number of the person calling. Caller ID lets you use your telephone like a pocket pager, enabling you to decide whether to take the call, return it later, or ignore it.

- **Busy number redial** continues to dial a busy number automatically until the line is free. The telephone then alerts you when the line is ringing.

- **Selective call acceptance** allows you to program your telephone with a list of only those people you want to contact you. When a person on that list calls, the call rings through to your telephone. No other calls are allowed to get through.

- **Voice message** enables callers to leave a message that you retrieve later, just like an answering machine. Voice message is similar to voice mail; however, no special equipment is required at a user's location.

◇ LONG DISTANCE SERVICES

There are many choices for long distance service. Besides AT&T, MCI, and Sprint, a host of smaller, regional long distance companies market themselves to specific parts of the country. These services may or may not have their own long distance networks. In many cases, they purchase blocks of long distance time from a common telephone carrier and then resell that time to small businesses and individuals.

Toll-Free Numbers

One long distance service can benefit your company's customers: a toll-free number, sometimes called a "watts" line. As the owner of an 800 number, your company pays for all incoming long distance charges. A toll-free number is an expense, true, but it's more than just a convenience for your distant customers. It can be a selling point in whether your company makes the first sale at all.

Because of the demand for toll-free numbers, telephone companies have made a variety of other three-digit prefixes available in addition to 800, including 888, 878, 877, and 866.

900 Numbers

The 900 prefix is often associated with information lines that require the caller to pay a per-minute fee for the time on the call. This fee is charged to the caller's telephone bill and paid to the owner of the 900 number. Some small businesses involved in mail order have tried using 900 numbers, but often it is reserved for technical help, not for customers who want to order a product.

Teleconferences

One way to reduce travel costs associated with meetings is to use teleconferencing. Teleconferences can be scheduled in advance with a long distance carrier. With a reservation, you can link up different callers from around the country at the same time.

There are two basic ways to conduct a teleconference. In the first, each caller dials a special telephone number at a designated time and is connected to the group teleconference one by one. The second uses an operator, who calls and connects each individual to the teleconference. The cost of the teleconference includes a setup fee and an hourly fee for each caller along with the long distance charges for each individual.

Teleconferences are often combined with Web conferences, where attendees are not only connected via the telephone but also view a presentation on the Web. (See Chapter 17 on Web conferencing.)

Figure 10–1. Apple iPhone

Courtesy of Apple.

◆ CELLULAR TELEPHONES

One of the most versatile ways your boss can communicate while away from the office is by using a cellular telephone. Cell phones use radio frequencies to communicate with a cellular telephone network, consisting of various microwave radio towers spaced throughout a city or region. These regions are called cells. When a call is being made, the telephone first establishes a radio link with one of the cellular transmission towers. The cell then connects the telephone with the regular telephone system to make the call. Calls are received in much the same manner.

There are many different types of cell phones. Some models include text messaging, small computer display screens, computer keyboards, and even digital cameras (see Figure 10–1). Various attachments allow a cell phone to be used inside a car. For example, power can be provided from the car's cigarette lighter, and an external antenna can be connected to increase the telephone's range. Many have a hands-free feature, which allows a speaker and microphone to be connected inside a car. Most cell phones also have memory for storing frequently called numbers.

Cellular Fees

Cellular service requires payment of a flat monthly fee plus a per-minute charge. Often, a telephone is provided as part of the basic package if your company agrees to a specific service contract of one to three years. Most cellular phone services include a home territory where calls can be made without long distance charges. When a user ventures outside the home territory, the phone uses another cellular service provider's network. This is called roaming and involves additional charges. Some service packages include free nationwide roaming and long distance.

Special Services

Personal communications services combine the power of a cell phone with a two-way radio. The rates paid while using the radio service are different from those paid while using the cellular service. Most service plans include a certain number of credits for both types of phone usage.

Another innovation, cellular data services, combines the power of computer communications with a cellular modem. By having a cellular modem installed inside a portable computer, you can connect your computer with various networks and databases while on the road.

PERSONAL DATA ASSISTANTS

Blurring the distinction between computer and cell phone are miniature computers called PDAs (personal digital assistants). Many PDAs (see Figure 10–2) are also equipped with cellular modems for wireless communications.

Some PDAs use a small keyboard for input. Others use a touch screen and a pen interface to access various menu choices. To enter text information or graphics, simply write or draw on the small screen. Built-in handwriting recognition software translates handwriting into computer text so it can be stored in the PDA's memory or later transferred to an office computer.

Some of the most sophisticated PDAs can be used as a cell phone for making or receiving voice calls. PDAs can also be connected to a personal computer for transferring data and e-mail messages.

PAGERS

Pagers have become an important business communications tool. The caller dials the pager's telephone number and then enters his or her telephone number or even a voice message. The owner of the pager is then notified by the pager's beeping or vibrating, and information about the call is displayed on the LCD display screen. The owner of the pager can then go to the nearest telephone to return the call.

Pagers are very useful when your boss must be away from the office for extended

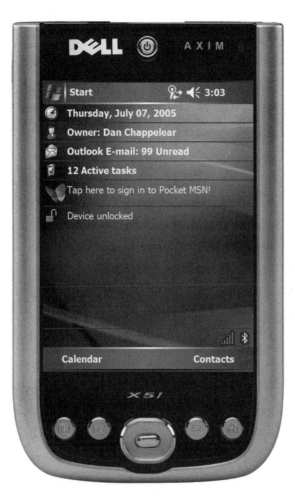

Figure 10–2. Personal data assistant.

Courtesy of Dell Inc.

periods of time. When there is an important call from a business associate or client, the pager can be used to pass on the caller's number. Most pagers function within the range of a city or a specific region. However, some systems, using satellite communications, can page a person anywhere in the country with just one call.

◇ FAX MACHINES

While faxes are increasingly being replaced by e-mail, there are still millions of fax machines (Figure 10–3) in use, and millions more faxes are sent annually.

Today's fax machines are faster and more versatile than ever. There are even products available that tie your fax machine to your office telephone's voice messaging system. Those products make it as easy to check for fax messages when you're out of the office as it is to check for voice messages.

Figure 10–3. Fax machine.

Courtesy of Xerox Corporation.

How to Select a Fax Machine

Selecting a machine begins with a clear understanding of how it is going to be used. Some of the factors to consider include:

- What type of documents will you send and receive?
- How many pages will each document have?
- How many locations will you send the same document to?
- Do you frequently send illustrations, photographs, or sketches?
- Are company employees often on the road? Would it be useful for them to be able to reroute fax messages to another fax machine? At any time of day or night?
- Does your company need more than one fax machine?
- Would it be more convenient and more efficient if employees could send and receive faxes right at their desks while at the same time transacting other business?

Low- and High-Volume Usage

Fax machines cost from several hundred dollars for basic no-frills machines up to thousands of dollars for more sophisticated models and plain-paper faxes. However, if you opt for a basic machine for the company or department, consider that usage often grows dramatically as employees become accustomed to the convenience of sending and receiving fax messages.

If you anticipate high usage, consider these factors:

- **Paper capacity**. Some fax machines use thermal paper, a glossy paper that comes in rolls ranging from 66 to 328 feet. Each foot equals approximately one page. Other fax machines can use regular office or copy paper and hold from twenty-five to five hundred sheets.

- **Plain versus thermal paper**. Plain-paper fax machines cost more than those that use thermal paper and have more moving parts that can malfunction. Many users reconcile a preference for plain paper with the cost benefits of thermal fax machines by copying thermal fax messages on plain bond paper as they come in. But whatever your choice, use only the paper the manufacturer recommends. Improperly coated paper—usually the cheaper brands available—can damage your fax machine.

- **Document feeder.** Document feeders can hold up to fifty pages at a time; however, approximately 60 percent of all fax messages transmitted today are three pages or fewer. If your company is small or you're buying only for your own department, a ten-page document feeder may be adequate for most of your needs.

- **Usage.** If your business sends or receives photos, illustrations, or graphics, consider purchasing a fax machine with grayscale (halftone) capability, which translates pictures into between eight and sixty-four shades of gray.

- **Resolution.** Most faxes have a normal resolution (picture sharpness) appropriate for most business correspondence and simple line drawings. If your business requires a sharper image, higher resolutions are available. Remember, however, that the machines at both ends of the transmission must have that capability.

- **Broadcasting.** If you send daily reports to satellite locations, broadcasting capability can be an important time saver. Broadcasting stores pages in the fax machine's memory for transmission to the locations you specify.

- **Automatic dialing**. This is another time saver that lets you store frequently called fax numbers in the machine's memory bank. The numbers can be dialed at the touch of a button individually or in groups.

- **Delayed send.** This money-saving feature lets you program a document for transmission at a specific time—for example, during off-peak hours—to take advantage of lower calling rates. It's also valuable to companies doing business overseas that want to schedule delivery during business hours in another time zone.

- **Polling.** Polling lets your machine retrieve documents stored in another fax machine's memory. If collecting sales figures from branch offices is a routine part of your business day, polling lets you retrieve the data whenever it's convenient for you via their fax machines.

Computer Fax Modems

In addition to dedicated fax machines, there are also fax modems available for personal computer systems. A fax modem connects your computer to the phone lines to send and receive data and allows your computer to send and receive faxes.

To send a fax, you first compose the document on the computer electronically. Then, without having to print out the document and take it to a fax machine, you access the software that comes with the fax modem and transmit the document just as a regular fax machine does. Incoming faxes are stored in your computer's memory like a graphic. You can read the fax using the software or print it out with your printer.

11

Computer Hardware

◇ OFFICE COMPUTERS

Companies of all sizes routinely use personal or desktop computers in the office. Computers allow employees to be more productive by automating many repetitive tasks, such as word processing, billing, and filing. When an office has only one computer, the administrative assistant may be its most frequent user. You may also be the person who investigates the different types of hardware and software and recommends which PC the office should buy.

Computers available for business uses range from powerful mainframes and minicomputers to networked systems to the personal computers (PCs) many people have in their homes. Personal or desktop computers are often used in most small businesses. They come in a wide variety of different configurations in both Microsoft Windows operating systems (those found in IBM-compatible computers) and Apple Macintosh operating systems.

When most people use a PC, what they are really using is a computer system. The computer itself may be no larger than a single integrated circuit chip soldered to a circuit board inside the computer's case. However, the user interfaces with a variety of other elements that together make up the computer system. These elements, called *peripheral devices*, include the keyboard, monitor, mouse, disk drives, and printer.

A true computer system usually consists of five elements:

1. An input device, such as a keyboard or mouse, that allows you to communicate with the computer.

2. An output device, such as a monitor or a printer, that allows the computer to communicate back to you.

3. A processor that allows for the manipulation of your data. The central processing unit (CPU) is the brains of the computer system.

4. A storage system, such as a hard disk drive, that allows you to save your work electronically.

5. Software that provides instructions for the computer in the form of programs.

◆ **HARDWARE**

How you operate your computer and what type of work it can perform depend on how your system is equipped. From the outside, the computer is just a case to house the electronic components. There are a variety of different computer designs, such as the desktop system that sits on a desk, the floor-standing tower system, and the portable or laptop computer (Figures 11–1 through 11–3).

All computers have a power switch on the system unit, located on the front of the case or on the back. Depending on which brand of computer you use, on the front there are also probably drives mounted inside the system unit or connectors for connecting various devices such as digital cameras.

The computer's operating system and programs are stored on a *hard disk* drive (Figure 11–4) that is mounted inside the system unit. In addition, most computers have a *CD-ROM* or *DVD-ROM* drive.

Each disk drive is given a letter, number, or name so that it's easy to load and save information to or from a particular drive location. On Microsoft Windows computers, the first diskette drive is called drive A, the second diskette drive is called drive B, and the hard drive is called drive C. The CD-ROM or DVD-ROM drive would be called drive

Figure 11–1. Apple iMac desktop computer system.

Photo (© 2007) Apple Computer. Courtesy of Apple.

Figure 11–2. Tower computer configuration.

Photo (© 2007) Dell Computer. Courtesy of Dell Inc.

Figure 11–3. Apple Macbook Laptop computer.

Photo (© 2007) Apple Computer. Courtesy of Apple.

D. On Apple Macintosh computers, the drives are given names or labels.

PCs are usually designed to be expandable. For this reason, it's possible to remove the case should you need to get inside to install a new component. Many people are afraid to open the computer case, yet the more familiar you are with your computer, the

Figure 11–4. Hard disk drives.

Photo (© 2007) IBM Corporation. Courtesy of International Business Machines Corporation. Unauthorized use not permitted.

better able you will be to troubleshoot little problems that arise from time to time. If you work for a small business, your boss is the person who probably bought the computer. Ask permission to open the case (or let the boss do so and look over his or her shoulder). Computer repairs and upgrades are simple skills to acquire, yet they are invaluable, especially in terms of time saved. Once a small company begins to rely on a computer to run its day-to-day business, the whole company can come to a screeching halt if the computer goes down.

Inside the system unit of a typical IBM compatible, you can see a metal box, which is the computer's power supply. This *transformer* converts the power from the wall outlet into electricity that can be used by the computer. You can see the hard disk drive that is mounted inside the case. And you can see the *motherboard*, which occupies most of the inside of the computer. This large circuit board contains various chips and your processor. On the motherboard, you can see various slots for plug-in expansion boards. For example, if you want to use a monitor or a printer with your computer, you may need to plug an interface card into one of these slots so that the device can communicate with the computer.

Expansion boards are available for a variety of different purposes. They easily plug into the motherboard expansion slots so you can add a device such as a modem or high-performance video card. Most computer motherboards have three or four *Peripheral Component Interconnect* (PCI) slots for connecting video display cards, modems, and other components. PCI cards and slots have "plug and play" capability. That means that when you install one of these cards, your computer automatically recognizes the card the next time it starts up. The *Accelerated Graphics Port* (AGP) slot is reserved for high-performance graphic cards for connecting your monitor to the computer.

The expansion slots in the motherboard provide a common electronic signal called a bus. A *bus* allows electronic signals to be passed from one part of the PC to another. There are several different types of computer buses available in your PC, which are often described in the specifications when purchasing a computer. Bus types include:

- **System Bus**—the pathway between the CPU and its memory
- **Backside Bus**—the pathway between the CPU and its internal cache memory
- **Frontside Bus**—the pathway between the CPU, main memory, and peripheral devices
- **Peripheral Bus**—part of the frontside bus that includes the ISA (Industry Standard Architecture), PCI, and AGP buses

Some expansion boards have a plug at one end where you can attach a device such as a disk drive or printer. These are called *ports*. Some ports are located on expansion boards, and some are connected directly to the motherboard. The two most common ports are the *parallel port*, used primarily for printers, and the *serial port*, used primarily to connect modems for telecommunications. Another useful port is the *Universal Serial Bus* (USB) port.

Looking at the back of a typical PC, you can see a parallel port for the printer, a serial port for the modem, another serial port for the mouse, and a video port for the monitor.

The term "expansion board" may appear to mean that all such boards are only options. However, there are several expansion boards found in almost all IBM-compatible models, such as the *display adapter*, which converts the computer's instructions into pictures on your monitor screen.

Many computers are now including built-in features that used to be available only as expansion cards. These systems feature display adapters, network adapters, and sound card capabilities built into the motherboard.

Other key components in your computer are the *memory chips* and the *processor chip*. The amount of memory your computer has determines the amount of workspace available for data. For example, if you are working with a large word-processing document or a large accounting program with a lot of data, you might eventually see messages on your monitor screen that the computer is running low or is out of memory. Most computers allow for upgrading the amount of memory. For most IBM-compatibles and Apple Macintosh computers, you can add to the computer's memory by plugging in memory chips, which are what provide your computer's memory. Memory chips can be plugged into slots on the motherboard of your computer to increase system memory. These memory chips are often called RAM, which stands for "random access memory." Your computer likely has between two and four slots for memory. Most modern computers should have at least 512 megabytes (MB) of memory, although at least 1 gigabyte (GB) of memory is preferred. Figure 11–5 shows a typical motherboard with the processor, expansion slots, and RAM slots.

Computer performance and speed are determined mainly by the type of processor chip included with your computer. In IBM-compatible computers, the main processors are made by Intel or AMD. Apple Computers now feature Intel processor chips.

Another performance enhancement enjoyed by many PC users is an internal *cache*, an extra bit of memory built into your processor that allows it to store certain instructions internally rather than using your computer's normal memory. This saves time and greatly increases speed.

Figure 11–5. A computer system with the case removed to see the motherboard, processor, expansion slots, and RAM.

Photo by Kevin Wilson.

Also important in evaluating speed and performance is the *clock speed* of your processor. Clock speed is the speed at which messages from the computer processor travel to other parts of the computer, such as the disk drives, hard drive, monitor, and printer. Many early model PCs had clock speeds of 4 to 8 megahertz (MHz). Speeds ranging up to several gigahertz (GHz) are available today.

The key point to remember when you're choosing a company computer is that better speed and performance usually translate into greater productivity. Therefore, an investment in a good computer system can help you do more in less time.

◇ MEMORY

Computer memory is often very confusing to new computer users because it implies that the computer remembers your data automatically. However, this is not the case: If you create a document with a word processor but don't save it and then turn off your computer, the document will be lost. Unfortunately, most computer users learn this lesson the hard way. Long-term storage of data is handled by the hard disk drive, not by the computer's memory.

Your computer's memory is that area where programs and data are temporarily copied from a CD, DVD, or hard disk drive so that you can use them. Moving programs and data into memory is called *loading* or, on some systems, *opening*. It is just like taking a document out of a file cabinet and putting it on your desk. Unlike this analogy, however, when a computer loads a program or a document into memory, it only takes a copy—leaving the original intact on the disk. You can modify the original by saving your latest work with the same name as the original, or you can retain the original and keep a new version by saving the new version with a slightly different name.

Random access memory (RAM) is the area of memory where your programs and data are loaded. Memory is measured in terms of bits, bytes, kilobytes, megabytes, and gigabytes.

Electronically, the RAM in your computer is made up of lots of little electric switches that are turned on or off. For programming purposes, "on" is given a numerical value of 1, and "off" is given the numerical value of 0. Therefore, programs and data are represented as lots of 1s and 0s. Each character in the alphabet is represented by a special code made up of 1s and 0s. The same is true for numbers and graphics on your monitor. Some computers use a 32-bit system. That means that it takes a combination of 32 1s and 0s to form each character or graphic. Other more advanced graphics computers use 64-bit systems.

Each group of eight 1s and 0s is called a *byte*; 1,024 bytes equal a kilobyte, 1,024 kilobytes equal a megabyte, and a gigabyte is 1,000 megabytes.

As previously stated, most computers are equipped with at least 512 megabytes of memory. However, this is barely enough to handle today's modern operating systems and applications software. For many applications and operating systems, 1 gigabyte of memory is preferred.

Another way some computers access even greater amounts of memory is to use *virtual memory*. Computers can use part of the computer's hard drive as if it were extra RAM. Virtual memory is slower than RAM memory and is used primarily when multiple programs are loaded and running at the same time. The program not being accessed by a user can be temporarily swapped to virtual memory.

Read-only memory (ROM) is another type of memory that is built into the computer and cannot be changed by programs. ROM chips contain a permanent set of instructions that support the overall operation of the computer. Essentially, they function automatically and require little attention from most computer users.

◇ INPUT DEVICES

In order to use computers, you need some way to communicate with them. This process is known as *input*. There are many types of input devices. Probably the most common is a keyboard. By simply typing on a typewriter-like keyboard, you send information to the computer for processing. In order to see what it is you have typed, most computers use a *monitor*. As characters are typed on the keyboard, they appear on the monitor screen.

Among the most familiar devices for input are game controllers such as *joysticks*. These devices allow a game player to communicate information to a computer informing it of key decisions necessary to play a game. A similar device is a *mouse*, a hand controller that is used in some software applications and operating systems for a variety of different computers (see Figure 11–6). A mouse is used to select menu choices and to move a *cursor*, or pointer, around on the monitor screen. A mouse consists of a rubber ball inside a plastic housing. By moving the mouse over a surface such as a desktop or a mouse pad, the ball moves, providing input to the computer to move a pointer on the display screen. An *optical mouse* uses an LED and photodiodes to detect movement relative to the underlying surface, rather than moving some of its parts—as in a mechanical mouse. Similar to a mouse is a *track ball*. Many small portable computers use *touchpads*, since the operator may be using the computer where there is no desktop available for a mouse.

Another useful form of input designed originally for disabled individuals is *voice recognition*. Voice recognition and natural language speech systems interpret the human voice into signals that a computer can understand as input. Voice recognition systems are now popular and can be used to select menu items in software and, in some cases, even to create text for a word-processing document or spreadsheet.

For graphic artists and designers and others who need to input precise drawings, a special drawing device called a *graphics tablet* is available. A graphics tablet consists of a plastic board containing a grid of fine electrical wires. A special drawing pen is used to draw. When the pen comes into contact with the grid of wires, information on the location of the pen is sent to the computer in order to create a graphics image on a monitor screen.

Another input tool used by graphic artists is the *scanner*. There are various models available. Some you hold in your hand; other desktop models operate much like a copy machine. With the desktop version, you place an original document into the scanner, and the scanner copies an image of the document or graphic into the computer's memory. When the document is text, special optical character recognition software is often used. This software takes the images input from a scanner and compares them against various text styles in memory. It then translates the scanner image into text for your word processor.

Finally, *digital cameras* can be used to acquire digital images that can be transferred into a computer and used in desktop publishing applications. (See Chapter 22 for more information on desktop publishing.)

◆ OUTPUT DEVICES

When you work with a computer, most of your attention is focused on output devices. This is where you see the results of your work. The most common output devices found on computer systems are the monitor and the printer. Both output devices are available in many different models.

Figure 11–6. Mouse and trackball.

Photo by Jennifer Wauson.

The Monitor

Monitors display information by painting the screen with tiny dots of color called pixels. Today, there are several different types of monitors to fit various needs. There are flat screen liquid crystal display (LCD) monitors (as shown in Figure 11–7) and traditional cathode ray tube (CRT) monitors. Monitors come in different screen sizes that are measured diagonally. Sizes range from 15 inches to 17, 19, 21, and even larger.

The crispness of the monitor's picture is measured in dot pitch, refresh rate, and resolution. Dot pitch is the distance between pixels. The better the dot pitch, the better the monitor can display lines and curves. The refresh rate is the speed at which the monitor repaints the screen. Refresh rates are measured in Hertz (Hz). A low refresh rate will produce a noticeable flicker on the monitor. Resolution is the screen image size that can be displayed on the monitor as measured in horizontal and vertical pixels. Typical resolutions used include 800×600 and 1024×768.

The Printer

Along with video display monitors, the other most popular form of output for a computer system is a printer. *Printers* produce a hardcopy paper version of what is on your display screen. There are several different types of printers available.

Ink Jet Printers

Ink jet printers produce letter-quality output by spraying ink through a series of tiny nozzles onto the paper to form each letter. Ink jet printers can print in black and white and in color. In fact, some ink jet printers can produce photographic-quality output that rivals traditional photographic film prints.

Laser Printers

Perhaps the most successful and popular method of producing letter-quality text is with a laser printer (see Figure 11–8). Although laser printers are more expensive than ink jet printers, their quality and speed have made them popular among all types of computer users. Laser printers function similarly to copy machines. A graphics image of the computer output is sent to the laser printer, which also has a computer processor. The laser printer then uses a laser to display an image on an electrically charged drum surface. Once the charged surface comes into contact with a powdered or liquid toner, the toner sticks in the image areas and falls off the non-image areas. When paper comes into contact with the drum, the toner is transferred to the paper, producing an image.

Color Laser Printers

Recent advances in color printing have resulted in laser printers that use multicolored toners for producing color output.

Figure 11–7. LCD monitor.

Courtesy of Dell Inc.

Printer Performance

The performance of a printer is determined by its resolution, memory, and speed. Printer resolution is the sharpness of the image the printer can produce on paper. Resolution is measured in dots per inch (dpi). For draft-quality text printing, a dpi setting of 300 is sufficient. For letter-quality printing, a dpi setting of 600 is good. For photographic-quality printing, a resolution of 600 dpi or better is needed.

Dpi settings affect the speed of the printer. Most ink jet and laser printers can print three to six pages per minute, depending on the type of image. Photographic-quality images may take much longer. Laser printers tend to be the fastest printers available.

Printers have built-in memory that helps speed up the printing process. If you print large documents or documents with complex graphics, having additional printer memory enhances printing speed.

Another device for reproducing computer output is a *plotter*, or large format printer, which draws the computer output in large format. This is often used in architectural and design offices.

◆ STORAGE DEVICES

The ability to store, search for, and retrieve specific information from permanent data storage media is ideal for helping secretaries organize the department or company—and keep it organized. Using the computer's electronic filing system, you should see a great time savings for yourself as well as an increase in your productivity and efficiency in day-to-day business activities.

A computer stores your work in two areas, one temporary and one permanent. The temporary storage is your computer's memory, its RAM. We've already discussed computer memory, but it's important to remember that information stored in RAM is stored only as long as the computer is turned on.

The Hard Drive

The main permanent storage device is the computer's *hard drive* (sometimes called a *fixed disk*), which can be either internal (mounted inside the computer case) or external (in its own case connected to the computer via a cable). A hard drive is actually a stack of disks coated with a magnetic coating, similar to audiotape or videotape. Information is saved on a hard drive much the same way a song is recorded on audiotape. The computer's electronic signals are recorded on the magnetic hard drive disk, and when you want the information back, the hard drive "plays back" those signals. Saving information on a hard drive is called *writing* to the drive; playing information back is called *reading*. It is also possible to erase information on a drive, which is called *deleting*.

Disk storage capacity is measured in units called *bytes*. As previously discussed, a byte is made up of 8 bits of information. A *kilobyte*, or K for short, is 1,024 bytes. A

Figure 11–8. Laser printer.

Courtesy of International Business Machines Corporation. Unauthorized use not permitted.

megabyte is 1,024 K. One thousand megabytes is a *gigabyte* (often called a "gig"). One thousand gigabytes is a *terabyte*. Hard drives can store billions of bytes. Typically, hard drives store anywhere from 20 to 80 gigabytes to several terabytes or more.

Tape Backup

One specialized storage medium is available solely for the purpose of making backups. Tape backup drives use a cartridge tape to back up your hard drive and all your data. A tape backup drive is much slower than a hard drive, so it's not very useful for normal day-to-day use as a storage medium. However, special software combined with a tape backup drive can automatically back up your data periodically so you are also protected in the event of hard drive failure.

Removable Drives

A removable cartridge drive acts like a hard drive, although it's somewhat slower in terms of reading and writing data. However, a removable cartridge can be taken from the drive and replaced with another, which offers great flexibility. When one cartridge is filled up, it can be replaced by another. It's like having a completely new hard drive. The removable cartridges are contained in a special housing that protects the sensitive media inside. Since these cartridges can store several gigabytes or more of programs and data, they must be handled very carefully and stored in a cool, protected environment.

CD-ROM and DVD-ROM

Another increasingly popular data storage medium is a *CD-ROM*. This system uses a compact disk to store computer data. Approximately 600 megabytes can be stored on one CD-ROM.

If you have a CD-ROM drive that can create—or "burn"—CDs, you can also use it for making backups of your data. These drives are often called CD Recordable (*CD-R*) or CD Read and Write (*CD-RW*) and can store approximately 600 megabytes of data.

Making the move from the entertainment center to the computer are *DVD-ROM* drives. These drives can store several gigabytes of data and are often used for viewing DVD movies on your computer.

DVD recordable (*DVD-R*) and DVD Read and Write (*DVD-RW*) drives are also available. They can record DVD data disks that can store 4 to 9 gigabytes of data.

Flash Drives

Flash drives are small portable devices that can connect to the USB port on your computer for storing and transferring data from one computer to another. Flash drives are about the size of your car keys and can store data for ten years or more without being plugged into a power source. These inexpensive devices come in a variety of sizes ranging from a few megabytes up to several gigabytes.

◇ LAPTOP COMPUTERS

Many offices use small laptop computers in place of desktop computers to give employees mobility and flexibility when using their PCs. With a laptop, everything is combined into one unit: CPU, monitor, hard drive, CD-ROM, modem, and network card, as well as other devices like speakers and microphones. Laptop computers can be upgraded with larger hard drives and additional RAM. You can connect them to printers, a phone line, and an office network, or to an external monitor, keyboard, and mouse. One nice feature of a laptop computer is the built-in battery. This battery can power the computer for several hours without needing to be connected to a power outlet.

While you can connect an external mouse to a laptop computer, a variety of built-in pointing devices are available. Most laptops use a touchpad with buttons or a pointing stick positioned next to the G and H keys that resembles the eraser of a pencil.

When you are in the office, some laptops can be connected to a port replicator or docking station. When connected to one of these expansion units, you can use an external monitor, keyboard, and mouse just like a desktop computer system.

◇ HAND-HELD COMPUTERS

Hand-held computers, often called *PDAs* (personal digital assistants), are rapidly taking the place of address books in many offices. Many executives use these devices to take notes, store contact information, and plan their schedules.

PDAs can be connected to your desktop computer using a cable or a wireless connection to download or upload information. In this way, a person can have portable access to much of the same information that is stored on his/her PC.

PDAs are normally pen-based computers. The user enters and accesses information using a stylus and a touch screen. The PDA accepts handwritten input and converts it to text. Small keyboards are available with some models.

◇ MAINTAINING YOUR COMPUTER

For the most part, there is little you need to do to maintain your computer system. However, as for any machine, there are a few things you can do that will help your computer last longer and operate smoothly.

Cleaning Your Mouse

As your roll your mouse around over a mouse pad, it picks up lint and dust particles that eventually clog the little wheels and rollers inside. If you notice the mouse beginning to operate erratically, check the user manual for how to remove the roller ball. You can then clean the ball with a soft dry cloth and wipe the three sets of rollers inside the mouse. Normally, when a mouse is dirty, the rollers are coated with a gunk that can be wiped off with a cloth or scraped off using your fingernail.

ScanDisk

ScanDisk is a utility that comes with your computer that can detect and fix hard disk errors that cause performance problems. In the latest versions of Windows, this utility is called CHKDSK. These utilities run automatically if a computer loses power unexpectedly. You can also run these utilities periodically to check the condition of your hard disk drive. To run the utility, double-click MY COMPUTER, then right–mouse-click your hard disk drive. From the pop-up menu, click PROPERTIES. On the Properties window, click TOOLS; then, in the Error-Checking section, click CHECK NOW.

Disk Defragmenter

As you use your computer, the files you save get divided and spread in different available spaces on your hard drive. The more spread out or fragmented they get, the more the performance of your computer is affected. A disk defragmenter recombines files and resaves them in one continuous location. This reorganizes your hard drive and improves disk efficiency.

Disk Cleanup

As you work with various documents, print, view Web pages, and so forth, temporary information gets stored on your computer. These temporary files can grow in size and eventually squeeze out room for other things. It's a good idea to delete these files from time to time.

Backing Up Your Data

If your hard drive fails, you could lose all your data. Since your hard drive is like a very large filing cabinet filled with important and often confidential data about the business you work for, protecting that information is very important. Therefore, you should back up your hard drive frequently by making copies of all data onto an external hard drive, a network drive, a backup tape, diskettes, a CD-R, a CD-RW, a DVD-R, or a DVD-RW.

Computer
Software

◇ THE BIOS

Unless you are a programmer and know how to write programming code that can communicate directly with the computer's hardware to perform a function, you need an operating system and software. But even a programmer needs a computer that has a basic set of software instructions installed. These basic instructions are the computer's Basic Input Output System (*BIOS*).

The BIOS is installed in a read-only memory (ROM) chip on the computer's motherboard. The BIOS is the first thing that loads when your computer is started. These basic instructions test the computer to make sure it is operating properly and then recognize the various components, including the CPU, memory, keyboard, and monitor.

After your computer is up and running, the BIOS continues to act as an interface between the computer and the operating system. The BIOS interprets commands to access hard drives, display information to the monitor, accept keystrokes from the keyboard, and monitor system conditions such as temperature.

Fortunately, most computer users never have to interact with their computer's BIOS. The only time you may need to access and use the BIOS directly is when you install a new hard drive or set the date after installing a new battery. You can access the BIOS by pressing the DELETE key on the keyboard just after starting the computer.

◇ OPERATING SYSTEMS

An operating system is the underlying software that allows other programs—such as word processors, databases, and spreadsheets—to operate with similar menu choices, processes, and functions. The operating system, sometimes called an OS, is a set of rules that other programs must follow. The operating system serves as an intermediary, handling communications between your software and the computer's hardware.

Microsoft Windows is the most widely used computer operating system. There are several alternative operating systems, including Apple OS for Macintosh, Unix, and Linux. Because Microsoft Windows is by far the most commonly used operating system in business today, we'll spend the next part of this chapter discussing the features of Windows.

◆ How Does Microsoft Windows Work?

Microsoft Windows is computer operating system software. It is the software that many computer manufacturers are installing on computers so that they do something more than act as a very expensive paperweight. As the operating system, Microsoft Windows provides instructions to the computer's "brain" for how to access disk drives, how to print, and even how to add 2 + 2. Think of the operating system as the interface between you and the computer components. Tell the operating system what you want to do, and it completes the task—if it is told in the proper way. So your job is to learn how to "communicate" with the computer operating system.

Microsoft Windows has a graphical user interface (GUI). In simple terms, everything can be done with a point and click from a mouse. Graphics are used to create an understandable interface with the user. With Microsoft Windows, you can graphically see what you need to do and can accomplish it through the graphic interface. The secret is to know what you want to accomplish.

There are a variety of versions of Microsoft Windows available, depending on the age of your computer and how often your business upgrades its computers. Versions include:

- Windows 95
- Windows 98
- Windows 2000
- Windows XP
- Windows Vista

◆ The Windows Desktop

The Windows Desktop is the screen you see when you turn on your computer and Windows loads. As you use Windows, you rearrange, remove, and place items on the Desktop, just like a real desktop. The Desktop includes a variety of features such as:

- Desktop icons like My Computer
- The Taskbar
- The START button

The Taskbar occupies the bottom edge of the Desktop by default. It can be moved to the top or either side, or it can be made to disappear and reappear when you need it.

Figure 12–1 shows a typical Desktop after newly installing Windows Vista. The Taskbar along the bottom contains the start button on the left and the time on the right. Open applications and folders are represented by buttons on the Taskbar at the bottom of the screen. These buttons come and go depending on which programs or folders you have open at any given time.

Figure 12–1. The Windows Vista Desktop.

Screen shot reprinted by permission from Microsoft Corporation.

The Start Menu

The Start Menu (Figure 12–2) is opened by clicking on the START button at the left-hand end of the Taskbar. As an operating system, Windows presents an interface to you, the user. The job of the interface is to give you the means of commanding the computer to perform actions like launching programs, copying files, and activating a printer. Normally, once the operating system is started, you're supposed to know what to do next. Of course, new users often do not know what to do next, so Windows provides a clearly marked starting place, the START button.

As a beginner, you will use the Start Menu as home base for most operations you perform in Windows. Later, as you gain experience, you'll be creating folders and icons and will have the option of not using the Start Menu as much. Be aware that like most things in Windows, the Start Menu may vary depending on certain programs and options that may be installed on your system. In addition, the Start Menu contains several options that have nothing to do with starting things. In fact, one command is Shut Down, the opposite of starting. Before we go any further, we need to mention two possibilities that may occur at any time, even though they may seem out of sequence at this point: (1) the computer may be shut down, and (2) individual programs, said to be "frozen," may be shut down.

Shutting Down Windows

One option on the Start Menu is Shut Down. Although there is nothing to stop you from just switching off the computer, doing so without choosing the Shut Down procedure

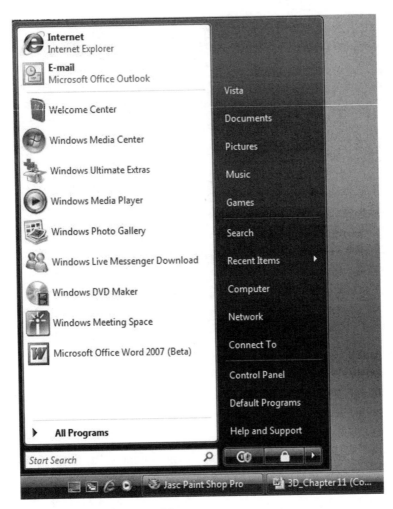

Figure 12–2. The Start Menu.

Screen shot reprinted by permission from Microsoft Corporation.

may result in lost data and corrupted files.

When you choose Shut Down, the screen dims and a new menu appears that gives you several options. You can click the YES button to shut down, or you can make another selection first and then click YES. If you choose to shut down, Windows spends a few moments closing files, then displays a screen informing you that it is OK to turn off the power.

Closing a Frozen Program

If you have had any experience with personal computers, you are familiar with the circumstance where the computer stops responding and becomes "frozen." Because Windows operates in protected mode with 32-bit applications (a technical term meaning that each 32-bit program can run independently of all other programs), it is often possible that the one program that is causing the problem can be closed, and others will continue to run normally.

Should your computer become frozen, you can press the CTRL + ALT + DEL keys simultaneously. When you do this, a list of tasks that are currently running appears in a dialog box called Close Program. From this task list, you can do one of four things: (1) You can end the task (stop the program) that is causing the problem, perform a normal shut down, reboot (i.e., restart) the computer immediately without a normal shut down, or cancel and return to where you left off; (2) To end the task, you would make a guess at which program is causing the problem, select it from the list, then click END TASK; (3) If this does not unfreeze the computer, you can try a normal shut down by recalling the task list (by pressing CTRL + ALT + DEL again), then choosing Shut Down; (4) If that doesn't work, you can press CTRL + ALT + DEL while the task list is displayed to force a system reset.

◆ STARTING A PROGRAM

The next option on the Start Menu that we'll look at is Programs. When the pointer is on Programs, a new menu appears to the right of the Start Menu.

As we'll discuss in more detail later, the little arrowheads to the right of some of the options means that another menu appears when you point to that option. To start a program, you select it from the Programs Menu with your mouse and then click. The program then loads and appears on your screen.

◆ RESIZING A WINDOW

If the program window occupies your entire screen with no part of the desktop background visible, it may be maximized. If your window is maximized, you see three buttons in the upper right corner of the window.

If the center button looks like it does in Figure 12–3 (two small overlapping windows), your window is maximized. Each time you run a program, you'll notice that a new button appears on the Taskbar at the bottom of the screen. The button is labeled with the program name. When the Taskbar becomes crowded, the buttons are automatically made smaller to accommodate more of them. When the buttons are too small to show the program name, you can point to a button and wait a second or two, and the complete caption appears in a little pop-up box.

To resize a window, you drag its border. You can do this by moving the mouse pointer to the border. When you are in the correct spot, the pointer changes to a two-headed arrow pointing left and right. You can then click and drag the window to a new size.

You can reshape both dimensions of a window by dragging the lower right corner. Position the mouse pointer over the corner until you see a diagonal sizing pointer. Then click and drag the mouse to change the dimensions. Some windows cannot be sized beyond certain limits. While using Windows, you frequently need to resize and move windows to arrange your desktop for efficiency.

Figure 12–3. Minimize, Maximize, and Close buttons.

Screen shot reprinted by permission from Microsoft Corporation.

MINIMIZING, MAXIMIZING, RESTORING, AND CLOSING WINDOWS

When you wish to get a window off the screen temporarily but have its program continue to run or its window instantly available, you can minimize it. To do this, you click the MINIMIZE button in the top right corner of the screen (see Figure 12–3). When you do this, you'll notice that the window appears to zip down to the Taskbar. Technically, the window is still "open," so it appears on the Taskbar. To restore it, just click its button on the Taskbar.

If you need more space to work in an application window, you can maximize it to cover the entire screen. Just click the MAXIMIZE button in the top right corner of the window. If you maximize a window, the three buttons in the upper right corner of the window change. The MAXIMIZE button is replaced by a new button, called the RESTORE button. If you click the RESTORE button, the window returns it its original size.

When you wish to close a program or folder, you click the CLOSE button in the upper right corner of the window. It is the button that is marked with an X.

USING SCROLL BARS

When the material inside a window won't fit the current window size, scroll bars automatically appear to allow you to move the view and reveal the rest of the space.

Within each scroll bar there is a scroll slider. At the ends of each scroll bar there are

Figure 12–4. Windows Explorer.

Screen shot reprinted by permission from Microsoft Corporation.

small arrow buttons. The length of the slider gives you some indication of the proportion of the whole that you are viewing. You use the scroll bars to move within the viewing space. To move a small increment at a time, you click on the arrow buttons at the ends of the scroll bars. You can also click and drag the slider up or down (or left or right on the horizontal scroll bar).

Using scroll bars is one of the basic techniques for using Windows. Scroll bars appear in windows, dialog boxes, and anywhere a screen display needs additional space for items.

USING EXPLORER TO VIEW FILES AND FOLDERS

The program you use to manipulate files is called Explorer. You can start Explorer by clicking the START button, then point to the Programs, and then click WINDOWS EXPLORER near the bottom of the Programs Menu. In Windows Vista, Windows Explorer is in the Accessories folder.

The window is divided into two panes (Figure 12–4). On the left is a tree diagram of disk drives and folders. On the right is a list of the files and folders contained within the selected folder in the tree.

◆ FILES AND FOLDERS

People talk about having information stored on their computers. The most common questions are: Where is the information stored, and how do you find it? Here are two definitions that you need to understand first:

1. **File.** A file is a document that has been created or an application that has been installed on the computer. Files are similar to piles of projects on your desk. They are the actual pieces with which you work.

2. **Folder or Directory.** A folder is a directory or the organizer for the files. Folders can be used to store all the pieces of a software package that are needed to run the software or to organize documents that are created. Folders organize files into logical groups. Folders can hold other folders. The first folder you come to is called the directory, and the folders inside the first folder are the subdirectories. The ultimate decision of how to organize a folder is up to you, since you have to find and access files and folders for later use.

Placing a File in a Folder

To place a file in a folder, you only need to drag and drop it. When you drag the file, be sure to point to the icon, not to the name of the file. Dragging by the name works, but sometimes you may try to drag a file that is already selected when you click it to drag it. If the file is already selected, clicking on the name switches to edit mode (so you can type a new name), and you can't drag it then. If you always drag the icon, you avoid this potential pitfall. When you drag to the target folder, that folder becomes highlighted when you are pointing at the correct spot.

Deleting a File or Folder

You use the same procedure to delete files and folders. When you delete a folder, all the files and other folders within it are also deleted. You can use one of three techniques to delete files or folders:

1. You can drag it to the Recycle Bin icon on your desktop.

2. You can open its context menu and click DELETE.

3. You can select it and press the DELETE key on your keyboard.

◆ WINDOWS HELP

There are two types of help: the online help for Windows itself, and the online help for the various applications running in Windows. Software manufacturers use the built-in facilities of Windows Help, so most applications have similar help features.

Table 12–1 lists ways you can call for help. Because applications differ, not all these methods are always available.

TABLE 12–1. Windows Help

Help about Windows	Open Start Menu, click HELP.
General help in an application	Open application's Help Menu.
Specific help about a current procedure	Press F1.
Help about a screen object	■ In some applications, click the Toolbar HELP button, then click the object.
	■ In some applications, press SHIFT + F1, then click the object.
	■ In some applications (and Windows itself), dialog boxes have a question mark button. Click it, then click the object in the box.
General help about a dialog box	Some dialog boxes have HELP buttons. Also try F1.

When you access Windows Help, you see three tabs along the top, labeled Contents, Index, and Find. Table 12–2 lists what they do. The most useful of these is the Index, since most often you know the topic you want help with.

TABLE 12–2. Windows Help Features

Contents	Presents help like a book or outline with chapters, topics, and subtopics.
Index	Searches for key words in topics, like a book's index.
Find	Full text search for words within the entire help system, including the body text of the help screens.

Help from Applications

Applications have their own help systems. Usually, they use the same model as Windows, so they should look and behave in a familiar manner.

In many applications, pressing the f1 key while something is selected or while you are performing some function gives you help about the object or procedure. Since you often need help to start a procedure, you may find that selecting help from the menu and using the search feature is the most often-used technique. Figure 12–5 shows the help screen in Microsoft Word.

Pop-Up Help

Some applications have automatic pop-up reminders to help you remember the functions of the various on-screen buttons. If you hold your mouse pointer over any of the buttons on a program's toolbar, a pop-up label appears, and a more detailed explanation is shown at the bottom of the window. Making the pointer remain still while pointing at an object is called hovering in some manuals. Many of the more recent Windows

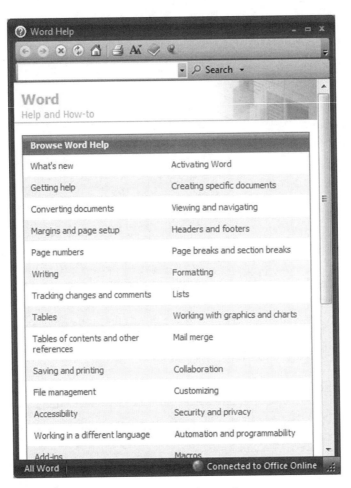

Figure 12–5. Help in Microsoft Word.

Screen shot reprinted by permission from Microsoft Corporation.

applications from different publishers use the pop-up help technique when you hover over a button.

MENUS

Most applications and folder windows have menu bars. A menu bar is a list of menus. When you click the name of a menu, it drops down. This is called opening a menu or pulling down a menu. The most common menu choices include File, Edit, View, Tools, Window, and Help. In some menus, an arrowhead appears to the right of some of the listed options. This means that when you point to it, another menu appears. Options that are followed by an ellipsis (three periods) display a dialog box. Options with nothing after them execute immediately.

Once a menu is opened, you can move to another menu with the mouse or with the left and right arrow keys. The same actions work vertically within each menu, so that you can point to an option with the mouse or use the up and down arrow keys to point to one.

You can close a menu without making a selection by clicking on the menu name again, clicking anywhere except on a menu option, or by pressing the ESCAPE key (on the keyboard) twice.

Sometimes menus can be used to make settings, and the settings can be indicated on the menu. If you decide not to display, say, the Toolbar, you can click that item. The menu closes, and the Toolbar disappears. The next time you open the View Menu, the Toolbar item will not be checked off.

Using Pop-Up Context Menus

The right-hand mouse button is used often in Windows. Usually, it produces a pop-up menu that is sometimes called a context menu because it contains options appropriate for the specific object you are pointing to. Most applications also use context menus.

Sometimes when a context menu appears, several of the options are grayed out. Grayed-out items do not work, because they are not appropriate for your current situation.

Objects on the Windows Desktop have their own context menus. If you point to any of the icons on the desktop and right-click, a context menu appears.

DIALOG BOXES

Often when you select an item from a menu, such as Print, a new small window appears on the screen (Figure 12–6). These windows are called *dialog boxes*. Dialog boxes are used to adjust various settings. For example, with the Print dialog box, you can select the quality of the printing, the size of the paper, the number of copies, and so forth.

Within a dialog box you often use what are called *radio buttons*. Radio buttons are round, and the selected one has a dot in it. Radio buttons are always in groups of two or more, and one of them is always selected. When you select another one, the previously selected one is deselected, just like when you punch a station button on a car radio.

Dialog boxes may also contain text entry boxes. When you click in one of these blanks, an insertion point (also called a cursor) appears, indicating where the next character you type will appear. You can use this technique to edit the default value. (Be aware that, typically in a numeric entry space, you will not be allowed to enter non-numbers.)

To close a dialog box, you can choose one of the command buttons. Usually, you have a choice of OK and CANCEL. Choosing OK closes the dialog box and accepts your entries. CANCEL closes the dialog box but ignores any changes you made. If the dialog box also has a CLOSE button in the upper right corner, it has the same effect as the CANCEL button.

SAVING FILES

While working on a document, you'll want to save it frequently to prevent loss of any of your work. The first time you save a new document, you are prompted to give it a filename, and you need to select a folder in which to save it.

You can save by opening the File Menu and choosing Save or Save As (Figure 12–7). In an application such as Microsoft Word, you can click the SAVE button on the Toolbar.

The first time you save an unnamed document, the Save As dialog box appears. Thereafter, each time you click the SAVE button, the document is saved immediately (no dialog box appears) under the same name. Should you wish to save it with a new name, you can open the File Menu and choose Save As.

The Save As dialog box is called a *common dialog box* because Microsoft provides it as a tool that can be utilized by anyone writing programs for the Windows operating system. Most Microsoft programs and many applications from other companies use the common dialog boxes rather than design their own. This is a great advantage to users, since once they have learned the standard common dialog boxes, they know how to perform the same function in many different programs.

The Save As and Open dialog boxes are very similar. They contain many of the features of the Explorer, including the ability to point to a drive and folder. In addition, the Save As and Open dialog boxes can be used for some file management tasks, such as deleting or renaming files and folders and creating new folders. While the basic function of the Open dialog box is to allow you to select or enter the name of the file you wish to open, the main function of the Save As dialog box is to allow you to choose where you wish to save a file and to give it a name of your choice.

The file is created on the disk. Once the file is saved the first time, you can continue to work on the document and save at intervals. When you click the SAVE button, the current version of the file is saved immediately in the same folder and with the same filename, overwriting the previous version. This happens without asking you for a filename.

Figure 12–6. The Print dialog box in Microsoft Word.

Screen shot reprinted by permission from Microsoft Corporation.

◆ PRINTING FILES

You can print a document by clicking the File Menu and then clicking PRINT. Many programs also have a print button on a toolbar. Sometimes this button causes the Print dialog box to open, but many times, the toolbar button makes the document print one copy immediately to the currently selected printer without displaying the dialog box.

On the Print dialog box, you can choose which printer you wish to use, in case you have more than one (such as you might on a network). You can also choose what portion of the document you want to print and the number of copies. Though this is the common dialog box for printing in Windows, other applications often use different, though similar, boxes. Usually, they offer additional options.

Windows also allows you to print by dragging and dropping a file icon onto a printer icon.

◆ FINDING A FILE

The Find program is a very useful tool, so we are going to cover it in some detail here. You can start it several ways, but the most convenient way is the F3 key. When you press F3 on the keyboard, the Find dialog box appears. When you command Find to locate a file, it begins searching from the folder or drive shown in the *Look in* blank. If you specify a folder as the starting point for the search, Windows finds it faster.

If you open a folder—either in Explorer or in its own window—then start Find with F3, that folder will be the *Look in* folder.

Here is an important note. The F3 key does not start Find unless the Desktop, Taskbar, a folder, or Explorer has the focus. In other words, if you are working in an application, that application's window will have the focus, and the F3 key will perform whatever function is assigned to it by the application. If the application does not use the F3 key, nothing happens when you press it. If you want to start Find while working in an application, be sure to click the Desktop or the Taskbar first. Some applications, such as the Microsoft

Figure 12–7. The Save As dialog box in Microsoft Word.

Screen shot reprinted by permission from Microsoft Corporation.

Office suite, have their own built-in Find-like features, so in actual practice, you will probably seldom use the Windows Find program while running an application.

Wildcard Searches

You can search for files by entering only part of the filename, or you can limit your search by using special symbols called wildcards (see Table 12–3). For example, you can find all files on drive C with "win" in the filename. A fairly long list of files should appear. The files can appear in several formats. The window containing the list of files acts exactly like a folder containing files or the Explorer. You can move and copy files, delete them, or work with them in the appropriate application. You can sort and reverse-sort the listed files by clicking on the column headers.

TABLE 12–3. Wildcards That Can Be Used with Find

Name	What will be searched for
★	All files and folders
★.★	All files and folders
★.	All files (not folders)
xyz	All files and folders with xyz in the name or extension
★xyz★	All files and folders with xyz in the name or extension
★.xyz	All files with the extension xyz
xyz.★	All files with the name xyz and any (or no) extension
?xyz	All files and folders where xyz is preceded by one or more characters
??xyz	All files and folders where xyz is preceded by at least two characters
x?yz	All files and folders where x is followed by one unknown character, then the letters y and z

You can also use wildcards similar to those used in old DOS to search for files. Although your system may be set so that it does not show all the three-character extensions for the filenames, they are still used, even with long filenames. For instance, if you wish to display all the executable program files, you can use the wildcard *.exe. That tells Windows to find all files, regardless of name, with the extension "exe."

Date Searches

Each time you create a file, the date and time are saved with the name. When the file is modified, the date and time are updated. Sometimes you might need to find a file whose name you do not remember, but you know you modified it in the last two or three days. The first place to look would be the Documents option on the Start Menu, since it remembers the last fifteen files you modified. Failing that, you can have Find show you files in a certain date period.

Advanced Searches

Finally, you can find files and folders based on type, size, or even text contained in the file. When searching for text, you should be aware that such searches may take a while, so you should narrow the search as much as possible by specifying a specific folder, if possible, or other criteria such as date.

 SHORTCUTS

Shortcuts are small files that "point" to other files, folders, and programs. When you open a shortcut, the object to which it points opens. This allows you to store objects in an appropriate place in the hierarchy of folders, but access them from another location, usually the Desktop or the Start Menu. So, for example, the Calculator program is stored in the Windows folder. It might just as easily be stored in some folder several layers deep. That might be the best place to keep it so that your computer is properly organized, but it makes it difficult to find when you want to use it. One solution to this problem is to place a shortcut to the Calculator program on the Desktop. You can place a shortcut in any folder.

The Desktop itself is actually a folder. The rule is that when you drag a program (application) object to a folder, such as the Desktop, the default action is to create a shortcut. However, when you drag a file or folder to a folder, the default action is to move (if the folder is on the same drive), or copy (if the folder is on a different drive). Since this can get confusing for many people, it is suggested that you always right-drag objects, then pick the action you want from the Menu.

How to Use Shortcuts

You should use shortcuts almost all the time. You can rename them all you want without affecting the original, and you can place copies in as many folders as you want. Almost all objects on the Desktop are shortcuts. You rarely place an original program, file, or folder on the Desktop.

DELETING FILES, FOLDERS, AND SHORTCUTS

You can delete files, folders, and shortcuts by selecting them and then doing one of the following: (1) dragging them to the Recycle Bin icon, (2) pressing the DELETE key on your keyboard, or (3) opening the right-click Context Menu and choosing Delete.

Recovering Deletions

If you wish to recover a file that you deleted, you can do so by just dragging it out of the Recycle Bin window (see also Table 12–4). The Recycle Bin can be set so that once the files in the Recycle folder occupy a certain percentage of space on the drive, the oldest files are automatically deleted permanently. You can also manually permanently delete files from the Recycle folder by selecting them in the Recycle Bin window and deleting them again, using either the DELETE key or the Delete command from the Context Menu. You can also right-click the mouse on the Recycle Bin and click EMPTY RECYCLE MENU from the Context Menu.

TABLE 12–4. What Happens When You Delete an Object

Object	What Happens When Deleted
File	The file is moved to a special folder called Recycle Bin.
Folder	All files in the folder, as well as files in subfolders, if any, are moved to the Recycle Bin. The folders are erased when you select Empty Trash.
Shortcut	The shortcut is moved to the Recycle Bin, but not the object to which it points. It remains untouched.

THE COMPUTER ICON

The drive icons are in the Computer folder, which is placed in the upper left corner of the Desktop when a new copy of Windows is installed on the computer. If you prefer to use the drive icons for file management, rather than the Explorer, it is a good idea to place shortcuts on the Desktop.

THE CONTROL PANEL

The Control Panel contains a group of utility programs that allow you to make adjustments to your computer, the Windows operating system, and the drivers for hardware devices. Certain icons are added to the Control Panel when you install programs and features in Windows. The key functions for which you use the control panel include:

- Changing your desktop background, color scheme, or screen resolution
- Setting the clock
- Installing a new printer
- Adding users to your computer
- Setting up security features
- Adding the computer to a network
- Backing up your computer's data

Depending upon which version of Windows your computer is running, there may be different icons and views for the Control Panel. The standard view is called *Classic View*. You can switch to Classic View by clicking Classic View on the Control Panel. Figure 12–8 shows the Windows Vista Control Panel in Classic View mode.

Date/Time

Your computer contains an internal clock and calendar. (You can make this same dialog box appear by right-clicking the clock on the Taskbar.) Date/Time allows the user to set the date and time on the computer's clock. The computer clock is used to label files with the date and time they are created and modified.

Display or Personalization

Your screen can be customized through the Display icon. (In Windows Vista, this is the Personalization icon.) This dialog box can also be accessed by right-clicking on the Desktop and choosing Properties or Personalize.

The desktop background can be set to a color and pattern, or you can make it display a graphic file. A graphic file displayed on the background is called *Wallpaper*. The Background tab allows you to set a pattern or choose a graphic file for wallpaper. Wallpaper graphics can be small or can fill the entire screen. If they are small, Windows gives you the option of repeating them to fill the entire screen. This is called *Tiling*. If you like, you can make your own wallpaper files in Windows Paint. Once you make the file, you just use the BROWSE button to tell Windows the name and location of the file.

Besides setting the colors of the standard parts of the Windows screen, you can set a number of other things, such as spacing of icons and the fonts used in title bars and menus. Once you have set your screen to the way you like it, you can just begin using Windows, and your settings will become the default. If you would like to change to other arrangements from time to time, you can save your settings as a *Theme* by giving it a name. Windows has a group of preset themes, too.

Screen Savers

Another popular feature is the Screen Saver. This is a screen that appears after a preset time period of no activity. The original purpose of screen savers was to prevent static images from burning in and damaging the monitor's screen. Modern monitors are rarely damaged by static images, but screen savers are a very popular way of personalizing computers, and most monitor manufacturers still recommend them.

Display Settings

The Display Settings is where you can change the resolution of your monitor and the number of colors displayed. Typical resolutions are 640 × 480, 800 × 600, and 1,024 × 768. Color resolution ranges from 16 colors to 32 bit (true-color).

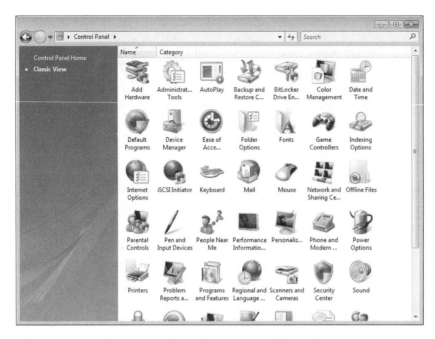

Figure 12–8. The Control Panel in Microsoft Windows Vista.

Screen shot reprinted by permission from Microsoft Corporation.

◇ MOUSE POINTERS

You can modify the settings of your mouse to make it comfortable for yourself. When you run the Mouse Utility, you see four tabs on the dialog box. The first tab, Buttons, allows you to reverse the buttons. Left-handed users may prefer to have the buttons reversed. The left button takes on the actions of the right button, and vice versa. You can also set the double-click speed, and there is a little test area to check the different double-click settings.

You can choose different mouse pointers, including animated ones. You can also save your choices in a scheme, just as you can for the appearance options.

Printers

You may have one or more printer icons, each one representing a printer that is available to you, either connected to your computer or through a network. Though you usually print while using an application, you can also drag a document file from the Explorer or a folder window and drop it on a printer icon. This causes the document's associated application to start and print the document.

In most cases, a print job is *spooled* first, which means the output from the application is sent to a temporary disk file, then to the printer. This allows large print jobs to be transferred to the spool file quickly, allowing you to go on working while the document is printed from the spooler. If you print several jobs in rapid succession, they form a queue, waiting for the printer to become available. Or, if you are attached to a network, several other people may be printing on the same printer, and all the documents form a queue.

The printer icon in the Control Panel allows you to view the queue. The window that appears is where the print queue would be shown. On networks, unless you are the system administrator, you cannot rearrange or cancel print jobs except your own.

APPLICATIONS SOFTWARE

In addition to your computer's operating system, there are many other software programs available for particular applications. These programs, often called *applications software*, are your primary tools in a business computing environment. They are designed to accomplish specific tasks or applications such as word processing, database management, or accounting.

Most applications software comes with reference manuals and even special templates for the keyboard. Some have online help and tutorials to help you learn how to use them. Most applications software is contained on a CD-ROM. If your computer is equipped with a hard drive, you install the applications software on your hard drive to make it easier and faster to access. To install, you copy the program from the CD to the hard drive. The exact way you install an application is discussed in the first few pages of the program's user manual. The installation process allows you to customize the software to your particular computer configuration. In this way, the software knows what type of printer you are using, what type of monitor, and where you want to save the data files it creates.

The following is a list of major types of applications software:

- Accounting
- Charting/graphing
- Clip art
- Communications
- Computer-aided design (CAD)
- Database management
- Desktop publishing
- Drawing
- Educational programs
- Electronic mail
- Integrated software
- Multimedia
- Music composition
- Optical character recognition
- Personal organizers
- Personal productivity
- Presentation graphics
- Programming tools
- Project managers
- Security
- Software emulators
- Software instruction
- Specialty printing
- Spreadsheets
- Statistics
- Virus detection
- Web browsers
- Word processing

13

Database Management

◇ CREATING AND USING A DATABASE

Database management systems are efficient tools for organizing and processing large amounts of information, for example, your company's accounting work, inventory customer records, and mailing lists. *Data* refers to individual items of information such as a customer's name, address, or phone number. A *database* is a collection of data, such as a mailing list. A *database management system* is computer software that allows you to store and manage the data in your database.

Although the various database programs available are different, the key to all of them is the way you organize your data. Let's say you want to keep a list of the company's customers. You might start with their names, addresses, and telephone numbers. With this list, you can easily look up telephone numbers or print out mailing labels to send out a marketing newsletter. But what if you wanted to know which customers purchased a particular product or service from the company or how much they spent? To do this, you would have to keep additional information about each customer.

◇ FIELDS, RECORDS, AND FILES

To begin creating your database, you need to define its structure. Most database management systems provide a screen that prompts you through this procedure. *To define the structure* means to determine the fields that go into your database. A *field* is a single category of information. Thus, the fields in an address database might include customer name, street address, city, state, zip code, and telephone number (Figure 13–1). Each of the fields needs to be defined individually and to be given a name. You must also tell the database whether the field will contain text information or numbers and what the maximum number of characters per field is.

Once all of your fields are determined, the next step is to enter information, or data, into your database. A *record* is a single entry of information. Thus, in a mailing list database, a single record is one person's name, address, city, state, and zip code (Figure 13–2). Most database management programs have enough room for thousands of records to be entered into the database, limited only by the amount of storage space available on your computer. You may view the data in your database by looking at individual records one at a time or by displaying a table showing your data arranged in rows and columns.

Figure 13–1. A database created using Microsoft Access.

Screen shot reprinted by permission from Microsoft Corporation.

To assist you in entering records, database management software programs provide a data entry form, although many programs allow you to design your own form. With the data entry display form on the screen, you only have to fill in the blanks. When one record is entered into the system, the program displays a new blank form.

Adding new records or updating previous records is relatively simple with most database programs. New records can be added to the end of your file of records. Changes to existing records can be made by accessing a record, erasing the current information, and then typing the update in its place.

SORTING AND SEARCHING

Sorting the Data

Once you've added some records, you can begin tapping the power of the database management software. One of the first things you may want to do is to sort the database (Figure 13–3). Indexing and sorting capabilities allow you to rearrange all the records in a meaningful order. Let's say you want to sort the records alphabetically by last name. In this case, the "last name" field would be the key or primary field, the field that determines the sort order. The first name may be the secondary field, the field that determines the sort order in a case where two last names are identical.

Another use for your database is to extract information that meets a specific criterion,

Figure 13–2. A record in a Microsoft Access database.

Screen shot reprinted by permission from Microsoft Corporation.

whether narrow or broad. You can choose simple criteria, such as displaying the address of a person named John Doe or locating the records for all persons who reside in the state of Texas. You can also use complex criteria. For example, in an accounts database, you may want a list of all persons within the 214 area code who have unpaid account balances as of September 1.

One advanced feature found on some database programs is the ability to perform mathematical functions. By creating a field that contains numerical information, a report can calculate totals for that field. This feature comes in handy when you are using a database program for keeping track of financial records.

Database management software handles all these tasks easily. You tell the database what type of information you need; the database extracts and displays only those records that meet your requirements. This process of extracting information is also called *querying the database*. You ask the database questions, and it gives you the answers.

Conducting a Search

The fastest way to find specific information in a database is to conduct a *search*. Most database management programs have a search feature that can be accessed via a keyboard command or a pull-down menu. When the command Search is selected, you are asked to type in comparison information. The program then searches the database for any records containing the comparison information and displays any that do.

Figure 13–3. Sorting a database with Microsoft Access.

Screen shot reprinted by permission from Microsoft Corporation.

To find more complex associations between your data, record selection rules (often called *arguments*) are used. These special commands combine the power of sorting with searching to find records that match a certain combination of criteria. Let's say you wanted a list of people who live in a certain state and have purchased a product or service from you but spent less than $100 on it. Many database management programs use Boolean logic to narrow down the selection. This involves the use of *and, or, not, less than, more than, equal to, not equal to, blank, not blank*, and so forth. For example, our record selection argument might be listed as following:

> State Field Contains: Texas
> Purchase Field Contains: Not Blank
> Purchase Amount Field Contains: <$100

To create a record selection, most database management programs use a menu system that allows a user to type in comparison information (arguments) and to select from various choices to combine arguments.

Printing the Information

Finally, a database management program organizes and prints the information you've selected in the form that you need it. Printed output from a database is referred to as a *report*. A report may be a list of names, a customer invoice, or a monthly statement. In any case, most database management programs allow you to design your reports to include as much or as little information as you want in a layout that suits your needs. Some programs are designed to display and print data on specific forms such as insurance forms, tax forms, and other business forms. Many office forms suppliers have a list of forms and compatible database software.

TYPES OF DATABASES

As an administrative assistant, you probably most often see two basic types of databases: the *file manager* and the *relational database*. The file manager is the simpler type of database, acting much like a regular filing cabinet. You use it when you need to organize a single group of information, such as a name and address file or a telephone record. Some database management applications are mainly designed for use with file manager software.

Other programs allow you to create a more complex type of database—a relational database. This type of system relates information in one database file to information in another by tying together key fields using a link such as a customer ID number. Suppose you had two databases: a customer address database and a customer order database. These two databases are linked by one common field: a customer ID number. When you type the customer ID number into an order, the order database retrieves the name and address of the customer from the address database. Thus, you would not have to type in the customer's name and address each time you completed a new order, saving you time and energy and reducing the opportunity for mistakes.

APPLICATIONS

In general, software applications that allow you to develop only file manager databases are less expensive and easier to learn and to use than those that develop relational databases. Here is a list of some common file manager and relational database programs:

- Microsoft Access
- Microsoft Works
- ACT! by Sage
- Lotus Organizer
- Lotus Approach
- My Mail List and Address Book by Avanquest
- My Database by MySoftware

Computer
Networking

◇ CONNECTING WITH OTHER COMPUTERS

Using a personal computer on the job can lead to substantial improvements in your productivity and organization. Being able to connect with other computers to share information or perhaps a printer can produce even more surprising results. There are two ways to connect computers together: telecommunications and networking.

Telecommunications involves connecting computers via telephone lines or a cellular telephone wireless connection. This is accomplished with a hardware device called a *modem*. The computer that receives calls from other computers and stores information that can be retrieved is often called the *host computer*. Other computers that access the host computer are called *remote computers*. These terms are used as a way to distinguish the two computers when they are connected.

Networking involves linking computers together using special coaxial cable or a wireless radio-like signal within an office or office building complex. Each computer connected to the network can communicate with any other computer on the network (Figure 14–1). This allows for sharing of files and printers and intra-office electronic mail. Usually, one computer is set up to provide storage for important data files and programs. This computer is called the *server*, because it provides access to needed resources whenever a computer user on the network needs them.

◇ MODEMS

There are two general types of modems: *internal* and *external*. External modems connect to your computer through one cable and to a telephone line through another cable. An internal modem is inserted inside the computer into an expansion slot or it may be built into the system. It does not require a cable to connect it to the computer, but you still must connect it to the telephone line.

The purpose of a modem is to convert data to a form that can be sent over telephone lines. At the other end, another modem receives the transmission and converts it back into data that a computer can understand.

Modem performance is measured in the number of bits of data that can be transmitted per second, called the *baud rate*. The baud rate can be measured in terms of bits of data per second.

Figure 14–1. A computer network.

Graphic by Jerome Brown.

A *broadband* connection is a fast connection capable of transmitting video, audio, and graphics. Many offices have a fast broadband connection that is shared by all the computers on the office network. In a small business or home, the connection may be DSL (Digital Subscriber Line, over the telephone lines) or a cable modem (using the cable TV system).

◇ WIRELESS CONNECTIONS

Wireless connections allow for ultimate freedom and connectivity. They allow computer users to access the Internet, printers, and shared data files without being connected to the network with a cable.

Wireless networks in an office usually involve a *gateway* computer that is physically connected to the Internet using a modem and cable. The gateway computer allows all the other computers on the network to share its connection. If the gateway computer is then connected to a wireless network hub or router, computers with wireless modems can access the network. Figure 14–2 shows a wireless network router.

Wireless connections are most often used by mobile users with laptops. A user can access the wireless network from a conference room or any other location in the building. There is a limit on the distance the wireless connection can travel. Most often, the signal is good only within the building. In some cases, the quality of the wireless network may vary from one part of the building to another. For that reason, many offices that have wireless

Left margin: 14 ■ COMPUTER NETWORKING

Figure 14–2. Wireless network router.

Courtesy of Dell Inc.

networks also continue to use wired connections for their fixed office computers.

Most computers equipped with a wireless modem recognize the wireless network automatically. Some wireless networks require the user to select the network from a list of available wireless networks and then enter a user ID and password.

NETWORKING

Computers within a single office or office building can be linked together, which is known as *networking*. Networking requires two main components: special network hardware and network software. Together, the parts of this system are known as a *Local Area Network* (LAN).

Networks are useful for sharing data, storing large amounts of information, and sharing expensive equipment such as laser printers. With a network, you can run multi-user programs such as database and order-entry and accounting systems. Each worker in the office using a computer connected to the network can add or retrieve information or share common peripherals such as the printer or hard drive.

The Physical Setup

The physical setup of a network is called its *topology*. The best-known topologies are named roughly for their descriptions: *ring, star*, and *bus*. A ring topology contains computers and devices set in a closed loop. In a star topology, computers and devices are connected to a central computer like spokes on a wheel. A bus topology connects the devices in a line with additions put at the end.

In a small business, a network may be just two computers linked together to share a printer. In small networks like this, each computer has equal status so that each person can access the disk drives of the other computer or the printer. This is called a *peer-to-peer* network. In larger businesses, there may be a central dedicated computer with a large-capacity disk drive to which all the other computers are connected. The central computer is known as a *server*, and the other remote computers are called *nodes*.

The benefits of networking are twofold: lower costs and greater efficiency. By having its employees share hardware, such as a storage server, a business doesn't have to purchase expensive devices for each user. Sharing software allows everyone who uses it to perform tasks in exactly the same way. Sharing software also allows multiple users to work on projects together. When working collaboratively, groups of users can complete large projects in less time. Improved communications using e-mail software allows users to coordinate schedules and encourages other efficiencies throughout an organization.

Networks can be configured using different hardware, protocols, and transmission media depending on the type of network being created. A protocol is a data transmission convention encompassing timing, control, formatting, and data representation. Most of the differences between network types are based on what protocol is used. Table 14–1 contains a list of network protocols and their speeds. Speeds are usually calculated in megabits per seconds: 100 megabits per second (100 Mbps) is equal to 1 megabyte (1 MB) per second, and 1,000 megabytes per second is equal to one gigabit per second (1 Gbps).

TABLE 14–1. Network Protocols and Their Speeds

Network Protocol	Speed
Token Ring Type 3	4 Mbps
10Base–T Ethernet	10 Mbps
Token Ring Type 1	16 Mbps
100Base–T Fast Ethernet	100 Mbps
Fiber Distributed Data Interface (FDDI)	100 Mbps
Asynchronous Transfer Mode (ATM)	155 to 622 Mbps
Gigabit Ethernet	1.25 Gbps
Fibre Channel	1.3 Gbps to 4 Gbps
SONET (Optical)	10 Gbps to 20 Gbps
Dense Wavelength Division Multiplexing (DWDM)	Up to 240 Gbps

Network Software

In order for a computer to communicate with other computers, it must use communications software. The software necessary for connecting to an office network or for communicating over telephone lines with a modem is usually built into the operating system. For example, Microsoft Windows has networking software called Network Setup Wizard that allows a user to configure his or her computer so it can connect to a network.

Most communications programs allow the user to select a *communications protocol*, a set of rules and procedures used for transmitting data between two computers. In most cases, the protocol you use is determined by the host computer. You must use whatever protocol and settings the host computer is using.

One of the main reasons to connect two computers is to transfer files. You might want to send someone a word-processing document or a spreadsheet so he or she can review it, or you might want to get a similar document from this person's computer. Most communications software has various commands that allow you to send or receive a file. When you send a file to another computer, it is called *uploading*. When you receive a file, it is called *downloading*.

When your computer is connected to an office network, you can view shared drives and folders on remote or host computers, just as if they were local drives on your own computer. You can then drag and drop or copy and paste files from one folder to another to upload or download files.

One common communications protocol used to access websites is called Hypertext Transfer Protocol, or *HTTP*. This protocol allows for viewing websites stored on remote computers on the Internet or an office network. When entering a Web address to be visited, such as the American Management Association, typing in http://www.ama.org is a way of using the HTTP protocol. The latest versions of the HTTP protocol allow a user to type a Web address without entering the http:// prefix.

Another communications protocol that is used to send and receive files between computers and a website is called *FTP*, which stands for File Transfer Protocol. Specialized FTP software allows you to sign into the website to access the files stored there. Web browsers such as Internet Explorer, FireFox, or Safari also function in FTP mode.

To manage the network, special LAN software is required. This software keeps up with the sending and delivering of information and manages use of the printer and other common peripherals.

Every user on a network has a password. You can connect to the network by typing in your name and your password. Once you are on, you have access to the extra disk drives and printers. You can run programs stored on other computers and access data files. In some cases, you can prevent other users from having access to certain confidential files stored on a particular computer. For instance, accounting records or personal data can be locked so that a special password is required for access.

Network Hardware

Network hardware usually consists of a network interface card along with special cables to link the computers together. Some computers, such as Macintosh computers with their Appletalk networking capability, have built-in network interfaces. All that is needed in these cases is cabling to link the computers.

Peer-to-peer LANs are usually smaller localized networks for a single workgroup, for example, a single office. A peer-to-peer network is usually the first type of network utilized by a workgroup, because it causes the least amount of disruption and is the least expensive. Users can continue working on their computers as they've done before the network was installed; however, they can now share resources and data.

A peer-to-peer LAN requires the following:

- A network interface card installed in each computer

- Cabling that links all of the network interface cards

- An operating system such as Windows or Macintosh OS

- Optionally, a network hub that may be used as a central connection point for all the computers on the network

Internet and Intranets

The Internet has existed for decades as a tool for scientists and the military. However, in 1989 a hypertext language with links was created that gave birth to the World Wide Web. The Internet is now a vast network of networks that link the world. It is accessed by hundreds of millions of users using dial-up modems, DSL, cable, wireless radio signals, and satellites. Web information is distributed to personal computers, palmtops, personal digital assistants, smart phones, set-top boxes, and televisions.

Intranets are networks connecting computer resources within an organization or company. Unlike the Internet, intranets are private and restrict access. Usually intranets are extended LANs using Ethernet or another dedicated network protocol.

15

E-Mail

E-mail is short for *electronic mail*. It involves the exchange of written messages sent over computer networks such as the Internet. In many offices, e-mail has replaced written memos, drop-by office visits, and even phone calls. E-mail provides a written record of office communications. You can send messages to groups of people simultaneously, attach files, and include hyperlinks to websites. E-mail is one of the most popular and effective tools for communicating with others over the Internet. With e-mail, you can send a message to anyone in the world who has e-mail access—and, barring technical difficulties, the message will be received in a matter of minutes.

◆ E-MAIL ACCOUNTS

An e-mail account allows you to connect to a network and the Internet. This is done through an Internet Service Provider, or *ISP*. The ISP helps you get connected to the network using a dial-up telephone connection, DSL, cable modem, or satellite modem. When you establish an account with an ISP, the ISP provides you with the following:

- **E-mail address.** In most cases, this is your name or nickname, followed by the @ sign and an ISP identifier that most commonly ends with the extension .com or .net.
- **POP server.** This is the name of your incoming mail server. POP stands for Post Office Protocol. This is the ISP's computer that receives incoming e-mail messages addressed to you.
- **SMTP server.** This is the name of the outgoing mail server. SMTP stands for Simple Mail Transfer Protocol. This is the ISP's computer that processes the e-mail messages you send.
- **User name.** This is usually the part of your name that appears in your e-mail address before the @ sign. Some ISPs use your entire e-mail address. The user name is used to access the ISP's system along with your password.
- **Password.** This is the secret code you use to keep your e-mail private.

In many offices, an administrative assistant obtains an e-mail account from the company's system administrator. This person assists you in setting up your computer to send and receive e-mail and provides you with your user ID, password, and e-mail address.

◇ PASSWORDS

Passwords can sometimes be case-sensitive. If your e-mail password is all uppercase letters, you need to press the shift key while entering your password.

You should never store your password around your computer. Your password should be something that is easy to remember. If you are assigned a password that is hard to remember, change it yourself. Most e-mail systems encourage you to change your password often. The best passwords combine letters and numbers and are at least six characters in length. Never use your name, your user name, your telephone number, your birthdate, your social security number, or family names as passwords. Also, never use any real word that can be found in the dictionary without combining it with numbers.

◇ E-MAIL PROGRAMS

E-mail can be accessed from a website. This is often called Web mail. You can also use e-mail software provided by your ISP. However, in most businesses, the most commonly used e-mail programs include:

- Microsoft Outlook Express
- Microsoft Outlook
- Windows Mail
- IBM Lotus Notes
- Macintosh Mail

All e-mail programs have similar features such as file folders for organizing mail, toolbars, a menu bar, a message list, and a message view window. The most commonly used toolbar or menu bar commands include:

- **New Message**—to create a new message
- **Print**—to print a paper copy of a message
- **Read**—to view a message in a separate window
- **Reply**—to reply to a particular message
- **Reply to All**—to reply to everyone copied on a previous message
- **Send and Receive**—to send out mail you've written and receive new messages
- **Forward**—to send an e-mail you've received to someone else
- **Attachment**—to send a computer file along with your e-mail message

Microsoft Outlook Express

Microsoft Outlook Express is provided with Microsoft Internet Explorer version 5.0 or later. It is designed for home users and small businesses that need a simple and easy-to-use e-mail program. Microsoft Outlook Express users can send plain text or HTML-formatted e-mail. HTML-formatted e-mail allows a user to format an e-mail using fonts, bullet lists, and so forth. Microsoft Outlook Express includes a customizable toolbar, an address book, Inbox filters, and support for multiple e-mail accounts. Figure 15–1 shows a screen image of Microsoft Outlook Express.

Microsoft Outlook

Microsoft Outlook is a more advanced e-mail management program that is included with the Microsoft Office suite of programs. Microsoft Outlook is one of the most common e-mail programs used by businesses today. In addition to sending and receiving e-mail, users can also manage their personal calendar, schedule meetings with co-workers, and manage contacts. Microsoft Outlook can also be integrated with voice mail systems so that voice messages can be retrieved and played on your computer. Figure 15–2 shows a screen image of Microsoft Outlook.

Windows Mail

Microsoft Windows Mail replaces Outlook Express in Vista, the latest version of Windows. Windows Mail functions similarly to Outlook Express with many of the same toolbar buttons and folders. Windows Mail includes a built-in search box that lets you search for specific content in all your e-mail messages. There is also a junk mail filter that helps reduce the amount of spam. Figure 15–3 shows a screen image of Windows Mail.

Figure 15–1. Outlook Express.

Screen shot reprinted by permission from Microsoft Corporation.

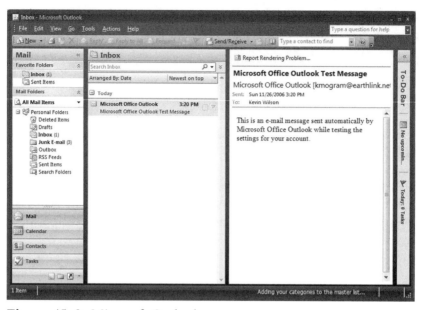

Figure 15–2. Microsoft Outlook.

Screen shot reprinted by permission from Microsoft Corporation.

IBM Lotus Notes

IBM's Lotus Notes is an e-mail messaging and collaboration program that includes e-mail, a schedule, a To-Do list, a calendar, an address book, a personal journal, Web pages, and databases. Lotus Notes can be integrated with voice mail, pagers, fax, and wireless devices such as cellular telephones and handheld PDAs. Figure 15–4 shows a screen image of IBM Lotus Notes with the various components identified.

Apple Macintosh Mail

Apple Macintosh Mail is a program that comes with the Apple OS X operating system used on Macintosh computers. Mail is a multifaceted program that allows for customizing mail messages with personalized stationary. It can be used as a memo pad and for keeping a To-Do list. Incoming e-mail messages can be easily added to a To-Do list in order for you to stay organized.

Mail is a full-featured e-mail application that includes most of the same functionality as Microsoft Outlook and Lotus Notes. Figure 15–5 shows a screen image of Macintosh Mail.

◇ MANAGING E-MAIL

When you receive mail, the e-mail program stores it in your Inbox. When you click the Inbox, you see a list of messages you have received. When you select a message from the list, the body of the message is displayed in a window. You may read other messages

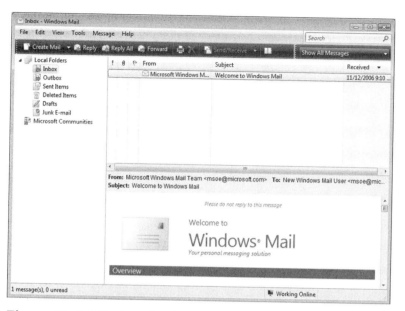

Figure 15–3. Windows Mail.

Screen shot reprinted by permission from Microsoft Corporation.

by clicking on the listings in the Inbox window.

The icon to the left of a message indicates whether or not the message has been read. In Microsoft Outlook and Windows Mail, unread mail has a sealed envelope to the left of the message. When you read a message, its icon automatically changes to an open envelope.

After you have read a message, it remains in your Inbox. You can reduce the clutter in your Inbox by moving the messages to other folders. You can also use menu items to move a message to the Deleted Items folder or, once the message is highlighted, you can simply press the DELETE key.

You can print a message by opening it and clicking the PRINT icon on the toolbar. To compose a new message, you click the NEW MAIL icon on the toolbar. A New Message window then appears. Figure 15–6 shows the New Mail window in Microsoft Outlook.

To send a message, click the SEND button on the toolbar. The message is stored in the Outbox folder until you click SEND AND RECEIVE. In Lotus Notes, you have to click REPLI-CATE to send and receive mail.

◇ SENDING ATTACHMENTS

Whenever you e-mail a message to someone, you have the ability to send additional files along with your message as an attachment. In Microsoft Outlook, you click the ATTACH icon on the toolbar. The Insert Attachment dialog box then appears. You can navigate to the appropriate file and attach it to the e-mail message. You then see the attachment list-ed or shown as an icon, along with your message.

When you receive an attachment, the e-mail program lets you know by showing you a small icon next to the message in your Inbox. In programs like Microsoft Outlook, an attachment shows up as a paper clip icon. When you open the message, you see a listing for the attachment or an icon embedded within the document. Double-clicking the icon opens the attachment file.

Reasons for Sending Attachments

There are a number of reasons why one chooses to send someone an attachment. Here is a partial list of reasons:

- The recipient can use the attached file to add, edit, or make revisions.
- You need a document to arrive ready to print and distribute.
- The recipient needs the document immediately.
- You need to send a single document to many different recipients.
- The recipient is going to distribute the document to others.

Alternatives to Sending Attachments

You should avoid sending attachments when they are unnecessary. You can avoid sending attachments by:

- Cutting and pasting word-processing data into your e-mail message.
- Placing the files on a website or File Transfer Protocol (FTP) site for downloading.
- Sending the files on a diskette or CD-ROM.
- Faxing the document.
- Printing the document and sending it via regular mail or overnight express.

Figure 15–4. IBM Lotus Notes.

Courtesy of International Business Machines Corporation. Unauthorized use not permitted.

Figure 15–5. Apple Macintosh Mail.

Courtesy of Apple.

Problems with Attachments

E-mail attachments can be big and take a long time to download if the recipient has a slow connection. There can also be translation problems when the recipient doesn't have the right program or the correct program version for opening and using the attachment. In addition, many viruses spread across the Internet through infected attachments.

E-Mail Protocol for Sending Attachments

Unless you send attachments to someone on a regular basis, you should always check with the recipient before sending an attachment. Make sure the person has the right software and can handle downloading the file.

When you send an attachment, use the e-mail message as a cover letter. Explain what the attachment is and why you are sending it. You can use compression software such as WinZip if you are sure the recipient also has the same software. Compression software reduces the file size and download times for users with slower dial-up Internet connections.

Always keep in mind that the formatting of a document may change on the recipient's computer. Many files, such as Microsoft Word documents, are printer-dependent. That means that their layout on the screen and on paper is dependent on what model printer is installed.

If you want to make sure a document will look the same on the screen and when printed on a recipient's computer, use Adobe Acrobat. Adobe Acrobat uses a file format called Portable Document Format (PDF). Adobe Reader, which lets you open and read PDF files, can be downloaded for no charge from the Adobe website at www.adobe.com. To create an Acrobat document, you need to purchase Adobe Acrobat creation software. After the software is installed on your computer, you will be able to create Acrobat documents

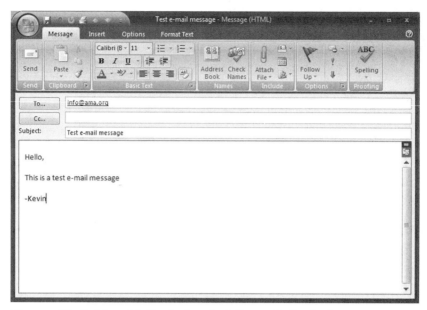

Figure 15–6. New Mail window in Microsoft Outlook.

Screen shot reprinted by permission from Microsoft Corporation.

by printing your document to the PDF printer, which acts as a software-only printer connected to your system. Instead of printing your document on paper, your document is printed as a PDF file and stored on your hard drive.

Attachment Protocol for Recipients

Don't get upset when you can't open an attachment. When this happens, send a reply and explain the problem. If necessary, ask for word-processing documents to be saved as text or have the document printed and mailed.

You should know what kind of attachments you can open. Each program has a file extension—a dot and three characters—added to the file name. The file extension is used by a program to identify its own data files. When you examine an attached file extension, it tells you what program is needed. The following is a list of common file extensions and the program needed to open them:

- doc—Microsoft Word
- txt—Microsoft Word, WordPad, or Notepad
- rtf—Microsoft Word
- pdf —Adobe Acrobat Reader
- xls—Microsoft Excel
- ppt—Microsoft PowerPoint
- pps—Microsoft PowerPoint
- jpg—Windows Paint
- bmp—Windows Paint

- gif—Windows Paint
- mp3—Windows Media Player
- mov—Quicktime Player
- avi—Windows Media Player
- zip—WinZip

Be careful with executable file attachments. These files are actually programs that could install a virus. File extensions like *exe*, *vbs*, *com*, *drv*, *dll*, *bin*, and *sys* can easily contain viruses. You should always use anti-virus software and keep it up-to-date. Don't open file attachments from people you don't know. Some viruses come embedded within legitimate files, such as Microsoft Word macro viruses. Because of this, you should always download file attachments to your hard drive and scan them with your anti-virus software before opening them.

Hyperlinks in E-Mail Messages as an Alternative to Attachments

There is a limit on how large an attachment you can send with an e-mail message. The maximum size varies depending on the recipient's Internet Service Provider. One alternative to sending a file attachment is to post the file somewhere on the Internet and to send a link to the file within an e-mail message. In most e-mail programs, when a World Wide Web address appears in the body of a message, it shows up as a hyperlink that the recipient can click to view or download.

 ORGANIZING YOUR E-MAIL

When you receive messages in your e-mail program, they automatically go to the Inbox. In time, the number of messages you receive may crowd the Inbox and make it difficult to keep track of information. You can create new folders to organize your messages. You can then drag and drop messages from the Inbox to the various folders to store and save them.

It is important for an administrative assistant to keep a good filing system for e-mail messages. You may want to create separate file folders for projects, personnel, clients, or subjects. You can create folders within folders to further organize your messages.

E-MAIL ADDRESS BOOK

All e-mail programs have an address book to help you manage your e-mail contacts. There are two ways to generate listings for the address book: You can enter the information manually, or you can add to a list through a menu command. Once you've added names to your address book, you should start using it to address messages.

NEWSGROUPS

Usenet is a series of newsgroups, maintained on host computers, that act as electronic bulletin boards open to the public. There are thousands of newsgroups. Some are designated for specific regions or cities, some are geared to specific pastimes and hobbies, and others are directed to specific fields of scientific inquiry. Any newsgroup that you subscribe to at work should be directly related to your job. You should check with your boss and get permission before you subscribe.

To join a newsgroup and read the messages, you must first subscribe. After you subscribe, messages from the newsgroup download into your e-mail program. You can then view and read the messages just like e-mail.

You can determine what a specific newsgroup is devoted to by its name. The naming structure is hierarchical, moving from general concepts to specific issues. The first part of a newsgroup name is used to designate the most general level of interest. For example:

- rec.—is used to indicate recreational groups
- soc.—contains newsgroups devoted to social issues
- chi.—is the prefix for groups centered around Chicago

The remaining elements of a newsgroup's name indicate more specific areas of interest:

- sci.physics—is a general science newsgroup about physics
- sci.physic.quarks—narrows the focus to the subatomic particles called quarks

Subscribing to newsgroups tells your e-mail program to keep track of those newsgroups you are particularly interested in following. While it's not required that you subscribe to a particular group to read and view messages, there are some distinct advantages to subscribing. Every time you open the newsgroup reader, your e-mail program loads all of the available newsgroups your provider carries. By subscribing to a specific newsgroup, you do not have to scan through all of the newsgroups to find the one you're looking for. Besides being a time-saving issue, subscribing to a newsgroup may also prove to be a money saver if your Internet online time is monitored.

The messages list window displays all of the postings and replies from other users of the newsgroup. The first column lists the subject of the message, containing a short description of the contents of that posting. The second column lists the name of the sender. The third column includes the date and time that the message was posted. The last column shows the size of the message.

MAILING LISTS

Like newsgroups, a mailing list is another message-board–like resource. People who are interested in a particular topic use a mailing list to carry on a group conversation. You can subscribe by sending an e-mail message to the list's subscription address, where you will be added to the list. As with newsgroups, you should subscribe only to mailing lists that are directly related to your work. Always check with your boss and get permission before you subscribe.

The first question that pops into most people's minds when they hear about sending an e-mail to a subscription address is: "Where do I find these addresses?" Mailing lists, unfortunately, are not as easily determinable through guesswork as Web addresses are. You'll soon find, however, that mailing lists are surprisingly accessible—you just have to know where to begin. A simple way to find a mailing list is to conduct a search using a search engine such as Google.com or Yahoo.com. Just type "mailing list" in the search box along with a specific subject word.

SIGNATURE FILES

A signature file is a small text file that can be added automatically at the end of your e-mail messages. Signature files are created in ASCII text format, which is a format that can be read by any program on any computer.

The content of this file should include your name, title, company name, address, phone number, company website, and your e-mail address.

RETURNED MAIL

Sometimes a message you send cannot be delivered. When this happens, you receive a message notifying you that your mail has been returned. There are a number of reasons why this could happen. Often, the cause may be temporary problems with your ISP, or the host server of the intended recipient may not have been online when your message arrived. In addition, you may have made an error in the intended recipient's address. Should a message be returned to you, read the routing information that appears at the top of the message. Verify that you sent the message to the proper address. If the problem persists, notify your ISP or the person you're trying to send mail to.

INSTANT MESSAGING

Instant messaging is a form of rapid response e-mail that allows a user to send multiple e-mail messages back and forth to another person when both parties are online at the same time. Rather than sending a series of e-mail messages that must read and replied to individually, instant messaging allows the two users to chat with each by typing short messages to each other.

Instant messaging allows you to store a list of people whom you want to contact with instant messages. This list is often called your buddy list or contact list. You can send a message to anyone on the list who is online.

When you send an instant message to someone, a message window opens where you and the other person can type messages that both of you can see. Figure 15–7 shows a screen capture of Windows Messenger.

There are a variety of instant messaging programs available, including:

- America Online Instant Messenger (AIM)
- Windows Messenger
- MSN Messenger
- Google Talk
- Yahoo Messenger
- ICQ

In addition to being able to type text messages back and forth, the most popular instant-messaging software allows for sending files, images, video, and sounds.

◇ E-MAIL PROTOCOL FOR ADMINISTRATIVE ASSISTANTS

Since e-mail is a written form of communication, you should follow proper e-mail protocols in order to look professional. You can do this by using proper language and accepted rules.

Addressing Your E-Mail

To send a message to someone, enter his or her e-mail address in the To field. Always verify the correct e-mail address of a recipient. Sending just one e-mail to the wrong person could be a disaster. If a person is already in your address book, many programs fill in the address automatically when you click on the name.

The CC field is for carbon copies. You should add recipients to this field when you want them to have a copy of a message but do not need a response from them. You should use this field sparingly, unless you are certain the recipient knows why he or she is receiving a copy of the message. Using this field can be confusing, since many people consider CC messages as FYI (for your information).

The BCC field is for blind carbon copies. When you add a recipient to this field, any recipients in the To or CC field will not know the person in the BCC field was copied. In most cases, you should not use the BCC field to send secret messages behind someone's back. This can be an e-mail etiquette disaster. Instead, use the BCC field to send messages to a list of people in order to keep their e-mail addresses private.

Subject Line

Most e-mail recipients decide when and whether to read a message based on the subject line. Always add a subject to the subject line. Some computer novices and ultra-busy executives forget to add a subject line. Even if you have to reply to a message you receive that does not have a subject line, always add one yourself.

Keep your subject short. Many e-mail programs limit the subject line message to forty characters or fewer. Avoid putting "RE:" at the beginning of your subject line. Many programs automatically insert "RE:" in the subject line when you reply to a message. You may want to capitalize the subject like a book title; if so, capitalize the first letter of each word except for articles and infinitives.

Always be very specific with your subject lines. A subject like "ISS Meeting on Tuesday" is better than "Meeting." Make the subject meaningful. If the message generates a back-and-forth conversation, you'll know what the message is about after you received it for the third time.

Message Greetings

E-mail should always have a personal greeting and include customized information. With e-mail, there's no need for the inside address, date, and all the normal things that go into a business letter. However, standard business letter protocol still applies with e-mail.

If this is the first time you have sent an e-mail to a recipient, introduce yourself and explain why you are writing. Be respectful of people you don't know.

Body of the Message

Be respectful of the recipient's time. Keep your messages short. If one sentence will do the job, use one sentence. If you have to switch subjects, it's best to send a separate e-mail so it can be filed separately.

Use the active rather than passive voice in your message. The passive voice incorporates various forms of the word followed by another verb. For example, "Documents were drafted by the committee" is passive. An active voice alternative is: "The committee drafted documents."

Keep your language gender-neutral. Avoid using sexist language such as, "The sales-

Figure 15–7. Windows Messenger.

Screen shot reprinted by permission from Microsoft Corporation.

man should configure his e-mail program." Instead, you could say: "The salesperson should configure the e-mail program."

If you make a request in an e-mail message, don't forget to add "please" to your request. If someone does something for you, a polite "thank you" is always nice.

Always spell-check your messages. Most e-mail programs have a built-in spell-check feature. Always proofread your messages before you send them. Many people don't bother to read their messages before they send them, and it shows. Most spelling and grammar errors can be eliminated if you read your messages before clicking SEND.

You can use common abbreviations and acronyms used in your business if you are certain the recipient understands them.

Avoid using all capital letters in the body of your message. In Internet tradition, this means yelling. However, if you need to emphasize a word like DANGER or WARNING, that's OK.

HTML Format Versus Plain Text

You can choose whether to send your messages in HTML format or plain text. In Microsoft Outlook, this feature can be set by accessing the Tools Menu, clicking OPTIONS, and then clicking the MAIL FORMAT tab. The HTML format allows you to format your message just like word processing; however, the recipient must be using an e-mail program that recognizes HTML format. Within an office where everyone is using the same e-mail program such as Microsoft Outlook or Lotus Notes, it's OK to send formatted messages using HTML format. With plain text messages, all formatting information is disregarded.

For external e-mails, you should assume that the recipient is using a plain text e-mail system. Therefore, when you send external e-mails, you should not use:

- Italics
- Underlining
- Bullets
- Tabs

- Bold
- Multiple colored or sized fonts
- Any special symbols or fonts
- Spacing to indent paragraphs

Even for internal e-mails, you should refrain from formatting your e-mail to look like a desktop publishing job. Your message format should be basic and easy to read. Use paragraphs, and double-space between them. Don't double-space after periods. Most people now use a publishing style that requires only one space after a period.

Emoticons

Emoticons are little sideways faces created using punctuation marks. For example, the emoticon :-) means smile. Emoticons are often used in online chat rooms and to signal to your reader that you are being sarcastic or making a statement with a tongue-in-cheek attitude. They can also be used to soften a message. Use emoticons sparingly. In general, they should be avoided at work.

Sign-Offs

For business e-mail, you should always end your message with a formal sign-off. *Sincerely, regards*, or *best wishes*, followed by your name, are the best salutations for formal messages. For informal communications, you can sign off with just your name. For external e-mails, always include your contact information: name, title, company name, address, e-mail address, and phone and fax numbers. Alternatively, include your contact information in your signature file.

When to Respond to E-Mails

In deciding how often to read and respond to e-mail, you must balance your workload between productive work and spending all day doing e-mail. Of course, your manager or a customer should get a quicker response than someone else if you are busy.

With most e-mails personally addressed to you, you should respond by the end of the business day. Even if the e-mail requires that you perform a task or do some research, you should let the sender know you got the message and when he or she can expect you to complete the task.

You can use templates for frequently asked questions, such as directions to your office. You can create a template message in your word processor and cut and paste it into your e-mail message. You can also use software like ReplyMate for Outlook.

When you send e-mail to external recipients, you should not expect a reply as quickly as you would with an internal e-mail. Unless a message is urgent, you should wait a few days, even up to a week, before resending the message. Remember, if a message is urgent, you can always call on the phone.

Messages Sent to the Wrong Address

If you ever receive an e-mail message by mistake, send a reply to the sender along with a copy of the message, and let the sender know that he or she used the wrong e-mail address. Of course, this does not apply to any junk e-mails you may receive.

Quoting from a Previous E-Mail

When you reply to a previous e-mail, send a copy of the previous message or a few lines as a quote. This helps the recipient know to which message you are replying. Most e-mail programs automatically copy the previous message if you click REPLY on the toolbar. You have the option of including the entire message or deleting everything except the section you want to reference. You should quote when you are answering a question, when you are commenting on a point made in a previous e-mail, or when you think it will be helpful. If you use selective quoting, you can mark the previous message by using two "less than" symbols (<<) and two "greater than" symbols (>>) on each side of the quote.

When you include a copy of a previous message or a quote, always type your message above the quote or copy. This prevents the recipient from having to scroll down to find your message.

Handling E-Mail Overload

When you find your Inbox swamped with messages, answer the most recent messages first. This helps you avoid answering questions or dealing with issues that may have already been resolved. In addition, by answering the most recent messages first, you maximize your appearance of promptness.

Don't spend all day reading and replying to e-mail. You should read and respond to all nonurgent messages at one time—perhaps after lunch or at the end of the business day. File or delete messages you have already read and responded to. This reduces the clutter in your Inbox.

Filtering Messages

There are filters built in to e-mail programs like Microsoft Outlook and Lotus Notes. Filters allow you to sort messages directly to specific file folders, bypassing your Inbox. Filters do take some time to set up, but they are well worth the time. Some ideas for filters include separating:

- Mail from particular people
- Internal e-mail from external e-mail
- Messages that do not include your company's domain name
- Messages where your e-mail address is in the CC or BCC field
- Messages from mailing lists or newsgroups
- Personal e-mail from family and friends

Figure 15–8 shows the Rules Wizard in Microsoft Outlook for setting up e-mail filters.

Urgent Messages

You should mark a message as "urgent" or "high priority" only when it really is. Never cry wolf with your e-mail by getting in the habit of marking all your messages "urgent." In fact, when you have an urgent message to send, you should consider whether e-mail is the best medium for the message. Perhaps a telephone call would be more effective.

Return Receipt

On an internal e-mail system, you can choose whether to be notified via e-mail when a recipient receives your message. When the message is read, you get a read receipt.

Return receipts are usually not supported for external e-mails sent over the Internet. In many cases, the receipt tells you only that the message made it to the recipient's e-mail server. There are delivery receipt options in Microsoft Outlook that give the recipient the option of acknowledging the delivery of the message.

Some e-mail programs allow you to read a message in a preview window without actually opening the message. If the recipient never actually opens and reads your message, you won't get a return receipt.

If you send a message with a return receipt and do not get a receipt, or if you request something and do not get a response, send out a reminder message. For internal messages, give the recipient until the end of the day to respond. For external messages, give the recipient several days to a week to respond.

Rules for Forwarding Messages

Forwarding a message can be both good and bad. It's good because it allows you to easily share information with others. It's bad because any message you forward may end up in public.

When is it OK to forward messages? Not as often as most people think. Unless a person gives you permission to forward a message, you should not forward it. There may be many reasons why someone would not want his or her message forwarded. The message may be for you only, the tone might not be appropriate for others, or the sender may not want to share his or her e-mail address.

If you don't want a message you send to someone to be forwarded, how should you let the recipient know? Make it clear that the message is just for him or her.

Before forwarding a message that contains a history of replies, check to make sure that everything in the message is appropriate before you forward. Remove any unnecessary or sensitive content.

Always keep in mind that e-mail is not private. Anything you write might be forwarded. Not everyone follows the correct protocols. One of the best rules to follow for e-mail communication is to not write anything in an e-mail that you would not want someone else to read.

You should never forward jokes and chain letters to anyone at work. You never know when someone might find them offensive. However, if you receive a lot of forwarded messages, you can set up a filter that looks for messages with FW on the subject line.

Is it necessary to reply to forwarded messages? The answer is usually no, unless you find that there is something in the message that specifically applies to you or one of your responsibilities.

Mass Mailings

Any time you need to send a single message to a group of people, you can always just add all of the addresses to the To and CC fields. However, this means you are sharing everyone's e-mail address with everyone on the list. To avoid this, you can either create a group or use the BCC field. When you use the BCC field, none of the e-mail addresses are revealed. You do need to put at least one e-mail address in the To field; however, that can always be your own e-mail address.

You should never use the BCC field to send a message behind someone's back. This is considered impolite.

Figure 15–8. The Rules Wizard in Microsoft Outlook.

Screen shot reprinted by permission from Microsoft Corporation.

Creating a Group

Many e-mail programs like Microsoft Outlook allow you to create a group of e-mail addresses from your address book and save the list with a unique name. When you send a message to the group, everyone in the list receives the message. Figure 15–9 shows how to create a group in Microsoft Outlook.

Some company e-mail systems have pre-configured groups. Be careful when sending e-mails to these groups. Know who these individuals are before you include them in a mass mailing.

Reply to All

If you receive a mass mailing and click REPLY TO ALL, everyone on the list gets a copy of your reply. This can be dangerous if Reply to All is used by mistake. When replying to a message, always make sure you click REPLY rather than REPLY TO ALL, unless you really do intend to send a reply to everyone on the list.

Some e-mail programs allow you to set a preference that prompts you when you click REPLY TO ALL. This feature helps prevent clicking REPLY TO ALL by mistake.

What Messages Are Appropriate for Business E-Mail?

E-mail is not always the best medium for a message. Sometimes it is best to use the telephone or speak with a co-worker in person rather than sending an e-mail message.

E-mail is appropriate in business communications for things like directions, requests, information to be saved, information to be copied, and company-wide announcements.

What Messages Are Inappropriate for Business E-Mail?

The following are examples of situations where e-mail is an inappropriate medium for communication:

- Thank you notes
- Long memos
- Yes or no answers
- Job praise
- Telling your boss you are sick
- Requests for raises, promotions, or resignations
- Jokes
- Flirting
- Gossip
- Anything illegal or unethical

The Tone of Your E-Mail at Work

When you e-mail your boss, do not use a casual tone, even if you are friends. Keep your e-mails businesslike. You never know when your boss may need to forward one of your messages to a superior.

Never write an e-mail when you are angry. Take time to calm down before you fire off a message you'll later regret.

International E-Mail

There are special rules that apply to international business e-mails. Start by addressing the recipient as Mr. or Ms. and his or her surname. Do not use the recipient's first name. Keep the tone of your e-mail formal, and avoid humor that might be misunderstood. Convert all your measurements to metric, and be careful about calendar dates. The date 2/06/08 means June 2, 2008 in Europe, not February 6, 2008. To be clear, always write out the month, day, and year.

If your message concerns money, be specific about what currency you are talking about. If you ask the international recipient to call you, provide him or her with the appropriate telephone country code. Also watch out for time-zone confusion. If you say you'll call the recipient at 5 p.m., make sure you are clear about whose 5 p.m. you mean.

Figure 15–9. Creating a group in Microsoft Outlook.

Screen shot reprinted by permission from Microsoft Corporation.

Auto-Respond Messages

When you are out of the office for longer than one business day and will not be able to respond to your e-mails, you should use an out-of-office notice that auto-responds to your e-mails. An auto-respond message can be set up in your e-mail program. It automatically sends a message to anyone who sends you a message while you are away. Your auto-respond message can inform the senders that you are away and will respond to their e-mails at a specific time when you return.

E-Mail Hoaxes

From time to time, you may receive forwarded hoaxes. You should be suspicious of any message that says, "Forward this to all your friends." Many times, these chain letters are simply ways to harvest e-mail addresses for junk e-mailers.

If you are suspicious that a message may be a hoax, you can check the following websites dedicated to exposing Web-related hoaxes:

- urbanlegends.about.com
- hoaxbusters.ciac.org

You can also do a search of the particular message content in Yahoo.com or Google.com.

Spam

Spam is another word for junk e-mail. These are the unsolicited sales offers and scams that try to trick the unsuspecting e-mail user. Many Internet Service Providers have filters that attempt to eliminate spam; however, many spam messages still slip through. You can reduce the amount of spam you receive by setting up filters that look for subject line phrases like *free, hot, money, hi, hello*, and *info*. You should also report any spam messages to your Internet Service Provider. You can also report spammers to the U.S. government's Federal Trade Commission or fill out a complaint form at www.ftc.gov.

Never reply to spam. This will cause you to receive even more, because now the junk e-mailer knows your e-mail address is real. Also, never click on any Web links in a spam message or call any telephone numbers listed.

E-Mail Viruses

There are many different types of computer viruses that spread via e-mail. These viruses can clog up your hard drive and slow down your computer, destroy files, compromise access to your computer, and automatically spread viruses to other computers.

One of the most common ways to get a computer virus is from an e-mail attachment. The attached file is either infected or is itself a virus. You should always use anti-virus software and keep it updated. Anytime you receive a file attachment, download it and scan it with your anti-virus software.

E-Mail Privacy

E-mail is not private. Not only may your messages be forwarded to others, but your company has the right to read anything you write or receive via e-mail. Because your employer pays for the computer, Internet connection, and your time, your business e-mail account belongs to the company. Even if you delete e-mail, it is still available for a company to view. The same rules apply for Web surfing and telephone usage.

16

Using the Internet

The Internet represents a vast global resource for collecting, disseminating, and distributing information. The Internet's underlying technologies enable instantaneous communication and collaboration across the entire globe. Individuals, businesses, educational institutions, communities, libraries, government bodies, and so on are able to share information like never before. The popular media have come to call this vast new digital world "cyberspace."

With the Internet, the possibilities are infinite. Businesspeople can check in with the home office from anywhere, or they can e-mail proposals to sales prospects instantaneously. In short, the Internet has changed our perception of time and space.

Simply put, the Internet is composed of millions of computers linked into tens of thousands of computer networks. These networks, which span the globe, are then connected to one another.

◇ THE WORLD WIDE WEB

Today, the World Wide Web makes up a very large percentage of total Internet traffic. Just about every for-profit and nonprofit company, university, library, school, and government, as well as millions of individuals, now have a presence on the Web. The Web uses the same underlying protocols as the Internet but has supplemented them with several additional technologies that have made the Internet far more accessible to computer users around the world. These include browser software, search engines, and HTML (HyperText Markup Language).

The Web was originally introduced to the Internet as a text-only system. With the release of the Mosaic browser—the first graphical browser—in 1993, the popularity of the Web grew. Soon after, Netscape appeared on the scene with its first Web browser, Netscape Navigator. Microsoft also developed its web browser, Internet Explorer. Both Netscape and Explorer were quickly accepted and surpassed Mosaic in use. Both browsers were faster, contained more features, and were easily acquired by downloading them from websites.

Today, Web documents can include text, graphics, video, and sound. The World Wide Web gives you access to true multimedia documents from all over the globe.

◇ CONNECTING TO THE INTERNET

In order to connect to the Internet, you need a modem, browser software, and an ISP (Internet Service Provider).

Modem

A modem is a device that translates and transmits signals sent over phone lines, cable, or radio signals. Many computers today have modems already built into them. For machines without a built-in modem, you can purchase a modem and attach it to your computer.

Browser Software

Once you have a modem installed, you need to add browser software to read the documents available on the World Wide Web. Browser programs read, interpret, and present documents. Netscape Navigator, Microsoft's Internet Explorer, FireFox, and Safari are some of the most widely accepted Web browsers.

ISPs

Internet Service Providers are companies or organizations that provide access to the Internet. ISPs maintain several *servers*, which are computers dedicated to providing high-speed access to the Internet. In one early way to connect to the Internet, your computer's modem dials a server at your ISP, which then establishes your connection to the Internet. This type of connection is called a *dial-up connection.*

The speed at which data can travel to and from your computer is determined by a number of factors including the processor in your computer, the speed of the ISP's servers, and the type of data line connecting computers along the way. Data can be carried on a standard phone line. However, improving technology has resulted in the creation of the ISDN line, which can carry data about four times faster than a standard phone line, and the T1 line, which can carry data about one hundred times faster than an ISDN line. Even faster is a T3 line. A T3 line represents twenty-eight T1 lines and has the "backbone" speed of major Internet connections in the United States.

Fast Internet connections are sometimes referred to as *broadband*. Broadband connections can be fifty times faster than dial-up connections. Broadband connections include the following:

- **DSL**—a digital subscriber line service that connects at high speed over a telephone line
- **Cable modem**—a high-speed connection provided by a cable television company
- **Satellite modem**—a high-speed connection provided by a satellite subscription service
- **Wireless modem**—a high-speed connection that uses radio and cellular telephone signals

Besides providing direct access to the Internet, some ISPs also contain several options to make your online activity user-friendly and more interesting. These options may include chat rooms, entertainment ideas, travel services, online catalogs for home shopping, and so forth.

◇ BROWSERS AND HTML

The software programs that allow you to view the Internet are called *browsers*. Netscape Navigator and Microsoft's Internet Explorer are two of the most common browsers in use today. Browsers are designed to read the content of Web pages and display the data on your screen.

The Web is based on the principle of *hypertext*. Hypertext is a method of navigating through documents using *links*. You've probably encountered hypertext even if you've never used the Web. For instance, CD-ROM encyclopedias often have highlighted terms in the text of the entries. Clicking on these terms connects you to a related entry or to a definition of a term. Similarly, the Help Menu that you can open in a software application usually presents you with a Hypertext Menu that links to various topics.

Hypertext is a "nonlinear" medium. That is, aside from a site's home page, there is no beginning, middle, or end to hypertext documents. You can link from a home page to a page that discusses the latest news and then link from that page to a different site altogether for related information.

Links are embedded into a Web page through a coding system called HyperText Markup Language (HTML). When you activate one of these links by clicking on it, the Web makes the connection to the host computer that houses the document you requested, and it retrieves the documents without involving the user in the underlying file-transfer process.

◇ WEB PAGES AND WEBSITES

A *Web page* is a document, almost like a word-processing document, that can be displayed by your Web browser. Web pages contain text, graphics, sounds, animation, downloadable files, and hyperlinks.

A *website* is an organized group of Web pages. For example, this book could be put on the Web and would be considered a website. Each of the chapters could be considered a Web page.

When you visit a website, the first page that appears is called the *home page*. The home page contains links to other pages on the website. If this book were a website, the home page would likely contain a table of contents, with each listing being a hyperlink that would take you to the chapter or page you select.

◇ INTERNET ADDRESSES (URLs)

How does the browser find a particular document? It employs an addressing method known as the Universal Resource Locator (URL). Each page on the Web has its own URL. A look at how a URL is put together might make it easier to visualize how documents are found.

Here is an example of a URL: http://www.videologies.com/assistant.htm. The first section (http) is the *protocol*. This indicates the type of Internet service the URL uses, in this case, hypertext transfer protocol—http. When typing a URL using a modern browser, you usually do not have to include the http:// prefix. It is automatically added when you access the site. The two slash marks (//) indicate that the next section of the URL is a domain name. In our example, the *domain name* consists of videologies.com. This is enough information to direct the browser to the host computer. When it reaches the site, it pulls up the default home page, unless a particular file is specified.

Each type of organization has its own domain. A few of the more common domains are listed in Table 16–1.

TABLE 16–1. Common Domains

Domain	Organization
.com	Business/Commercial
.org	Organization
.gov	Government
.edu *or* .k12	Educational institution
.net	Network provider
.mil	Military agency
.co	Country level domains
.info	Commercial and personal sites
.biz	Commercial
.name	Personal

The last section of the URL—after the slash (/)—specifies a file located within that domain. If you do not enter a specific file name, the URL generally takes you to the home page of the site you are requesting. In this case, we want to reach a particular file named assistant.htm.

◇ USING A WEB BROWSER

Many of the features and functions of the Microsoft Explorer browser are the same or very close to those of Netscape Navigator. The features you will use the most often include:

- Menu bar
- History list
- Help
- Status bar
- Toolbar
- Favorites
- Address box

Figure 16–1 shows a Web page in Microsoft's Internet Explorer.

The Menu Bar

Menu bars are common to most Windows and Macintosh applications. They include categories of functions you'll use the most often when working. The menu bars for Netscape Navigator and Microsoft Internet Explorer have different choices. Netscape Navigator includes choices for File, Edit, View, Go, Bookmarks, Tools, Windows, and Help. Microsoft Internet Explorer includes menu bar choices for File, Edit, View, Favorites, Tools, and Help.

The Toolbar

The toolbar includes buttons for the most common functions you'll use when browsing the Web. Like their differences in menu bar choices, the toolbars for Netscape Navigator and Microsoft Internet Explorer differ slightly in their look. Toolbars can be customizable with features you use the most often; however, the default versions of the programs include the following:

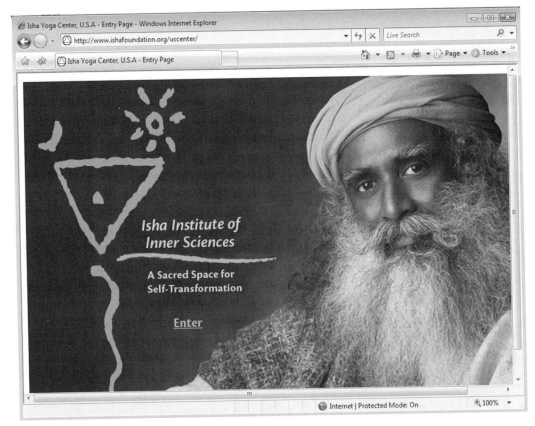

Figure 16–1. Microsoft Internet Explorer.

Screen shot reprinted by permission from Microsoft Corporation. Content courtesy of Isha Foundation (www.ishafoundation.org).

- **Back**—to view the last Web page you viewed
- **Forward**—to return to the original Web page after you have clicked the BACK button to view a previous Web page
- **Stop**—to stop loading a Web page
- **Refresh**—to reload a Web page to check for an update
- **Home**—to load the starting Web page that opens whenever you start your browser
- **Search**—to access the browser's Web search function
- **Favorites**—to access a website you have added to your list of favorite websites
- **History**—to access any of the Web pages you have viewed in the past

BOOKMARKS

Both Netscape Navigator and Microsoft's Internet Explorer feature a bookmark function that keeps an electronic record of favorite pages. (In Explorer, the bookmark feature is called Favorites.) No matter what it is called, the feature maintains a list of URLs that can be accessed whenever you want to return to your favorite websites.

PRINTING A WEB PAGE

There are two ways to print a Web page. You can click the printer icon on the browser's toolbar. If you are using Internet Explorer or Netscape Navigator, you can also click the File Menu and then click print. Depending on the type of Web page, the Print window may ask which frame you wish to print. Frames are a way of dividing up the information on a Web page so that it almost looks like a magazine page layout. You can choose to print one particular frame or all of the frames on the page.

SAVING A WEB PAGE

You can download and save a Web page to your computer's hard drive. By doing this, you can view the page again without having to be online.

To save a Web page in Internet Explorer or Netscape Navigator, click the File Menu, then click SAVE AS. The Save Web Page window appears and allows you to browse to a location where you want to save the page.

DOWNLOADING AND UPLOADING FILES

When you are viewing Web pages with your Web browser, your browser is *downloading* files to your computer. These files are stored temporarily in your computer's memory as you view them. As just described, you can choose to save a Web page to your hard drive in order to access it when you are offline.

Downloading involves the transmission of a file from the Internet to your computer. Sometimes you find links to files on Web pages that are available for downloading. These files may be data files, new programs, drivers for particular devices, graphics, music, and so forth.

Uploading is the opposite process. You transmit a file from your computer to another computer on the Internet. For example, if you apply for a job online, you might want to upload your resumé. In most cases, this is done by clicking the appropriate link to upload a file, then browsing your computer's hard drive to locate the file you want to send.

If you are involved in publishing documents and other information for websites, you need to use an FTP (File Transfer Protocol) program. An FTP program works similarly to Windows Explorer. After logging onto a website with a user name and password, you will see two windows on your screen. One window shows the files on your computer's hard drive. The other window shows the files on the website. You can then drag and drop files using your mouse from your computer to the website in order to start the FTP process.

COOKIES

Whenever you visit a website, your browser stores information about your visit on your computer. This information is called a *cookie*. A cookie stores information, such as your user ID and user preferences, so you don't have to retype them the next time you visit the site. Cookies are often used by Web marketers to learn your likes and dislikes so they can try to sell products. Unfortunately, this means your privacy is at risk.

You can set your browser to disable cookies if you wish. You can do this by viewing your browser's Preferences or Options Menu.

SEARCH TOOLS

There are millions of pages on the World Wide Web. How do you begin to find the information you're interested in? Various companies have developed programs that search the Web for the information you're looking for. A number of different sites on the Internet that provide this service are commonly called *search engines*.

Search engines serve as a sort of automated reference librarian. Search engines find pages on the Web based on key words you provide. There are a variety of engines and tools to help you find what you're looking for. For example, Google.com, MSN.com, Ask.com, Lycos.com, Yahoo.com, and Altavista.com can help you find sites on the Web.

Yahoo! organizes listings into categories and subcategories. It is among the most popular search tools because it allows users to register their own websites. You can find the latest additions to the Web using Yahoo!

The list of categories in a Web guide is most useful when you have a broad subject in mind. The guide's hierarchical structure can help you narrow your topic as you go along. For instance, you could search an extremely broad topic, such as "weather," using the categories provided by a Web guide.

16 ▪ USING THE INTERNET

The following is a list of popular search sites:

- About.com—www.about.com
- AltaVista—www.altavista.com
- Ask—www.ask.com
- Dogpile—www.dogpile.com
- Excite—www.excite.com
- Go.com—www.go.com
- Google—www.google.com
- HotBot—www.hotbot.com
- LookSmart—www.looksmart.com
- Lycos—www.lycos.com
- Mamma Metasearch—www.mamma.com
- Northernlight—www.northernlight.com
- Search—www.search.com
- Snap—www.snap.com
- Suite101—www.suite101.com
- WebCrawler—www.webcrawler.com

◆ CONDUCTING A SEARCH

Because of the sheer volume of information on the Web, broad searches generate a great number of results. Yahoo! provides the very useful service of breaking the results down for you.

Some search engines don't return results based on categories and concepts. Instead, they look for the occurrence of the key words you put in your search request within all the documents in their registries. This approach has both advantages and disadvantages.

The main advantage is breadth. A search for the key word "hurricane" may turn up interesting documents that refer to hurricanes but are not entirely devoted to hurricanes. For instance, a general science magazine may have a good article on hurricanes. While you may not find it in a directory search, because it wouldn't be listed under the category "hurricanes," you would likely find it in a key word search. A disadvantage is that in addition to useful references, you also pull up every page with the word "hurricane," whether it's relevant or not.

The simplest way to get good results from a search engine is to determine in advance precisely what you are looking for and then enter as many words as you can think of to describe it.

Thus, while searching for "hurricanes," you should use the engine AltaVista. AltaVista ranks the search findings by matching them to the search text. If your search text involves a number of words or phrases, AltaVista ranks Web pages that have all the search text requirements above those that contain only a single element of the search text. For example, Web pages containing all the words of the search text "hurricane, radar, image, Atlantic, ocean," will be ranked above those that contain only one or two of those words.

Effective Search Strategies

Two key terms used in comparing search engine performance are *recall* and *precision*. Having a high recall rating indicates that a search engine returns a great number of documents from a search. High precision refers to the percentage of returns that actually match your search criteria. The goal on which to focus is to increase the precision of your searches.

You can achieve more efficient search results through the use of *search syntax*. There are a few simple syntax elements that can greatly help you to refine your search. Incorporating search syntax into your queries makes each search far more effective in finding the information you want. In other words, it increases the precision of your search.

Advanced searching alerts the search engine to the relationship between your key terms. You can specify that *all* your terms must appear, *any* of your terms must appear, or that the terms must appear in a specific order. Moreover, you can specify that certain words do not appear. This feature would be helpful if you were searching for information on pythons and wanted to exclude documents dealing with the British comedy group Monty Python.

You indicate the relationships between your key terms by placing *operators* between them. For example, adding a plus sign (+) between words in your search produces results that include all of the words in your search. *Note: Be sure to refer to a search engine's Help page before doing an advanced syntax search. The Help page indicates which operators are recognized in that search engine.*

Boolean Searches

AltaVista and HotBot also let you perform Boolean searches. This is the search syntax that professional research librarians use. While Boolean searches can get complicated, knowing a few of the operators involved helps you refine your searches. The following are some useful operators. (Note that they are typed in all capitals.)

AND Placed between two words to indicate that the document must contain both words

OR Placed between two words to indicate that the document can contain one or both words

NOT Placed before a word to indicate that this word must not appear in the document

NEAR Placed before a word to indicate that these words must occur within ten words of each other

Searching Within a Site

You've seen that there are many ways to search. However, just because you have found a good site doesn't mean that the search is over. You'll find that even good sites contain a lot of filler. The goal is to cut through the filler and find the material that is useful and helpful to you. It is easy to get lost in a large website. Here are some standard rules for searching a very large website:

- Clearly identify the desired information. In other words, clarify the search.
- Think through the possible search terms that could be used.
- Remain focused in your search. Don't be pulled into surfing if you are trying to find something specific.

◇ ERROR MESSAGES

When using a browser, an error message can come up for a number of reasons. Different problems generate different error messages.

The Web is a dynamic and ever-changing environment; while pages are constantly created, others are removed. If you encounter a page, or a site, that does not exist, you receive an error message. Here are some of the error messages you may encounter:

- **Unable to Locate Server**—If the browser is unable to locate a particular host computer (also called a server), you receive a message indicating the situation.

- **Page Does Not Exist**—If you try connecting to a specific Web page that does not exist, you receive another type of error message. Rather than a dialog box, an actual Web page appears, advising you that the site you requested is not a valid URL.

- **Server Busy or Unavailable**—When there is too much traffic on the Internet, or if you try to access an overwhelmingly popular site, you may receive an error message.

◇ PLUG-INS

Your Web browser has various features that allow it to display graphics, play sounds, and run animations. Some specialized tools are required to access content on certain websites. For example, some sites provide streaming audio or video content. These sites usually require a special plug-in be installed in order to access the content.

Some of the most common plug-ins include RealNetworks' RealPlayer, Apple Computer's QuickTime Player, and Adobe's Shockwave, Flash, and Acrobat Reader.

◇ WEBSITES OF INTEREST TO ADMINISTRATIVE ASSISTANTS

The following websites may be of special interest to administrative assistants:

- **1-800-Flowers**—www.1800flowers.com—An online florist

- **All One Search**—www.allonesearch.com—A search engine for finding reference sources, quotes, and other language usage resources

- **Amazon.com**—www.amazon.com—An online bookstore that is searchable by title, author, or topic; also sells CDs, DVDs, and other products

- **American Management Association**—www.amanet.org—Resources and training information for administrative assistants and their managers

- **Ask An Expert**—www.askanexpert.com—Specialized answers to questions ranging from business and industry to science and health

- **Bankrate.com** —www.bankrate.com—A listing of mortgage rates across the country

- **Barnes & Noble**—www.barnesandnoble.com—An online bookstore that is searchable by title, author, or topic; free online courses are also available from this site

- **Better Business Bureau**—www.bbb.org—A list of Better Business Bureau services

- **BusinessTown.com**—www.businesstown.com—A site dedicated to business resources that includes sample letters and forms, travel information, accounting and finance, and office procedures

- **CareerBuilder.com**—www.careerbuilder.com—A listing of thousands of job postings, resumé listings, and employer information

- **CitySearch**—www.citysearch.com—A listing of entertainment, restaurants, hotels, and shopping for various U.S. cities

- **CNN**—www.cnn.com—An online news resource

- **Cool Jobs.com**—www.cooljobs.com—A listing of job postings

- **Cybershop.com**—www.cybershop.com—An online shopping resource for corporate gifts

- **Dictionary**—www.dictionary.com—An online dictionary and thesaurus

- **EDGAR Online**—www.edgar-online.com—A repository of corporate filings by public companies to the Securities and Exchange Commission

- **E-Trade Financial**—www.etrade.com—An online stock trading resource

- **Expedia Travel**—www.expedia.com—An online travel agency for booking airline flights, hotels, and car rentals

- **Federal Express**—www.fedex.com—An express shipping service for overnight letters, packages, and freight

- **FindLaw**—www.findlaw.com—A directory of legal resources, law firm listings, and legal news

- **Fodor's Online Travel Guides**—www.fodors.com/reviews—A listing of restaurant and hotel reviews for various cities around the world

- **Foreign Languages for Travelers**—www.travlang.com/languages—A list of common phrases in various foreign languages

- **Idea Café**—www.ideacafe.com—A collection of resources available for small businesses

- **InfoSpace**—www.infospace.com—A search engine that finds telephone numbers, addresses, and e-mail address of people nationwide

- **Insurance.com**—www.quotesmith.com—A website with information on various types of insurance products

- **Internal Revenue Service**—www.irs.gov—The website of the IRS, with downloadable tax forms and tax information

- **Learn2.com**—www.learn2.com—An extensive resource with online courses on many different subjects

- **MapQuest.com**—www.mapquest.com—An online map service that can provide driving directions between any two streets in the United States

- **Monster.com**—www.monster.com—A listing of job postings

- **MSN Encarta**—www.encarta.msn.com—An online encyclopedia

- **National Fraud Information Center**—www.fraud.org—Information on common scams

- **New York Times**—www.nytimes.com—An online newspaper

- **Office Depot**—www.officedepot.com—An online office supply store

- **Office Max**—www.officemax.com—An online office supply store

- **Priceline.com**—www.priceline.com—A resource for purchasing air travel, hotels, and car rentals at reduced prices

- **Small Business Administration**—www.sbaonline.sba.gov—A listing of resources available for starting, financing, and running a small business

- **Staples**—www.staples.com—An online office supply store

- **Travelocity**—www.travelocity.com—An extensive travel guide for booking air travel, hotels, and car rentals anywhere in the world

- **True Careers**—www.truecareers.com—A listing of job postings

- **United Parcel Service**—www.ups.com—A shipping service for packages

- **U.S. Census Bureau**—www.census.gov—A website with statistical listings for individuals and businesses

- **U.S. Federal Government**—www.fedworld.gov—A resource listing U.S. federal government websites, publications, agencies, tax information, and jobs

- **USA Today**—www.usatoday.com—An online newspaper

- **Wall Street Journal**—www.wsj.com—An online newspaper

- **Weather Channel**—www.weather.com—An online weather report for anywhere in the world

- **WebMD** —www.webmd.com—A website with an extensive library of health-related information

- **Zip Codes**—zip4.usps.com/zip4—A site that lets you locate zip codes by typing in an address and a city

Web Conferencing

◇ OVERVIEW OF WEB CONFERENCING

Web conferencing is growing in popularity as a way to hold meetings with people from different locations without having to leave the office. A Web conference (sometimes called a webinar) allows the meeting to take place at a central online location so participants can share PowerPoint slides, view software demonstrations, or brainstorm ideas using a shared whiteboard. By combining a Web conference with an audio teleconference—where participants interact over the telephone—a Web conference can almost replace the need for in-person meetings.

Typically, an administrative assistant handles all aspects of setting up and running a Web conference, while his or her manager is a speaker or presenter. Having someone who focuses solely on the technology aspects of the Web conference frees the presenter to focus on the content and interactions with the participants.

Businesses often use Web conferencing for marketing meetings, sales presentations, training sessions, human resources announcements, employee orientations, and shareholder meetings. Web conferencing can help slash travel budgets, save travel time, and encourage more interaction between distant groups of people. The lack of face-to-face interaction can be solved by adding interactive polling, question and answer sessions, software application sharing, and video cameras.

Web conferencing vendors provide the software necessary for hosting a Web conference, as well as providing the support necessary for teleconferencing. By signing up with a vendor, you can get an account, install the software, and begin hosting your first Web conference in a matter of minutes. Some of the most popular Web conference vendors include:

- **InterCall**—www.intercall.com
- **WebEx**—www.webex.com
- **GoToMeeting**—www.gotomeeting.com
- **Citrix**—www.citrix.com
- **Inter-Tel**—www.linktivity.com
- **Microsoft Live Meeting**—office.microsoft.com/livemeeting

◇ WEB CONFERENCING APPLICATIONS

Many Web conferencing vendors offer feature-rich applications that allow for a dynamic interactive experience. Some of these features include:

- **Application Sharing**—Allows for sharing a software application on the presenter's desktop with the participants of the Web conference. Control of the application can be passed to conference attendees to demonstrate features, make changes, or collaborate. Application sharing is often used in training sessions, where the presenter acts as an instructor demonstrating how to use new software.

- **Screen Sharing**—Allows for sharing anything on the presenter's screen with the participants of the Web conference. This is often used when the presenter wants to demonstrate features of the computer's operating system or show two or more software applications simultaneously.

- **Presentation Sharing**—Allows the presenter to upload a PowerPoint slide presentation to share with the conference participants.

- **Whiteboard**—Allows the presenter and participants to draw diagrams and write notes on the screen.

- **Monitoring**—Allows the presenter to see a roster of attendees, to control access to shared documents and shared applications, and to grant co-moderator status.

- **Audio Controls**—Allows the presenter to mute or un-mute the participants' phone lines.

- **Web Tours**—Allows the presenter to display Web pages and share them with the conference participants.

- **Annotation Tools**—Allows the presenter and attendees to control an on-screen pointer, highlight parts of the screen, draw objects and diagrams, and type text on the screen.

- **File Transfer**—Allows the presenter to share files with the participants.

- **Chat**—Allows the attendees to type messages to the presenter or to each other. This feature is often used by the presenter to take participants' questions throughout the Web conference.

- **Polling**—Allows the presenter to provide a set of questions with multiple-choice answers to quiz the participants or to get feedback.

- **Recording**—Allows the presenter or individual participants to record a presentation in order to watch and listen to it later.

- **Web Camera**—Allows the presenter and participants to add webcams to the Web conference in order to see each other.

- **Reporting**—Allows the presenter to see a report following the Web conference showing the roster, participant activity, chat, and polling results.

- **Virtual Computer Lab**—Allows the presenter to send participants to specially configured computers for hands-on training.

◇ ORGANIZING A WEB CONFERENCE

To hold a Web conference, you need a computer with an Internet connection, Web conferencing software, and a telephone line. The conference participants can access from a dial-up Internet connection if that's all they have available; however, it's recommended that the presenter have a high-speed Internet connection such as a DSL, a cable modem, or a T1.

To start a meeting, you use the Web conferencing software to schedule a specific date and time. The software then lets you send out invitations to attendees that includes information on how to join the Web conference. The attendees can then join the conference by following the instructions in their invitation to sign on to a particular website or by clicking a hyperlink that automatically connects them to the conference. The attendees may need to install the Web conferencing software, which is a process that takes only a few minutes the first time they use the service.

Securing Your Meeting

One way to make sure that only invited participants attend your Web conference is to require a conference password. You can specify a password for each meeting and include it in your invitation. Since you may use the same account for many Web conferences, it is possible that someone who attended a previous session could attend a current session if you fail to password-protect the conference.

Another way to secure your meeting is to schedule an unlisted meeting. Unlisted meetings do not show up on the meeting calendar for your account.

You can also require your attendees to register for the meeting. You can then accept or reject each registration request.

Teleconference Information

Most Web conferencing vendors also offer teleconference services that provide you with a toll-free call-in number along with an access code and personal identification number. The call-in number and access code are included in the conference invitation. The presenter calls in first and uses the personal identification number to start the call.

One low-cost option is to use an Internet phone conference, using Voice over Internet Protocol (VoIP) technology. With this technology, the audio portion of the Web conference is transmitted over the Internet. The presenter and participants must use microphones and speakers connected to their computers in order to talk and listen. Usually, a VoIP teleconference is best if only one person, usually the presenter, is talking.

Microsoft Outlook Integration

Many Web conferencing vendors have software that integrates with Microsoft Outlook's meeting scheduler. By installing the Outlook integration software, a presenter can schedule a meeting in Microsoft Outlook and include Web conference information in the meeting request. The meeting request serves as a conference invitation to the participants. The request also schedules the meeting automatically on the presenter's Web conference account calendar.

Participant Systems Check

A systems check is a quick process that participants need to go through in advance of the Web conference. This process usually involves having the participant do a pre-meeting installation of the Web conferencing software. Most Web conferencing vendors have a link on their websites that allows new users to install the necessary software before the Web conference.

To reduce the number of technical issues at the beginning of your Web conference, you should provide step-by-step instructions in your invitation that encourage participants to perform a systems check and to install any necessary Web conferencing software. Even if participants have attended Web conferences using the same system in the past, it is still a good idea to have them test their system. Changes to the vendor's software, upgrades to a user's computer, or even operating system and browser security updates could cause the Web conferencing software to suddenly stop working.

Some participants may have trouble installing the Web conferencing software during the systems check because of restrictions on software downloads put in place by the IT department. These restrictions are usually put in place for security purposes and to help prevent the spread of computer viruses. If this happens, the user may try to install the Web conferencing software and nothing happens. If possible, the presenter should contact the IT department and find out if any of the participants will have this issue. If so, then make sure you consult with the IT department to authorize the download and to provide instructions for participants on how to work around this issue.

Sample Meeting Invitation

Figure 17–1 is a sample invitation for a Web conference using WebEx.

⬦ **PLANNING YOUR WEB CONFERENCE**

As you plan your Web conference presentation, use the following checklist:

- Determine the discussion topics first. Remember, less is more, so try not to cover too much information in one session.
- Decide how much time should be spent on each discussion topic. It's best if the Web conference lasts no more than sixty to ninety minutes. It is difficult to keep participants' attention beyond this length.
- Think about what the participants will see on the screen for each of your discussion points. Try to spice up the presentation visually, rather than just using text bullets for every discussion point. Use pictures or charts when possible to illustrate points.

Hello,

You are invited to attend a Web conference using WebEx.

Session Details

Topic: Isha Foundation
Date: September 23, 2009
Time: 10:00 a.m. EST
Session Number: 46297
Session Password: Sadhguru
Teleconference Number: 1-800-555-2973
Teleconference Pass Code: SJV101

To access the conference, you will need to conduct a systems check well in advance of the meeting to ensure you are able to view the Web content. Even if you have attended a Web conference using WebEx before, it's important to conduct a systems check. Site configuration changes, such as an upgrade, can affect your computer's ability to access the Web conference.

To Perform the Systems Check

1. Go to http://www.webex.com
2. Click the **Training Center** tab.
3. Click **Set Up** on the left-hand side of the screen.
4. Click **Training Manager**.

You will be prompted through a short software set-up to determine if you computer is compatible. If your computer fails the system check, contact WebEx technical support at

_____.

To Join the Session on the Internet

1. Log on to http://www.webex.com
2. In the box under the words "if you know your meeting number, join here," type the session number and then click **Join**.
3. Follow the prompts for a short software download to access the Web conference.
4. Dial into the audio portion of the call.

Thank you.

Figure 17–1. Sample Web conference invitation.

- Identify ways to add interactivity to the meeting so you can test the participants' understanding. You can use polling and chat questions, breakout sessions, or a shared whiteboard, or you can turn over control of a software application to the participants.

- If more than one person will be facilitating the Web conference, decide who will present each portion of the presentation. Decide how you will transition from one person to another. Will you all be in the same room, or will each of you be connected to the conference separately?

- Identify in advance who will field questions from the participants. You may want to line up several subject matter experts and have them join the conference in order to answer questions.

Sample Web Conference Agenda

Because a Web conference can get fairly complicated to produce, it's a good idea to create an agenda for the facilitators in advance of the conference. This is especially important if you plan to utilize tools such as a shared presentation, application sharing, polling questions, and so forth. Table 17–1 is a sample agenda for a new product rollout.

TABLE 17–1. Sample Web Conference Agenda

Time	Discussion Topic	Presenter	What Participant Sees	Test for Understanding
10 min	Welcome / Introduction	Jennifer		
	• Welcome		• PowerPoint Slide 1	
	• Conference guidelines		• PowerPoint Slide 2	
	• Agenda		• PowerPoint Slide 3	• Sign in using Chat
	• 4 Ps of marketing		• PowerPoint Slide 4	• Polling Questions
15 min	Product	Kevin		
	• Definition		• PowerPoint Slide 5	
	• Features		• Shared Browser	• Allow participants
	• Future enhancements		• Shared Browser	to direct
	• What's in it for me?		• PowerPoint Slide 6	
5 min	Pricing	Jim		
	• Packages		• PowerPoint Slide 7	
	• Marketplace fit		• PowerPoint Slide 8	• Polling question
15 min	Promotion	Jennifer		
	• Marketing efforts		• Shared Browser	• Allow participants
	• Advertising		• Shared Browser	to direct
	• Talking points		• PowerPoint Slide 9	• Download
	• Ask for the sale		• Sale Document	document
5 min	What Happens Next	Kevin		
	• Launch date		• PowerPoint Slide 10	• Polling question
	• Your role		• *Your Role* Document	• Download
	• Our role		• *Our Role* Document	document
10 min	Open Forum / Questions	All		
	• Feedback		• Whiteboard	• Polling question
	• Questions		• Chat	
	• How to log out			

◇ PRESENTING AT A WEB CONFERENCE

Keep the following tips in mind in preparing for the Web conference, running it, and handling post-conference tasks.

Preparing for the Web Conference

Always test your access to the conference software, the presentation, and other features that you intend to use before the actual conference. Hosting a conference in a conference room away from your regular computer may result in technical issues that should be resolved in advance.

Make sure all the files and documents you want to share are organized in a single folder so you can easily locate them during the meeting. Always clear your Web browser's cache before beginning a meeting. It's also a good idea to restart your computer before launching the Web conferencing software. This ensures that there aren't any conflicts from other applications you may have been running earlier.

If you plan to use polling, create all the questions before the meeting start time. Some Web conferencing software allows you to create and save your polling questions. Other systems may require that you enter them manually during the conference. If you have to enter them manually, you should type them into a word-processing document and then be ready to copy and paste them into the Web conferencing software.

Always join the Web conference and teleconference at least ten to fifteen minutes before the scheduled time. Be prepared to help participants join the Web conference. You should be familiar with the steps for installing the Web conferencing software for first-time attendees and assisting users whose computer skills may be lacking.

The administrative assistant should assist the presenter in driving the presentation and interacting with the Web conferencing software. This allows the presenter to focus on the message rather than the technology involved. The assistant can also monitor the chat window to see questions and respond to them without bothering the main presenter.

Include a welcome slide for your presentation that includes the title and teleconference access number. This gives the participants something to see when they first join the Web conference. Include meeting guidelines and technical assistance information on the second slide in your presentation.

Running the Web Conference

During the presentation, minimize background noise by telling participants to turn off their cell phones. Remind the participants to avoid sidebar conversations, or use the audio controls to put the participants on mute. If you will be un-muting their phones at the end of the conference to take questions, remind the participants not to put the conference call on hold. If their telephone system plays background music, everyone will hear the music.

Remind everyone how to use the Web conferencing software's features to ask questions, raise their hand, or to send chat messages.

During your presentation, use the annotation tools to point to areas on the slide, highlight text, and write notes. When you move from one slide to the next, wait a few moments for your participants' screens to catch up.

When sharing a presentation or document, open the application with which it was created and share the application. For example, if you have a PowerPoint presentation, rather than uploading the slides, you can open the presentation in PowerPoint on your desktop and then share the open PowerPoint application. This allows you to make edits if necessary.

Use Web browser sharing to take participants on a Web tour, rather than giving them a Web address and asking them to review the site later on their own. By taking them on a tour, you can ensure that they see the features you want. Use the full-screen mode when showing slides, sharing applications, or conducting Web tours.

If a brainstorming discussion occurs, use the whiteboard feature to take notes. This keeps everyone focused on the Web conference and allows everyone to follow along. In addition, most Web conferencing software allows you to save the whiteboard text at the end of the conference.

Provide handouts to participants at the beginning of the meeting. If a PowerPoint slide presentation is being conducted, you can share the presentation and allow participants to print a copy. You can improve the performance of presentations by limiting the number of animations, slide transitions, and screen captures. Try to limit the number of slides in a presentation to no more than thirty slides. If you must have more slides to cover the content, create a separate presentation and switch presentations in the middle of the conference.

Keep a watchful eye on the time. If discussions get too lengthy, participants should be asked to hold their questions until the end.

Give participants a break if the Web conference is going past ninety minutes. Everyone needs a chance to stretch and use the restroom after ninety minutes, so add an "intermission" to longer conferences. Just tell everyone to leave the Web conference running and return to the conference at a specified time.

It's always considerate to record the presentation for invited participants who are unable to attend. Most Web conferencing vendors allow you to record the on-screen activities and combine them with the telephone audio for access at a later time. Some vendors require special equipment in order to capture the telephone audio, so make sure you check with your vendor before you attempt to record a session. If you decide to make a recording, make sure everyone knows the call is being recorded.

If by accident you are kicked out of your own conference because of some technical glitch, don't panic. Just communicate what happened over the audio part of the call and then log back in. This is also good advice to share with participants who may have the same thing happen to them. If they lose the audio or Web portion of the conference, they should simply log back on or call back in.

Handling Post-Conference Tasks

When the conference ends, thank everyone for participating. If you made a recording of the presentation, let everyone know when the recording will be available. You can send out a post-meeting e-mail to the participants that includes a hyperlink to the recorded version.

Be sure to hang up the phone and close the Web conferencing software when you are finished. Be careful about making any comments about what happened during the conference, in case you are still connected and some of the participants are still listening.

When you close the Web conferencing software, save the chats, polling questions, and whiteboard text that was created during the conference. Some systems save these items for you automatically.

Spreadsheet Software

◇ **What Is a Spreadsheet?**

Many administrative assistants use computerized spreadsheet software to handle accounting chores, assist with budgets, and perform similar tasks. Spreadsheet software takes the place of the columnar pad that was so popular in the past. A columnar pad is divided into columns across the top and rows that run down the side. The rows and columns intersect at a small box. Altogether, there are hundreds of these little boxes on each page. An electronic spreadsheet is a large grid of columns and rows. A box where a column and row intersect is called a cell. Each *cell* has a unique *address*. Most spreadsheets label columns using letters, and rows using numbers. Therefore, the cell at the intersection of column C and row 5 is cell C5.

The largest spreadsheet can contain millions of cells depending on the memory size of the computer running the software. However, most of the applications you'll be working with use only five hundred to one thousand cells.

The most commonly used spreadsheet program is Microsoft Excel. Figure 18–1 shows a screen image of Microsoft Excel.

◇ **Navigating Around a Spreadsheet**

When you are using a spreadsheet, one cell is always active—that is, ready for you to input data. This cell is designated by a cell pointer, highlighted area, or flashing cursor. To make another cell active, you use the arrow keys, numeric keypad, or mouse to move to another location. Because of the limits on screen size, only a small group of cells can be displayed at any one time. If you wish to view additional cells, use a mouse or the arrow keys to move even farther on the spreadsheet.

Navigating around on a spreadsheet is much like looking through a window. Moving the window around to view additional cells is called *scrolling*. There are also special commands that take you to predefined locations on a spreadsheet, such as the bottom or top.

To make using a spreadsheet as simple as possible, most spreadsheet software programs have some type of control panel. Some have the control panel at the bottom of the screen, and others have it at the top. The control panel displays information about the active cell and has a space where the user can type information into the active cell. In addition, it displays menus for activities such as saving, printing, and loading, as well as

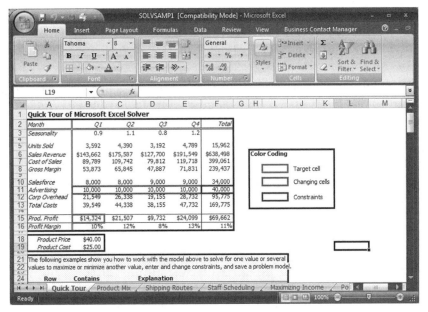

Figure 18–1. Microsoft Excel.

Screen shot reprinted by permission from Microsoft Corporation.

in some cases a list of special built-in functions. To select a choice, you move the cursor around using the arrow keys, numeric keypad, or mouse to highlight your choice, and then press ENTER/RETURN or click the mouse.

 SPREADSHEET DATA

Any entry into a cell can be one of three possible items: a label, a number, or a formula. A *label* is a word used to describe information in your spreadsheet. For example, you might want to calculate a budget for office expenses. Therefore, you would create a list of those expenses: paper, pens, computer supplies, stamps, and so forth. These words describe the numbers in another column or row, which is why they're called labels.

The actual expenses for the office supplies are the *numbers*. In order to add up a total of all the expenses at the bottom of the list, you need to enter a *formula*, a combination of cell addresses connected by mathematical symbols, for instance, A1 + A2 + A3.

To enter a label, number, or formula into a cell, place the cursor on the cell you want to make active, then begin typing. As you type, the information you enter is displayed in the control panel. When you are ready to put that information in the active cell, you either click the mouse or press ENTER/RETURN on the keyboard.

Formulas

A formula will work correctly only with numbers. Therefore, in order for a spreadsheet to distinguish labels, numbers, and formulas, most spreadsheet software programs use special predefined characters so that a user can specify the difference. For example, if the first character you type in a cell is a number, the spreadsheet assumes that entry is a number. If the first character you type is a letter, the spreadsheet assumes the entry is a label. And if you type in a special software-defined character such as " = ", the spreadsheet assumes your entry is a formula.

Spreadsheet formulas can get complicated. Formulas can link information from one area to another so that totals from one group or section can be added to an overall summary. For example, an accounting system could be set up that allows you to enter expenses into various accounts. One formula would calculate the total expenses for each account; another would be used to link the total of a particular account to an overall profit-and-loss statement.

The simplest formula is one that moves the data from one cell to another. Say you entered the following formula in cell A1: " =Sum(A2) ". Whatever amount appeared in cell A2 would automatically also appear in A1.

The use of parentheses is an important aspect of formulas. For example, a formula such as " =Sum(A1:A10) " would provide a total of all the numbers in cells A1 through A10. When combined with other mathematical symbols for division, multiplication, and subtraction, a formula containing multiple sets of nested parentheses could be created, for example, " =Sum(((A1:A10) * A20) – A30) ".

In order to create a formula correctly, you must know the order in which the mathematical operations will be performed by the computer. The natural order is to perform any calculation involving exponents first, followed by multiplication and division, and then addition and subtraction. For example, you do the following to solve the formula =Sum((2^2 ∞ 10) + ((144/12) – (5+6))) :

- 2^2 — First square the 2 to get 4 =Sum((4×10) + ((144/12) - (5+6)))
- 4×10 — Multiply 4 by 10 to get 40 =Sum(40 + ((144/12) - (5+6)))
- 144/12— Next you divide 144 by 12 to get 12 =Sum(40 + (12 - (5+6)))
- Then do the addition and subtraction, starting inside the parentheses: 5 plus 6 equals 11 =Sum(40 + (12 - 11))
- 12 minus 11 equals 1 =Sum(40 + 1)
- To finish, 40 plus 1 equals 41 =Sum(41)

Whenever a continuous group of cells is involved in a formula such as a row or column or block of numbers, rather than type in each individual cell address, a *range* is specified instead. For example, A1:A10 specifies a range of cells from cell A1 to cell A10 including all cells in between. A range can be as small as two cells or as large as the entire spreadsheet. It can be a row, a column, part of a row or column, or a block of several rows and columns. Most often, a range is specified by identifying the beginning cell, followed by a colon or an ellipsis, followed by the ending cell.

Automatic Recalculations

One of the nice features of a spreadsheet is the ability to recalculate formulas automatically if you change any of the numbers in the cells included in the formula. If you have formulas that link various columns, rows, or sections, changing one number in a cell can cause numbers to change throughout the entire spreadsheet as each formula automatically recalculates. This recalculation feature is extremely useful for performing a "what-if" analysis.

If you want to see the effect of a change in one particular area on a spreadsheet, enter the new number, and see what it does to the overall total. This feature allows you to build what are sometimes called *spreadsheet templates*. For example, if you create a spreadsheet to keep track of petty cash or a project budget, once you create the spreadsheet and the formulas, you can go back and change the labels and the numbers and have a whole new spreadsheet with a lot less work. By saving the new spreadsheet with a new name, both the old version and the new version are stored for future use.

Functions

Spreadsheets have a variety of built-in functions that can replace complicated formulas. One of the simplest is the *sum function*. It allows you to calculate the total of a range of cells. Functions are identified by first typing either " = " or " @ " depending on the particular software and then the function name. This lets the software know that the entry is a function and not a label. Some spreadsheet programs allow users to select functions from a pull-down menu. Functions are available for many different mathematical, statistical, and financial formulas.

◆ **EDITING SPREADSHEETS**

Another feature that can save you much time is the spreadsheet's ability to copy labels, numbers, and formulas from one location to another. For example, you might want to list your petty cash expenses by months, with each month in a separate column. Rather than recreating the labels and formulas for each month, you could copy the entire first month's information and paste it into the next column or the next group of columns. The spreadsheet software automatically compensates for the differences in cell labels from column to column and row to row; it also adjusts the new column so that the formula calculates the numbers in the new column, not in the original month column. The commands for selecting, copying, and pasting can all be found in the control panel of the spreadsheet.

Arranging Layout

Arranging your layout to look the way you want is another useful feature of an electronic spreadsheet. You can change the contents of any cell; add or delete rows or columns; and copy, cut, and paste data from one cell, row, column, or block to another similar area.

Editing Commands

Most spreadsheets have editing commands listed in their control panels. The simplest editing feature is to access the contents of a single cell and to alter the data there. When you make a cell active by selecting it with the cursor or mouse, its contents appear in the control panel. There you can insert text, type in completely new text, change a number—or do anything else.

You create new cells by inserting a new row or column. The Insert command or Create New Column or Row command allows you to do this easily. You select a column to the left of where you want to insert a new column and then select the insert command from the control panel. For inserting rows, you select the row where you want the new row to appear. Pointing to the very top of a column or the extreme left of a row with a mouse allows you to select it. If you do not have a mouse, position your cursor at the top of a column or on the cell on the far left of a row and choose SELECT from your Control Panel Menu. Then move your cursor to highlight the row or column.

To delete a row or column, select the entire row or column, and choose DELETE from the Control Panel Menu.

Whenever you insert or delete a row, it's important to note that some cells and formulas will move in the spreadsheet to a new cell address. Most spreadsheets automatically adjust to compensate for these moves so that you don't have to go back and make changes. Therefore, if you have a formula that adds up the total of a column of ten cells, and you insert five new rows in the middle, the formula is automatically changed to add up a total of fifteen cells instead.

Formatting features help you align the numbers and text to make your spreadsheet look good when printed out on paper. Formatting commands, found in the control panel, allow you to justify the text in a document, center text or numbers, or make them flush left or flush right. You can format individual cells or rows to specify how many decimal points are displayed or to create dates, dollar signs, commas, percentages, and scientific notations. You can change the width of a cell or column in order to display more information, such as a long label or a very large number. Some of the newest spreadsheets allow you to change the spacing of rows, the typeface style, and even the type size of your text and numbers.

◇ **OTHER SPREADSHEET FUNCTIONS**

Saving and Printing

When you get your spreadsheet looking the way you want, you may print it or save it. Printing and saving are commands you can select from the control panel. If you select SAVE, you are asked where you want to save your spreadsheet and to give it a name. You choose the disk drive where you want to save the file and then type in the name. Whenever you work with a spreadsheet that has been saved previously and you wish to save it again, it is automatically saved under the same name on the same disk or drive. If you want to save two or more different versions of a spreadsheet, you need to change the name slightly. This can be accomplished by selecting save as from the control panel or by selecting NO when asked if you want to save the file with the same name.

When you wish to print a spreadsheet, you are given an opportunity to determine how much of your spreadsheet you want printed, whether you want a header or footer, if you want borders or a grid, column and row numbers, and so forth. Some spreadsheets display a menu asking if you want to print the spreadsheet to a printer or to a file. Printing to a file is a way of saving a spreadsheet on a CD or hard drive so that it can later be incorporated into another program such as a word processor.

Online Help

Many spreadsheets are equipped with online help features, which provide detailed explanations of spreadsheet commands, functions, and procedures. These online help files can be accessed while you are in the middle of working on a spreadsheet by choosing Help from the spreadsheet's control panel and selecting the topic you need help on.

Templates

To help get you started, many spreadsheets have built-in *templates*, which are pre-built spreadsheet models for common applications in business such as budgets and financial analysis. By loading a template, you can edit the spreadsheet to customize it to your particular business. This can be a great time saver.

Spreadsheet Macros

Spreadsheet macros are another great time saver. As you may already know from your word-processing work, a *macro* is a way to minimize repetitive keystrokes. You can create a macro by selecting Macro from your spreadsheet's control panel. You are then asked to type in the keystrokes you want to record. Once these are recorded, you are asked to assign a simple keyboard command to trigger the macro. Many spreadsheets come with built-in macros that you can customize and access with special keyboard commands.

CHAPTER 19

Data Security

◇ INFORMATION = PROFIT

Information about your company is valuable, not only to your company but also to unscrupulous people outside your company. Such information includes confidential records such as bank transactions or corporate credit card numbers. It also includes paper or computer files about customers, new products, sales strategies, and so on. Consider how damaging it would be to your company if such records were lost or destroyed or if they were stolen by a competitor. That's why data security is critical to protect computer information from theft, misuse, and disaster.

The misuse of computer information ranges from unauthorized use of computer time to criminal acts like sabotage. It all falls under one general category that many people call "computer crime." Surveys show that more than half of the government departments and industrial organizations in the United States have experienced some form of computer crime. Because of this growing epidemic, it's important that you understand the different types of computer crime in order to protect yourself and your company's information.

◇ DETERMINING WHAT IS A CRIME

There are different degrees of computer crime, from breaking into other people's computers in order to steal or sabotage data, to making illegal copies of software to give to a friend. All of it is wrong.

Probably the most often committed offense is theft of computer time. It ranges from the innocent borrowing of someone's computer without permission to the theft of computer time from a business for personal use and gain. Theft of computer time—especially involving large computers, such as one running an office network—can easily translate into a theft of money. Besides the theft of time, unauthorized use of a computer also involves unnecessary wear and tear on the equipment and software.

The best way to judge whether a personal activity might be considered a criminal act is to compare it with the use of a company vehicle. Would it be wrong to borrow a company car or truck without asking? Would it be wrong to use the company car on the weekend for personal use? Would it be wrong to fill up one's personal car with gas and charge it to the corporate account? We know your answer is "Yes, it would be wrong," so keep this comparison in mind when using business computer equipment and software yourself and when overseeing others' use of it.

THREATS FROM OUTSIDE

Today's companies are using computer communications in ever-increasing ways, and these same applications are in the hands of criminals. Working from the privacy of their own homes, would-be criminals often gain access to an organization's computers for the purpose of stealing or altering information. This electronic trespassing or vandalism has several variations, which are referred to by their own slang terms:

- **Hacking**—Breaking into computer systems to gain access to restricted or private information
- **Freaking**—The defrauding of a telephone company using stolen long-distance access codes or credit cards
- **Crashing**—Breaking into a computer system in order to shut it down or turn it off
- **Trashing**—The altering or erasing of a computer's data files
- **Viruses**—Malicious computer programs that destroy data or open unauthorized access to a computer

THREATS FROM INSIDE

One of the most serious threats to the security of business data comes from insiders: those working within a company who decide to misuse computer or data files as a form of vengeance or for financial gain. This type of computer crime is extremely harmful, since it may involve information worth thousands and thousands of dollars. If a computer crime happens in your company, any insider could be a suspect. However, there are certain individuals who are likely to be investigated first:

- Disgruntled employees often take their vengeance out on the computer system in the form of sabotage.
- A competitor or an employee who has recently quit or been terminated may be responsible for theft of computer data or software.
- Outside users of a computer system via a communications system may attempt authorized sale of information, such as customer lists.
- Computer programmers may attempt to take their programs with them or to create hidden embezzlement schemes.
- Computer operators may alter or erase data on purpose.
- Computer system engineers may attempt to alter security information or passwords.

◇ SOFTWARE PIRACY

Software piracy is another major computer crime problem. Individuals are sometimes allowed to make copies of their programs for protection purposes, but the sale and/or the distribution of those copies to friends and other computer users is a violation of federal copyright laws.

With the growing concern over the copying problem, many software publishers have been forced to devise elaborate copy protection schemes. Piracy may not affect your company directly, but the cost of combating piracy is eventually passed along to you as the consumer.

◇ APPREHENDING CRIMINALS

Computer criminals have often been hard to apprehend as a result of a lack of understanding on the part of law enforcement agencies and the judicial system. However, things are beginning to change. Many states are leading the way with special legislation aimed at stopping software piracy. Other new laws make it a crime to trespass electronically on a computer system even if there is no damage or theft. Many cities are establishing special police units to combat computer crime.

◇ PROTECTING YOUR COMPANY'S DATA

Audit Logs

There are steps you can take to protect your company's data from these human threats. Audit logs are a record of who has been using a computer system. As a user logs onto a computer, it records the time, the name of the user, the files that person accesses, and when the person logs off. The computer then keeps the data in a special security file.

In some cases, an audit log can tell whether files have been altered. The use of audit logs is usually provided as part of security password software that can be installed on individual computers. If a computer crime occurs, the log can furnish the authorities with evidence they might need to prosecute.

Codes

Special data encryption techniques code your data files and your communications automatically. Someone who is attempting to intercept and manipulate the information would receive a file that looks like random symbols, thus preventing use of the data.

19 ■ DATA SECURITY

◇ COMPUTER VIRUSES

One type of computer crime that is a big concern to even the smallest business is the computer virus. A virus is a program developed by a computer vandal who finds pleasure in creating havoc. This program "infects" other programs, causing them to malfunction or to fail completely. Viruses are passed from computer to computer via e-mail and by copying files from one computer to another. Some viruses will only display messages; others can damage your hard drive and the files stored there. Some virus programs even try to extort money from victims in order to receive a software antidote.

To combat the rapidly growing virus problem, there are a variety of virus protection software programs available on the market. (See Table 19–1.) The key to selecting and using one of these programs is to purchase the most current edition and then update it on a regular basis.

TABLE 19–1. Anti-Virus Software

Company	Internet Address	Anti-Virus Software
Aladdin Knowledge Systems	www.aladdin.com	eSafe
Alwil Software	www.asw.cz	Avast
AVG Anti-Virus	www.grisoft.com	AVG Anti-Virus
CA	www3.ca.com/securityadvisor	eTrust
Cat Computer Services	www.quickheal.com	Quick Heal
Central Command Software	www.centralcommand.com	Vexira Antivirus
CyberSoft	www.cyber.com	waVe AntiVirus
DialogueScience	www.dials.ru	SpIDer Guard
Frisk Software International	www.f-prot.com	F-Prot Antivirus
F-Secure	www.fsecure.com/	F-Secure Anti-Virus
Kaspersky Lab	www.kaspersky.com	Kaspersky Anti-Virus
McAfee	www.mcafee.com	McAfee Anti-Virus
NetZ Computing	www.invincible.com	InVircible AV
Panda Software	www.pandasoftware.com	Panda Antivirus
Per Systems	www.persystems.com/antivir.htm	Per AntiVirus
Proland Software	www.pspl.com	Protector Plus
Softwin	www.bitdefender.com	BitDefender
Sophos	www.sophos.com	Sophos Anti-Virus
Sybari Software	www.sybari.com	Forefront
Symantec	www.symantec.com	Norton Antivirus
TREND Micro	www.trendmicro.com	Trend Micro AntiVirus

Most virus protection programs are designed to look for and destroy viruses that are known at the time the program was written. As new viruses appear, an older virus protection program may fail to detect them.

Symptoms of Viruses

When a virus attacks your computer, you may see the following effects:

- The virus continuously makes a copy of itself and uses up all the free space on your hard drive.
- A copy of the virus may be sent to all of the addresses in your e-mail address list.
- The virus may reformat your hard drive and wipe out all your files.
- The virus may install hidden programs that allow people to access your computer without your knowledge or permission.
- You experience a sudden degradation in system performance.
- Your anti-virus software stops working for no reason.
- Strange messages appear on your screen.
- Strange music or sounds play from your speakers.
- A program installed on your computer suddenly disappears.
- Your computer will not start.
- There is a lot of communications activity.
- The computer takes a long time to start.
- You get "out of memory" error messages.
- You cannot install new programs.
- A disk utility such as ScanDisk reports serious errors.
- A disk storage partition suddenly disappears.
- Anti-virus software indicates a virus has been found.

Firewalls

The only way to make a computer completely secure is to not use other people's data files and to completely disconnect from the Internet. Obviously, this is not practical. A firewall is a security system that protects a computer from attacks. It blocks access to a computer's communications ports, monitors the installation of new software, and controls which programs have access to the Internet.

There are both hardware and software firewalls available. Hardware firewalls are usually available within network routers and broadband modems. Software firewalls are available within Microsoft Windows and as add-on software products.

Firewalls block both incoming and outgoing threats. Incoming threats come in the form of communication port scans that look for an entrance into a computer in order to affect it with a virus. An outgoing threat occurs when a computer becomes infected with a virus or spyware. These malicious programs attempt to communicate with other computers on the Internet to spread themselves and steal information. A firewall limits access only to the programs the user authorizes.

Windows Firewall is available with Windows XP Service Pack 2. Windows Defender is a firewall that is available with Windows Vista. Internet security programs, such as Norton Internet Security and ZoneAlarm, are also available.

◇ **MAINTAINING YOUR COMPUTER'S SECURITY**

To prevent virus infections, hacker attacks, and other types of computer crime, do the following:

- Always use anti-virus software and keep it updated with the latest virus signature files.
- Install operating system security updates and software updates.
- Install and use firewall software.

Acts of Nature

Mother Nature can be an enormous threat, even causing a computer system to fail and lose data permanently. Floods, lightning, tornadoes, hurricanes, and fires could completely destroy your office computer and all your data files, resulting in the failure of the business and loss of everyone's job, since business records, client lists, accounting records, and much more would all be lost.

Electrical surges or voltage spikes can damage the computer's important electronic components. These surges can also disrupt and scramble data storage media like the hard drive. A complete power outage can shut down a computer system, causing loss of all data in the memory. (Steps you can take to prevent such problems can be found below.)

Mechanical Problems

Mechanical problems can cause storage media such as the hard drive to fail, resulting in the loss of all data stored there. Sudden changes in temperature or humidity, or bumping or dropping a computer system when the hard drive is operating, can result in what's called a head crash—or hard drive failure. (Again, steps to prevent such problems appear below.)

A Security Checklist

Following is a variety of ways to protect your company's data and make it more secure from both human and natural threats. You may wish to use some of these methods for your own computer. If you have office management responsibilities, you may also want to make changes for your entire department or company.

- Investigate theft prevention devices, which can lock a computer to a desktop.
- Prevent electrical noise and power surges from damaging your computer system through the use of surge suppressors. A surge suppressor plugs into the wall, and the computer system plugs into it for power.
- Get even more security with a device known as an *uninterruptible power supply*. It will power your computer system for a limited period of time in the event of a power outage. Then, if an outage does occur, you'd have ample warning to save your data.

- Make a backup copy of all data stored. The methods to back up your data range from printing out your files on paper to making regularly scheduled backups of your files on CD-ROM or DVD-ROM.

◇ COPING WITH DISASTER

It is a good idea to insure your company's computer system and software. If you work in a small company, you may want to check with your boss to see if he or she has this insurance. But in the case of a disaster, getting reimbursed for the cost of the equipment can't ever replace the valuable data that the business relies on.

Most large organizations have disaster plans that shift data-processing jobs from one location to another and protect data by storing them in two or more different locations. A small business should also have a disaster plan just in case. As secretary, you can get the ball rolling.

A good disaster plan should consider the following points:

- Is backup computer equipment available?

- Are backup software and data files available?

- What should employees do in the event of a disaster?

- What projects and tasks have priority?

- Are essential business supplies available?

Taking the time to create a disaster plan and to inform all employees in the company about it is essential. If the company is very small, even having an extra computer system, software, and supplies at someone's house may be a good start. It's like an extra insurance policy, and it may help all of you keep your jobs should disaster strike.

20

Keyboarding Skills

◇ KEYBOARDS

Whether you use a computer, a dedicated word processor, or a typewriter, you are using a keyboard. There are many differences in keyboards depending on the particular system you use. There are also differences in typing on each. For instance, computers and word processors require greater sensitivity than the heavy stroking needed on a regular manual typewriter.

No matter what keyboard you use, basic typing skills are a must. If your typing skills are not up to the level you feel are necessary for your job, computer programs such as Mavis Beacon Teaches Typing can help. If you don't use a computer, there are various touch-typing books that can provide assistance.

Since computer keyboards are growing fastest in importance, the focus of this chapter is on these. In many cases, electronic typewriter keyboards now have many of the same functions, and we compare these at the conclusion of the chapter.

Common Keyboards

The most common keyboard layout is the QWERTY keyboard, which gets its name from the first five alphabetical keys on the top left-hand corner of the keyboard. Most people learn touch-typing with a QWERTY style keyboard. (See Figure 20–1.)

If you examine a typewriter and a computer keyboard side by side, you find many similarities. For instance, you see on each the normal alphanumeric keys, along with a space bar, an ENTER or RETURN key, TAB keys, SHIFT keys, a CAPS LOCK key, and a BACK-SPACE key. The alphanumeric keys can be used to type letters or numbers. Typing a SHIFT along with a letter or number key produces an uppercase letter or, in the case of numbers, a special symbol. If you want to type all uppercase letters, you select the CAPS LOCK key once rather than holding down the SHIFT key. Touch the CAPS LOCK key again, and it toggles back off.

On both a typewriter and a computer keyboard, the TAB key moves your next keyboard entry to the next tab stop. However, with a computerized word processor or a modern electronic typewriter, tabs are no longer set mechanically. Instead, you use special software commands, menu or ruler choices, or a special key on the keyboard to set tabs and release them.

Esc key   Function keys   Editing keys   Navigation keys

Control key   Alt key   Cursor control keys   Numeric keypad

Figure 20–1. QWERTY style keyboard.

Photo by Jennifer Wauson.

The space bar adds spaces between words or characters, and it can insert spaces between words and characters typed previously. The ENTER or RETURN key on a computer keyboard may look similar to the carriage return found on a typewriter, but it is used much differently. On some typewriters, you type a RETURN at the end of a line in order to begin a new line of type. However, with a word-processing computer or modern electronic memory typewriter, a special feature called *word wrapping* is standard. This automatically moves your text to the next line when it will not fit at the end of the previous line. The ENTER or RETURN key is used only to skip lines, such as when starting a new paragraph.

Function Keys

Because of the increased functionality of a computer over a standard typewriter, a variety of extra keys have been added to computer keyboards to use with word-processing software, electronic spreadsheets, and database applications. Early computer systems had just a few extra keys, but most modern keyboards have many special-purpose keys.

Numeric Keypad

The numeric keypad is a set of number keys just like those you might find on a calculator. In fact, it is often used for computerized accounting and electronic spreadsheet applications. Many computer systems have built-in calculator software that can be called up on the monitor screen, allowing the user to make quick calculations and then return to another application to insert the result. The numeric keypad is also sometimes used for navigational purposes in some software applications. For example, if you want to move a pointer up on the screen, you hit the number 8 key. If you want to move down, you hit the number 2 key. To go left, hit 4. And to go right, hit 6.

The numeric keypad includes several mathematical function keys as well. The " + " key is used for addition, the " - " key for subtraction, the " * " key for multiplication, the

" . " key for decimals, " / " key for division, and the " = " key for equals or totals. There's also usually an extra ENTER key, which is used similarly to the TOTAL key on a calculator. In addition, you may find a NUM LOCK key. The NUM LOCK key, which stands for "number lock," toggles the numeric keypad so that it can be used to navigate or to type numbers. When the NUM LOCK is on, the numbers are entered when typed.

Navigation Keys

Along with the numeric keypad's navigational features, there are special-purpose navigation keys on many keyboards. Most have some form of arrow keys, allowing you to move a pointer on the screen up, down, left, or right. Other navigational keys include the HOME, PAGE UP, PAGE DOWN, INSERT, and DELETE keys. These may also have special functionality in certain applications. For example, in some word-processing programs, pressing the HOME key takes you to the beginning of your document. In a spreadsheet program, pressing HOME takes you to the top left-most cell, A1, sometimes called the *home cell*. The PAGE UP and PAGE DOWN keys in a word-processing application cause your document to scroll up or down one page at a time. The INSERT key is useful in some word processors for editing and inserting text in the middle of an existing sentence. The DELETE key works similarly to a BACKSPACE key. It can also be used to eliminate entire blocks of text that have been previously selected.

Special Function Keys

The special function keys found on many computer keyboards are usually labeled F1 through F10 or F12, although some keyboards have fewer than ten function keys. Located across the top of the keyboard or along the left side, special function keys are used in many applications to allow easy menu selection or to perform common tasks like saving documents, loading documents, printing, and editing. In addition to assigning one command to a particular function key, additional commands are available by pressing the SHIFT or the ALT keys along with a function key. Without the guidance of the software, these keys have little purpose. However, when specially programmed by a particular software application, they can have a multitude of uses.

There is no real standardized method for assigning commands to particular keys, although F1 is often the HELP key. To find out the assignments, check the manual for the software you're using. Some software publishers and other third-party vendors make keyboard templates available that connect to the top of your keyboard. These quick reference templates list the commands for each function key as well as other special key combinations.

Special Command Keys

The special command keys found on most computer keyboards include keys like ALT, CONTROL, and ESCAPE. The ESCAPE key is often used to back out of a series of menu choices or to leave a program. The ALT and CONTROL keys are often used on computers without special function keys. By pressing the ALT or CONTROL key and another designated key, a variety of commands, such as printing or saving, can be given from the keyboard.

For keyboards with special function keys, using the ALT or CONTROL keys in combination with the special function keys provides access to additional commands.

IBM-Compatibles vs. Macintosh

Perhaps the greatest differences between computer keyboards are those between IBM-compatible and Macintosh computers. Most of the keys we have been describing are common to IBM-compatibles. Macintosh computers have different special function keys such as the OPEN-APPLE COMMAND key and the OPTION key. These are used in combination with another keystroke. For example, pressing the OPEN-APPLE COMMAND key along with the s key saves a document. A list of these keyboard commands is available in the software manual as well as in the pull-down menus. Many of the Macintosh command key combinations have been standardized and are the same from one program to the next.

Keyboard Macros

In addition to using special function and command keys to access specific commands from the keyboard, users can define their own keyboard commands with the help of special keyboard shortcut software. There are a variety of these accessory programs available for both IBM-compatibles and Macintosh computers. These programs allow a user to assign a particular series of commands or keystrokes to a single multi-key combination. For example, use OPTION-C as a user-assigned command to bring up the calculator. Use OPTION-D to type today's date automatically.

Another similar keyboard shortcut tool, available in many software applications on both IBM and Macintosh, is the *macro*. A macro can be used to record a long series of keystrokes and menu choices. The recording of these keystrokes and commands can be saved and given a name. In addition, a user-definable key combination can be assigned to call up and play the recorded macro automatically.

The Mouse

Both IBM-compatibles and Macintosh computers use a mouse as an addition to the computer keyboard. A mouse is a hand controller that contains a small, round ball connected to a series of sensors. When you move the mouse around on your desk, the ball inside rolls, and the sensors translate this into movement of a pointer on the monitor screen. Thus, if you pick up the mouse and move it in the air, it does not affect the monitor screen at all.

An alternative is the wireless optical mouse. This type of mouse does not use a roller ball or a cable. Instead, it uses a special light-emitting diode to scan your desktop or mouse pad (a piece of foam rubber that gives the mouse extra traction) for movement. Signals from the mouse are transmitted via radio waves to a receiver connected to the computer.

Today, it's impossible to discuss keyboarding skills without also discussing the use of a mouse. Most people use a mouse in conjunction with a mouse pad. The amount of movement on the screen that a mouse can produce can be controlled by the computer's operating system. On IBM-compatible Windows-based systems, the mouse control is found in the Control Panel folder. With Macintosh computers, the mouse control is found in the control panel under the Apple pull-down menu option.

The IBM-compatible mouse has two or three buttons. The left mouse button is used for making selections. The right mouse button is used for accessing special function menus. If the mouse is equipped with a third button, it can be programmed to perform special functions. A left-handed user can switch the functionality of the mouse buttons. The Macintosh mouse usually has only one button that is used for making selections.

A wheel mouse differs from a standard mouse in that it includes a little wheel between the two buttons. When you roll the wheel, you can scroll up or down on the screen without having to click the scroll bars. This comes in handy when viewing long documents.

As an alternative to a mouse, track balls are available. They are almost like a mouse turned upside down. By rolling the ball with your fingers, you can move a pointer on the screen. Track balls are common with some laptop computers where operating conditions make it difficult to access a mouse.

Another alternative to a mouse and track ball is the track pad found on many laptop computers. The pressure-sensitive pad allows you to move the cursor around on the screen by moving your finger over the pad. The track pad usually includes two buttons that act like mouse buttons. Some laptop computers also include a pointing stick positioned in the middle of the keyboard keys. By pushing or pulling the pointing stick with your finger, the cursor is moved on the display screen.

◇ USING TYPEWRITERS

Modern electronic typewriter keyboards provide many of the same features found on IBM-compatibles and Macintosh computers. In addition to the common keys such as TAB, SPACE, SHIFT, BACKSPACE, and RETURN, there are special navigation, function, and command keys. Depending on whether a typewriter has memory capability, the number of special keys varies. They also vary greatly by manufacturer. However, even the most modest electronic typewriters now have some small amount of memory available and thus several additional keys for editing.

Common keyboard layouts include correction keys for correcting a character, word, or line, along with navigational keys for moving around within a document. Typewriters with built-in spell-checkers usually have a key for turning this feature on or off. Special formatting keys can justify text in several different ways. A special command or code key is often used to access additional formatting commands as well as special symbols.

Word Processing

The use of word processing can greatly improve your overall productivity. Although there are great differences between word-processing software programs, almost all allow you to create documents, edit and format these documents, and print them. Other features include spell-checkers, style and grammar checkers, mail-merge features, and the ability to store documents electronically.

The most common word processors found in businesses are personal computers equipped with word-processing software. When the word-processing program is run by the computer, the computer becomes an intelligent typewriter with the ability to create, edit, format, and store documents. Figure 21–1 shows a screen displaying Microsoft Word, one of the best-known word-processing programs.

◇ CREATING DOCUMENTS

In order to get started using a word processor, you must first create a fresh blank document. Some word processors require the user to create a new document and to name it right away. However, most allow you to wait until you save the document for the first time before assigning it a name.

Typing

When a new document has been created, you can begin typing and entering data. Some types of word processors, such as those for the Macintosh or Windows environment, allow you to begin typing immediately. As you type on the keyboard, the letters and words appear on the display screen. The text or data you type are stored in the computer's memory temporarily, until the document is saved or discarded or the power is turned off.

Positioning

On the screen, a pointer called a *cursor* shows where text will appear when typed. Cursors can take many forms: a vertical line, an underscore, or a rectangle. They may also flash on and off; it depends on the particular word-processing software used. You can move the cursor from one character to another, up or down, or left and right in order

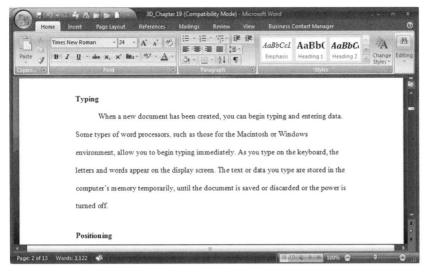

Figure 21–1. Microsoft Word.

Screen shot reprinted by permission from Microsoft Corporation.

to make corrections, edit, or format the text. To move the cursor, some word processors employ the arrow keys on the computer keyboard. On keyboards that don't have arrow keys, special combinations involving the number keys on the numeric keypad or two or more keys pressed simultaneously also moves the cursor. Some word-processing software programs allow the use of special function keys on the keyboard or special key combinations to jump to the top or bottom of the page.

You can also use a mouse to move around your document. By moving the mouse, a pointer moves on the screen. When you click the mouse, the cursor jumps to that location. If you want to change a word a few lines up from where you're currently typing, do the following: move the mouse up to that line, click, delete the incorrect word by using the BACKSPACE or DELETE key, and retype a new word in its place.

As you continue typing, you'll notice one of the main differences between word processors and typewriters when you reach the end of a line of text. On a typewriter, you type a carriage return and start a new line. Other more advanced typewriters with built-in computer memory automatically move a word that does not fit down to start the next line. This is a feature common to all word processors called *word wrap*. Thus, when typing on a word processor, you never have to type a carriage return unless you want to begin a new paragraph.

◇ EDITING DOCUMENTS

For administrative assistants, one of the best time-saving features of word processors is the ability to make changes very easily, without retyping the entire document. Many administrative assistants start a document by typing without regard to the format or the look of the finished document. They then come back, make revisions, and change the format. By coming back to spell-check, proof, and make corrections, they can remove most typos and sentence structure problems prior to printing out a copy of the document on paper.

Type-Over and Inserting

For some word processors, a user must first select the proper editing mode in order to make revisions. This is done by typing a special function key, such as the INSERT key, or a key combination. One editing function is the type-over mode that allows a user to type over mistakes. New characters appear on the screen in place of existing characters. If new characters or words must be inserted instead, an insert mode is available. When the insert mode is activated by pressing the INSERT key, new characters appear when typed, and all characters and words to the right of the cursor move to the right to make room.

Word processors written for Windows and Macintosh are always in insert mode by default. The user does not have to type any special function keys or key combinations to turn on insert mode.

Deleting Text

To delete text from a document, several choices are available. Some keyboards have BACKSPACE keys, and others have a key marked DELETE. When you type the BACKSPACE key, the cursor moves to the left one space and erases the character that was displayed there. When you type the DELETE key, the character that occupies the same space as the cursor is erased. Some word processors require you to move the cursor to highlight the specific character to be deleted and then to type the DELETE key.

Undo

In case you inadvertently delete something you did not mean to, most word processors have an Undo function. This can be accessed via a special function key or key combination or, in the case of Windows and Macintosh, a pull-down menu choice. When you delete text, it's stored in a temporary buffer memory. The buffer stores the last thing you deleted, such as a word, sentence, paragraph, or even whole pages. Select the Undo function, and your text is restored.

Cutting and Pasting

Moving text from one location to another is one more useful feature of word processors. For Windows and Macintosh environments, just click and drag the mouse to highlight a block of text such as a sentence, paragraph, or group of paragraphs. Once the text is highlighted, select CUT or COPY from a pull-down menu to put the text (or a copy of it) into the temporary memory buffer. Next, use the mouse to navigate through the document to the location where the text should be inserted. By clicking the mouse on this location and selecting PASTE from the pull-down menu, you remove the text from the memory buffer and insert it into the new location. Thus, moving text from one location to another is called *cutting and pasting*.

Searching

Most word processors provide the ability to search for and find a particular string of characters or words anywhere in a document. This feature comes in handy for finding names in a mailing list or other specific information in a document. Some word processors call this a *Search* function, others a *Find* function.

In order to search an entire document, position the cursor at the beginning of the document. On Windows- and Macintosh-based word processors, a Search or Find function is available on a pull-down menu. Once search has been selected, you are asked to type in the characters or words you want to find.

Searching and Replacing

A related function is *Search and Replace*. Many users save time by using Search and Replace like a macro. If these users frequently have to type a long, complicated word or phrase in a document, they type substitute characters instead, such as "xxx." Since "xxx" would normally not appear in a document, the user can later access the Search and Replace function. This function then finds "xxx" and allows the user to type in a replacement string—the long, complicated word or phrase.

◆ FORMATTING DOCUMENTS

Many users of word processors start by typing in text and later go back to make adjustments to the way the document will look when printed on paper. This is a process known as *formatting*. There are many different ways to format a document, for example, by changing the margins, the line spacing, or the type style and size of the characters.

Margins

All word processors allow you to set the left and right margins. Most often, a ruler is used to show where on a piece of paper the text will be positioned when printed. For Windows and Macintosh, margins are set by moving a margin guide on the ruler, and tabs are positioned by moving a tab guide—both with the mouse.

Line Spacing

For the Windows and Macintosh environments, the line spacing is changed by selecting a choice from the ruler or menu bar. There are icon choices for single spaced, double spaced, and triple spaced. They can be selected at any time when entering text; the text entered after the selection will be spaced according to your choice. You can also alter the spacing of already existing text by first highlighting the text with a mouse or pointer, and then selecting your line spacing choice from the ruler.

Tabs

Word-processing programs let you set tabs and can be programmed to indent a specified number of spaces at the beginning of a new paragraph automatically. Windows- and Macintosh-based word processors use pointers, which can be placed on the ruler at various points to determine tab stops and indentations.

Justification

The remaining line-formatting option is justification. Any block of text can be aligned flush with the left margin or the right margin. Another choice is full justification, which aligns the text flush with both the left and the right margin—like typesetting in a book. This is done by adding spaces between the words of each line. A fourth option is centered justification, used to center titles and other text in the middle of a line.

For Windows- and Macintosh-based word processors, select your justification option from the ruler or pull-down menu with the mouse or pointer. A previously written block of text may be justified by first highlighting the block with the mouse, and then selecting the justification choice from the ruler or pull-down menu.

Character Formatting

Another major document-formatting tool is the character format. Text can be printed in a variety of different styles, such as underlined, bold, and italics. In addition, the characters themselves can be printed in many different sizes and typefaces called *fonts*.

Often, word-processing programs come with a limited number of fonts and font sizes already installed. Additional fonts can be purchased as software to increase your number of choices. Some fonts are used to display text on the screen, and others are used by the printer. Some printers print only fonts that are installed in the printer hardware.

Windows and Macintosh word processors use pull-down menus to select font style choices, which appear on the monitor screen almost the way they'll appear printed on paper. The font and size of existing text can be changed by highlighting the text with the mouse or pointer, and then selecting the font choice from the pull-down menu.

Page Formatting

Additional formatting options are available for entire documents and sections of a document. For example, the page format determines the top, bottom, left, and right margins for all text on a page. In addition, headers and footers can be inserted on each page for page numbers, the date, or the name of a document.

Styles

If you create a specialized format for a document, rather than manually format each section, you can create what are called *styles*. Styles allow you to define individual formatting characteristics such as margins, justification, font size, and font style and give them a name that can be accessed from a menu on the ruler.

PRINTING DOCUMENTS

When a document has been created and formatted, getting that document printed on paper is the ultimate goal for most word-processor users. The Print function allows you to specify additional information about the way the document should appear on paper, for example, which pages of the document are to be printed, whether the printing itself should be draft mode or letter quality, how many copies should be made, page orientation (portrait versus landscape), paper size, and whether the printing will be one-sided or two-sided.

Most word processors have a print-preview feature, which displays on the monitor the overall layout of the printed document on paper. In this way, you can see the formatting options before time and paper are wasted printing an incorrect document. Before printing any document, it's important that you first save the document on a CD or the computer's hard drive. Since printing involves a hardware connection between two different devices, occasionally there are problems that cause a computer to "hang up" on the printer. If you have not saved your document, you could lose it if this happens.

Some of the biggest problems for many word-processing users are printer related. The printer might print something you didn't intend, or perhaps it might not print at all. In order for the computer to communicate with a printer, print driver software is required. This software is usually supplied with the printer but can also be found included with some word-processing software. It's important that you specify the type of printer you are using and how it's connected to the computer. For Macintosh and Windows word processors, this can be done from the pull-down menus.

SAVING AND LOADING DOCUMENTS

One of the main benefits of using a word processor is the ability to save your documents electronically and to retrieve them to use again. In this way, common business documents such as letters, invoices, and contracts can be created once, saved, and then customized as needed. This feature eliminates having to recreate a letter or document every time it is needed.

Saving a document is an electronic way of recording the data on a CD or on the computer's hard drive. Before you can save a document, you are asked to name the document and to designate where you want to save it. Some word processors limit the number of characters that can be used in a name, so many people resort to using codes that can be easily remembered, such as M92608 for "memo written on 9-26-2008." Other word processors allow longer names.

If your computer is equipped with multiple hard disk drives, you must specify on which drive you want to save the document.

Loading or opening a document that has been previously saved involves specifying the name of the document you want to open and telling the computer which drive it is saved on. When a document is loaded from a CD or hard drive into the computer's memory, only a copy of the document is loaded. The original saved version is still stored on the disk. If you make changes to the document and save it again using the same name, only the most recent version is saved on the disk. The original version is wiped out, and the new version is saved in its place. To save both versions of a document, you need to alter the name of the new version. Even if you change just one letter or character in the name, the new version is saved in a different space, and the original version is still intact on the disk.

Fortunately, most word processors have built-in protection that warns you when an original version of a document is about to be *overwritten*. The word processor tells you that a previous version of the same document already exists and asks you to confirm that you really want to wipe out the old version. Other word processors use Update, Replace, or Revise commands to wipe out or protect your original version of a document.

◆ ADVANCED WORD-PROCESSING FEATURES

Many word processors have advanced features that may be of use to you in your job. For example, if you create long manuscripts or reports, features such as indexing, sorting, footnote tracking, automatic hyphenation, and tables may be of help. Check the manual for your word-processing software if you wish to employ these powerful tools.

Spelling and Grammar Checkers

Spell-checkers automatically look for spelling errors. Grammar and style checkers analyze the mechanics of your writing. Thesaurus programs can provide synonyms for words used in your document.

Just because you use a spelling, grammar, or style checker to analyze a document doesn't mean that you shouldn't proofread the material, too. Many times a word or phrase that appears correct to the computer is not correct in a given context.

Mail Merging

One of the most useful business-related features, *mail merging* allows you to create a single form letter and to merge it with a list of names and information to create individualized letters. For example, you might want to send a personal letter to customers telling each one about your company's new product or service. First you create a document containing the names and addresses of your customers. Then you create a form letter with special symbols or commands inserted where the customer's name and address and the greeting would normally go. These special symbols or commands are determined by your particular word-processing software. These commands link the form letter with your address list so that, when you print out the form letter, it automatically picks up elements of the list, such as name and address, and positions them in the proper place. The result is individualized letters by the dozens or even hundreds, while you typed only one.

The exact procedures for creating a mail merge vary; the software manual outlines the steps for your particular program.

Macros

Many word processors utilize macros to help customize and shorten repetitive processes. A macro is a way of recording a series of keystrokes or commands and recalling them by using a single keystroke or key combination. For example, you might have to type a long medical term repeatedly throughout a document. Rather than type it over and over, you might create a macro that with just a two-key combination automatically types the longer word.

Macros can also be created for a series of command choices from a menu, such as those required to select special formatting. Word processors such as Microsoft Word call these special formatting macros *style sheets*. Style sheets can be very helpful when the format changes often within a document. By highlighting a particular block of text, you can assign a name to this style, and it will be assigned a place on the ruler or pull-down menu, where it can be easily selected in the future.

◆ POPULAR WORD-PROCESSING SOFTWARE

Here is a partial list of popular word-processing software available:

- Microsoft Word
- Corel WordPerfect
- Lotus Word Pro

22

Desktop Publishing

Desktop publishing allows you to create brochures, fliers, newsletters, advertisements, and manuals without having to visit a print shop. Many administrative assistants use desktop publishing software to create high-quality publications that can be printed one at a time in the office or taken to a local print shop for mass duplication. Many desktop publishing programs have predefined templates that allow you to add your own text and graphics to quickly customize a publication. You can create your own letterhead, business cards, and business forms with the help of desktop publishing.

While it is similar to word processing in theory, desktop publishing focuses on the layout of text and graphics on a page. Some sophisticated word-processing programs, such as Microsoft Word, can be used for desktop publishing. However, there are other more specialized tools available for creating graphics, adding special effects, and laying out multi-page brochures.

In addition to desktop publishing software, you need an office computer system complete with a keyboard, monitor, and mouse. Optional desktop publishing hardware includes a graphics tablet, a color printer, a scanner, and a digital camera.

There are five general types of software used for desktop publishing: (1) word processing, (2) page layout, (3) illustration, (4) photo and image editing, and (5) font and image management utilities. These programs make up your desktop publishing toolbox.

Word Processing

Word-processing programs such as Microsoft Word and Corel WordPerfect are used to type and edit text, check spelling and grammar, and format text. These programs are best suited for working with words, not for page layout. Word-processing programs can be used in conjunction with page layout software to create text and then export it to the page layout program. Figure 22–1 shows a simple desktop publishing layout created in Microsoft Word.

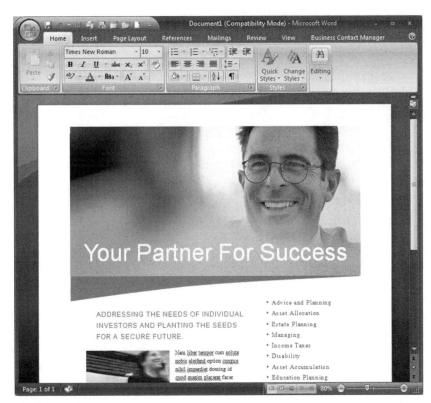

Figure 22–1. A page layout in Microsoft Word.

Screen shot reprinted by permission from Microsoft Corporation.

Page Layout

Page layout programs such as Adobe PageMaker, QuarkXPress, and Microsoft Publisher are the software most closely associated with desktop publishing. Page layout software allows for the integration of text and images on the page, manipulation of the page elements, and creation of artistic designs. High-end or professional-level tools available within these programs include separations, imposition, and typographic controls. Figure 22–2 shows a page layout in Adobe PageMaker. Figure 22–3 shows a page layout in Microsoft Publisher.

Illustration

Illustration programs are vector-based drawing tools for creating artwork, logos, and other drawings made by hand. Art can be created by drawing with a mouse or by using a graphics tablet. The most popular illustration programs include Adobe Illustrator and CorelDRAW. Figure 22–4 shows a screen from Adobe Illustrator.

Photo and Image Editing

Bitmap graphics, such as photographs, are manipulated using photo editing software. These photo-realistic images can be obtained by scanning photos, by using a digital

Figure 22–2. Adobe PageMaker.

Screen shot reprinted by permission from Adobe Systems, Inc.

camera, or by purchasing stock digital images. These programs allow you to color-correct images, crop them, manipulate them by copying and pasting elements, add text, combine and layer images, and add special effects. The most popular photo editing programs include Adobe Photoshop and Corel PhotoPaint. Figure 22–5 shows a screen from Adobe Photoshop.

Font and Image Management Utilities

The various text styles available for desktop publishing projects are called *fonts*. There are thousands of font choices available, and special tools are needed to manage them. Adobe Type Manager and Bitstream Font Navigator are used to organize and group fonts into families, so they can be more easily selected. Image management programs such as ThumbsPlus and HiJaak make it easier to locate pictures and do batch conversions or cataloging.

◆ TYPES OF DESKTOP PUBLISHING DOCUMENTS

The first step in desktop publishing is deciding what type of document is going to be produced. Will you create a brochure, a newsletter, or a business card? Depending on the document, the general format may already be predetermined. For example, if you need to create a business card, the document size and general characteristics are already known. You might use a business card template available in a program such as Microsoft Publisher and customize it with your company's logo and text information.

Figure 22–3. Microsoft Publisher.

Screen shot reprinted by permission from Microsoft Corporation.

There are a variety of desktop publishing documents you may be asked to produce as an administrative assistant including advertisements, direct mail pieces, holiday messages, an identity package, and sales information.

Advertising Information

Advertisements come in many different sizes, so the first step is determining the type of ad. Is it a Yellow Pages display ad, a small newspaper ad, an online ad for a website, or a flyer? Figure 22–6 shows a template available in Microsoft Publisher for creating an advertisement.

Direct Mail

Direct mail marketing can take various forms ranging from postcards to flyers to letters to brochures. You must decide which format is best based on the amount of information you want to include, the purpose of the mailing, and the budget for postage.

Holiday Messages

Customized corporate greeting cards are popular, but so are holiday newsletters, customized calendars, and postcards. Explore the templates available in your desktop publishing program or create something new.

Figure 22–4. Adobe Illustrator.

Screen shot reprinted by permission from Adobe Systems, Inc.

Identity Packages

Business cards, letterhead, and envelopes are the first steps in creating a corporate identity, and all three can be created using desktop publishing software. In addition, you can also create note cards, notepads, Rolodex cards, fax forms, and custom invoices.

Sales Information

If your company is involved in sales, you may be asked to help create a sales brochure. The type of product, the size of your marketing budget, and the amount of information you need to include determine the size of the brochure. Other sales-related documents include fliers, price lists, catalogs, and online catalogs.

◇ THE DESKTOP DOCUMENT

While there are a variety of processes and procedures involved in desktop publishing, the basic desktop publishing techniques involve six different areas: (1) design, (2) setup, (3) text, (4) images, (5) file preparation, and (6) printing.

236

Figure 22–5. Adobe Photoshop.

Screen shot reprinted by permission from Adobe Systems, Inc.

Design

Design is an ongoing process that begins prior to creation of the document. During this phase you may:

- Determine document format and type
- Create rough drafts
- Select fonts
- Conceptualize and brainstorm
- Select colors
- Select images

Document Setup

This is the phase where desktop publishing begins. During this phase you may:

- Select a template
- Set up columns and grids
- Customize the color palette
- Set page size and margins
- Set up master pages
- Create paragraph styles

Text and Fonts

The text used in your desktop publishing document can take many forms. Text may be created by typing directly into the page layout software or by using a word processor and then exporting the text. During this phase you may:

- Create text
- Compose the text layout
- Apply paragraph style settings
- Import and place text
- Select fonts

Figure 22–6. Advertisement template in Microsoft Publisher.

Screen shot reprinted by permission from Microsoft Corporation.

Images

Depending on the type of document and the elements you are using, image creation and selection can occur at any point in the process. While working with images you may:

- Take digital photographs
- Scan images using a scanner
- Browse and select images from clip art and stock photo collections
- Create and edit photo-realistic bitmap graphics using an image editor
- Create vector-based artwork graphics using an illustration program
- Convert images to the proper graphics file format
- Import and place graphics into the page layout
- Create boxes and add callouts, captions, and titles to images

File Preparation

After you get your desktop publishing document looking the way you want it, you must prepare the file to make sure it will print as planned. This is known as the *prepress phase*. During this phase you may:

- Do soft- and hard-copy proofs
- Embed fonts

- Specify color trapping
- Verify color specifications
- Package fonts and graphics with the file
- Impose the file
- Create a PostScript or Adobe Acrobat PDF file

Printing

With the creation process complete and the file prepared for printing, the last step is to print. During this phase you may:

- Print to a desktop laser or inkjet printer
- Deliver the digital files to a commercial printer
- Finish the document by trimming or folding

◆ DESKTOP PUBLISHING SOFTWARE TOOLS

Most desktop publishing software programs share certain common tools. They allow you to arrange and format text and graphics. Of course, each program has its own procedures, but there are four basic tools that almost all desktop publishing programs have available: (1) selection, (2) text, (3) graphics, and (4) magnification. You can find these tools in your program's toolbox.

Selection

The selection tool, also known as the *pointer*, is the most basic tool in any desktop publishing application. It is usually represented by an arrow and is used to select one or more page elements and move them around on the page. The selection tool can also be used to resize page elements.

Text

The text tool is usually represented by a T or A in the program's toolbox. It is used for adding text to your layout. By selecting the text tool, you can position your cursor on the page and then click your mouse. You are then able to use it to draw a text box and enter text. You can also use this tool to select a text box to change the formatting to a different size, color, font, or style.

Graphics

Most desktop publishing programs have graphics tools for drawing boxes and lines and for importing graphics. The toolbox may have tools for drawing freehand and for making circles, rectangles, lines, and curved lines. Some graphics tools allow you to format the shapes by changing their size, color, texture, transparency, and shape.

Magnification

In order to see your page layout up close for fine tuning, most desktop publishing programs have a magnification tool for zooming. Usually the tool is a magnifying glass.

◇ TYPOGRAPHY

The style, size, and type of text used in desktop publishing is known in the printing world as *typography*. In the computerized desktop publishing world, we call them *fonts*.

Fonts are measured in picas and points. *Picas* measure the length of a line of text. *Points* are 1/12 of a pica. Font sizes are measured in points. The larger the number, the bigger the type.

Leading is the space above and below the characters in a font for ascenders and descenders so they do not touch the next line. *Kerning* refers to the space between letters in a word. Both leading and kerning are adjustable in most desktop publishing programs and word-processing programs such as Microsoft Word.

There are two main classifications of typefaces: serif and sans-serif. *Serif* fonts have tiny trailing lines that finish the stroke of each character. These fonts are generally used for normal text because they are easier to read. Popular serif fonts include Times Roman. *Sans-serif* means no serif. This type is clean and is normally used for headings within documents. Helvetica is the most popular sans-serif font.

◇ PAGE LAYOUT

A master page layout is a common design that is used throughout a publication. For example, the master page layout determines:

- The number of columns
- The use of horizontal and vertical bars
- The placement of illustrations and logos
- The settings for page size
- The settings for portrait versus landscape page orientation
- The page margins
- The use of facing pages or single-sided pages
- The use of footers and headers
- The page numbering

◇ GRAPHICS FORMATS

Graphics come in a variety of file formats, and not all are suitable for every purpose. Some are best for the Web; others are more suitable for printing. Table 22–1 lists graphic formats and their applications.

TABLE 22–1. Graphic Formats and Their Applications

File Format	Application
BMP	Screen display in Windows.
EPS	Printing to PostScript printers and image setters. Best choice for resolution printing of illustrations.
GIF	Screen display, especially for the Web. Best choice for publishing illustrations and screen shots online.
JPEG	Screen display on the Web. Good choice for online publishing.
PICT	Screen display on the Macintosh and for printing to non–PostScript printers.
TIFF	Printing to PostScript printers. Good choice for high-resolution printing of images.
WMF	Screen display under Windows or printing to non–PostScript printers. Good choice for vector graphics.

◇ WHAT IS POSTSCRIPT?

One of the things you may have noticed in Table 22–1 is the term *PostScript*. PostScript is a programming language that was developed by Adobe, one of the leading producers of desktop publishing software. PostScript is used to communicate between a computer and a printer. The language describes what a page should look like to the printer. Printers print tiny dots on the paper. How these dots are arranged determines what your finished document looks like. A PostScript printer uses the language to translate the digital document created by your desktop publishing software into an image a printer can print.

Some sophisticated documents with an intricate combination of graphics and fonts are best output when using PostScript. PostScript is generally device-independent, that is, it prints just about the same on any PostScript-compatible device.

If your desktop publishing work consists of letterhead, business cards, and simple brochures, you probably don't have to worry much about PostScript. You can use a non-PostScript printer and achieve pleasing results. If you need to send your desktop publishing files to a commercial printer for output, you may need to use a PostScript printer to proof your documents in advance.

You may also need a program called Adobe Acrobat. Using Acrobat is one way to confirm that your document will print the same anywhere it is printed. Acrobat generates special files called PDF (Portable Document Format) files. PDF files include all the PostScript information necessary to make sure your desktop publishing documents are truly portable.

Adobe Acrobat allows you to print to the Acrobat Distiller. This is a software-only printer that converts your print output into the PDF file. Figure 22–7 shows a screen from Adobe Acrobat.

◇ SCANNERS

Scanners have become an important part of the modern office. Not only can they be used to scan photographs into digital images for use in desktop publishing applications, but they can also be used to digitize images of paper documents so they can be stored electronically. In addition, optical character recognition software can examine a scanned image of text and convert that text into digital text for editing and use in a word processor or desktop publishing application. Some office machines combine the features of a scanner, printer, and copier into one unit. Figure 22–8 shows a combination scanner, printer, and copier.

The most common types of scanners used in business are flatbed or desktop scanners and handheld scanners. For most business applications, a flatbed scanner capable of scanning legal-size documents is the best choice.

Scanners use a photographic process similar to digital cameras. They use Charge-Coupled Device (CCD) arrays. These are light-sensitive diodes that convert light into an electric charge. When a document is placed on the glass plate of a scanner and the cover is closed, a lamp shines a bright light on the document. The CCDs are located on the scanning head, which is moved slowly across the document. By using a series of filters and mirrors, color information is captured.

Scanners vary in resolution and sharpness. Resolution is measured in dots per inch (DPI). The scanner's DPI is determined by the number of sensors in the CCD. Most scanners have a DPI of at least 300. For most business applications, a resolution of 600 DPI is best. This allows you to scan and reproduce full-color photographs, as well as use optical character recognition (OCR) software to convert hard-copy text to digital text.

Scanners can increase the perceived resolution using a technique called *interpolation*. This is accomplished by creating extra pixels or dots between the ones scanned by the CCD. When evaluating a scanner for your business, you should focus on true DPI resolution and not interpolated resolution.

Another term associated with scanning is *bit depth*, which is also called *color depth*. This refers to the number of colors the scanner is capable of reproducing. Each pixel requires 24 bits to create true color, and almost all scanners support this. Some scanners offer 30- or 36-bit depth; however, for most business applications, a scanner with a bit depth of 24 is sufficient.

Images are transferred from the scanner to your computer using one of three connections:

1. **Parallel**—Connects through your printer parallel port and is the slowest transfer method available

2. **Universal Serial Bus (USB)**—Connects to your computer's USB port and is fast and affordable

3. **FireWire**—Requires a FireWire port or interface card on your computer and is the fastest transfer method available

One additional component in a scanning system is the scanning software. You need a driver and scanning application installed on your computer. Most scanning software is used in association with another application, such as a drawing program or a word-processing program. Scanners speak a language called *TWAIN*. The TWAIN driver acts as an interpreter between any application that supports the TWAIN standard and the scanner. For example, Microsoft Word and Adobe Photoshop both support the TWAIN standard.

✧ DIGITAL PHOTOGRAPHY

Digital photography is rapidly replacing the film camera and has many applications in business. You can use a digital camera to take pictures and then import your pictures into your computer for use in desktop publishing applications. You can create images for high-quality newsletters, photo ID cards, and websites for your company with a digital camera.

The key difference between a digital camera and a film-based camera is that the digital camera has no film. Instead, it has a sensor—a CCD similar to a scanner or a CMOS (complementary metal-oxide-semiconductor) chip—that converts light into a digital form. Images can be saved as a graphic file format, typically JPEG.

The key features you need to consider when choosing a digital camera include:

- Resolution
- Storage
- LCD
- Lens
- Exposure control
- Focus
- Movie mode
- Flash

- Sensor technology
- Compression formats
- Optical viewfinder
- Interface to the computer
- Image stabilization
- Macro
- Batteries
- Image-processing software

Resolution

The resolution of a digital camera is measured in megapixels. Pixels are the image elements in a CCD or CMOS chip. The more pixels, the better the image quality. Today's digital cameras range from 3 megapixels to 8 to 10 megapixels. For most business and home applications, you need at least 3 megapixels. This allows you to take a picture that is 2048 × 1536 pixels in size, and allows you to reproduce a large 8 × 10 inch image.

Even though a camera is capable of 8 to 10 megapixels, you can take pictures at different resolutions. For example, if your images are only going to be published on the Web, you can use a resolution of 640 × 480 pixels. This allows you to store more pictures in your computer's memory without having to offload them to your computer.

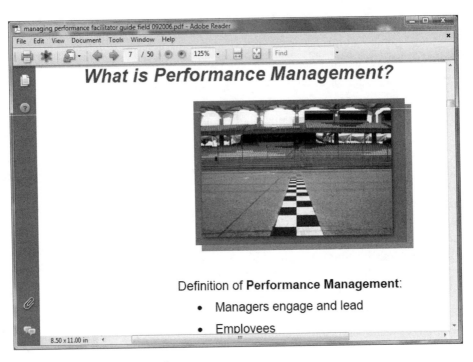

Figure 22–7. Adobe Acrobat.

Screen shot reprinted by permission from Adobe Systems, Inc.

Sensor Technology

The choice in sensor technology is between CCD and CMOS sensors. CCDs have more pixels and take better pictures in low light. However, they tend to be more expensive and use more power.

CMOS sensors are lower resolution and don't work as well in low light. However, if you need a low-end camera suitable for photography to be published on the Web, a CMOS-equipped, low-cost camera may be a good option.

Storage

Images are stored in the camera's memory. Most digital cameras use some form of storage device. Some common choices include CompactFlash, SmartMedia, and Memory Sticks. Removable memory cards are sold with a specified amount of memory.

Compression Format

Images are typically compressed by the camera as they are saved on the memory card. In uncompressed mode, a 3-megapixel image is approximately 3 megabytes in size. Most cameras store images in JPEG graphics file format. Some high-end cameras also support the TIFF format. JEPGs are compressed images, while TIFF's are not.

Figure 22–8. Combination scanner, printer, and copier.
Courtesy of Xerox Corporation.

LCD

Most digital cameras have a Liquid Crystal Display (LCD) screen that allows you to view a picture right away. If you don't like the image, you can delete it and take another picture.

Viewfinder

Some cameras do not have an LCD display and instead use an optical viewfinder. Other digital cameras have both an LCD display and a viewfinder. By turning off the LCD, you can save power and make your batteries last longer. In addition, sometimes in bright sunlight it is difficult to see the LCD. In that case, you can use the optical viewfinder.

Lens

The more expensive the digital camera, the better the lens, number of pixels, and other features. An optical zoom is better than a digital zoom. An optical zoom has an adjustable focal length lens. A digital zoom expands the image by enlarging it electronically. Some cameras combine both an optical and digital zoom.

Overall, you will find four different kinds of lenses on digital cameras:

1. Fixed-focus, fixed-zoom
2. Optical-zoom with automatic focus
3. Digital-zoom
4. Replaceable lens systems

Interface

The interface with your computer allows you to transfer images from your camera to your computer for image processing and desktop publishing applications. There are four different interfaces available:

1. **USB**—A cable connects from your camera to the USB port on your computer.
2. **Serial**—A cable connects from your computer to the serial port on your computer. This is a slow way to transfer images.
3. **Disk**—The camera uses a writeable CD or DVD to store images. You can put the CD/DVD into your computer's CD/DVD drive to read the graphic files.
4. **Flash Memory Slots**—A flash memory reader is attached to the computer that allows you to remove a memory card from the camera and insert it into the reader in order to transfer the images to your computer.

Exposure Control

Most digital cameras have automatic exposure. Some cameras offer manual exposure control and special settings for specific situations such as sports, landscapes, and portraits.

Image Stabilization

Some cameras offer a special feature to steady the camera to help you take clearer pictures. This feature is popular on video camcorders.

Focus

Most digital cameras have fixed focus—where you can't adjust focus at all—or automatic focus. Some digital cameras have a manual focus option.

Macro

If you plan to take extreme closeup pictures, you want a camera that has macro focusing capability. This feature allows you to move a camera very close to a subject and still be able to focus.

Movies

Many digital cameras offer an MPEG movie feature that allows you to take short movies with the camera.

Batteries

Digital cameras, especially those with CCD sensors and LCD displays, use a lot of power. Rechargeable batteries can help lower the cost, but the batteries themselves are expensive. When evaluating a digital camera, check to determine whether it uses standard-size rechargeable batteries.

Flash

Most digital cameras have a built-in flash. The normal modes of operation are automatic, forced flash, fill flash, and no flash.

Software

A digital camera usually comes with some type of software for use in downloading images from the camera into a computer. Microsoft Windows comes with software for transferring images from digital cameras, so no additional software is necessary.

Using PowerPoint

What Is Multimedia?

Multimedia in a computer context is defined as the integration of more than one medium, such as animation, audio, graphics, text, and video. Multimedia is a step beyond traditional presentation graphics used by many people in business. Rather than just use a software program such as Microsoft PowerPoint to create overhead transparencies, the computer is used as the presentation tool. When the computer is connected to a video projector, the presentation can be presented as a slide show and projected on a screen for everyone in a meeting to see. When you add graphics, animation effects, audio, and video files to the presentation, you've created multimedia.

The term *multimedia* was used long before computers appeared in the office. Originally, multimedia was a term to define presentations or lectures that included any elements other than just the spoken or written word. Slide projectors, audiotapes, movies, and pictures were often combined with a lecture or demonstration to provide a more dynamic presentation.

Why Is It Called Multimedia?

Today, the term *multimedia* has come to mean something different to different types of users. To the computer industry, multimedia often refers to a computer system that includes a CD-ROM and a set of speakers. To a computer game enthusiast, it may mean being able to "walk" through a virtual world and interact with characters. To an Internet user, multimedia could mean having the ability to click on a link on a Web page that provides a picture or audio file. To someone in business, it might mean using PowerPoint to provide a visual presentation for a lecture.

While these specific uses of multimedia vary slightly in emphasis, the basic elements remain much the same. They all include the combination of text, sound, graphics, and/or video delivered through or controlled by a computer.

A related term often heard these days is *hypermedia*. Hypermedia is multimedia whose sequence is determined by the learner or user. For example, most World Wide Web pages provide *hot links* to other documents or websites that provide additional information. It is up to the user whether to jump out of the linear presentation of information and explore in other directions.

While all hypermedia is also multimedia, not all multimedia is hypermedia. A PowerPoint presentation, which consists of a series of slides, typically is a very linear (non-hypermedia) type of multimedia.

◇ PRESENTATION AND AUTHORING PROGRAMS

Multimedia presentation and authoring software are tools that allow the user to bring all the multimedia components into a coherent presentation or product. While there is some overlap between presentation and authoring tools, a comparison of the two is valuable.

Presentation programs like Microsoft PowerPoint are typically called slide show programs. They are simple to use and basically present information in a linear fashion, one slide after another. On any slide, you can attach a media file with an image, animation, or sound. Some of them allow very simple branching out of a linear sequence.

Authoring programs have the distinct advantage of allowing more sophisticated branching. They also allow numerous media elements with overlays and logic attached. The disadvantage is that they are typically harder to learn to use. On the other hand, third-grade students have successfully created wonderful interactive multimedia presentations.

This chapter focuses on the use of Microsoft PowerPoint because it is well established as a business presentation tool and is relatively easy to learn.

◇ USING MICROSOFT POWERPOINT

Microsoft PowerPoint is included as part of the Microsoft Office Suite of software that is very popular in business today. If PowerPoint is installed on your computer, you can create a multimedia presentation or an overhead slide presentation by using one of PowerPoint's many templates. (See Figure 23–1.)

Using Views

PowerPoint allows you to view your presentation in several different ways. The view selection buttons are along the bottom left edge of the presentation window.

Slide View is used for designing the look of the slides. Here, you can work with the various fonts, colors, backgrounds, drop shadows, and so on.

Outline View is best for working with text only. You can see your presentation in context, since you see the text of a number of slides at once. Also, Outline View gives you a sense of the relative importance of the various points you're making. Finally, you can easily add, rearrange, or delete slides in this view.

In Slide Sorter View, you see all the slides in reduced size. This view is used for arranging slides in the sequence you want as well as setting transitions, builds, hidden slides, and other features.

In Notes View. you can compose notes about each slide. The notes can be used to print a script for yourself or handouts for your audience.

In Slide Show View, the screen changes radically to show only the slide. This is the

Figure 23–1. Microsoft PowerPoint.

Screen shot reprinted by permission from Microsoft Corporation.

view you use to present your presentation if you are going to do so on a computer screen or computer projector. In this view, since there are no toolbars or menus available, you primarily use keys to operate the show. For example, use the SPACEBAR key to move to the next slide. After reaching the final slide in a presentation, the program exits from Slide Show and the screen returns to the view you had before running the slide show.

Getting Help in PowerPoint

The primary Help feature of PowerPoint is the Office Assistant, which is designed to suggest Help topics based on your current activity as well as provide answers to your specific questions. The Office Assistant displays possible Help topics based on your search criteria. Sometimes the Office Assistant appears with a light bulb on it. This is to let you know that the Office Assistant has a tip relating to your current action. To see the tip, just click on the light bulb.

Another way to access Help is through PowerPoint's Help Menu, which conforms with the standards for most Microsoft Windows software. There are several navigational and control functions that can help you better use the Help program.

If you need help on a certain screen feature, such as a button, the status bar, or the ruler, you can click on the WHAT'S THIS? button. It activated the Help pointer. Then point to the item in question and click on it.

Moving Through Slides in Slide View

When you are in Slide View (where you are likely be most of the time), you can move through the slides by using the scroll bar on the right. You can click on the small buttons with double-arrowheads at the bottom of the scroll bar to move among slides. The up-pointing button moves to the previous slide, and the down-pointing button moves to the next slide. Depending on your Zoom setting, you can also click in the gray area above and below the slider to move between slides.

Using Zoom

While working with slides in Slide View, you can change the size of the image to make it more convenient to work with. Near the right-hand end of the toolbar is a drop-down list of percentages, called the Zoom Control. By clicking one of the percentages in the list, you can enlarge or shrink the size of the slide.

Working with Multiple Presentations

Like many Windows programs, PowerPoint permits you to work with more than one file at a time. You can open several presentation files at once in PowerPoint, and each can occupy its own window within the PowerPoint application window. Each window is called a document window.

Working with Outline View

In Outline View, each slide is represented by the slide icon that appears just to the left of the slide title. From Outline View you can add new slides, delete slides, edit the text of slides, and rearrange the sequence of slides. The floating window labeled Color displays a miniature version of the slide you're working on. It allows you to see the effects of your changes without having to switch back to Slide View. (See Figure 23–2.)

Adding a New Slide

You can add a new slide by selecting where you want the new slide to be and clicking on the NEW SLIDE button. Another way to create a new slide is to begin a new line in the outline at the top level. You begin a new line by pressing ENTER at the end of the previous line. The first text you type will be the title of the slide. When you press ENTER, you start a new line of text.

Moving Text

If you need to move text from one slide to another, you can easily do it by selecting the text and dragging to another slide in Outline View. When you release the mouse button, the text is pasted into the second slide.

Figure 23–2. Outline View in Microsoft PowerPoint.

Screen shot reprinted by permission from Microsoft Corporation.

Adding Text to a Slide

If you need to add some additional text to an existing slide, the easiest way to do that is to press CTRL and ENTER at the end of the title line. This automatically makes a bullet appear and allows you to enter the next line.

Demoting and Promoting Lines

One of the most common features of a PowerPoint presentation is bulleted text or numbered lists. You can also have lines of text that are indented below another line. Indenting text is called *demoting*. Moving indented text out even with the rest of the lines or bulleted list is called *promoting*. For example, if you need to demote a new line to become an item under the title, you can do that by clicking on the DEMOTE button.

As you might guess, you can promote items using similar methods (except that you use the PROMOTE button, of course). If you promote an item all the way to the top level, it creates a new slide and becomes the title of the slide.

Rearranging Slides

To change the sequence of a slide, you should switch to Slide Sorter View (see Figure 23–3). You can do this by clicking the SLIDE SORTER VIEW icon. This gives you a thumbnail view of the various slides in your presentation. To rearrange the order of your slides, you simply drag a slide icon to the new position. For example, if you wanted to move slide number 3 to the second position, you would click on the icon for slide number 3 and drag it until a horizontal line appears beneath slide 1.

Deleting Slides

To delete a slide in Slide Sorter View, you select it and press the DELETE key. As with most Windows applications, you can undo a deletion (or any action) by using the UNDO command.

Using Transitions

Slide Sorter View also permits you to create transitions between the slides in your presentation. These transitions—which can take the form of fades, dissolves, and wipes—are applied to the "incoming" (next) slide in a sequence. The Slide Sorter View has a button that is used for this purpose, called the SLIDE TRANSITION button.

The TEXT PRESET ANIMATION button can create new slides for individual items on a bulleted list. Remember that transitions are applied to the incoming, or following, slide.

The Slide Transition dialog box is where you specify the type of transition, the speed at which it occurs, and whether to advance automatically or under your manual control. There are several types of transitions available. All are previewed in the upper left corner of the dialog box.

The Slide Transition dialog box not only specifies which effect is to be used; it also allows you to see the effect of the transition before you use it. Each time you click on the TRANSITION icon, the slide previews what the transition will look like in your final presentation.

Figure 23–3. Slide Sorter View in Microsoft PowerPoint.

Screen shot reprinted by permission from Microsoft Corporation.

23 ■ USING POWERPOINT

Using Build Effects

In PowerPoint terminology, a *build* is a sequence of slides that displays each point, one at a time, in a bulleted list. While you could create each slide individually, using the build feature allows you to concentrate on other aspects of your presentation. To use a build effect, you first select the slide, then select an animation effect from a list.

When you return to the Slide Sorter View screen, you see an icon beneath the slide. This is a visual indication that you have an animation effect active for that slide.

The ANIMATION EFFECT icon does not respond to a click the way the TRANSITION icon does, but that's only because PowerPoint doesn't support previewing build effects while in Slide Sorter View mode. You can see the effects when you run the slide show.

Saving a Presentation

Once you've created a presentation, you'll want to save it to the disk. If you've used any Windows applications before, you already know how. You click the SAVE AS icon on the toolbar. You may have seen this Save As dialog box in other Windows applications. It's called a *common dialog box* because it's used throughout the Windows environment and in other Windows applications.

The Summary Info dialog box permits you to add comments and other descriptive text to your presentation file that you can search later. You might add some comments about how you created the presentation or the names of departments that can use the file. Other data you can track include the author's name, key words, and the title of the presentation.

Switching to Slide View

In Outline View, you can concentrate on the content of the presentation—the text and arrangement. To work with the appearance of the presentation, use Slide View. To switch to Slide View, click on the SLIDE VIEW button.

This view shows you the appearance of the slide, permitting you to inspect it visually. From here you can see if the colors are what you want and if the general look and feel of the slide is proper.

Notes Page View

In Notes Page View, you can create notes about each slide in your presentation. These notes can be printed to serve as a script or as handouts for the audience. To switch into Notes Page View, click the NOTES PAGE VIEW button. (See Figure 23–4.)

The slide appears on a representation of a sheet of paper, with an area below it for notes. To type a note, you can click inside the notes box to make a cursor appear. However, at this size it is difficult to read your note as you type it. To solve that problem, you can use the Zoom feature. The Zoom Control appears on the right side of the standard toolbar.

Running the Slide Show

One nice feature about PowerPoint is that you can run your slide show at any time while you're in the process of creating it. It's so simple to preview the show at any time that you may find yourself running the slide show often just to be certain that the effects come out right and the look is just what you want.

Table 23–1 gives a list of keyboard commands that you can use while in the slide show. The table is taken from the online Help screen, which you can display by searching for KEYBOARD SHORTCUTS, then choosing SLIDE SHOW SHORTCUTS.

TABLE 23–1. Slide Show Keyboard Commands

To do this . . .	Press . . .
Go to slide <number>	<Number> + ENTER
Black/unblack screen	B, . (period)
White/unwhite screen	W, , (comma)
Show/hide pointer	A, =
Stop/restart automatic show	S, +
End show	ESC, CTRL + BREAK, – (minus)
Erase screen annotations	E
Use new time	T
Use original time	O
Advance on mouse click	M
Advance to hidden slide	H
Go to slide 1	Hold both mouse buttons for two seconds
Advance to next slide	Mouse click or space bar
Return to previous slide	Press BACKSPACE

Your screen will go blank for a few moments while PowerPoint prepares to run the slide show. To move from slide to slide, use the space bar. Because different computer systems work at different speeds, you may experience a slight delay in getting to the first slide. Just be patient.

Using Fonts in Your Presentations

Fonts are usually thought of as the specific typeface design for letters, numbers and other characters that make up the text of a slide. Windows supports an almost unlimited array of fonts, so using the correct one for the job is a fairly important issue.

For a moment, picture the front page of a typical newspaper in your mind. There are headlines that are presented in larger, bolder fonts than the rest of the page, designed to catch your eye as you read. Smaller sub-headlines may punctuate sections of an article and allow the reader to browse through the content more quickly. The text of the stories is in a smaller, less dramatic font so that reading them won't become tiring on the eyes.

The point here is that fonts should be used as a design element to make your work more easily absorbed by the audience. When you make presentations with a tool like

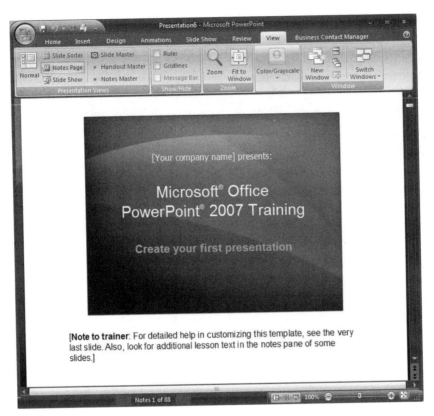

Figure 23–4. Notes Page View in Microsoft PowerPoint.

Screen shot reprinted by permission from Microsoft Corporation.

PowerPoint, you want your material to be easily understood with enough pizzazz to keep everyone's attention long enough for you to make your point. Fonts can go a long way toward getting your point across to an audience.

Changing Fonts

When you choose a template, an appropriate font is selected for you. You can easily change the font for the entire presentation by making the change on the Slide Master, which we'll discuss later in this chapter.

As a general design rule, you should stay with one font for all of the presentation. A single font gives your work a cleaner, more consistent look. If you mix fonts, you may end up with very tacky looking slides.

Although there are many different styles of fonts available, many of them fall into two basic categories called *serif* and *sans serif*. A serif is a short line or stem at the end strokes of individual letters. This lends a particular flair or style to the typeface design. Sans serif means without the serif. A sans serif font has letters with no end strokes. Studies show that serifs help guide the eyes and make text easier to follow. For this reason, publications with dense text, such as books, magazines, and newspapers, almost always use serif fonts. Typical examples of serif fonts include Times Roman, Times New

23 ■ USING POWERPOINT

Roman, New Century Schoolbook, Bookman, Palatino, and Courier (typewriter font).

For screen design, where text is kept to a minimum, a sans serif font may provide a cleaner look to your presentation. This is why television commercials and magazine ads frequently use sans serif fonts. Examples of sans serif fonts include Helvetica, Swiss, Arial, Avant Garde, and Modern. At least a few, if not all, of these fonts should be available on your particular computer system.

For presentations, you may use either a serif or a sans serif font, but you should avoid mixing them.

Changing the Font Size and Color

You can set each font type to a number of different sizes measured in units called *points*. The title of the slide is in a larger point size than the body text. To see the point measurement for the font size, simply look at the toolbar.

To increase or decrease the size of the currently selected text, simply click on one of the font size buttons until you get the font size you want. Each time you click this button, the text becomes a bit smaller, shrinking to the next smaller point size available on your system. The other button does just the opposite—that is, it makes the selected text get just a bit larger.

Color is an important aspect of character formatting. You have to be careful here. The chosen template uses appropriately coordinated colors. To help protect you from choosing an inappropriate color, the template uses a color scheme. A small drop-down box appears with several colors shown. There's a reason there are so few colors shown: These are colors matched to the color scheme you're using for the current slide, and they will blend in easily. Other colors are available, in case you need them, from the More Font Colors... option.

There is another button on the toolbar that gives you the ability to set shadows behind your text.

Changing Alignments

With PowerPoint, you can use various paragraph alignments to reposition text. You can change the alignment for any text area, or for any individual paragraph, to centered, left, right, or justified.

While text is an undeniably important aspect of your presentation, the way your text is presented is also very important. PowerPoint allows you to modify the background to use a wide variety of colors and gradients, or fill patterns, to make your presentation as visually appealing as possible.

Shading the Background

Shading means displaying a color that ranges from a lighter shade to a darker shade. Sometimes, shading is performed by adding what is called a *gradient*, which means a gradually changing range of colors. Gradients can display a range from light to dark, or one color to another, and in general add to the visual depth of your presentation. An example of shading is shown in the Slide Color Scheme dialog box. You can make adjustments to the shading in several different ways:

- The Color Scheme dialog box lets you adjust the color scheme for shadows, background, fills, etc. You can also select different colors from this dialog box.
- The Slide Color Scheme option allows you to specify colors for each component of the slide.
- The Variants section offers four versions for shading: from top to bottom, from left to right, from right to left, and from the center to each corner.

Changing the Color Scheme

Changing the color scheme can dramatically influence the look of your presentation. Unlike a template, a color scheme can be applied to individual slides as well as to the entire presentation.

The Color Scheme dialog box gives you several choices for changing colors. When you view this dialog box, notice that the upper right corner of the dialog box displays buttons for applying any changes to the current slide only (Apply) or to every slide in the presentation (Apply to All).

There may be instances where you want to use different schemes for different slides as a sort of color-coding method. In the absence of careful planning, however, varying schemes may cause problems with visual consistency, which may in turn annoy or distract your audience.

Using the Slide Master

The Slide Master controls the format for each slide in your presentation. For instance, when you want to change the size of the title on each slide, you simply have to change the title area one time on the Slide Master.

PowerPoint lets you look at different masters that correspond with different ways of viewing your work. There's a Slide Master, a Notes Master, and a Handout Master. The master shows you sample text to indicate the area size and placement of the title and body text. This helps you eye the layout of the template and gives you a way to reformat text on the master level.

Notes Master

The Notes Master gives you the ability to format your speaker notes. You can see your slide and type notes into the area shown to help remind you of important items to be covered in that slide, and any other related issues that may not be shown on the slide.

Handout Master

The Handout Master is used to add text and artwork to your audience handouts. You can see the master slides by holding down the SHIFT key while clicking on one of the buttons in the lower left-hand corner of the PowerPoint window.

PowerPoint Templates

A template is a presentation whose color schemes and layout formats can be applied to another presentation. PowerPoint comes with dozens of professionally designed, prebuilt templates you can use when creating your own slide shows. In fact, new presentations can be patterned after a default template called Blank Presentation.pot, or you can select from a variety of templates. (See Figure 23–5.)

After creating your presentation, you can even save its look and feel and use it again in another presentation by applying the template to the new file.

Changing a Template

Changing templates is a very powerful way to instantly reformat your entire presentation. When you change templates, all formatting revisions you've made to the Slide Master—including font types and sizes, colors, and text position—are reset. However, changes that you made on individual slides remain intact. Again, any formatting changes you made to individual slides remain even though you changed templates.

Inserting Visuals

The word *visuals* implies images, and educators know that a picture is frequently worth at least a thousand words. Visual media, which include graphics, photographs, movies, and animations, can be added to multimedia productions in a wide variety of ways. These can come from commercial sources, such as the wide variety of computer clip art or CD-ROMs full of images or from photographic or computer supply companies. Clip art is one of the most commonly used sources of images for multimedia developers.

When PowerPoint is first installed, the clip art files are placed in a subdirectory on your hard drive. To open any of these files, use the CLIP ART command on the Insert Menu.

PowerPoint may take a few moments to compile available images the first time you use the INSERT CLIP ART command. Be patient if you see several dialogs with a meter showing the progress of the operation.

Each clip art category contains a number of different images related by subject, as suggested by the titles. The Microsoft Clip Gallery is actually a miniature application within PowerPoint. You can add your own images and create your own categories, to better organize your clip art collection.

You can use the Clip Gallery program to preview clip art you wish to use in a presentation. Each image is represented by a *thumbnail* or tiny version of the real thing. You might not be able to see all the detail in each picture, but you can get an overall idea

Figure 23–5. Microsoft PowerPoint templates.

Screen shot reprinted by permission from Microsoft Corporation.

about content, layout, and colors used from the thumbnail.

Once you've found the clip art that really complements your presentation, you may find that a small amount of tweaking is needed to get it just right. PowerPoint, like many other Windows-based drawing programs, allows you to resize and move your graphics in almost any way you need.

You can also insert clip art images using the AutoClipArt tool. This feature searches your presentation for concepts and then suggests images in the Clip Gallery you might use to express your ideas.

Moving and Sizing Clip Art

Once an image is pasted on your slide, you can manipulate it by moving it or resizing it to fit your needs. As a general rule, you should avoid using more than one clip art image per slide. Too many images can clutter a slide and detract from your message.

Inserting Charts

Since your presentations cannot be dependent on clip art alone, it's nice to know that you can insert other types of graphic images into your slides. Charts can communicate mathematical relationships in a visual way. PowerPoint actually has a graphing module built into the program, and whenever you need it, all you have to do is click on a button on the toolbar.

When the datasheet is on the screen, you're actually using Microsoft Chart, a program included with PowerPoint. You could think of it as a (much) scaled-down version of Excel or some other Windows-based spreadsheet application.

Organization Charts

One other type of chart you can use in PowerPoint is the organization chart, often simply called an *org chart*. These are frequently used to show the relationships between departments or other groups within an organization. Inserting an org chart is just as easy as inserting a chart, and it's done almost the same way—by clicking a button on the toolbar. From here, you can build a chart that reflects the structure of the organization.

Creating Artwork

In addition to using clip art, graphics can be created from scratch on the computer by using simple paint programs such as Microsoft Paint, or more complicated drawing programs such as Adobe Photoshop. They can also be created outside the realm of the computer by pen, pencil, paint, crayons, photography, or any other media, and then brought into the computer for editing and incorporation. You can digitize images with a scanner, shoot digital photos with a digital still camera, or have your camera film processed and the images digitized on a PhotoCD.

Drawing with AutoShapes

Another special tool, called AutoShapes, gives you the ability to create less conventional shapes such as stars and arrows. You can find it on the Drawing toolbar.

The AutoShapes tool can help when you need something other than a simple rectangle or oval, and PowerPoint treats an AutoShape just like any other object. You can move and resize AutoShapes, type text onto them, or copy them for use elsewhere in your presentation. Using the SHIFT key *constrains* your drawings—rectangles will become squares, ovals will become circles, and so on. Use the SHIFT key whenever you want symmetrical images.

Using Videos

You can incorporate videos in your presentations as simply as you can place graphics on the screen. Videos can be shot with a digital camcorder and transferred to the computer using a special cable or a video capture card. You can then edit the video using a program such as Adobe Premiere and export it for use in the PowerPoint presentation.

Using Sound Media

In addition to still images and video, sound is another powerful medium. Audio in a multimedia presentation, just as graphics, can originate from a wide variety of sources—from commercial prerecorded music or historical speeches, to stand-alone sounds or part of a video, to narration recorded with a microphone connected to your computer.

Playback of audio usually involves a sound card, now built into most multimedia Windows systems. The quality of the sound varies drastically depending upon whether the sound card supports 8-bit or 16-bit sampling resolutions. Most multimedia computers include 16-bit sound cards as a standard feature. Without getting too technical, a comparison between the two is similar to the difference between AM radio and compact disc audio.

PLANNING A PRESENTATION

Consider the following guidelines as you plan your presentation:

Determine Your Goal and Objectives

Begin by defining your goal. What do you hope to accomplish? Is your goal to persuade or merely to inform? Persuasion may require getting your audience emotionally involved in your argument, getting them to care. On the other hand, if you are simply making a report, you may want your audience to remain objective, clear-headed, and somewhat emotionally detached.

Define your objectives. What topics will support your thesis?

Keep It Simple

Regardless of the purpose of your presentation, always try to keep it simple and focused. A simple, clear message can be delivered with greater impact to your audience and is more likely to achieve results. A complicated or muddled message will leave your audience confused and frustrated, which may severely hinder your chances for success. Keep the number of topics to a minimum. When expounding on each topic, make sure the information on each slide is clear and easy to understand.

Design for Flow

Outline your content in a topical format with a beginning, middle, and end. Try to keep your ideas focused and organized toward a logical conclusion. While sound reasoning and logic are not the only ways to effectively communicate or persuade, they are tried and true methods.

Design for Drama

Timing is everything. Design your presentation with a dramatic curve in mind. Peak your audience's interest toward the end and deliver the central conclusion of your message when you have everyone's full attention.

Plan Your Media Selection

Be sure to plan your media selection so that it's appropriate to the environment and audience. Do you need to prepare slides, overheads, or handouts?

Think and Plan Ahead

If you plan to use handouts along with a screen or slide show, consider whether you want to give them out before or after the presentation. If you give the audience handouts before the show, they can follow along, write notes directly on the handouts, and have an immediate reference should they have trouble seeing the screen. In some cases, however, saving the handouts till the end may help avoid giving away any surprises you may have planned.

Consider the Subject Matter

Consider your subject matter. Are you presenting a training seminar, a presentation to managers or employees, or a sales presentation? This may determine the scope of your presentation and the tone you want to set.

Consider Your Audience

Consider your audience. Is it made up of employees, customers, businesspeople, professionals, or mixed? Is it conservative or progressive? Formal or informal? Are they people you know personally or total strangers? Consider the audience's familiarity with the subject matter. If they are unfamiliar with it, or if the subject is somewhat technical, present one concept at a time and move in progression.

Both subject matter and audience should help you determine the tone of your presentation. Do you want a lot of humor or a more subdued approach?

Consider the Size of Your Audience

Larger audiences may dictate the need for more structure and formality. A smaller audience may be less formal, giving you more room for improvisation and one-on-one interaction.

Consider the Environment

Are you giving the presentation in an office, small conference room, or hotel meeting room? How visible is the screen from each part of the room? If visibility is questionable, you may want to include handouts with printed versions of each slide. If you're not familiar with the equipment, try to arrange time for setting up and rehearsing your presentation before delivering the real thing.

Practice

Practice delivering the presentation to a co-worker or friend. Your friends can offer helpful critiques by letting you know if your presentation is clear and focused, if your style and manner are tasteful, and if your treatment is interesting enough. They can also help you smooth over some of the rough spots.

◇ **PRESENTING YOUR PRESENTATION**

Once a multimedia presentation has been created, you need to prepare to present it to your audience, and then follow up once the presentation is complete. Below is a set of steps you might follow for this process. These guidelines will help you become a better developer and presenter. It's really true: Practice does make perfect in the world of multimedia development.

Step 1: Set Up

Now that a multimedia presentation has been created, you are ready to deliver the presentation. The first step is to set up the necessary equipment.

Step 2: Test Run

Make a test run through the presentation. This is especially necessary if the presentation was prepared on a computer other than the one you usually work on. If the presentation is a long distance from the original computer, be sure to move and test the presentation before traveling.

Step 3: Backup Plan

Develop a plan B. If the computer breaks or does not make it to the room in which the presentation is take place, what will you do? Having a backup plan is always a good idea!

Step 4: Deliver

Deliver the presentation. This may seem obvious, but don't be afraid to just do it! If everything goes perfectly, you are lucky. If not, relax, smile, and work through the problems.

Step 5: Evaluate

Take time to reflect on the experience now that the presentation is over.

- What went well?
- What needs to be improved?
- What was frustrating?
- What was exciting?
- What did you learn from the process?

Troubleshooting Computer Problems

There is nothing more upsetting than being in the middle of an important project and having trouble with your computer. Almost every computer user has experienced times when his or her computer didn't operate properly. Perhaps the computer crashed and lost your work before you saved it. Perhaps the computer started running very slowly or wouldn't turn on at all. In many cases, just turning a computer off and back on does the trick. This process, called rebooting, resets the computer's memory, processes, and programs.

Sometimes, though, you need to do more than reboot, but you must determine what you should do. Many people are afraid to troubleshoot computer problems; the solutions, however, to some of the most common problems can be quite simple. With some help, you can diagnose and correct most problems.

In most large offices, a computer Help Desk is available. If you experience a problem, you can call the Help Desk and they will send someone to take a look at your computer. In smaller businesses, you may have to call an outside vendor, who may first attempt to troubleshoot the problem over the telephone. Whether you work for a large or small business, though, the result is the same: lost time.

Hopefully, this chapter will help you troubleshoot some of the most common problems yourself so you can get back to work without waiting for a service technician. There are separate sections for Windows PC troubleshooting and Macintosh troubleshooting. Make sure you consult your owner's manual before you open your computer and attempt any repairs yourself.

◆ MICROSOFT WINDOWS PC TROUBLESHOOTING

Computer Won't Turn On

If your computer won't turn on, you first need to check the simple stuff. Check to make sure the power cord has not come loose from the wall or the back of the computer. Check the switch on the surge protector. Make sure the surge protector is turned on and plugged in. Has the surge protector blown a fuse? If so, you may be able to push the reset button to reset the surge protector. Make sure there is power to the wall outlet where the computer or surge protector is plugged in. Will anything else work in this outlet?

Computer Freezes or Crashes

Freezing occurs when the computer becomes completely inactive. There are no error messages, the mouse doesn't move, and the computer does not respond to keyboard commands. Crashing is similar to freezing, but the computer usually displays some type of error message. A program may close unexpectedly, but the rest of Microsoft Windows continues to function.

If your computer freezes or crashes frequently, it could be the sign of a hardware problem. Sometimes this is the result of a device that is not installed properly, such as a new video card, memory, or hard drive. Sometimes a component fails after the machine has warmed up.

Usually, it's a good idea to have a computer technician examine your computer when you experience frequent freezing and system crashes.

Computer Comes on with a Blue Screen

If you turn on the computer and a blue screen appears that says the computer was not properly shut down, it normally begins doing a scan for errors. This occurs when the computer was improperly shut down the last time you used it. The system scans for errors on the hard disk drive that can occur when you turn off the hardware without shutting Microsoft Windows down properly. To properly shut down the system, always go to the Start Menu on the taskbar and click SHUTDOWN from the pop-up menu.

Computer Runs Very Slowly

There are several reasons why your computer might start running very slowly, ranging from viruses to the system not having enough memory or hard drive space. Use anti-virus software to help combat viruses. To check your system memory, click START, CONTROL PANEL, and SYSTEM. The System window tells you how much memory your system has. It is recommended that your system have at least 1,000 MB or 1 GB of RAM. If your system has less, see about getting more memory. Figure 24–1 shows the System window.

While viewing the System window, you can adjust the performance of your Windows XP or Vista system by clicking ADVANCED. There you will find a setting for performance. Click the SETTINGS button for Performance. You can then adjust the visual effects for better performance. On the ADVANCED TAB of the Performance Options box, you can adjust the processor settings, memory usage, and virtual memory. Virtual memory is necessary, but the use of it by your computer slows your system. With virtual memory, when your computer system runs low on RAM, it offloads some of its memory to your hard drive. Since your hard drive is much slower than RAM, your computer is forced to slow down.

Another thing to check when your computer appears to be running very slowly is the space available on your hard drive. Double-click on MY COMPUTER, then right-click on the C: drive icon, and then click PROPERTIES. The Properties box shows the capacity of the C: drive as well as how much space is used and how much space is still available. Figure

24–2 shows the C: drive Properties box.

If most of your C: drive is being used, this can cause your system to run slowly. If this is the case, try using the Windows Disk Cleanup program, which will suggest files you can delete. To access Disk Cleanup, click the START button on the taskbar, and then click PROGRAMS, ACCESSORIES, SYSTEM TOOLS, and DISK CLEANUP. The Select Drive window opens. Select the C: drive and then click the OK button. Windows then checks the drive and the Disk Cleanup program begins to run. The Disk Cleanup program tells you how much space can be freed and displays a list of files that should be deleted. To set Disk Cleanup to run automatically, click the SETTINGS tab and check the box next to the statement "If this drive runs low on disk space, automatically run Disk Cleanup." You should manually run Disk Cleanup once a month to manage the space on your hard drive if you do not run Disk Cleanup automatically.

Another thing you can do to improve your computer's performance is defragment your C: drive. Over time, the files on your computer begin to get fragmented and stored on various open spaces on the drive, rather than being stored as one contiguous file. Because the files are broken up over multiple locations, this process is called fragmentation. When the computer goes to access one of these fragmented files, it takes longer to load. The Disk Defragmentation tool optimizes the performance of your computer by reorganizing the files on your hard drive into contiguous blocks. You should defragment the files on your hard drive once month.

To run Disk Defragmentation, exit all the programs and turn off your screen saver. To turn off your screen saver, right-click on your Windows Desktop, and select PROPERTIES from the pop-up menu. Click the SCREEN SAVER tab, then click the drop-down arrow

Figure 24–1. System window.

Screen shot reprinted by permission from Microsoft Corporation.

Figure 24–2. C: drive Properties box.

Screen shot reprinted by permission from Microsoft Corporation.

to select NONE. Click the APPLY button, then click the OK button. Double-click MY COMPUTER, then right-click on the C: drive icon. Then click PROPERTIES. Click the DERAGMENT NOW button to begin the process.

The Monitor Is Blank

Many computers have a built-in energy saver that puts the system to sleep after a period of time. The monitor appears to be off, while the power light goes from green to amber. To wake up your system, just move your mouse around or type a key on the keyboard. After a few moments, the system will power back on.

If the system is not in sleep mode, check to make sure the power switch is turned on. When the power is turned on for a monitor, the power light usually shows green or amber. Green tells you that the monitor has power and is receiving a video signal from the computer.

If you can't see the power light, check to see if the power cord is tight in the back of the monitor and to the power strip or wall socket. Also make sure the monitor video cable is tightly connected to both the back of the monitor and to the back of your computer.

If the power is on and all the cables are OK, check to make sure the monitor's brightness and contrast controls are not turned down. These controls are on the monitor; however, the location varies depending on the manufacturer.

Before assuming the monitor is broken, you might want to try another monitor connected to your computer. If that monitor works, then you can probably isolate the problem to your original monitor. If the replacement monitor also doesn't work, then the problem is likely with your computer's video card.

No Signal Input Sign on Monitor

Sometimes the monitor comes on and you see a box on the screen with red, green, and blue stripes, along with the message "No signal input." This means that the monitor is on but it's not receiving a signal from your computer. Just turn on the computer first, before turning on your monitor.

Mouse Won't Work

If your computer's mouse won't work or stops working while you are in the middle of a project, try the following troubleshooting steps. Check to make sure the mouse is connected to the computer. If the mouse cable is disconnected, reconnect it and, if necessary, restart your computer.

If the mouse uses a roller bar on the bottom, it may be dirty. Open the circular ring on the bottom of the mouse that surrounds the ball. Remove the ball and clean the little wheels that control the mouse movement using your fingernail. Many times, a gummy substance collects on these small rollers.

Sometimes just turning your computer off and then back on causes a non-functioning mouse to start functioning again. You can also try using a different mouse. If there is an unused computer around the office, try borrowing its mouse to conduct a test. If the replacement mouse works, then you've isolated the problem to your old mouse. It's probably time to buy a new one.

If you just installed a new mouse and it doesn't work, you must also install the new mouse software.

If you are in the middle of working when your mouse stops working, you can press the CTRL + S keys on the keyboard to save your work. Table 24–1 shows the keyboard shortcuts if your mouse stops working.

TABLE 24–1. Keyboard Shortcuts If the Mouse Stops Working

Keys to Press	Action It Causes
Windows logo key or CTRL + ESC	Opens the Start menu located on the taskbar
CTRL + ALT + DELETE (DEL)	Opens the Close Program dialog box, which contains a list of applications to be closed and command buttons for Ending Task, Shutting Down, and Cancel
ALT + F4	Closes all open programs and shuts down
Windows logo key + R	Opens the Run dialog box
Windows logo key + M	Minimizes all open windows
SHIFT + Windows logo key + M	Undoes minimizing of all windows, tiles horizontally, tiles vertically, or cascades windows
Windows logo key + E	Opens Windows Explorer, My Computer
Windows logo key + D	Minimizes all widows and undoes minimizing of all windows
TAB	Moves focus to next option in open window
ENTER	Chooses the OK button, opens a window selected using Window key + TAB
ESC	Closes a dialog box, cancels
Windows logo key + BREAK	Opens the System Properties box
Windows logo key + TAB	Selects the taskbar buttons
CTRL + N	Opens a new document
CTRL + O	Opens the Open File dialog box
CTRL + S	Opens the Save dialog box
CTRL + P	Opens the Print dialog box
UP arrow or DOWN arrow	Selects the previous or next item
PAGE UP or PAGE DOWN	Selects the item up or down one screen
HOME or END	Selects the first or last item in the list box

Keyboard Won't Work

If your keyboard stops working, check to make sure the keyboard is connected to the computer. If the keyboard cable is disconnected, reconnect it and restart your computer.

Another thing you can do is press the CRTL + ALT + DEL keys on the keyboard at the same time to bring up the task list. Use the mouse to select a program that says "not responding" and click the END TASK button. Repeat this process until all the tasks are ended. Check to see if the keyboard starts working again.

Sometimes just turning the computer off and back on causes the keyboard to START working again. If your mouse is still working, click start on the taskbar, and then click SHUT DOWN from the pop-up menu. Unplug the keyboard connection from the back of the computer and reinsert it tightly. Wait a few moments and then restart the computer.

Number Keypad Doesn't Work

The NUM LOCK must be on for the number keypad to work. If you press the NUM LOCK key on the keypad, the NUM LOCK button will light on the keyboard. The NUM LOCK key is located in the upper left corner of the number keypad.

Keyboard Error or No Keyboard Found

If you start your computer and see a message that says "Keyboard Error" or "No Keyboard Found," then the computer is not seeing the keyboard. Check to make sure the keyboard cable is connected to the computer. If you use a USB keyboard, make sure the USB cable is connected to the computer and to the keyboard.

Check to see if any lights display on the keyboard. Press the NUM LOCK button on the number keypad of your keyboard and see if the NUM LOCK light appears.

Try switching keyboards with another computer. If the replacement keyboard works, then it's probably time to toss your old keyboard and get a new one.

Printer Won't Work

If the printer isn't working, you need to determine if the problem is with the printer, the cable, or your computer. Check the printer's owner's manual for information on how to use the printer's built-in self-test mode. When the printer is in self-test mode, it will print a test page. If the self-test is successful, you can assume the printer is OK.

Test the connection between your computer and the printer by clicking START, SETTINGS, and PRINTERS, and then right-click the icon of the printer that is not responding. Click PROPERTIES and then click the PRINT TEST PAGE button. If Windows can't print a test page, then click the printer cable and make sure it is connected.

If multiple printers are available, try printing to another printer. If you can print to another printer, then your computer is OK and there's a problem with the connection to the other printer or with the failing printer itself.

Check to make sure the printer isn't having paper feed problems. Check to make sure the printer doesn't need a new ink jet or toner cartridge.

Is the printer shared on the network? If so, then usually a shared printer is connected to another computer on the network. That computer must be turned on before the shared printer is accessible.

Diskette Won't Work in Diskette Drive

If the diskette won't work in the diskette drive, either the diskette is bad or the drive is having problems. Does the drive make a sound? Try the diskette in another computer to confirm if the diskette is bad. Try another diskette in the computer to confirm that the drive is having problems.

Non–System Disk or Disk Error

If your computer has a diskette drive, you may have left a disk in the drive upon startup. Remove the disk and press a key on the keyboard to restart the computer. If the computer makes a funny sound, your hard disk drive may have failed. Contact your Help Desk or call a computer repair company.

Operating System Not Found

If you receive a message that the "operating system was not found," this usually means there is a problem with the hard drive or with your installation of Microsoft Windows. Try running the Windows Install CD to repair your Windows installation.

Numeric Error Code Displayed on Screen

When the computer displays a numeric error code, there could be a problem with the hardware settings stored in the computer's BIOS (basic input-output system). Turn the computer off and restart it. If that doesn't help, call your Help Desk or contact a computer repair company.

FDD or HDD Controller Failure Message

When the computer displays a message indicating that there is an error with the FDD or HDD controller, there is a problem with the fixed diskette drive (FDD), the hard disk drive (HDD), or the cables that connect them. Turn the computer off and restart it. If that doesn't help, call your Help Desk or contact a computer repair company.

Hard Drive Won't Save or Load Files

One of the first symptoms that your hard drive is having a problem is that it has trouble saving or loading files. One way to check the health of your system is to run the ScanDisk utility. If your computer was not shut down properly, when the system restarts, ScanDisk automatically runs to check for errors. You can also run ScanDisk yourself, performing either a Standard scan, which checks files and folders for errors, or a Thorough scan, which tests files, folders, and the disk surface for errors.

To start the ScanDisk tool, exit all programs and turn off the screen saver by right-clicking the WINDOWS DESKTOP and selecting PROPERTIES from the pop-up box. Click the SCREEN SAVER tab, and then select NONE from the drop-down box. Click the APPLY button and click OK. Then click the START button, PROGRAMS, ACCESSORIES, SYSTEMS TOOLS, and then SCANDISK. Select the drive you want scanned, and click the radio button for THOROUGH. Also click the box to check "Automatically Fix Errors." Click the START button to begin.

Beeping Noises During Startup

Beeping sounds usually mean there is a problem with the computer's hardware, such as the video card or memory. Turn the computer off and restart it. If that doesn't help, call your Help Desk or contact a computer repair company.

WINDOWS PC SOFTWARE TROUBLESHOOTING

Program Locks Up

When a program locks up while you are in the middle of work, test to see if the keyboard is still responding by pressing the CAPS LOCK key. Try typing CTRL + Z to undo whatever you just did, or press the ESC key.

If necessary, restart the computer by typing CRTL + ALT + DEL. This brings up the Windows Task Manager. You can then check the status of the running applications. If any of the programs have a status of Not Responding, click that program, and then click the END TASK button. The bad news is that whatever you were doing on the program since the last time you saved will be lost. If necessary, restart the computer by typing CTRL + ALT + DEL to bring up Windows Task Manager. Then click SHUT DOWN from the menu, and then click RESTART.

If nothing else works, press the START button on your computer and hold it for ten seconds to restart the system.

Computer Starts in Windows Safe Mode

Windows Safe Mode is a limited version of Windows that loads when your computer is having trouble. Windows is smart enough to know when there's a problem and will automatically run Safe Mode, or give you the option to load Safe Mode, when your start the system.

In some cases, you may want to force the computer to load into Safe Mode. You can do this by holding down the F8 key on the keyboard just before Windows would normally start loading. You'll see the Windows Startup Menu and you can select Safe Mode from the list of options. You can tell you are in Safe Mode because the screen resolution will be VGA standard 640 × 480 resolution with 16 colors and you'll see the words "Safe Mode" on the screen.

In Windows Safe Mode, the system loads with a minimum set of device drivers so the PC can function at a basic level. You won't be able to print or use the Internet, but you can still do some troubleshooting. For example, if you installed new software that caused a problem, you could load Windows in Safe Mode in order to uninstall the program.

Not Enough Virtual Memory Message

If your computer has been on for a while and you have used several different programs, you may need to restart your system. If you repeatedly get a message that there is not enough virtual memory, you may need to have additional memory installed in your computer.

As stated earlier in this chapter, virtual memory is actually hard drive space that is used as system memory when your computer runs out of RAM. You can adjust the amount of hard drive space that is used for virtual memory by clicking the START button, CONTROL PANEL, and SYSTEM. Click the ADVANCED TAB, and then on the Performance section, click the SETTINGS button. On the Performance Options box, click the ADVANCED tab. In the Virtual Memory section, click the CHANGE button. You can click the drive you want to use for virtual memory and the amount of space you want to use for this purpose. When you are finished, click the SET button, then click OK. Click OK again on the Performance Options box, followed by OK on the System Properties box.

Fatal Exception Error

If you are running a program and suddenly a blue screen appears with the message "Fatal Exception Error," the only way to respond is to restart your computer. Anything you were working on before your last save will be lost. Fatal exception errors can occur when you are working on a file from a diskette or CD-ROM and you remove it before the system has finished reading from it. Sometimes a particular program causes fatal exception errors on a regular basis. You might also get fatal exception errors after installing a new program or a new device. If this happens, use Windows Safe Mode to uninstall the program. Check the software or hardware vendor's website for the correct software or drivers for your operating system. If you install incompatible software or hardware drivers, it could be the cause of fatal exception errors.

Missing Program Error Message

If you normally start a program from a shortcut icon on the desktop and suddenly one day get a Missing Program error message, this usually means that the program has been deleted or moved or become corrupted.

If you moved the program, delete the old shortcut on your desktop and create a new one. The program may have been accidentally deleted. Search your computer for the missing program by clicking the START button, then clicking SEARCH. If you find the program, try running the program from its new location. If the program appears to be missing, you may have to reinstall the program.

Erasing Text Rather than Inserting

One common problem you may experience while working with a word-processing program such as Microsoft Word is that you try to insert text in the middle of a document. Rather than inserting the new text, your typing actually erases the existing text as you type. This happens when the INSERT key is toggled to the off position. Click the Edit menu on the menu bar, and then click UNDO to get back to the point where you were before you started erasing text. Now press the INSERT key on the keyboard and try again. This time, you should be able to insert rather than overtype.

One way to tell whether you are in Insert or Overtype mode is to check the OVR letters at the bottom of the program window. If the letters OVR are grayed out, the Insert is toggled on. If the OVR letters are black, Insert is toggled off.

Using System Restore

System Restore allows you to take your computer back in time to a point where you know it was working OK. To use this feature, you must first enable it by scheduling restore points. To access System Restore, click START, PROGRAMS, ACCESSORIES, SYSTEM TOOLS, and SYSTEM RESTORE. Choose CREATE A RESTORE POINT, and then click NEXT. Name the Restore Point, then click the CREATE button. When the process is finished, click CLOSE.

To restore the system back to your restore point, start System Restore, and then choose RESTORE MY COMPUTER TO AN EARLIER TIME. Click the NEXT button, and then pick the date of your restore point. Click NEXT, and then click NEXT again. Click the OK button. You can set System Restore to automatically create Restore points at various times each week.

APPLE MACINTOSH TROUBLESHOOTING

Apple Macintosh systems can also experience problems ranging from system startup issues to software issues. Make sure you consult your owner's manual before you open your computer and attempt any repairs yourself.

System Does Not Start

If your Macintosh won't start when you turn on the power, first check the power cord at both ends. Make sure it is securely connected to the back of the Mac and to the wall outlet or power strip. If the computer is connected to a power strip, make sure the power strip is connected to the wall outlet and turned on. Check to make sure the power strip hasn't blown a fuse. You can check this by bypassing the power strip and plugging your Mac's power cord directly into a wall outlet.

Check the other cables and connections, such as the keyboard and mouse cables, and any network cables. Check all the cables carefully for bent pins. Sometimes a bent pin causes the system to short electrically and the system won't power on to protect itself.

Also check the screen brightness and make sure the brightness and contrast are not turned down low.

System Starts and Freezes

If your Mac starts up and then freezes, try restarting the system. Unplug all peripheral devices except for the mouse and keyboard. For example, unplug any printer, network cables, scanners, or other USB devices. Then try restarting the system again. If it starts, you can troubleshoot which peripheral device is having problems by reconnecting them one by one and restarting each time.

Sometimes programs add plug-ins to the system. These plug-ins are called *extensions* in the Macintosh world. To see if a software extension is causing the problem, restart the computer while holding the SHIFT key down. This turns the extensions off. If the computer restarts, then remove all the extensions and add them back one by one. Restart the Mac after each addition. You can manage your extensions using Extensions Manager.

System Starts with Sad Mac

If the system starts with a sad Mac icon, restart the system using the Mac OS operating system disk and reinstall the system. Then run a hard disk drive checking tool such as Disk First Aid, MacCheck, or Norton's Disk Doctor.

Applications Unexpectedly Quit

If you have an application that quits functioning, close all your applications and restart the computer. If the program continues to quit periodically, try reinstalling the program. Check online and make sure the program is compatible with the system software you are using. Check the stats for the amount of memory needed to run the application.

Application Busy or Missing

If you try to open a data file and get the message "Application Busy" or "Application Missing," you should locate the application and start it first, then try opening the file. If the application won't open, try reinstalling it. If there are two copies of the application, delete one.

System Locks Up

If you are in the middle of doing something and the system locks up, type COMMAND - OPTION + CONTROL + ESCAPE and then select YES to force quit. Save all documents, quit all applications, and then restart the Mac.

To prevent system crashes, add more memory to the system, check for duplicate system folders, or duplicate applications.

You should also use Extension Manager to look for any extension conflicts. If necessary, use the installing disks to install a clean version of the operating system and any applications.

Time and Date Incorrect

If the time and date are incorrect, and you make changes but the changes won't stick, you may need to reset the PRAM (Parameter Random Access Memory) or rebuild the desktop. Control Panel settings that won't stick can also be a signal that the system board is going bad.

COMPUTER PROBLEMS

Control panel settings are stored in PRAM. To reset the PRAM, turn off the system completely and then turn it back on. As the system is powered on, hold the COMMAND + OPTION + P + R keys until the system makes two chimes.

To rebuild the desktop, restart the system while holding the COMMAND + OPTION + SHIFT keys until a message appears. Then click OK.

Hard Drive Problems

If your hard drive makes a funny sound or if you have trouble reading or saving files from your hard drive, restart your Macintosh and run the Disk Utilities program. If you can't access the hard drive, try to reinstall the Macintosh operating system from the installation CD-ROM.

Also try resetting the PRAM and rebuilding the desktop. To reset the PRAM, as the system is powered on, hold the COMMAND + OPTION + P + R keys until the system makes two chimes. To rebuild the desktop, restart the system while holding the COMMAND + OPTION + SHIFT keys until a message appears. Then click OK.

Monitor, Printer, Keyboard, and Mouse Problems

To troubleshoot monitor, printer, keyboard, or mouse problems on the Macintosh, follow the same procedures outlined earlier for troubleshooting problems with a Windows PC.

Diskette or CD Won't Eject

If you have a diskette or CD that is stuck inside the Macintosh, press the SHIFT + COMMAND + 1 key. Then restart the computer. While restarting, press the mouse button. If this doesn't work, try inserting a paper clip in the small hole in the front of the diskette or CD-ROM drive.

Office
Ergonomics

You can think of ergonomics as a way of designing tools and equipment to suit individual needs. For a number of years, there have been efforts to improve ergonomics, primarily in manufacturing and product design. But improvements can also be made for office workers.

Ergonomics addresses three aspects of your workplace: the physical, the environmental, and the personal. An example of a physical aspect is creating a good fit between you and your computer workstation. An example of an environmental aspect is eliminating glare on your monitor screen by improving the lighting in your work area. An example of a personal aspect is the need to take periodic breaks throughout the day to restore your energy and improve comfort.

Early recognition of physical symptoms allows you to make adjustments, seek help, and eliminate further discomfort. So how can you recognize the early signs and symptoms? Well, only you can listen to what your body is telling you. If you feel any fatigue, tension, or discomfort in any part of your body, take immediate action to relieve it. It's important to pay attention to the early signs and symptoms to avoid conditions that may lead to further discomfort.

Other symptoms include limbs that feel heavy or in which you feel a dull ache. You might also have joint or muscle discomfort. Be aware of problems with your eyes, including dry or itchy eyes, redness, aches, or blurred vision. You can also get headaches from eyestrain.

How can you recognize the advanced signs and symptoms of work-related problems? Consider the following:

- Do you notice tingling, numbness, or coldness in joints and extremities?
- Is there a loss of strength or dexterity in your hands?
- Do you have difficulty turning door knobs, grasping things, or holding onto things?

What should you do if you experience these symptoms? Remember first that these symptoms are likely temporary and might have nothing to do with your work. For example, these symptoms might result from recreational activities, such as sports, hobbies, and home projects, or from medical conditions, such as arthritis, diabetes, pregnancy, or obesity.

Whatever their source, it's important to address these symptoms early and seek appropriate medical attention. Early intervention is the key to avoiding prolonged discomfort.

Whether at work or play, examine the risk factors in your activities.

- Are you involved in prolonged, intensive activities without breaks?

- Is your desk arranged so that you must extend yourself to reach the phone or reference materials?

- Do you often sit in one position without moving about? Often do not take rest breaks? Rarely if ever stretch? You should take a break at least once each hour.

- Do you use too much force when gripping a pen or pencil?

- What about leaning or rubbing against hard surfaces such as the edge of a desk?

- Do you perform visually intensive tasks without breaks?

- Do you work in an area where there are wide temperature shifts, drafts, breezes, poor or irregular lighting, or excessive noise?

◇ YOUR DESK AND CHAIR

There are three preferred ways to sit at your desk. First, sitting upright is perhaps the most familiar posture when working at a computer. When seated, the angle between your upper and lower body should be approximately 90 degrees. Your back should be supported and erect. Your feet should be supported by the floor or a footrest. This is a good all-around posture for working at the computer.

A second popular sitting position is called reclining. In this position, you lean back in your chair. Make sure your back is fully supported and your buttocks are not shifted forward, which causes your lower back to not be supported. Your feet should be supported by the floor or a footrest. This is a good posture for viewing information on your monitor or for reading documents.

The third way to sit is called declining. In this posture, your upper body is upright while your thighs are declining slightly and your feet are firmly on the floor or a footrest. The seat back is adjusted almost vertically to provide back support. This is also a good posture for keyboarding work.

To enhance your comfort, you can make four main adjustments to a chair. These are adjusting the seat pan height, the backrest height, the backrest tilt, and the armrests. Let's look at each of these adjustments in more detail. (See also Figure 25–1.)

You should adjust the seat pan height so that your elbows are approximately at keyboard height when your elbows are next to your body. Your thighs should be approximately parallel to the floor with your feet resting firmly on the floor. If your feet are not resting firmly on the floor, you need a footrest. This seat pan height adjustment prevents your thighs from being compressed so blood flow is not restricted. This reduces fatigue in your legs. This adjustment also encourages you to sit more erectly and to use the backrest of your chair, which reduces stress on the lower back.

The backrest height adjustment makes sure that your lower back is supported. For most people, their lower back is at the same height as their elbows when the elbows are next to their body. When adjusted correctly, the lumbar support of the backrest should fit the curvature of your lower spine. This adjustment helps your lower back to maintain its natural curvature and thereby provides even compression on spinal disks and less fatigue of your back muscles.

Figure 25–1. Ergonomic desk chair.

Photo by Jennifer Wauson.

The backrest tilt adjustment involves the angle between the backrest and the seat pan. It should be no less than 90 degrees. You should avoid adjusting the backrest too far back to where your arms are stretched out to reach the keyboard. You should also avoid adjusting the backrest too far forward where you are too close to the keyboard and cause too much bend in your elbow.

The armrest adjustment involves adjusting the height of the armrests so that the elbows rest naturally on the armrests without slouching or shrugging your shoulders. If possible, you should adjust the width between armrests so that the armrests are directly underneath your elbows. The correct adjustment of the armrests reduces the loading of the arm on the shoulder.

What if you must use a nonadjustable chair? Just because the chair is "nonadjustable" doesn't mean you can't still make adjustments. You can make an existing chair more ergonomically sound by physically adjusting the height and adding lumbar support. You can adjust the height by adding a cushion on top of the seat pan. Finally, you can add a back support cushion, pillow, or even a rolled up towel to give yourself lumbar support.

You can lower the height of your work surface by obtaining a lower-height work

Figure 25–2. Positioning your keyboard.

Photo by Jennifer Wauson.

surface, or, as a last resort, have Facilities or a similar group cut down the height of the legs. You might also consider adding an adjustable-height or lower fixed-height keyboard tray to your work surface.

You can raise the height of a work surface by obtaining a higher-height work surface or by adding blocks under the workstation's legs.

◇ POSITIONING YOUR COMPUTER KEYBOARD AND MOUSE

The keyboard and mouse are typically the main interface between a user and a computer system. Therefore, if you work with a computer system, you probably use your keyboard and mouse extensively.

How can you set up your keyboard and pointing device to maximize comfort? There are several things you can do. You can place them properly and, if necessary, you can acquire keyboard and mouse accessories.

To set up your keyboard properly, start by placing it directly in front of the monitor with the home position keys, G and H, centered to the screen. Sit so that your elbow angle is approximately 90 degrees. Maintain a straight line across the hand and forearm. This might require you to lower the keyboard off the rear legs. Placing your keyboard properly helps you maintain a neutral posture, thereby improving comfort (see Figure 25–2).

Pointing devices such as a mouse, trackball, or glidepoint should be positioned to maximize comfort. You should place the device at the same height as the keyboard and as close to the keyboard as possible. For right-handed people who don't use the ten-key numeric keypad, you might want to consider using a keyboard without this keypad. Positioning your pointing device correctly helps you maintain a neutral posture, thereby improving comfort.

Several keyboard and mouse accessories are available that can assist you with your comfort. Adjustable keyboard trays and platforms are designed to position the keyboard at various heights to help keep your wrists and arms in a neutral, relaxed position. Adjustable keyboard trays can slide in and out from underneath a work surface. Some models have a separate height and tilt adjustment.

Palm rests (Figure 25–3) can be helpful in the use of both keyboards and mice. These soft foam or gel strips are designed to raise your palms and keep your wrists straight. If you use a palm rest, it should not be used while keying but only to rest your palms between periods of keying.

◇ POSITIONING YOUR COMPUTER DISPLAY

The location and orientation of your display depends on the lighting characteristics in your work area, the viewing distance and angle, and glare control.

Glare control is key to avoiding eyestrain and the accompanying discomfort it can cause. You should keep in mind that the best way to correct screen reflections is to remove their source. The need for antiglare screens (Figure 25–4) suggests that the workplace is not arranged or lit properly.

Many sources that can cause glare reflections on a properly positioned display are

Figure 25–3. Keyboard and mouse palm rests.

Photo by Jennifer Wauson.

Figure 25–4. Antiglare screen.

Photo by Jennifer Wauson.

likely to cause distracting glare in a person's normal field of vision. Screen glare can result from too much light falling on the screen (for example, light from windows or lamps), or bright areas of the environment that reflect onto the screen (such as a white shirt or blouse).

If possible, choose a workplace setup location where the screen is perpendicular to any windows and away from any bright light sources such as lamps. You should consider using an antiglare screen if it is impossible to control the source of the glare.

You should also adjust the monitor's contrast, brightness, and color controls to suit your individual comfort level. This may require changing these controls during the day as room light varies.

Special screen cleaners are available to clean dust, dirt, and fingerprints from the display or antiglare screen. You can also try a damp cloth.

After you've located your display properly in your work area to avoid glare, you need to fine-tune the position in relationship to your body. Your display should be centered behind your keyboard. The height of your display depends on your eye height while seated. The top of the display, not the top of the screen, should be even with or a little lower than your horizontal line of sight.

For people of shorter stature, you should avoid placing the display on top of your desktop computer system. This makes it nearly impossible to position the keyboard and display properly. Either the monitor will be too high, or the keyboard will be too low. If, in your work, you look primarily at source documents, place the source documents directly in front of you and the display slightly off to the side.

If you need to raise the display, stands are available that can provide a comfortable viewing height in order to reduce eye and neck discomfort.

If you wear glasses with bifocals, trifocals, or progressive lenses, and you find yourself looking through the bottom or top of your glasses to view the screen, you should adjust the display until you don't have to tilt your head up or down to see the screen. What if you have a laptop instead of a monitor? In a fixed office setting, you might consider getting a "Y" connector and using an external keyboard and mouse. You can then set the laptop on a raised platform behind the keyboard to raise the screen to the proper height. Another option is to obtain a separate display for office use.

The distance between your eye and the display should be whatever is comfortable for you. You should be able to easily read the characters on the screen. You should not have to lean forward or back to read the screen. One good rule of thumb is to sit at an arm's length from the display with your hand in a fist position.

You can tilt the display up or down as necessary. Try to maintain a 90-degree angle with your line of site. Also be careful not to pick up glare from overhead lighting. By following these simple placement guidelines for displays, you can avoid possible eyestrain, awkward neck positions, and neck and back discomfort.

◇ ARRANGING YOUR WORKSTATION

The way you organize the elements of your workplace to fit your individual needs is an important consideration in working comfortably. Make sure you have sufficient desk area to allow you to position your keyboard, pointing device, display, and other items in a way that works best for you.

Organize your desk to reflect the way you use work materials and equipment. Place the equipment you use most often, such as your telephone, within the easiest reach. Avoid placing objects where they reduce your freedom of movement. For example, don't place a computer tower or boxes under your desk too close to your legs. The key here is to maintain an orderly desktop to reduce unnecessary movements or awkward postures. This will help to improve your comfort.

Proper lighting is really a relative term. Lighting that is good for one task may be inappropriate for another. The general attitude in most offices is that more is better, but this is not necessarily true for working at your computer. If you are reading paper documents, you need bright light, but if you are viewing a display, you need less light. The best solution for most offices is to reduce the overhead lighting so that the screen is more easily read. Task lamps can be used to provide lighting for reading documentation or to illuminate specific work areas. You should be careful when placing task-specific lighting to avoid glare on the screen and to avoid getting direct light in your eyes. Having the proper lighting helps you reduce eyestrain and its accompanying discomforts.

If your job involves working with documents, you should place the source documents properly to avoid eyestrain and awkward neck positions. One useful accessory is a document holder. When positioned properly, a document holder reduces the amount of movement required when looking back and forth between the screen and the document. Some document holders sit on your desk and are adjustable. Other models attach to the side of the display.

You should position the source document at the same distance as your display and next to your display. The main thing is for the document to be on the same plane and angle as the display.

If you spend most of your time transcribing, you should position your source documents directly in front of you and place your display off to the side.

How many times a day do you pick up a telephone? It's probably a lot, right? The main thing here is to avoid cradling the handset between your ear and shoulder, which can lead to neck discomfort. If you use a telephone for the majority of your day, you should consider obtaining a telephone headset. A variety of sizes and types of telephone headsets are available. You should find one that fits you comfortably and is compatible with your telephone. If you are unsure of compatibility, consult the telephone manufacturer's literature.

◆ SUSTAINED WORK

No matter how well your workstation is set up, you should take frequent breaks. These breaks in your work are important as they help you to avoid fatigue. Frequent ergobreaks are important when you perform sustained, intensive, or highly repetitive work. Even if you just change positions or stand up and stretch at your workstation, it will help.

When working at your computer, it is recommended that you take a short break at least once each hour. These breaks can be from thirty seconds to five minutes long and can go a long way toward reducing fatigue. If you do take a short break from your workstation, don't just go somewhere else to sit. It is more beneficial to get up and move around. For example, stand while taking a phone call. Stand while having a face-to-face conversation with a colleague. Go make copies at the copy machine. Or just take a break from the keyboard and change your position in your chair and read mail or other documentation.

It is also a good idea to rest your eyes occasionally throughout the day. Your eyes can become fatigued; however, this is a temporary condition and is not harmful to your eyes. The muscles in your eyes that work to focus on near and far objects become fatigued when they focus for extended periods of time on near objects. Your eyes experience the least stress when they are focused on objects twenty feet away or farther.

Computer display users tend not to blink as frequently as people performing other reading tasks. Eye dryness from this staring effect is increased by low humidity in the office.

If you have difficulty reading your screen, consider increasing the default font size or improving the screen resolution.

If you wear glasses, keep the lenses clean and keep your prescription current. In fact, even if you don't wear glasses, you should have periodic eye exams. Most people's vision changes over time.

◆ KEYBOARDING

The ergonomic principles behind proper keyboarding technique start with your body position relative to the keyboard. Maintain a relaxed and neutral hand and arm posture to improve comfort. Your shoulders should not be hunched up. Your arms should be comfortably at your side with your elbows bent at approximately 90 degrees. The keyboard should be approximately at elbow height, which allows the forearm and hand to be in a straight line and parallel to the floor.

The proper keyboarding technique involves a few guidelines you should keep in mind while you are working. If you notice that you are doing something incorrectly, you should stop and make adjustments.

Keep a soft touch on the keyboard. Use as little pressure as possible. Your hands should glide over the keys. If your hands remain in a fixed position, your fingers tend to overreach for the keys. Keep your fingers in a relaxed posture similar to when you rest your hand gently and naturally on a table. Try not to extend your pinky fingers and thumbs while typing. Avoid resting your hands on the palm rest while typing. Use the palm rest only when you are not typing. To reach the keys that are farthest away, such as the function keys, move your entire hand instead of reaching with your fingers.

Glossary of Computer Terms

A

Accelerator key   A keyboard equivalent of a mouse click, signified by an underlined character in a menu or dialog box. You can press the key (often in combination with the ALT key) instead of clicking with the mouse.

Access   To get to, to bring up and display, as "to access a file" or "to access a menu." In computer terminology, *access* is a verb.

Active window   The application or document window to which the next keystroke or mouse click will apply. Sometimes called the *foreground window* or *current window*. See *Window*.

Address book   A feature of a browser that holds personal information (for example, name, e-mail address, phone number) for reference.

Alphanumeric   Refers to any combination of the letters of the alphabet and the ten numeric digits. Contraction of *alphabet* and *numeric*.

Append   To add to the end of existing text or an existing file.

Apple, Inc.   A major developer of microcomputers that chose to use a different type of microprocessor chip from those found in IBM machines and their compatibles. Software designed for Apple computers does not work on IBM machines, and vice versa.

Applet   A small-scale application that is included with Windows. Examples include Write, Paintbrush, Notepad, Cardfile, Calendar, Clock, and Calculator.

Application   A computer program. Examples include word processors, spreadsheets, and database management systems. Sometimes, applications are differentiated from programs that perform a task like computer operation and maintenance, which are called utilities or applets. See also *Applet, Utility program.*

Application window   A window containing a running application, along with its work area and menu bar. An application window may contain multiple *document windows*.

Applications   See *Applications software*.

Applications software   An organized collection of computer programs that provides powerful tools for performing a variety of tasks in a specific area, for example, word processors, spreadsheets, and database management systems.

Argument   Additional information added to a command to define the scope of an operation. In a spreadsheet, an argument tells a function the values to use in a calculation. Compare *Parameter*.

ARPAnet (Advanced Research Project Agency)   A wide area network developed in the 1960s by the Advanced Research Project agency of the U.S. Department of Defense.

ASCII   The American Standard Code for Information Interchange, a 7-bit character set almost universally available on all personal computer systems. It is a common denominator for exchanging data between computers. Files that consist only of ASCII characters are called *text files*.

ASCII file   A text file made up of only letters, numbers, or symbols.

Associate   To identify a document or data file with a particular application through the file's extension. When you open a file in Windows Explorer with an extension that has been associated with a particular application, that application starts automatically.

Attachment   A graphics, text, or HTML file sent with an e-mail message.

Attributes   Hidden codes that assign certain properties to files. For instance, there are attributes to make a file read-only, to make a file hidden, or to indicate if the file has been modified since the last backup. You can display and modify a file's attributes by selecting the file in Explorer, then pressing ALT + ENTER.

B

Back up   To copy the information stored on the hard disk onto another medium, such as a set of floppy diskettes; this is usually done as a safeguard against malfunction of the hard disk. Used as both a noun and a verb.

Background   In a multiprocessing environment, the program that runs unattended while another is running in the "foreground." Typically with Windows you might print a document in the background while working with another application.

Backslash   The " \ " character; represents the root directory in DOS paths and serves as a separator between elements of a path name.

Batch file   See *Batch processing file*.

Batch processing file   A file containing DOS instructions to be performed automatically or with little input from the user.

Baud rate   A measure of speed referring to movement of serial data, usually applied to modems and serial printers.

BCC   Blind Carbon Copy. When you BCC an e-mail message recipient, other recipients cannot see that you have sent a copy of the message to this person.

Binary   A system of counting using only two digits, 1 and 0.

Binary file   A file that is in machine-readable form, like an executable program.

Bit   Short for "binary digit"; the smallest unit of information.

Bitmap   An image or graphic produced by paint programs such as Paint.

Block   In word processing, text that is highlighted and treated as a unit.

Bookmark   A way that a Web browser can keep a permanent record of Internet addresses.

Boolean operators   Operators that are designed to put conditions on a search. The most common Boolean operators are AND, OR, and NOT.

Boot   Starting (or restarting) a computer. Since a computer must start itself by loading its own startup software, it is said to "lift itself by its own bootstraps." When you boot the computer, Windows starts.

Border   Any of the four sides of a window that serves as the boundary line for that window. The border can be used to reshape and resize a window.

Browse   To look through drives and folders for a file. Some dialog boxes have a BROWSE button that lists available drives and folders from which you can select the appropriate folder and file.

Browser   A software program that requests, interprets, and presents World Wide Web documents. Frequently used browsers include Netscape Navigator, Internet Explorer, Lynx, and Mosaic.

Buffer   Temporary storage in memory for data or other information. A disk cache and a print buffer are two examples.

Bus   A pathway or channel between multiple devices.

Bus topology   A network arrangement connecting computers together along a common set of electrical conductors so that each can communicate with the others. Compare *Ring topology, Star topology*.

Button   A graphically defined clickable area of the screen.

Button bar   See *Toolbar*.

Byte   A unit of computer data, usually equivalent to one alphanumeric character.

C

Cache   The storage area on a person's computer that has copies of original data stored so that the computer doesn't have to go to a remote server to get information every time it is requested.

CAD   See *Computer-aided design*.

Cascade   A way of arranging open windows on the desktop so that they overlap but still show each window's title bar.

Categorical directory   A search tool that contains a directory in which the contents are organized by category, for example, Yahoo!

CC   The Carbon Copy message header. This field contains the e-mail addresses of additional message recipients.

CD-ROM   Compact disk read-only memory, an advanced storage medium capable of holding up to 550 megabytes of data.

Cell   In spreadsheets, the intersection of a row and column. A cell may contain a value, a label, or a formula.

Cell address   The identification of a spreadsheet cell by its row and column coordinates.

Central processing unit (CPU)   A term often used interchangeably with the microprocessor of a personal computer.

Character   A single letter, number, or symbol (including a space). Sometimes used interchangeably with *byte*.

Character set   The letters, numbers, and symbols available for use by personal computers and printers. The first 128 of these symbols are standardized and referred to as the *ASCII character set*. They include letters A–Z and numbers 0–9, among others.

Character string   A group of alphanumeric characters treated as one unit. A text string can be a single character, several characters, or many words.

Check box   A small square box appearing in dialog boxes denoting an option that can be set. An "X" or checkmark in a check box means that option is turned on.

Chip   A small electronic component that contains microscopic electronic circuits.

Choose   To begin an action using either the mouse or the keyboard.

Circuit board   A nonconductive surface on which electronic paths or circuits are imprinted.

Click   To quickly press and release a mouse button without moving the mouse, usually to select an on-screen item. Compare *Double-click*.

Client   A computer or software program that can access particular services on a network.

Clipboard   The temporary storage area used by Windows to transfer text and images between applications and/or documents. It is a holding area within the computer's memory.

Clone   Informal term for an IBM-compatible computer.

Close   To remove an application or document window from the desktop.

Close button   A small button at the right end of the title bar that closes a window.

Column   In spreadsheets, the vertical divisions of the worksheet. On a computer monitor, one character space; most monitors display eighty columns. Compare *Row*.

Command   An instruction that controls the activity of a computer system, normally entered by the user through the keyboard.

Command button   A rectangular button found in a dialog box and labeled with the action it carries out.

Compatible   A computer that is functionally identical to a competitor in appearance, operation, or both; a clone.

Compound document   A document that contains data created in more than one program, usually employing links to other files through OLE or DDE.

Computer-aided design (CAD)   Software application commonly used by engineers, designers, and architects to simplify their work.

Conference   An application developed to provide real-time conferencing over the Internet. It includes live audio transmission, Internet chat, a whiteboard, file transfer, and collaborative browsing.

Control menu   In application windows, this list of options allows Restore, Move, Size, Minimize/Maximize, Close, and Switch To other applications. The menu appears when you click the tiny icon at the left end of a window's title bar.

Control panel   A utility program that permits system-wide adjustments to Windows.

Copy   A frequently used operation to duplicate text, data, or a file without disturbing the original. Compare *Move*.

CPU   See *Central processing unit*.

Cross posting   A method by which you can post a single article to multiple newsgroups.

Cursor   A blinking bar indicating where characters will appear when typed. Usually called the *insertion point* in Windows.

Cursor control keys   The arrow keys, PAGE UP, PAGE DOWN, HOME, and END keys.

Customer support   Telephone assistance provided by software manufacturers to address problems arising from specific user situations.

Cut   To place a copy of text or other data in the Clipboard and remove the original selected text from the screen. Compare *Copy, Paste*.

D

Data   In general, any information being processed by the computer system.

Data file   One of the two primary types of files that DOS works with. Data files are generally created by the user or by computer programs themselves. Compare *Program file*.

Database   An organized collection of related information (data) stored on the computer's hard disk.

Database management system   Applications software that contains tools for defining, organizing, storing, and retrieving data.

Database manager   See *Database management system*.

Database structure   The basic, initial design of the database according to the wishes and needs of the user; what different items of information are included in a database.

DDE Dynamic Data Exchange, which allows application programs to pass commands and data to other applications. With DDE, one program can remotely control another.

Default   A value assigned or an action taken automatically by a software program unless another is specified. Can be thought of as a "factory setting."

Default button   In some dialog boxes, this is the button Windows selects automatically if enter is pressed, shown with a bold border.

Delete   To erase or remove data from a computer's memory or disk storage.

Desktop   The main screen. The desktop is any part of the screen not appearing within a window.

Desktop computer   Another term for microcomputer.

Desktop publishing   A powerful type of applications software for manipulating text and graphics, allowing a computer user to prepare near print shop–quality documents.

Device   A component of the computer's hardware system, like a mouse, a printer, a disk drive, or a modem, among others.

Device driver   A software program that controls communications between the computer and a device attached to it.

Dialog box   A rectangular box that opens temporarily and requests additional information or provides command options.

Digital   The representation of information using only arrangements of binary numbers (1 and 0) to represent all characters and values.

Directories   Structures on a disk or website that contain files or other subdirectories.

Directory   A convenient logical division for storing related files. See *Folder*.

Directory path   The route from one area on a disk to another through the levels of directories and subdirectories.

Directory tree   A graphic (or imagined) representation of levels of hierarchical directories. Similar in shape to a family tree.

Disk   See *Diskette*.

Disk cache   Memory buffer set aside for temporarily storing data being read from or to be written to a disk. Its purpose is to make the computer operate faster.

Disk controller   The circuitry (often an expansion board) that directs the operation of the disk drives and their respective read/write heads.

Disk operating system (DOS)   See *Operating system*.

Diskette   A single disk of recording material that is a portable but relatively limited form of data storage.

Display   A video display device, often called the "monitor" or the "screen."

Display adapter   The circuitry (often an expansion board) that converts the computer's commands to "show this" to a visible picture on the display.

DNS (Domain Name System)   The addressing protocol that lets computers connected to the Internet find each other.

Document   A general term for most types of work created with applications. In many contexts, *document* is synonymous with *file*.

Document icon   Graphic representation of a document window that has been minimized.

Document window   Window within an application window containing a document created or modified by that application. In many applications, there can be more than one document window within the application window.

Documentation   The collection of books and other materials that explains the use and operation of a software program.

Domain name   The name given to any computer registered on the World Wide Web as an official provider of information and files. Domain names are usually two or more terms separated by periods. Examples include Microsoft.com or www.mus.edu.

DOS   Disk operating system.

DOS prompt   See *Prompt*.

Double-click   To quickly press a mouse button twice in succession without moving the mouse. Used to choose an item or start a process. Compare *Click*.

Download   To copy data or files from another computer. Compare *Upload*.

Drag   To move an object onscreen by pointing at it, then pressing a mouse button and moving the mouse while keeping the button pressed.

Drag and drop   A process in which you use your computer's mouse to click and hold objects on the monitor, move them around while continuing to hold the mouse button, and release the mouse button when you have moved the object to the desired location.

Drop-down list box   A single-line text box (sometimes with a default value already highlighted) that opens to display a list of additional choices.

Drop-down menu   A list of command options that drops down from a menu bar.

DVD   A storage medium capable of storing 4 to 9 gigabytes of data.

E

E-mail   Electronic mail sent from one computer to another over a network or by telecommunications.

E-mail address   A unique address assigned to a person allowing him or her to receive e-mail messages. It consists of a user ID, followed by an @ sign and a domain name. An example is athomas@nasa.gov.

Embed   To insert data created from one document into another, and allow the embedded object to be edited (through OLE) just by double-clicking on it.

Emoticons   Short for emotional icons. These character combinations are one way of trying to get across emotion in what you say. For example, :) is a smile.

Enhance   In word processing, to make specific text stand out from the rest, for example, by underlining or using boldface type.

Enter key   The key pressed to begin the execution of a command. Also called the *return key*.

Erase   See *Delete*.

Executable file   A file that starts programs. You can start an executable file in Explorer by double-clicking its name. The following extensions are reserved for executable files: .EXE, .COM, .BAT

Expansion board   Additional circuit boards to enhance the performance or capabilities of the computing system.

Expansion card   See *Expansion board*.

Expansion slot   An opening along the data bus for the addition of expansion boards.

Extension   For Macintosh computers, extensions are software plug-ins that add additional functionality. See *Filename extension*.

F

FAQ   Frequently Asked Questions. Many times, newcomers to a newsgroup ask questions that the old-timers have heard over and over again. FAQs are written and posted periodically to reduce the number of redundant questions.

Field   In a database, an item of information; similar to a blank on a form.

File   A named collection of information stored on a disk or other storage device. Files include text, programs, graphics, and databases.

File manager   In older versions of Windows, an application that organizes, copies, deletes, and renames files and directories, and runs programs. Windows uses an updated version called Explorer.

File server   A central computer that supervises the operation of a network. Compare *Node*.

Filename   A number or letter designation assigned to a file.

Filename extension   An optional one- to three-letter addition to a filename separated from that filename by a period. Application programs use the filename extension to identify compatible files.

Fixed disk   IBM's term for a non-removable hard disk.

Flame   An Internet message that often uses profanity or otherwise berates and belittles the recipient.

Flat file   A simple database management system used to organize a single group of information. Compare *Relational database*.

Floppy disk   An informal term for a diskette.

Folder   A container object that holds files and other folders. Also called a *directory*.

Font   A set of letters, numbers, and symbols that are a particular size and design. Usually available in a range of sizes and a variety of styles.

Footer   Repeated text that appears at the bottom, or "foot," of each printed page.

Foreground   Area of the screen occupied by the active window. This is always the application with which you are currently interacting.

Format   The basic layout or appearance of a document or spreadsheet, including such things as margins, line spacing, and column width.

COMPUTER TERMS ■ 26

Formatting   The process of preparing a disk or diskette to receive data; a new disk must be formatted before it can be used. When a disk is formatted, all previous data is erased and replaced by new sectors and tracks.

Frames   A feature available on the World Wide Web that presents text, links, graphics, and other media in separate portions of the browser display. Some sections remain unchanging, while others serve as an exhibit of linked documents.

Freeware   Free software that is available on the Internet and can be downloaded, used, and redistributed at no cost to the user.

FTP   An abbreviation for File Transfer Protocol, a set of rules for transferring files on the Internet.

FTP site   A location on the Internet where one can either download or upload files, using FTP.

Function keys   Programmable keys whose purposes depend on the software program being used.

G

Gigabyte (G or GB)   Roughly, a billion bytes.

Global   An operation that affects an entire document or spreadsheet.

Graph   A visual representation of data, such as a bar graph or pie chart. Should not be confused with *Graphics*.

Graphic interface   The use of pictures, symbols, and icons to provide a menu of operations and applications available to the user. Usually, a mouse is used to point to a particular icon to run that program.

Graphics   The production of lines, angles, and curves by a computer on a monitor display or printer.

Graphics mode   A way of presenting visual data in which the screen is treated as an array of tiny dots. Anything shown on the screen (pictures or alphanumeric characters) is built up from these dots. Compare *Text mode*.

H

Hard disk   An internal, usually non-removable data storage device.

Hardware   A general term referring to all of the physical and electronic components of the computer system.

Header   (1) Text within a Web page, e-mail message, or newsgroup message that indicates the main point of a document or a section within it. (2) Repeated text that appears at the top, or "head," of each printed page.

Help   In applications software, a set of instructions or operating reminders that can easily be displayed onscreen.

Hierarchical directories   The formal term for the arrangement of directories and subdirectories in a directory tree.

High density   Diskettes that have increased storage capacity.

Hits   (1) When you are conducting an Internet search on the Web, the term applied to each result of a particular search. (2) The number of visits to a website. Each time a website is accessed by a viewer, there is one additional hit to that website.

Home page Frequently, this term refers to the cover of a particular website. The home page is the main, or first, page displayed for an organization's or person's World Wide Web site. Sometimes also called a ***Start page***.

Hover To place the mouse over an area of the screen (but not clicking).

HTML An abbreviation for HyperText Markup Language, the coding language for the World Wide Web that informs browsers how to display a document's text, links, graphics, and other media. This language forms the foundation for all Web pages.

HTTP HyperText Transfer Protocol. The way information gets exchanged between HTTP servers and their clients.

Hyperlink Sometimes called a link, a pointer within a document that, when clicked, transports you somewhere else.

Hypertext Text that is organized by means of links from one piece of information to another.

I

I/O (Input/Output) A general term to describe any input/output device or the data that flows to or from it.

IBM International Business Machines, Inc.

Icon A graphic symbol or picture used to represent various objects or options, such as applications, documents and devices.

Inactive window An open window that is not currently selected or being worked within.

Inbox The place a person goes to get his or her incoming messages within his or her e-mail program.

Ink jet printer A type of letter-quality printer that "paints" its characters by squirting tiny drops of ink onto the paper.

Input Any data or information that goes into the computer.

Insert In insert mode, characters typed at the cursor push existing text to the right as the new characters are typed. Compare ***Overwrite***.

Insertion point The place text appears when you type. Usually shown as a flashing, vertical bar or line. Sometimes referred to as a *cursor*.

Integrated circuit A large number of electrical components and connections densely and microscopically placed on the surface of a semiconductor. Often called a *chip*.

Integrated software A comprehensive applications software package, usually including word processor, spreadsheet, database manager, and communications programs.

Interactive Requiring input or responses from the user.

Interface The point where two data processing components meet, for example, where a printer cable plugs into a parallel port. The user interface refers to how information is conveyed to the human user, such as the design of the screens and the functions of the keys.

Internet The global network of computers that enables people all over the world to electronically communicate with each other.

Internet phone An application that transmits a user's speech across a network (in this case, the Internet) to another user's machine.

Internet Service Provider (ISP)   An organization or company that provides users with access to the Internet.

Intranet   A network of computers that is set up like the Internet, except that only certain people, like those who work for a company, are given access.

J

Joystick   An input device often seen with computer and video games.

Justification   In word processing, arranging and spacing words and letters so that margins are aligned. Left justification (that is, along the left margin) is common, right justification less so.

K

Keyboard   Most frequently used input device; resembles a typewriter keyboard.

Keyboard shortcut   Special key sequence used to choose a command directly without first highlighting and displaying a menu.

Keypad   Supplemental set of keys resembling a calculator keypad. Convenient for entering a large amount of numerical data. *Cursor control keys* are superimposed on the numerical keypad and may be *toggled* back and forth with the NUM LOCK key.

Kilobyte (K or KB)   1,024 bytes.

L

Label   In spreadsheets, the contents of a cell beginning with either a letter or one of several text characters. Although they may contain numerals, labels are not affected by arithmetic operations. Compare *Value*.

LAN   See *local area network*.

Laser printer   A sophisticated, letter-quality printer that combines laser and photocopying technology.

LCD   Liquid crystal display, a popular technology for flat-screen monitors and laptop computers.

Light pen   An input device that optically scans and "reads" data, often in the form of a bar code.

Link   Short for hypertext link. A link provides a path that connects a user from one part of a World Wide Web document to another part of the same document, a different document, or another resource. In spreadsheets or databases, two or more separate files may be linked through a common field.

Linked object   The visual representation of a drawing, a sound file, or other media element that can be embedded, updated, and accessed from within a document through OLE.

ListBox   Column of available choices arranged in alphabetical sequence. Usually only one, but sometimes more, can be selected.

Listserv   An e-mail address that is configured to forward every message it receives to the e-mail addresses of those who have subscribed to it. You can think of it as an electronic, interactive newspaper.

Load   To place or copy a program into memory in preparation for running it.

Local Area Network (LAN)   A group of computers connected together to allow users to share resources and files.

Login   The name or identity used when you access a remote computer system.

M

Macro   Macro instruction. A work-saving procedure in which a series of frequently used keystrokes and commands are recorded by a software program to be "played back" later by just pressing one or two keys.

Mail merge   A word-processing feature allowing information from two files (such as text in a form letter and addresses from a mailing list) to be combined quickly and simply so that each form letter looks individually typed.

Mailbox   A place where your e-mail program stores mail.

Mailing list   See *Listserv*.

Mainframe computer   A very large computer, usually requiring specialized staff and support.

Maximize   Enlarge an application window to occupy the entire desktop, or enlarge a document window to fill the entire application window in which it resides.

Maximize button   Small button located near the right end of the title bar. It enlarges the window to its maximum size.

Megabyte   1,048,576 bytes, or roughly one million bytes. Abbreviated "M" or "MB"; often referred to as a "Meg."

Memory   The high-speed working area of the computer where both the program currently being run and the data being processed are temporarily stored.

Menu   In applications software, a list of several options or commands available to the user.

Menu bar   The row beneath the title bar that lists the names of command menus that are available.

Merge   See *Mail merge*.

Message box   An information-only type of dialog box that requires a single user response, usually the selection of an OK or CANCEL button.

Message headers   The part of an e-mail message (or newsgroup posting) that contains basic information such as sender, receiver, and subject.

Microcomputer   A small, relatively inexpensive, freestanding computer designed for individual use. Also known as a *personal computer*.

Microprocessor   The small computer chip in a personal computer that interprets programs and performs instructions.

Minimize   To reduce an application or document window to an icon. Some windows cannot be minimized.

Minimize button   Small button near the right end of the title bar. It shrinks the window down to an icon and places it on the desktop.

Modem Modulator-demodulator, a device that allows computer data to be fed back and forth over telephone lines.

Moderated listserv Just as a debate has a moderator to make sure both sides stick to the rules, so too do some listservs have a human moderator who makes sure the rules of the listserv are being followed. These listservs are called moderated listservs.

Moderated newsgroup A newsgroup that features a human moderator to review messages before they are posted.

Moderator Anyone who moderates, or filters, the content on a listserv or newsgroup.

Monitor The computer's video display.

Mother board The primary board of the computer; contains the main circuitry, including the microprocessor.

Mouse An input device that controls pointer movement by sliding on a flat surface. It has one or more buttons used to initiate actions.

Move The transfer of text, data, or files from one location to another. The original material is then erased. Compare *Copy*.

MS-DOS A proprietary *operating system* distributed by the Microsoft Corporation. Usually simply called *DOS*. PC-DOS is a licensed version distributed by IBM that is functionally equivalent. The functions of DOS are built into Windows, so a separate version of DOS is not required.

Multimedia The combination of a variety of media, including sound, animation, video, text, and graphics.

Multitasking The capability of some computers to perform more than one task or run more than one computer program at a time.

Multiuser The capability of some computers and computer systems to support several interactive terminals at the same time, with the appearance that each terminal is enjoying exclusive use of the system.

N

Netiquette The acceptably polite method of talking via electronic communication.

Network A group of computers connected through cables or telephone lines for the purpose of transferring information from place to place. See *Local Area Network*.

Newsgroups Topical areas of Usenet that operate much like bulletin boards for the discussion of topics regarding recreation, society, culture, business and computers. Currently, there are more than 12,000 newsgroups available.

Newsreader Software designed to download, display, and transmit newsgroup postings.

Node Peripheral computers connected to a network. Compare *File server*.

Number crunching Informal term for a spreadsheet's ability to take a large table of related numbers and formulas and perform multiple calculations in a short time.

O

Object   An item such as a file, folder, or icon that is visually represented on the screen. Objects have properties and usually can be manipulated as in copying, deleting, or modifying.

OLE   Object Linking and Embedding, the inclusion (embedding) of data from one program, such as a table, chart, or drawn object, to another data file. OLE permits changes to embedded items by simply double-clicking on them in the current document.

Online   To be currently connected to a remote network or computer.

Online services   Services provided to connect your computer to the Internet.

Open   To make a document available for revision or printing, or to enlarge an icon to a window. Also, to start an application.

Operating system   A program that supervises and controls the operation of a computer, the operation of other software programs, and the user's communication (interface) with the computer. Windows is an operating system.

Operators   Anything that modifies a term or equation. In the equation $2 + 2 = 4$, the plus sign is an operator. When searching on the Web, you can often use special symbols or words to build a search "equation" that is often more effective than searching for a single word or phrase.

Option board   See *Expansion board*.

Option button   Round button in a dialog box used to select an option. Within any group of option buttons, only one button can be selected. Sometimes called *radio buttons*.

Outbox   The place within an e-mail program where messages are queued, ready to be sent.

Output   Any information or results from the computer for the user.

Overwrite   In overwrite mode, any characters typed at the cursor erase preexisting text as the new characters appear. Compare *Insert*.

P

Parallel port   A connection or outlet on the system unit that can transmit 8 bits at a time. Usually connected to printers. Compare *Serial port*.

Parameter   An addition to a command that governs software, selects options, or establishes limits. Compare *Argument*.

Parent directory   The directory one level higher than another.

Password   In applications software, a specific word required to gain access to protected information.

Paste   To insert *cut* or *copied* text from the Clipboard into a document.

Path   See *Directory path*.

PC   Abbreviation for personal computer. See M*icrocomputer*.

Peer-to-peer   A network arrangement whereby each computer has equal status and access to all resources.

Peripheral device   Any external piece of equipment attached to the system unit; same as an *I/O device*.

Peripherals   See *Peripheral device*.

Personal computer (PC)   See *Microcomputer*.

PIF   Program Information Files, which tell Windows how to control and run DOS (non-Windows) applications.

Pixels   The smallest graphic unit that can be displayed onscreen. Also called *picture elements* (PELS).

Platform   A particular computer environment with specific operating protocols. Windows, Macintosh, and UNIX are platforms.

Plotter   A specialized printer used to draw pictures, graphs, schematics, and other pictorial representations.

Plug-in   A small program that enhances the capabilities of a Web browser. Plug-ins enable browsers to display file types beyond images and text.

Point   To move the mouse until the tip of the pointer rests on the item to be selected or chosen.

Pointer   Usually an arrow-shaped cursor that indicates the current mouse position, and the screen location where your next click will take effect. Can also be a double-headed arrow, I-beam, hourglass, crosshair, small hand, or other shape, depending on what you are currently doing.

Pointing device   Any control that allows the user to position the cursor, select items, or perform commands. Examples include a mouse, a trackball, and a joystick.

Port   Connections used for transferring information between peripheral devices and the system unit. See *Parallel port, Serial port*.

POST   Power On Self Test, a self-checking program automatically run every time the computer is switched on.

Post   A message to a newsgroup. When you submit messages (also called articles) to newsgroups, you are said to be posting a message.

Printer   A peripheral device for producing permanent printed copies of computer output.

PRAM   Parameter Random Access Memory. This is where system settings are saved in an Apple Macintosh.

Program   A complete set of coded instructions that tell a computer how to do something.

Program file   A complete set of coded instructions that tells the computer how to do something. In Windows, a program usually has a file extension of .COM, .EXE, .BAT, or .PIF.

Program icon   A graphical representation of a program.

Programming   The process of writing coded instructions for a program.

Prompt   A message or symbol (such as the DOS prompt) displayed by interactive software, requesting information or instructions from the user.

Properties   Attributes of an object. For instance, a text object might have a particular font, a certain color, and a certain size.

Protocol   A set of rules. On the Internet, this translates into the set of rules computers use to communicate across networks.

R

RAM   See *Random Access Memory*.

Random Access Memory   RAM, the temporary computer memory that can be read or written to. It is the workspace of the computer and its contents are lost when the computer is shut down.

Read   The ability or process of acquiring data from memory storage, or a peripheral device. Compare *Write*.

Read-Only Memory   ROM, the permanent memory that can be read but not written to except by special means. It contains instructions for starting the computer, as well as special routines that perform many functions of the operating system.

Read/write slot   The exposed area on a diskette where the disk drive head can read and write data.

Reboot   To restart the computer and reload the operating system. See *Boot*.

Record   One complete entry in a database file.

Relational database   A database management system that allows two or more files to be linked together, forming relations on common data or "tables." Compare *Flat file*.

Resolution   The degree of clarity of characters on a video display or printer.

Restore   To return a window to its size and position prior to being minimized or maximized.

Restore button   Small box at the right end of the title bar that makes the window resume its prior size and location on the screen.

Return key   See *Enter key*.

Ring topology   A type of network whereby each node receives and passes along all messages in a closed loop until the messages reach their destinations. Compare *Bus topology, Star topology*.

ROM   See *Read-Only Memory*.

Root   See *Root directory*.

Root directory   The highest level folder in the system of hierarchical folders; the one that is automatically created when a disk is formatted.

Row   In a spreadsheet, the horizontal division of a worksheet. On a computer monitor, the vertical space for one line of text; most monitors can display twenty-five rows.

Run   To start or execute an application program or other process.

S

Save (to disk)   To write data to a disk or other storage device.

Scroll   The action of moving through text and graphics in order to see parts of the file or list that cannot fit on a single screen.

Scroll bars   Bars in the right-hand and bottom borders of a window representing a document's current position on the screen. Boxes within the scroll bars (called *scroll boxes* or *sliders*) may be dragged with a mouse to move the cursor more rapidly.

Search   To look for a specific character string of information.

Search and replace   To look for specific information and replace it with different data.

Search engine   A computer program that indexes a database and then allows people to search it for relevant information available on the Internet.

Search syntax   The phrasing and symbols used in directing a search tool.

Sector   A subdivision of a track on a disk constituting a unit of disk storage space.

Select   To mark an item by highlighting it or clicking on it. In Windows, objects are selected prior to an action, which will be applied to the selected object. For instance, if you select text, then press the DELETE key, the selected text is deleted. In Explorer, if you select an icon (single-click), then open the File menu, the options on the menu will apply only to the selected icon.

Serial port   A connection or outlet on the system unit that can transmit only 1 bit at a time. Used for a variety of peripheral devices, including modems, printers, and mice. Compare *Parallel port*.

Server   Any computer that delivers or transmits information and data.

Shortcut key   A key combination that carries out a command or action without first accessing a pull-down menu.

Signature   A small text file that contains information your e-mail or newsgroup client automatically attaches to the bottom of every message you send.

Software   The set of instructions that make computer hardware perform tasks. Software includes both the *operating system* as well as application programs.

Sort   To arrange records or data in a particular order.

Split bar   Used to divide a document window into panes when dragged with the mouse. Usually located at the top of a vertical scroll bar, or to the left of a horizontal scroll bar. Explorer uses split bars to separate the directory window from the file contents window.

Spool   To store a print job on disk so that it can be printed at the same time you are working with another application or document. Abbreviation for *simultaneous peripheral operation online*.

Spreadsheet   Applications software that is an electronic version of the traditional financial analysis tools: the columnar pad, the calculator, and the pencil. The spreadsheet is represented on the screen as a grid of columns and rows.

Star topology   A network arrangement in which all lines converge on a central "host" computer. Compare *Bus topology, Ring topology*.

Start page   Frequently, this term refers to the cover of a particular website. The start page is the main, or first, page displayed for an organization's or person's World Wide Web site. Sometimes called a *home page*.

Status bar   The horizontal bar near the bottom of the typing screen showing the cursor's current position, and which special function keys (if any) are active. Not found in all Windows applications.

String   See *Character string*.

Sub domain   A distinct section contained within a domain.

Subdirectory   Lower-level directories subordinate to a parent directory.

Subscribe   To add a discussion group to your subscription list.

Surfing the Internet   Slang expression for using the Internet. Also called "surfing the Web."

System board   See *Mother board*.

System reset   See *Reboot*.

System unit   Hardware unit that houses the majority of the computer's electronic components, including the microprocessor and the disk drives.

T

Task   A running program; an open application or active process.

Task List   A window that is used to show all open applications and switch between them. Can also arrange windows and icons and terminate any running programs or processes. Sometimes called *task manager*.

Task switching   The act of suspending one program's operation while running another. Only one program is actually running or active at a time, as opposed to *multitasking*, where two or more programs are running simultaneously.

TCP/IP   A set of protocols that applications use for communicating across networks, including the Internet.

Telecommunications   Data communications via telephone circuits.

Template   In some applications software, a template is a predesigned form automatically set up to receive certain information or to perform specific procedures. Also, a plastic or paper cutout to be placed on or near the keyboard to remind users of key operations and procedures.

Text attribute   An enhancement of text, such as underlining or boldface, for adding emphasis.

Text box   An area within a dialog box where data needed for a chosen command is typed. May contain default text or be blank. The standard Windows editing keys can be used while typing here.

Text editor   A program that is used to create, edit, and view text files (ASCII). Notepad is an example of a Windows-based text editor. See *ASCII*.

Text mode   A way of presenting the entire character set quickly by having all characters built in to the computer's memory. Compare *Graphics mode*.

Thread   A series of newsgroup articles all dealing with the same topic. Someone replies to an article, and then someone else replies to the reply, and so on.

Thumbnail image   An image that is a smaller version of a larger one.

Tile   A way of arranging open windows on the desktop so that none overlap and all are visible. Each window occupies a portion of the screen.

Time slice   Amount of processing time allocated to an application by the computer while multitasking, usually expressed in milliseconds.

Title bar   The horizontal bar located along the top of a window that contains its title.

Toggle   An action typical of certain keys allowing a function to be alternately turned on and off by pressing the same key (much like a light switch).

Token ring   Local area network software methodology that works with networks arranged in a ring topology.

Toolbar   A row of graphical rectangles that suggest pushbuttons. Each pushbutton represents a command that can be executed directly by clicking the appropriate button. Also called *button bar, icon bar, tool palette*, and other names.

Topology   The design and physical arrangement of a network.

Touchscreen   A combination input device/monitor that allows information to be conveyed to the computer by touching specific areas on the monitor screen.

Track   A logical concentric circle on a disk for storing information.

Trash   A folder containing unwanted messages that can be emptied when the person desires.

True Type fonts   Scaleable fonts that can be sized to any height and print exactly as they appear onscreen.

Tutorial   Practice sessions that are frequently provided by software manufacturers as an aid to learning their software. Tutorials may be printed in a book or displayed onscreen.

U

UNIX   A multiuser, multitasking operating system, developed by AT&T and originally designed for use of minicomputers. Versions of UNIX are now available for the more powerful versions of microcomputers.

Upload   To copy data or files to another computer. Compare *Download*.

URL   An abbreviation for Uniform Resource Locator. A URL serves as identification for all Internet documents.

Usenet   A large network of computers that are home to the message forums called newsgroups.

User   Commonly used term for the person currently operating the computer and its software.

User interface   See *Interface*.

Utility program   A general-purpose computer program that performs an activity not specific to any one applications program. Often used for computer "housekeeping" operations, such as managing files.

V

Value   In spreadsheets, the contents of a cell beginning with either a numeral or one of several symbols. Values can be manipulated by arithmetic operations. Compare *Label*.

Veronica   An acronym for the Very Easy Rodent-Oriented Net-Wide Index to Computerized Archives. This is a search engine designed to search Gopherspace.

VGA   See *Video graphics array*.

Video graphics array (VGA)   An advanced color display adapter that allows for 16 colors (from a palette of 256), high-resolution text, and graphics.

Videodisc   A disk-based medium for storing and accessing video and audio information. Also called *laserdisc*.

Virtual memory   Hard disk space used to swap tasks and other information when actual system RAM runs low. Allows applications to work as if there were more RAM installed than actually present in the system.

Virus   A program designed to interfere with the normal operations of computers.

VoIP   Voice over Internet Protocol, a technology for telephone-like voice communications over the Internet.

W

Web guide   A type of search tool for locating information on the Web. Yahoo! is an example of a Web guide.

Web page   An HTML document that can be browsed and edited.

Web phone   See *Internet phone*.

Website   A collection of World Wide Web documents, usually consisting of a home page and several related pages. You might think of a website as an interactive electronic book.

What-if   A powerful feature of spreadsheets using formulas and functions to compute the values at cell addresses rather than computing the values themselves. Once the spreadsheet has been constructed, new data can be introduced and the entire spreadsheet recalculated to show the effect of the new data.

Window   Rectangular area on the desktop containing an application or document file. Windows can be sized and moved, minimized and maximized, opened or closed.

Windowing   The division of a single display screen into more than one viewing area.

Windows application   Programs designed for the Windows environment that can run only with Windows.

Wizard   A step-by-step procedure to help lead you through what might otherwise be a complex set of steps.

Word processor   A powerful applications package for creating, revising, and printing text documents.

Word wrap   A word-processing feature that automatically breaks a line of text at an appropriate point, continuing to the next line.

Workspace   The main work area in an application window that displays the program and any documents being used. Also called *drawing area, layout area*, or *client area*.

World Wide Web   The graphical interface portion of the Internet.

Write   The ability or process of moving information from one place to another and saving it at the destination, such as in memory or on disk. Compare *Read*.

Write-protect feature   A method of protecting storage media (diskettes) from being accidentally altered or written over.

X

XENIX   A version of UNIX.

BUSINESS DOCUMENTS

SECTION THREE

A manager discusses a business document with her assistant.

Photo by Jennifer Wauson.

The Business Letter

◇ APPEARANCE

Despite constantly improving forms of communication such as e-mail, the business letter still exerts enormous influence and deserves your close attention. Business letters are more formal and personal than e-mail. They are also more private.

Very few customers of a business ever see the home office or a branch office; this is often true even of small businesses. What customers do see is company correspondence. An untidy or ungrammatical letter gives the instant impression that the company's product or service is equally flawed. On the other hand, upon receiving a handsomely spaced, well-constructed, and well-organized letter, a customer unconsciously assumes it has come from an up-to-date, well-organized, and successful business.

Letter writing occupies at least one-third of all office work, and good writing is the most effective advertisement of your capability. Any skills you can acquire or improve in this area do double duty: They help you work more quickly and effectively while advancing your career.

Besides the skills you need for your own writing, you need to learn techniques of letter writing to handle your boss's correspondence. Most successful businesspeople have already mastered the mechanics of language, but many in authoritative positions lack such skills. They rely on their administrative assistants to see that their letters are satisfactory.

Any letter that comes from your keyboard—whether composed by you or your employer—must have a businesslike appearance that does not distract from the message it has to convey. The letter must be neat and symmetrical, and it must not have any typographical, grammatical, or spelling errors. Its language should clearly and simply go to the heart of the matter discussed. Its language and appearance should also be within the conventions of the commercial world. That is the reason each company selects its own style for presentation to its public.

The way in which a company is known to its customers, its good name, its reputation, and the quality of its products or services all comprise the corporate image. Image is very important, and many companies spend fortunes to have the image instantly recognized by the consumer, so no matter what style the company uses, use it consistently. This helps make the company's correspondence characteristically its own. That consistency also translates into dependability in the customer's mind.

◇ PARAGRAPHING

If you are new to the company, it's not likely you'll be invited to decide on which style of letter to use. A certain style may have already been selected long ago after various experiments. In accordance with that style, you'll be instructed to indent paragraphs or to block them and to put a double-space between paragraphs that are single-spaced. Your boss will no doubt also tell you his or her way of closing a letter, perhaps with the company's name and his or her signature with title below. You should conform to your employer's preference without question.

At the same time, you'll be told about *open punctuation* (no marks at the end of each line outside the text of the letter) or *closed punctuation* (marks after the date line, after each line of the addressee's name and address, after the complimentary close, and after the signature). Closed punctuation is usually used with blocked paragraphs.

◇ PARTS OF A BUSINESS LETTER

The various parts of a business letter (Figure 27–1) include:

- **Dateline**—Two to six lines below the last line of the printed letterhead. The date should be written out in this form: January 1, 2008.

- **Reference line**—A numerical file number, invoice number, policy number, or order number should appear on a new line below the date.

- **Special mailing notations**—Special notations such as "confidential" should appear two lines below the date.

- **Inside address**—Should include the addressee's title and full name, business title, business name, and full address.

- **Attention line**—If the letter is not addressed to any specific person, skip one space after the inside address and add "Attention: _____." You can make the letter go to the attention of a department.

- **Salutation**—One line after the attention line or the inside address. Examples include: Dear_____, Ladies and Gentlemen, Dear Sir or Madam, Dear (company name).

- **Subject line**—Gives an overview of what the letter is about. Can be used in place of a salutation.

- **Message**—The body of your letter with paragraph breaks; optional indentations for paragraphs, bullet lists, and number lists.

- **Complimentary close**—Appears two lines below the last line of the message. Either left justified or five spaces to the right of center.

- **Signature block**—Justified with the complimentary close with options of typed name and title, signature, or just signature.

- **Identification initials**—The initials of the typist appear left-justified two spaces below the signature block.

- **Enclosure notation**—Located with the identification initials or in place of them with the a notation such as: enc, encl, enclosures (3), 3 encs.

- **Copy notation**—Left-justified two lines below identification initials with the notation: cc: (person's full name or initials).

- **Postscript**—Two spaces below the last text on the page with a P.S. and then a short sentence.

◇ BEGINNING THE LETTER

The Date Line

Some offices show the *standard date line* near the body of the letter, ending at the right margin two spaces above the name of the addressee, which is written flush with the left margin. If the *centered date line* is chosen, it is placed two spaces below the letterhead as though it's part of the letterhead and centered exactly. This is an effective and well-balanced look if the company name and address in the letterhead fall in the center. If the letterhead is spread out across the whole top of the page ending at the right margin, then the standard date line seems more graceful and more balanced. When paper without a letterhead is used, the date line must be standard and must be a part of the three-line heading. This consists of the address of the writer and the date of the letter:

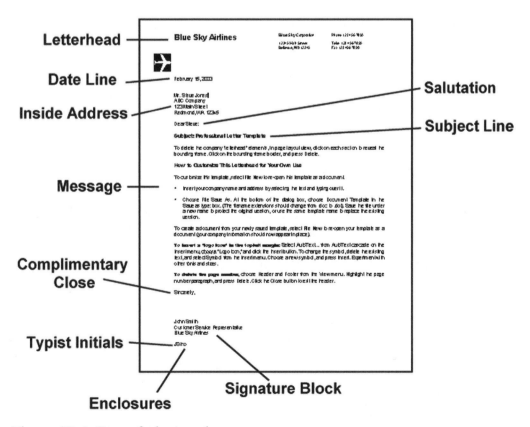

Figure 27–1. Parts of a business letter.

1501 Guadalupe Street
Austin, Texas 78702
May 27, 2008

Never place the name of the writer in the typewritten heading of the letter, for that belongs only at the end of the letter.

In typing the date line, never abbreviate the name of the month or use figures for it. Also, use numerals only for the day of the month; never add *nd*, *d*, *rd*, *st*, or *th* to the numerals. These sounds are heard but are never written.

WRONG:	**RIGHT:**
May 27th, 2008	May 27, 2008
June 22d, 2008	June 22, 2008

The Inside Address

The name and address of the addressee should be exactly as typed on the envelope.

If a street address is long enough to require two lines, place the less important of the two above:

Student Union Building
Northwestern State Teachers College
Alva, Oklahoma 76021

If an individual in a company is addressed, show the individual's name (and title) with the company's name below that, single-spaced. If there is a long address that must be carried over to a second line, indent the second line three spaces:

Mr. Rick Ritenour, President
San Francisco National Bank and
   Mortgage Association
1200 Market Street
San Francisco, California 99001

Never abbreviate part of the company name unless the company's registered name uses an abbreviation (Co., Inc., or &) and such abbreviation is shown on the company's official letterhead.

Figures are used for all house numbers except "one" (which is spelled out). If there is a numerical street number, separate the house number and street number by a dash:

3780–87 Street (Note: no *th* after 87)

Names of cities are never abbreviated; the names of states are also never abbreviated. There is one exception: Use the official U.S. Postal Service postal state abbreviations on the envelope address. (See Chapter 4 on mail services and shipping.)

Never use an abbreviation such as a percentage mark for "care of"; always spell the words out. Never use "care of" before a hotel name if the addressee is a guest there, and never use it before a company name if the addressee is employed there. However, if the addressee is temporarily receiving mail at the office of the company, "care of" may be used before the company name:

> Mr. Steve Eichman
> Care of The Rockwell Corporation
> 60 Wall Street
> New York, New York 10022

Titles

An individual's name is always preceded by a title, for example, Mr., Ms., Mrs., Miss, Dr., or Col. It's permissible to place initials denoting a degree after the name of an addressee; in that case, always omit the beginning title:

WRONG: **RIGHT:**

Dr. Gary K. Wilson, Ph.D.   Gary K. Wilson, Ph.D.

Reverend and *Honorable* are titles of respect and are preceded by the word *The. Mr.* is omitted:

WRONG: **RIGHT:**

Rev. John Wilson   The Rev. John Wilson

Reverend Jim Seckman   The Reverend Jim Seckman

Women and Men

In addressing a woman, it's useful to refer to previous correspondence from the individual to see whether she included a courtesy title when she typed or signed her name. If you have no previous correspondence, use these general guidelines: *Miss* is used for an unmarried woman; *Mrs.* is used with her husband's full name (if known) for a married woman or a widow. If a divorcee retains her married name, use *Mrs.* plus her own name, not her husband's. *Ms.* is used in any of the above cases if the woman prefers it; it's also used if you do not know the woman's marital status or if you're addressing a divorcee who has resumed her maiden name.

Address a professional woman by her title, followed by her given and last name:

> Dr. Bernice Wilson

The previous custom was to use *Mr.* as the title when the gender of the addressee was in doubt. The current custom, to avoid giving offense, is more likely to use the addressee's full name without a title, in both the address and the salutation:

Dear Toby Wilson

However, if the letter has some importance, it's worth making a quick call to the other party to get the proper title. Simply say to whoever answers the telephone: "I'm addressing a letter to Pat Richardson. Is that Mr. Richardson or Ms.?" This can save you and your employer much embarrassment later on.

Business Titles

Business titles are never abbreviated:

WRONG:	RIGHT:
Mr. Mark Giddens, Sr. Ed.	Mr. Mark Giddens, Senior Editor
Ms. Julie Seckman, Asst. Mgr.	Ms. Julie Seckman, Assistant Manager

When you are writing to a person holding more than one office within a company, use the highest title, unless you are replying to a specific letter signed by him or her under another title as applying to the subject covered. When you are writing to a department of a company, rather than to a person within the company, place the company name on the first line and the department on the second line:

MB's Department Store
Electronics Department
120 Irving Mall
Irving, Texas 76022

Attention Line

An *attention line* refers the letter to the person or department in charge of the situation covered. The word *Attention* is followed by the name of the individual or department. Do not abbreviate the word *Attention* or follow it with a colon.

The attention line is placed two spaces below the last line of the name and address of the addressee, either flush with the left margin of the letter or in the center of the page when paragraphs are blocked. When paragraphs are indented, the attention line is placed in the center of the page.

The attention line is never used in a letter to an individual but only in a letter having a plural addressee, in which case the letter is written to the entire company and not to the person named in the attention line. The salutation must always agree (singular or plural) with the name of the addressee, not with the name on the attention line. For example:

Johnson Smith & Company, Inc.
1500 Main Street
Greenville, Texas 75401

Attention Mr. Horace Wauson

Gentlemen:

Salutation

The salutation is typed two spaces below the addressee's address or the attention line, flush with the left margin. The first word of the salutation begins with a capital, as does the name of the addressee. In business letters, the salutation is followed by a colon. In personal letters, the salutation is followed by a comma:

Dear Governor Thompson:

My Dear Mrs. Thomas:

Dear Jane,

Sometimes you are required to write a letter addressed to no particular person or company (such as a letter of recommendation); then you use capitals for the salutation:

TO WHOM IT MAY CONCERN:

Subject Line

The *subject line* of a letter is an informal way of categorizing or titling the letter. Many letters in business must begin with a subject line after the salutation, a valuable aid in the distribution of mail that also facilitates filing. The subject line can be centered, but when the paragraphs are blocked, it is flush with the left margin.

Do not type "Re" or "Subject" before the subject line. Underline the subject line, but if it occupies more than one line, underline only the bottom line, letting the line extend the length of the longest line in the subject.

Be sure to word the subject line so that it is helpful. If the letter is about an order of silk, a subject line reading simply "Silk" would contribute nothing. If, however, the subject line should read

Silk Returned, Our Shipping Order 8939

the clerk opening the letter could promptly route it to the person within the organization best able to reply.

◆ CONTENTS

With the body of the letter, first consider its appearance. You must judge how long the letter will be and how much space it will occupy in order to place it on the page as within a picture frame—never too high, never too low, always with proper side margins. If you create the letter with word-processing software, you can add spaces to the top of the letter or change the page margins after you have written the letter.

The body of the letter should be brief and straightforward. The letter should have the same ease as a personal conversation. Although you must write whatever your boss dictates, many times while typing you can ease the language a bit to improve its impression on the reader; it's possible to do this with just a word or two more or less that won't call attention to any change. Of course, you should always have your boss approve your revisions. It's your responsibility to see that the letter going forth is creditable in every way to your employer's interests.

The length of the letter should be in accordance with its importance. If the letter is too short, it may have a curt tone and may seem to slight the recipient. If the letter is too long, the recipient's attention may wander after the first page, and he or she may not read the letter in its entirety.

CLOSING THE LETTER

Complimentary Close

When the salutation has been "Dear Sir" or "My Dear Sir," no personal connection exists between the writer and the recipient. Thus, the complimentary closing can be "Yours truly" or "Very truly yours." "Sincerely" or "Sincerely yours" is appropriate when there is an established personal as well as a business relationship, but it is used only in letters to individuals, never to a company. "Respectfully yours" appears only on letters addressed to a person of acknowledged authority or in letters of great formality.

Avoid the use of such complimentary closes as "Yours for lower prices" or "I remain" and other hanging phrases. In addition, "Cordially yours" is not suitable in a business letter. It is often used but this is incorrect since the phrase is too familiar for business. Avoid it.

The Signature

If in the body of the letter the writer has referred to *we*, *us*, or *ours*, the company—and not an individual in the company—is writing the letter. Consequently, the signature would then consist of the typed name of the company under the complimentary close, the space for the writer's signature, and the typed name of the writer with his or her title. The whole signature is typed in block form beginning under the first letter of the complimentary close. In some blocked paragraph letters, the complimentary close begins at the left margin; then the signature also begins at the left margin.

> Very truly yours,
> GRAM'S QUILT COMPANY
> Evelyn Wauson, President

Never put a line for the writer's signature. This is a superfluous and old-fashioned practice.

When the writer has referred within the letter to *I, me, my,* or *mine,* this means that he or she—not the company—is writing the letter. Therefore, the writer's name is typed with his or her title, omitting the company name entirely.

Very truly yours,

Evelyn Wauson, President

A woman may include a courtesy title in her typed signature, so as to allow the recipient of the letter to reply appropriately. Parentheses may be used:

(Miss) Louise A. Scott

Ms. Tina Anderson-Tate

Mrs. Pat Brueck

The courtesy title is blocked with the complimentary close, not extended to the left of it. For a married woman, the signature may consist of either the woman's first name and her surname or her husband's name preceded by Mrs. (no parentheses).

Sincerely yours,
Mrs. Ruth Wilson

A widow may sign as though her husband were living. A divorced woman no longer uses the given name or initial of her former husband. She may use whatever courtesy title she wishes, whether or not she keeps her married surname.

Other Elements

Reference Initials

It's no longer considered necessary to type reference initials—the initials of the letter writer and the typist. However, if the company requires identification of this kind for its files, show these on the file copy only and not the original. The writer's initials are typed in capitals, the typist's in lowercase. To separate the two, use a colon or a slash. Many companies require only the typist's initials since the writer's initials are obvious from the signature of the letter.

When using a word processor, write the initials or name of the person dictating the letter on the office file copy.

BUSINESS LETTER

Enclosures

Mention of enclosures should be placed two lines below the reference initials. It may seem to serve no purpose to add "Enc. 2" if the body of the letter mentions the enclosure of two papers. However, the mailing department may find this notation helpful to sort outgoing mail. In addition, as the recipient of such mail, this helps you keep the contents of letters together as you prepare to distribute them without having to read every line.

Postscript

Sometimes the letter writer takes advantage of the postscript—following the initials, "P.S.," two spaces below the signature or reference initials—to dramatize some bit of information. This is acceptable. However, you should never use the postscript to add something that was forgotten during the writing of the letter. Instead, rewrite the letter.

◆ A LAST LOOK

Before you consider the letter finished, decide if it looks like a picture on the page; that is, have you centered the whole thing? Ask yourself: If you received this letter, would you be favorably impressed? Then check your grammar, spelling, and punctuation again.

A business letter should be folded neatly and precisely. The side edges must match, the typing inside the folds must seem to be protected, and only the fewest folds for the perfect fit into the envelope must be used. Upon taking the letter from the envelope, the recipient should be able to begin reading the letter immediately and should find it attractive. Remember that this is the reader's first impression of your organization.

◆ LETTERS WRITTEN BY THE ADMINISTRATIVE ASSISTANT

Letters written over your own signature usually include acknowledgments of correspondence received while your boss is away, letters requesting appointments, follow-up letters, and letters requesting information that another secretary can furnish. While these letters are an excellent opportunity to show your capability and initiative, always keep in mind that service to your boss and the company is the main factor in deciding which letters to write without dictation.

Many of the routine letters described in this chapter may be handled electronically through e-mail. However, because business letters are more formal, personal, and usually generate results better than e-mail, many executives prefer them over e-mail for certain types of correspondence. Regardless of whether the document is printed on paper or transmitted as an e-mail or fax, you should follow the same guidelines.

Planning the Letter

Good ideas can be clouded by verbosity, while clear and forceful words make for quick understanding. Therefore, plan your letters before you write a word. You'll save yourself precious time and effort and add to the company's bottom line because the time element is the greatest cost connected with writing a letter.

To begin, ask yourself: Is this letter supposed to serve the writer, the reader, or both? Will the letter give information, or will it request information? Will it ask for action? What other data must it contain? Before you write, be sure that you have all necessary information on the subject, so you can readily refer to previous correspondence or double-check your information. If you're hazy about the subject of the letter, the reader will be as well.

In the first sentence, mention your purpose in writing so that the reader immediately knows what the letter is about. Then follow with whatever explanation is necessary, using a positive tone at all times—that is, words chosen to evoke a positive response. Speak directly to the reader from his or her own point of view, not from yours. The reader must see the advantages of replying favorably.

Use concise language, but be as natural as possible, as though you were speaking to the other person. Reserve the last sentence to request a response if there is to be further correspondence on the subject. Always make that last sentence complete, never hanging. A hanging statement is one that leads into the signature, such as "Hoping this meets with your approval, I am . . . " If that's the thought you wish to express, state it instead as, "I hope this meets with your approval."

In a business letter, there's no place for cute or clever remarks or for slang. Your use of slang may be misinterpreted as your not knowing the correct English equivalent. Also avoid exaggeration, sarcasm, or any remarks derogatory to any person or to any product—even competitors.

Letters Written for the Employer's Signature

Your boss may prefer that all letters be written over his or her name rather than having some letters written over yours. This may be true even if you compose the letters and have permission to sign the boss's name yourself.

When you're composing such a letter, use the boss's characteristic language and style. If your employer usually dictates in a short, concise manner, word the letter in the same way. If your boss usually goes into detail, do the same. And when you sign your employer's name, try to duplicate his or her handwriting as nearly as possible. In other words, make the reader think that your employer took the time to dictate the letter and sign it. To do less is an insult to the recipient.

Never write "Dictated but not read" or "Signed in Mr. Wilson's absence." It's insulting to the recipient, implying that your employer either didn't have the time or didn't take the time to read and sign the letter personally. It also hints that you could not be trusted to write what your employer asked you to write.

For the same reasons, don't sign the boss's name and then add your initials beside it. If you find it useful to show the true writer and true signer, make a notation on only the file copy for future reference.

When you write a letter on your employer's behalf but in your own name, sign it, but do not type your name below the signature line. Instead, type:

Sincerely yours,

Secretary to Mr. Wilson

◆ ROUTINE LETTERS

Encourage your boss to trust you with routine correspondence by emphasizing the enormous time savings it will produce. Then, when the boss discovers that you can prepare such letters for signature without dictation, he or she may reward you with more challenging correspondence. Following are the types of routine letters you should be able to handle with ease.

Appointments and Acknowledgments

You may write letters that request an appointment for your boss or acknowledge letters requesting an appointment with him or her. In each letter, always refer to the reason for the appointment and the suggested time. Always request a confirmation.

If a certain time has been requested and your employer approves, confirm the appointment accordingly. If your boss will be occupied at the requested time, suggest another and ask for confirmation. Be sure to keep a record of appointments suggested and not yet confirmed. If there is ever a disagreement over whether your employer broke an appointment, you will have proof otherwise in writing For this reason, if the back-and-forth process of setting an appointment moves from the letter to the telephone, always send a letter to confirm it in writing.

Reservations

In writing for hotel reservations, state the type of accommodation desired, the name of the person desiring it, and the date and time of arrival, with the probable date of departure. Then request confirmation.

Usual reservations for plane or train travel may be made through a travel agent who understands your employer's requirements and makes every effort to satisfy. Travel agents can be invaluable to a business, and their services are free because their fees are paid by the airline or hotel. When using a travel agency, a telephone call will substitute for a letter to request arrangements; however, do request written confirmation once arrangements have been made.

Follow-Up

In some offices, secretaries use a follow-up file (or a tickler file) to check on delayed replies after a certain lapse of time. When you write a follow-up letter, refer to the previous correspondence, identifying the last letter by date as well as content, and perhaps enclosing a copy if it contains a great deal of detail that could be useful

Dear John:

I have just read in *The Wall Street Journal* of your promotion to General Sales Manager. I don't think that Smith and Company could have chosen a better person for the job.

Sincerely yours,

[signed] Phil

Dear John:

I appreciate your generous letter about my promotion to Executive Vice President. Such good wishes and kind words will help me do a better job, I'm sure.

Thanks for your note and for your valued friendship.

Sincerely yours,

[signed] Phil

Figure 27–2. Sample letters of congratulations and acknowledgments.

should the original not be available to the addressee.

If you have many follow-up letters to write, instead of composing separate reminders, prepare a form request that can be duplicated on the copier machine or in your word processor. When follow-ups are sent outside the company, often the enclosure of a stamped return envelope will speed a reply.

Sample Model Letters

When a letter is typical of ones you send out frequently, make an extra copy, and place it in a special binder or keep a copy in the memory of your computer so you can refer to it as a model when you have to write that sort of letter again. On a typed letter, note the space plan for margins and center measurements so you have the format already arranged. With a computer or word processor, these margins and center measurements are much easier to reset.

Personal Letters

You'll find that many of the letters in this "letter bank" will be from your boss to another businessperson, yet the subject will be personal in nature. These letters are among the most difficult to write, since they must display sincerity in a variety of situations: sending congratulations, declining invitations, offering condolences, and the like.

Figures 27–2 through 27–4 are samples of personal letters to business associates that you may adapt for your own use. Such letters should use the salutation that your boss would normally use for the recipient. For the signature, use the name the employer is called by that recipient.

Dear Mrs. Wilson:

It is with great regret that I just read of your son's passing.

I know no words of mine can console you in this sorrowful time, but I do want you to know of my deepest sympathy. You have many friends who are thinking of you.

Sincerely yours,

Philip Brown, President

Dear Mr. Crenshaw:

All of us at Thorne and Sons were saddened to learn of your wife's death. We know there is nothing we can say to help you in this time of grief, but we do want you to know that we extend to you our very deep sympathy.

Sincerely yours,

Philip Brown, President

Dear Mrs. Holmes:

We at Liberty Oil Company were sorry to read of the tornado that struck your Denison factory. We know the loss was very great, but we know also that you will rise and go ahead with rebuilding.

If we can be of service in helping you overcome your present problems, please call on us. We have enjoyed doing business with R. G. Holmes Corporation and look forward to resuming our enjoyable relationship in the near future.

Sincerely yours,

Philip Brown, President

Figure 27–3. Sample letters of condolences.

Personal Service and Hospitality

When a person has done your employer a personal service or has entertained the boss without financial remuneration when he or she is out of town, that person should be thanked in a letter that can be written by you (Figure 27–5).

Introductions

Letters of introduction written by you for the boss's signature may be mailed or prepared for delivery in person. Such letters should contain the name of the introduced person, the reason for the introduction, the personal or business qualifications of the person, and a courtesy statement (Figures 27–6 and 27–7).

Dear Henry:
    Your card and beautiful bouquet of roses helped a great deal to make last week bearable.

    I am back at the office and feel I shall be good as ever very soon. The accident was a shock, but with good friends like you, I know the days ahead will be brighter.

    You may be sure that I appreciate your friendship all the more at a time like this.

Sincerely yours,

[signature only]

Figure 27–4. Sample letter of thanks.

Dear Janet:
    If it hadn't been for your keen mind and able assistance, our recent sales meeting might have been a complete flop. Because I had never before conducted such a meeting, I certainly was lucky to have your help.

    Thank you for your good judgment and wise suggestions.

Sincerely yours,

[signature only]

Figure 27–5. Sample letter of personal service and hospitality.

Invitations

Letters of invitation should be gracious without undue formality. Always tell when, where, and why the event will take place. (See Figures 27–8 and 27–9.)

Acceptance of Invitations

Letters of acceptance should be brief, appreciative, and enthusiastic. If the letter of invitation failed to include complete details, the letter of acceptance should ask for specific information (Figure 27–10).

Declinations

Letters declining an invitation should express appreciation and enthusiasm, with an assurance of regret or an explanation (Figures 27–11 and 27–12).

    Because this cancellation comes so close to the date of the speech, this letter would immediately be delivered by messenger or would be faxed or e-mailed if the addressee is in another city. It is wise to follow up with a phone call.

Dear Mr. Fielding:

This will introduce a good friend of mine, John August, who is associated with our state's Department of Commerce. He has heard of the fine work you are doing in Ohio and hopes he will have a chance to talk with you for a few minutes when he visits Cincinnati next Tuesday, March 22.

I have asked Mr. August to telephone you upon his arrival in Cincinnati to learn whether you can see him on that day. If you can, I shall appreciate it. I think you will enjoy meeting him.

It was great to see you at the Boston convention, and I look forward to the Buffalo convention in September.

Sincerely yours,

Philip Brown, President

Figure 27–6. Sample letter of introduction to a business associate.

Dear Tom:

A very good friend of mine, John August, will be passing through Nashville on his way to Boston next Tuesday, and I have asked him to stop by your office. John is a fellow you will enjoy meeting.

I shall appreciate any courtesy you may extend to him while he is in Nashville—his first visit to your great city, by the way.

Sincerely yours,

[signature only]

Figure 27–7. Sample letter of introduction to a personal friend.

◇ INTEROFFICE MEMORANDUMS AND E-MAILS

If the company you work for is large, much of your correspondence is with other departments or perhaps with branch offices scattered throughout the company. The office memorandum, commonly called a memo, is a popular and inexpensive method of communicating with these fellow employees.

In many offices, paper memos have been replaced by e-mails. However, there are many types of communication that are inappropriate for e-mail. For example, confidential information or information that should not be forwarded should be printed on paper and not sent as e-mail.

Memos should be directed only to persons within the organization and should be signed or initialed by the sender. If a memorandum is confidential in nature, enclose it in a sealed envelope. If copies are sent to individuals other than the person or persons addressed, a notation to that effect should be made at the lower left comer of the form. If

Dear Mr. Brueck:

The American Consolidated Life Insurance Company is holding a dinner next Thursday evening honoring its million-dollar-a-year salespeople. Will you join us as our honored guest?

Since you would be seated at the head table, we are asking you to join us in Room 200 of the Waldorf Hotel at seven-thirty, so that we may arrive at the banquet room in a group.

Sincerely yours,

Nora Drake, President

Dear Roger:

Arthur Whitfield is coming to town next Friday, and Mary Smith and I are entertaining him at a luncheon at the Ritz. We hope you can set aside a couple of hours so as to join us. I am sure Arthur will be happy to see you, as Mary and I shall also.

The luncheon will be held in the Persian Room at twelve-fifteen.

Sincerely yours,

[signature only]

Figure 27–8. Sample invitations to attend a luncheon or dinner.

Dear Mr. Lee:

As President of the Chicago Rotary Club, I have been asked to arrange the program for our next Thursday noon meeting. I know that all of our Chicago Rotarians would like to hear the address you gave in Detroit last week (I was privileged to be in attendance there) on the subject of "The International Situation."

Next Thursday's meeting will be held in the Venetian Room of the Drake Hotel. I hope you will be with us to give our members the same treat you afforded the Detroit Rotarians.

Sincerely yours,

Philip Brown, President

Figure 27–9. Sample invitation to give an address.

you wish to create memo forms from scratch, use plain white paper. If your office is equipped with a word-processing computer, store the basic form in the computer's memory and retrieve it when needed. Figure 27–13 contains an example.

◇ PAPER SELECTION

Paper selection is important for some written communications. Paper and envelopes come in various sizes, colors, and qualities. One way to rate a particular paper is by its basis

Dear Miss Brett:

It is a pleasure to accept your invitation to attend the dinner next Thursday evening honoring your million-dollar-a-year salespeople.

I shall be in Room 200 of the Waldorf Hotel promptly at seven-thirty, as you request.

Thank you very much for your invitation.

Sincerely yours,

Philip Brown

Dear Mr. Brown:

I shall be delighted to speak to the Chicago Rotary Club next Thursday. Thank you for inviting me.

Your suggestion that I repeat my Detroit address means that I won't have to prepare a new one.

I shall look forward to seeing you in the Venetian Room at noon.

Sincerely yours,

Barry Lee

Figure 27–10. Sample acceptances of an invitation.

weight. For example, 20 lb paper is often used in copy machines and laser printers, while 100 lb paper can be used for report covers.

Paper with rag content and cotton is more expensive than other varieties and is often a choice for letterhead. The standard size for letterhead is $8\frac{1}{2} \times 11$ inches.

ENVELOPES

Envelopes come in a variety of sizes. Security envelopes have extra thickness so that documents cannot be read through the envelope by holding it up to a light source. Windowed envelopes have a clear plastic window that allows an address to show through. Typical envelope sizes include:

- No $6\frac{3}{4}$—$3\frac{5}{8}$ inches × $6\frac{1}{2}$ inches

- No 9—$3\frac{7}{8}$ inches × $8\frac{7}{8}$ inches

- No 10—$4\frac{1}{2}$ inches × $9\frac{1}{2}$ inches

Addressing Envelopes

Envelopes can be addressed by using a typewriter, by printing on sheets of adhesive-backed labels, or by using the envelope feature of your word-processing software.

Dear Miss Brett:

Only yesterday, I accepted an invitation to speak in Boston on July 12, the date of your dinner meeting honoring your million-dollar-a-year salespeople. This will make it impossible for me to be your guest that evening.

It was kind of you to invite me, and I regret my inability to attend. I hope the occasion will be a very successful one.

Sincerely yours,

Steve Wauson

My Dear Mrs. Scott:

In reply to your letter of May 3 inviting me to participate in your association's fund-raising campaign, I appreciate your thoughtfulness in writing to me.

I am familiar with your association's good work, and in the past it has been my pleasure to contribute to it. It is with regret, therefore, that I must tell you that all my available funds for purposes of this nature have been pledged. It is not possible for me to be a party to your worthy program at this time.

You have my best wishes for a highly successful campaign.

Sincerely yours,

Mrs. Susan Wilson

Figure 27–11. Sample letters of declination.

Regardless of which method you use, the address should contain the following:

- Name
- Company
- City, State ZIP + 4

- Title
- Street address, suite or apartment number

You should capitalize the first letter of every word in the address, except prepositions (*of* and *for*), conjunctions under four letters, and articles. You should leave one space between the state name and zip code. The state name can be spelled out, or you can use the two-letter abbreviation (which is preferred by the Postal Service). The next to the last line in the address should be the street address, P.O. Box, rural route, or highway address.

Word-Processing Envelope Feature

When using the envelope feature in your word processor, you should accept the defaults for the envelope size. This ensures that the address falls within the OCR read area for the U.S. Postal Service. If the software allows, include USPS POSTNET bar code above or below the address block.

In Microsoft Word, you can access the envelope feature by clicking the Tools Menu, then clicking ENVELOPES AND LABELS. On the Envelopes and Labels dialog, you can enter the delivery address and return address. If you click the OPTIONS button, you can click the

Dear Mr. Bryson:

I dislike writing a letter that will cause someone inconvenience, but this one falls within that category, to my regret.

This morning, I was advised that a close relative had passed away in Denver, and I shall be leaving this afternoon to attend the service tomorrow, the day of your meeting.

I am sorry that I shall not be able to speak to your group and especially that you will have to find a speaker to replace me at this late date. I hope you understand that I am helpless to avoid this trip.

I hope your meeting will be successful in every way.

Sincerely yours,

Nora Drake, President

Figure 27–12. Sample letter of declination.

TO: Mary Anne Scott, Shipping Department Manager
FROM: Bob Brueck, President
DATE: May 12, 2008
SUBJECT: Meeting to discuss various overseas carriers

A meeting has been scheduled for Tuesday, May 12, in my office to discuss with several carrier representatives suggested methods and costs to deliver our products to international markets. Your attendance is requested.

Distribution:
Tom Alberton
Martha Reeves

Figure 27–13. Sample interoffice memorandum.

check box to add Delivery Point Barcode to the envelope or label. Figure 27–14 shows the Envelopes and Labels dialog in Microsoft Word.

Creating Envelopes by Merging an Address List

With Microsoft Word, you can print envelopes for a mass mailing by merging addresses from an address list. The first step is to create a new blank document. On the Tools Menu, if you click MAIL MERGE you can view the Mail Merge dialog. It allows you to select a main document and a data source, and then to merge the two documents. The Mail Merge function can be used to print form letters, address labels, or envelopes. Figure 27–15 shows the Mail Merge dialog.

Figure 27–14. Microsoft Word Envelopes and Labels dialog box.
Screen shot reprinted by permission from Microsoft Corporation.

Windowed Envelopes

When using windowed envelopes, adjust the placement of the inside address so there will be a 1/8-inch clearance around the edges of the address inside the window.

Return Addresses

A return address should always be included; however, the writer's name is not necessary. The return address should include the company name, street address, city, state, and zip. It should be aligned at the left about a half-inch from top and a half-inch from the side of the envelope. Any special notations such as *confidential*, *personal*, or *hold for arrival* should be typed three spaces below the return address.

Folding Letters

The standard way to fold letters is to fold them into thirds. Start by bringing the bottom third of the letter up and then making a crease. Fold the top of the letter down to within 3/8 inch of the bottom crease. Then make a second crease. The second fold side goes into the envelope first.

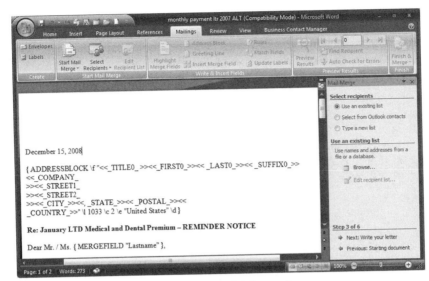

Figure 27–15. Microsoft Word's Mail Merge feature.

Screen shot reprinted by permission from Microsoft Corporation.

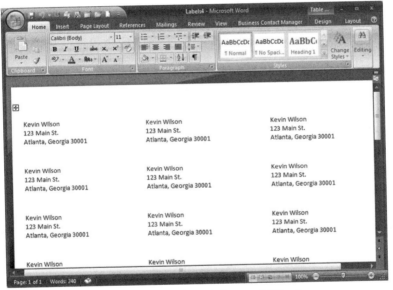

Figure 27–16. A page of labels in Microsoft Word.

Screen shot reprinted by permission from Microsoft Corporation.

 LABELS

You can use the labels feature of a word-processing program just like the envelope feature. You can purchase adhesive label sheets from companies such as Avery and set the word processor to match the label number.

You can type single addresses or a page of the same address (useful for creating return address labels). Figure 27–16 shows an example of the labels ready to print in Microsoft Word.

Other Written Communications

◆ REPORTS

As an administrative assistant, you may be asked to create a variety of different reports for your boss. Some of the reports will be routine and will be created from various sources already available. Other more formal reports will require input from your boss in the form of dictation, supplied documents, and a series of reviews and revisions. There are four general types of reports that will be created by administrative assistants. They are:

1. Memorandum report
2. Letter report
3. Short report
4. Formal report

Memorandum Report

The memorandum report is a routine and informal report that might be prepared on a weekly basis to, for example, report the status of projects to upper management. This report is objective and impersonal in tone. There may be some introductory comments; however, they are very brief. Headings and subheadings are used for quick reference and to highlight certain aspects of the report. Usually, the memorandum report is single-spaced and printed on plain paper; however, in some businesses, this report may be sent as an e-mail or e-mail attachment.

Letter Report

The letter report is normally a one-page letter that is printed on company letterhead. Letterhead second sheets are used for continuation pages. The letter report is most often sent outside the company to consultants, clients, or the board of directors. The report should have headings and subheadings to organize the content.

Short Report

The short report differs from the memorandum and letter reports because it has a title page, a preliminary summary with conclusions and recommendations, authorization information, a statement of the problem, findings, conclusions, and recommendations. The short report may contain tables and graphs and can be either single- or double-spaced. Headings and subheadings are used to organize the content and to emphasize certain aspects.

The title page has the name, title, and address of the person or company to whom the report is being submitted. In addition, the title page includes the preparer's name, title, and address. Long report titles are divided and centered.

Formal Report

The formal report is more complex and has a greater length compared to the short report. Included in the formal report are the following:

- Report cover
- Title fly
- Letter of authorization
- Foreword or Preface
- Table of contents
- List of figures
- Report body
- Appendix
- Bibliography

- Flyleaf
- Title page
- Letter of transmittal
- Acknowledgments
- List of tables
- Synopsis
- Endnotes or footnotes
- Glossary
- Index

There are specific margin settings for a formal report. The top margin for the first page should be 2 inches, and the top margin for subsequent pages should be 1 inch. Bottom margins on all pages are 1 inch. The left and right margins on all pages are 1 inch. For bound reports, the left margin should be 1½ inches to allow extra room for the binding.

Spacing for the body of the report can be single- or double-spaced. Set-off quotations should be single-spaced, as are footnotes.

Paragraph indentations should be 5 spaces. Long quotations should be indented 5 spaces in from body. Numbered and bullet lists should also be indented 5 spaces in from body. Footnotes should match paragraph margins.

Primary headings should be left justified, bold, with additional space above and below. A 20- to 24-point sans serif font such as Helvetica should be used. Secondary headings should be left justified, bold, with a 16- to 18-point sans serif font. Third-level headings should also be left justified, bold, with a 12- to 14-point sans serif font.

There should be no page number on the title page, although a page number should be assigned for numbering purposes. The front matter should use small roman numerals for numbering. The body of the report should use Arabic numerals starting with 1. Page numbers should be either centered or in the right margin, ½ inch to 1 inch from the top, or ½ inch from the bottom.

Headings and Subheadings

You should use a numbering system for headings. You can use numbers or a combination of numbers and letters. Figure 28–1 shows two alternative heading numbering systems.

Headings and subheadings should be parallel in structure. The following are examples of nonparallel and parallel structure.

Nonparallel

1. Reading the Manual
2. The Instructions
3. How to Install the Software

Parallel

1. Reading the Manual
2. Following the Instructions
3. Installing the Software

Report Cover

The cover should have the title and author's name. The title should be in all capital letters. The cover may optionally be printed on card stock paper.

Flyleaf

The flyleaf is a blank page that is inserted after the cover. A flyleaf is also sometimes added to the end of the report just before the back cover.

```
1. Main Heading
        1.1  Subheading
        1.2  Subheading
                1.2.1   Third-level heading
                1.2.2   Third-level heading

I.  Main Heading
        a.   Subheading
        b.   Subheading
                1.      Third-level heading
                2.      Third-level leading
```

Figure 28–1. Heading numbering systems.

Title Fly

The title fly is a single page with just the report title in all caps, centered on the upper third of the page.

Title Page

The title page should include the title of the report in all caps, followed by the subtitle if there is one. It should also contain the recipient's name, corporate title, department, company name, and address. The page should also include the preparer's name, corporate title, department, company name, and address. The date the report is submitted should be included on the title page as well.

Letter of Authorization

The letter of authorization should be printed on letterhead and should explain who authorized the report and any specific details regarding the authorization.

Letter of Transmittal

The letter of transmittal is a cover letter for the report. It explains the purpose of the report, its scope, limitations, research used, special comments, and acknowledgments. The letter of transmittal may take the place of a Foreword or Preface.

Foreword or Preface

The Foreword or Preface contains the author's statement about the purpose of the report. This is an optional section that is used to provide background on the project or to thank individuals who supported it.

Acknowledgments

The acknowledgments page should list individuals, companies, or institutions that assisted in creating the report.

Table of Contents

The table of contents should include headings, subheadings, and third-level headings with page numbers. You can use an outline style with a heading numbering system. If you are using a word processor, you can automatically generate a table of contents based on the heading styles.

List of Tables

If tables are used in the report, you should include a list of tables in the front matter. The list should include table numbers, page numbers, and the descriptions that are used as table titles in the body of the report.

List of Figures

If illustrations are used in the report, you should include a list of figures in the front matter. The list should include figure numbers, page numbers, and the captions that are used with the figures in the body of the report.

Synopsis

The synopsis is a brief summary that presents the main points to be covered later in the report.

Report Body

The body of the report should include an introduction to the report, an introduction to the major sections (headings, subheadings, and third-level headings), and a summary at the end of major sections. The body should include normal paragraph breaks, bullet lists, numbered lists, illustrations, and tables.

Endnotes or Footnotes

A footnote is a note of text written at the bottom of a page in a report in order to cite a reference or make additional comments on content in the main body of the text. A footnote is normally labeled with a superscript number. Endnotes are similar to footnotes, but rather than being on the bottom of a page, they are listed at the end of a section or at the end of the report.

Appendix

If there are supplementary reference materials or sources of research, you can include them at the end of the report in a separate section, the Appendix.

Glossary

The glossary should include technical terms with definitions along with any abbreviations. Abbreviations should be spelled out the first time they are used in the body of the report.

Bibliography

The bibliography should list all sources of information that were used to compile the report.

Index

An index is optional for many reports. If you are using a word-processing program such as Microsoft Word, an index can be generated automatically similarly to the way a table of contents is created. However, you need to mark index entries throughout your document before you ask the program to create the index.

Indexes are an alphabetical listing. The first word of each entry has an initial capital letter. The rest of the words lowercase. Subentries in the index are like subheadings and are indented one or two spaces. Cross-references direct the reader to another location in the index. Punctuation is kept to a minimum.

◇ DOCUMENTING SOURCES

You should always acknowledge the work of other writers to allow the reader to judge the quality of the information based on the quality of the source, and to enable the reader to verify information. Some writers use parenthetical references to document sources; others include footnotes or endnotes.

Footnotes and Endnotes

Footnotes are short notes set at the bottom of the page. Endnotes are placed at the end of the report. In one common method for documenting sources, both footnotes and endnotes are numbered, with a small number inserted at the end of the text being referred to. The corresponding footnote appears at the bottom of the page; the corresponding endnote appears at the end of the report.

Footnotes and endnotes should include the author's name (or authors' names), the title of the source, the place of publication and publisher, the date, and the page reference. For example:

> James Stroman, Kevin Wilson, and Jennifer Wauson, *The Administrative Assistant's and Secretary's Handbook* (New York, AMACOM Books, 2007), page 201.

You can also document sources by inserting parenthetical references within the text. The parenthetical references generally include only author names and the page being cited, for example: (Stroman, Wilson, and Wauson, p. 201). Full publication information appears in a bibliography (or list of works consulted) at the end of the report.

Bibliographies

Bibliographies list all works citied in the report footnotes/endnotes or parenthetical references. You may also include research that was not cited as a specific reference but was used to create the report. The bibliography listings are ordered alphabetically by author's last name. If there is no main author, then the book title is used. The author's surname comes first. Additional authors are listed first name, last name. For example:

> Stroman, James, Kevin Wilson, and Jennifer Wauson, *The Administrative Assistant's and Secretary's Handbook* (New York, AMACOM Books, 2007), page 201.

◇ REPORT TEMPLATES

If you are using a word-processing program such as Microsoft Word, you can create a report by using one of the report templates that are available. By clicking FILE, NEW, and then clicking the REPORTS tab, you will see three default reports that you can choose from:

1. Contemporary Report

2. Elegant Report

3. Professional Report

◇ PRESS RELEASES

When writing a press release, start with the main idea first, followed by major details related to the idea, followed by minor details, and then finally supplemental information. The major elements to include are the five Ws: who, what, when, where, and why. Also, don't forget to explain how.

A press release should be factual, interesting, and informative. All the details should be carefully verified and proofread.

Press releases should be printed on normal size office paper and double-spaced. All margins should be 1 inch.

The top of the press release should include contact information, with name, address, phone number, and e-mail. The words *Press Release* and *For Immediate Release* or *For Release* (and then the date) should also be included.

If a press release is longer than one page, *MORE* is typed at the bottom of the first page in all capital letters, centered or on the right side. Subsequent pages are numbered and should include a short title caption, left justified.

At the conclusion of the press release, type five number signs ##### or *-end-* or *(END)* .

◇ TABLES

Tables are a good way to organize information into a compact, easy-to-read form. Word-processing software programs, such as Microsoft Word, have features for creating and formatting tables.

The default table has horizontal and vertical grid lines. You can determine the number of rows and columns as you create the table. You can also add additional rows or columns as needed. The table grid will be the same width as regular paragraphs. (See Table 28–1.)

TABLE 28–1. A Table Grid			

You can click within a table cell and move the column spacers in the ruler to make columns wider or smaller.

Column headings are usually added at the top of each column. The first row of each column can be merged to form a single row. This is where the title should be listed. The table title should be bold, often in all capital letters. (See Table 28–2.)

TABLE 28–2. Sample Table with Data			
SALES BY REGION			
North	**South**	**East**	**West**
$123,000	$145,221	$132,010	$90,321
$133,210	$111,301	$112,101	$99,781
$141,210	$98,989	$156,287	$101,341

Other table cells can be merged to create cross-headings that span several columns or several rows. To do this, select the cells, then click the Table Menu, then click MERGE CELLS.

Data in a default table are left justified. You can select a row and then click on a different justification using the icons on the toolbar. Some types of data—such as money—are often presented right justified.

Heading text, as well as other text, can be made bold, italics, or both. You can change the color of the text and add shading to rows or columns.

You can change the height above and below the text within the table by selecting the table, then clicking FORMAT, PARAGRAPH, and then adjusting the settings for Spacing Before and After.

Using the borders and shading feature in the Format Menu, you can select the entire table or parts of the table and change the size or style of the grid lines. You can also remove the grid lines completely if you want. (See Table 28–3 as an example of changing the format of a table.)

TABLE 28–3. Table with Formatting Features			
SALES BY REGION			
North	**South**	**East**	**West**
$123,000	$145,221	$132,010	$90,321
$133,210	$111,301	$112,101	$99,781
$141,210	$98,989	$156,287	$101,341

You should capitalize the first word of each item in a table, plus any proper nouns or proper adjectives. Table text can include numbered lists and bullets, just like regular document text.

When placing tables within a report, the table should appear as soon as possible after it is mentioned in the text. Tables should always be introduced in the text. Avoid breaking a table at the end of a page and running it onto the next page. Start the table at the beginning of a new page if necessary.

Add two spaces after the last normal paragraph text before inserting the table. Leave two spaces after the table before resuming with the next paragraph.

◆ EDITING AND PROOFREADING

Editing a document requires checking for the following:

- Grammar
- Punctuation
- Style
- Spelling
- Accuracy

The traditional lines between copyediting and proofreading have blurred with the use of computers in business. Many administrative assistants must proofread and edit their own documents before they are distributed. In some large offices, a technical writer or documentation specialist may edit reports that will be distributed to wide audiences within the company or communications destined for outside the company.

Sometimes a boss proofreads and copyedits documents and sends them back with corrections. Depending on who is performing these tasks, an administrative assistant may need to make corrections to documents that contain proofreading symbols and abbreviations. (See Tables 28–4 and 28–5.)

TABLE 28–4. Common Proofreading Symbols

Symbol	Meaning
⌄	insert a comma
⌄	insert an apostrophe or single quotation mark
∧	insert something
⌄ ⌄	use double quotation marks
⊙	use a period here
℘	delete
∿	transpose elements
◡	close up this space
#	a space is needed here
¶	begin new paragraph
No¶	no paragraph

TABLE 28–5. Common Proofreading Abbreviations

Abbreviation	Meaning
Ab	a faulty abbreviation
Agr S/V or P/A	agreement problem: subject/verb or pronoun/antecedent
Awk	awkward expression or construction
Cap	faulty capitalization
CS	comma splice
Dgl	dangling construction
DICT	faulty diction
– ed	problem with final -ed
Frag	fragment
‖	problem in parallel form
P/A	problem with pronoun/antecedent agreement
Pron	problem with pronoun
Rep	unnecessary repetition
R-O	run-on sentence
Sp	spelling error
– s	problem with final -s
STET	let it stand
S/V	problem with subject/verb agreement
T	verb tense problem
Wdy	wordy
WW	wrong word

Copyediting

Use the following checklist when copyediting a document or manuscript:

- Are the headings and subheadings consistently used?
- Is the spelling correct?
- Are all proper names accurate?
- Are all lists parallel in structure?
- Do all nouns and verbs agree?
- Are numbered lists correctly numbered?
- Are all dates correct?
- Are all alphabetical lists in alphabetical order?
- Is all punctuation correct and consistent?
- Is all capitalization correct and consistent?
- Are all bibliographical references accurate and consistent?

Proofreading

Use the following checklist when proofreading a document or manuscript:

- Are all headings and other text elements consistent in style and layout?
- For letters, is the dateline, reference line, initials, enclosure, and carbon-copy notation accurate?
- Are all cross-references accurate?
- Are all margins consistent and proper?
- Are all tables aligned correctly and consistently?
- Have any footnotes been omitted?
- Are all end-of-line word divisions accurate?
- Are there any accidentally repeated words in the document?
- Are the page numbers correct?
- Are headings and captions separate?

Electronic Revisions

Rather than make edits on paper, you can make edits electronically on a word-processing document. By using the Track Changes feature (Figure 28–2) in a word-processing program like Microsoft Word, you can allow multiple people to add revisions and comments. Revisions show up in a different color font. After you have reviewed the revisions, you can accept them one at a time or reject them.

Figure 28–2. Revisions in a Microsoft Word document.

Screen shot reprinted by permission from Microsoft Corporation.

29

Forms of Address

Using the correct form of address helps to create a favorable impression, whether you are communicating in a letter, by telephone, or in person. This chapter provides a list of the correct forms in alphabetical order by the title of the person being addressed.

Chart Code:

EA	Envelope address
S	Salutation of a letter
C	Complimentary closing of a letter
SP	Speaking to
WR	Writing about

Abbot

EA	The Right Reverend Jackson Thomasson, O.S.B., Abbot of _____
S	Dear Father Abbot
C	Respectfully yours
SP	Abbot Thomasson *or* Father Abbot
WR	Father Thomasson

Alderman or Selectman

EA	The Honorable Horace Wauson, The Honorable Julie Seckman
S	Dear Mr./Mrs./Miss/Ms. Wauson
C	Very truly yours *or* Sincerely yours
SP	Mr./Mrs./Miss/Ms. Wauson
WR	Mr./Mrs./Miss/Ms. Wauson

Ambassador (United States)

EA	The Honorable Regina A. Strauss, American Ambassador (*but in Central or South America*: The Ambassador of the United States of America)
S	Sir/Madam *or* Dear Mr./Madam Ambassador
C	Sincerely yours *or* Very truly yours
SP	Mr. /Madam Ambassador
WR	the American Ambassador *or* the Ambassador of the United States

Ambassador (foreign)

EA	His Excellency Tom Jowers, Her Excellency Rosemary Boyd
S	Excellency *or* Dear Mr. /Madam Ambassador
C	Respectfully yours *or* Sincerely yours
SP	Mr. /Madam Ambassador
WR	the Ambassador of Spain *or* the Ambassador

Archbishop (Roman Catholic)

EA	The Most Reverend Archbishop of New York *or* The Most Reverend John C. Terrell, Archbishop of New York
S	Your Excellency *or* Dear Archbishop Terrell
C	Respectfully yours *or* Sincerely yours
SP	Your Excellency
WR	the Archbishop of New York *or* Archbishop Terrell

Archdeacon

EA	The Venerable Paul A, Morgan
S	Venerable Sir *or* My dear Archdeacon
C	Respectfully yours *or* Sincerely yours
SP	Archdeacon Morgan
WR	the Archdeacon of Los Angeles

Assembly Representative (see Representative, State)

Attorney General (of the United States)

EA	The Honorable Daniel Jones, Attorney General, Washington, DC 20503

S   Dear Mr./Madam Attorney General

C   Sincerely yours *or* Very truly yours

SP   Mr./Madam Attorney General *or* Attorney General Jones

WR   the Attorney General *or* Mr./Mrs./Miss/Ms. Jones

Attorney General (of a state)

EA   The Honorable Marsha Smith *or* Attorney General of the State of Kansas

S   Sir/Madam *or* Dear Mr./Madam Attorney General

C   Sincerely yours *or* Very truly yours

SP   Attorney General Smith

WR   the Attorney General *or* the State Attorney General *or* Mr./ Mrs. Miss/Ms. Smith

Bishop (Roman Catholic)

EA   The Most Reverend Phillip Johnson, Bishop of _____

S   Your Excellency *or* Dear Bishop Johnson

C   Respectfully yours *or* Sincerely yours

SP   Bishop Johnson

WR   Bishop Johnson

Bishop (Episcopal, not presiding)

EA   The Right Reverend Mark Lessing, Bishop of _____

S   Right Reverend Sir *or* Dear Bishop Lessing

C   Respectfully yours

SP   Bishop Lessing

WR   the Episcopal Bishop of _____

Bishop (Episcopal, presiding)

EA   The Most Reverend Peter Brown, Presiding Bishop

S   Most Reverend Sir *or* Dear Bishop Brown

C   Respectfully yours *or* Sincerely yours

SP   Bishop Brown

WR   Bishop Brown

Bishop (Methodist)

EA	The Reverend Andrew Carter
S	Reverend Sir *or* Dear Bishop Carter
C	Respectfully yours *or* Sincerely yours
SP	Bishop Carter
WR	Bishop Carter

Brother (of a religious order)

EA	Brother Robert, S.J.
S	Dear Brother Robert
C	Respectfully yours *or* Sincerely yours
SP	Brother Robert
WR	Brother Robert, S.J.

Brother (superior of a religious order)

EA	Brother Thomas, S.J., Superior
S	Dear Brother Thomas
C	Respectfully yours *or* Sincerely yours
SP	Brother Thomas
WR	Brother Thomas

Cabinet Officer of the United States (current; addressed as "Secretary")

EA	The Honorable Timothy Dutton, Secretary of State, Washington, DC 20044
S	Sir/Madam *or* Dear Mr./Madam Secretary
C	Very truly yours *or* Sincerely yours
SP	Mr. /Madam Secretary
WR	the Secretary of State, Timothy Dutton

Cabinet Officer of the United States (former)

EA	The Honorable James Barker
S	Dear Mr./Mrs./Miss/Ms. Barker
C	Very truly yours *or* Sincerely yours

SP	Mr./Mrs./Miss/Ms. Barker
WR	Mr./Mrs./Miss/Ms. Barker

Canon

EA	The Reverend Thomas R. Milford
S	Dear Canon Milford
C	Respectfully yours *or* Sincerely yours
SP	Canon Milford
WR	Canon Milford

Cardinal (Roman Catholic)

EA	His Eminence John Cardinal Simonton, Archbishop of Chicago (*plus address*)
S	Your Eminence *or* My dear Cardinal Simonton *or* Dear Cardinal Simonton
C	Respectfully yours *or* Sincerely yours
SP	Your Eminence *or* Cardinal Simonton
WR	His Eminence Cardinal Simonton *or* Cardinal Simonton

Chairperson of a Committee U.S. Congress

EA	The Honorable John Brown, Chairman, Committee of the United States Senate/House
S	Dear Mr. Chairman/Madam Chairwoman
C	Sincerely yours *or* Very truly yours
SP	Senator/Congressman/Congresswoman Brown *or* Mr. Chairman/Madam Chairwoman
WR	Senator Brown *or* Congressman/Congresswoman Brown *or* the Chairman/Chairwoman of the Senate/House Committee on _____

Chancellor of a University (see University Chancellor)

Chaplain (of a college or university)

EA	The Reverend Dean A. Augustine, Chaplain
S	Dear Chaplain Augustine
C	Respectfully yours *or* Sincerely yours
SP	Chaplain Augustine
WR	Chaplain Augustine

Charge d'Affaires ad interim, United States

EA	Gary K. Wilson, Esq., American Charge d'Affaires ad Interim (*or in Central or South America*: United States Charge d'Affaires ad Interim)
S	Dear Mr./Mrs./Miss/Ms. Wilson
C	Sincerely yours
SP	Mr./Mrs./Miss/Ms. Wilson
WR	the American Charge d'Affaires in France (*or in Central or South America*: the United States Charge d'Affaires in France)

Clergy, Lutheran

EA	The Reverend Arthur Anderson (*plus address of church*)
S	Dear Pastor Anderson
C	Respectfully yours
SP	Pastor Anderson
WR	Pastor Anderson

Clergy, Protestant (no degree, excluding Episcopal)

EA	The Reverend Donald Reese (*plus address of church*)
S	Dear Mr./Mrs./Miss/Ms. Reese
C	Respectfully yours
SP	Mr./Mrs./Miss/Ms. Reese
WR	The Reverend Mr. Reese

Clergy, Protestant (with degree)

EA	The Reverend Dr. William Johnson
S	Dear Dr. Johnson
C	Respectfully yours
SP	Dr. Johnson
WR	The Reverend Dr. Johnson

Clerk of a Court

EA	Elizabeth Pym, Esq. *or* Clerk of the Court of _____
S	Dear Mr./Mrs./Miss/Ms. Pym
C	Sincerely yours *or* Very truly yours

SP	Mr./Mrs./Miss/Ms. Pym
WR	Mr./Mrs./Miss/Ms. Pym

Congressperson (see Representative, Congress)

Consul (United States or other)

EA	John Robert Henderson, Esquire, American (*or other*) Consul
S	Dear Sir/Madam
C	Very truly yours
SP	Mr./Mrs./Miss/Ms. Henderson
WR	The American Consul in Brazil

Dean (of a cathedral)

EA	The Very Reverend John C. Majors *or* Dean John C. Majors
S	Dear Dean Majors
C	Sincerely yours *or* Respectfully yours
SP	Dean Majors
WR	Dean Majors

Dean of a University or College (see University or College Dean)

Doctor of Dentistry/Divinity/Medicine/Philosophy

EA	Deana Fate, D.D.S. *or* Deana Fate, D.Div. *or* Deana Fate, M.D. *or* Deana Fate, Ph.D.
S	Dear Dr. Fate
C	Sincerely yours *or* Very truly yours
SP	Dr. Fate
WR	Dr. Fate

Governor (of a state)

EA	The Honorable Penny Corson, Governor of New York
S	Dear Governor Corson
C	Respectfully yours
SP	Governor *or* Governor Corson
WR	Governor Corson

Governor-elect (of a state)

EA	The Honorable Diane Jennings, Governor-elect of Ohio
S	Dear Mr./Mrs./Miss/Ms. Jennings
C	Respectfully yours
SP	Mr./Mrs./Miss/Ms. Jennings
WR	Mr./Mrs./Miss/Ms. Jennings

Governor (of a state, former)

EA	The Honorable Elizabeth Rietz
S	Dear Mr./Mrs./Miss/Ms. Rietz
C	Sincerely yours
SP	Mr./Mrs./Miss/Ms. Rietz
WR	Mrs. Elizabeth Rietz, Former Governor of Ohio

Judge

EA	The Honorable George Smithers, Justice (*plus name of court*)
S	Sir/Madam
C	Sincerely yours *or* Very truly yours
SP	Judge Smithers
WR	Judge Smithers

King

EA	His Most Gracious Majesty, King Philip
S	May it please Your Majesty
C	Respectfully
SP	Your Majesty (*initially; thereafter*: Sir)
WR	His Majesty *or* King Philip

Lawyer

EA	James Robert Judd, Esq. *or* Mr./Mrs./Miss/Ms. Judd
S	Dear Mr./Mrs./Miss/Ms. Judd
C	Very truly yours *or* Sincerely yours
SP	Mr./Mrs./Miss/Ms. Judd
WR	Mr./Mrs./Miss/Ms. Judd

Lieutenant Governor (of a state)

EA	The Honorable Mary Brown, Lieutenant Governor of Maine
S	Madam/Sir *or* Dear Mr./Mrs./Miss/Ms. Brown
C	Respectfully yours *or* Sincerely yours
SP	Mr./Mrs./Miss/Ms. Brown
WR	Lieutenant Governor Brown

Mayor

EA	His/Her Honor the Mayor *or* The Honorable Alison Starnes, City Hall (*plus city, state*)
S	Sir/Madam
C	Very truly yours *or* Sincerely yours
SP	Mayor Starnes
WR	Mayor Starnes *or* Mayor of Raleigh

Military Enlisted Personnel (United States)

EA	rank, full name, address
S	Sir/Madam *or* Dear Sir/Madam
C	Very truly yours
SP	Sergeant Smith, Airman Jones, Private Jackson
WR	Sergeant Smith, Airman Jones, Private Jackson

Military Officer (United States)

EA	rank, full name, address
S	Sir/Madam *or* Lieutenant Banks, Admiral Banks
C	Very truly yours
SP	Lieutenant Banks, Admiral Banks
WR	Lieutenant Banks, Admiral Banks

Minister, Protestant (no degree)

EA	The Reverend Richard W. Fate
S	Dear Mr./Mrs./Miss/Ms. Fate/Reverend Fate
C	Respectfully yours *or* Very truly yours
SP	Mr./Mrs./Miss/Ms./Reverend Fate
WR	Mr./Mrs./Miss/Ms./Reverend Fate

Minister, Protestant (with degree)

EA	The Reverend Robert R. Foley, D.D.
S	Dear Dr. Foley
C	Respectfully yours *or* Very truly yours
SP	Dr. Foley
WR	Dr. Foley

Monsignor, Roman Catholic

EA	The Right Reverend Monsignor Johnson
S	Right Reverend Monsignor Johnson
C	Respectfully yours
SP	Monsignor Johnson
WR	Monsignor Johnson

Pope

EA	His Holiness the Pope, Vatican City, Italy
S	Your Holiness *or* Most Holy Father
C	Respectfully yours
SP	Your Holiness
WR	His Holiness *or* the Pope

Premier

EA	His/Her Excellency (full name), Premier of _____
S	Dear Mr./Madam Premier
C	Sincerely yours
SP	Your Excellency
WR	The Premier of _____ *or* The Premier

President of the United States (current)

EA	The President, The White House, Washington, DC 20500
S	Mr. /Madam President *or* Dear President Jackson
C	Respectfully yours
SP	Mr./Madam President *or* Sir/Madam
WR	The President *or* President Jackson

President of the United States (former)

EA	The Honorable Stephen Murray
S	Sir/Madam *or* Dear Mr./Mrs./Miss/Ms. Murray
C	Respectfully yours
SP	Mr./Mrs./Miss/Ms. Murray
WR	Former President Murray *or* Mr./Mrs./Miss/Ms. Murray

President of a University or College (see University or College President)

Priest, Episcopal

EA	The Reverend Ann Thomason *or if degreed*: The Reverend Dr. Ann Thomason
S	Dear Mr./Mrs./Miss/Ms. Thomason *or* Dr. Thomason *or* Reverend Thomason
C	Respectfully yours
SP	Mr./Mrs./Miss/Ms. Thomason *or* Dr. Thomason *or* Father/Mother Thomason
WR	Father/Mother Thomason *or* Dr. Thomason

Priest, Roman Catholic

EA	The Reverend Leland Smith (*plus initials of his order*)
S	Reverend Father (*formal*) *or* Dear Father (*less formal*)
C	Respectfully yours
SP	Father Smith
WR	Father Smith

Prime Minister

EA	His/Her Excellency, Prime Minister of _____
S	Excellency *or* Dear Mr./Madam Prime Minister
C	Respectfully yours
SP	Mr./Madam Prime Minister
WR	The Prime Minister of _____

Prince

EA	His Royal Highness
S	Sir *or* Your Royal Highness
C	Respectfully
SP	Your Royal Highness
WR	His Royal Highness *or* Prince George

Princess

EA	Her Royal Highness
S	Madam *or* Your Royal Highness
C	Respectfully
SP	Your Royal Highness
WR	Her Royal Highness *or* Princess Mary

Professor

EA	Professor *or* Dr. (*if Ph.D.*) Gary Keith Wilson, Department of Chemistry, Vanderbilt University, Nashville, Tennessee 37235
S	Dear Professor Wilson
C	Very truly yours *or* Sincerely yours
SP	Professor *or* Dr. Wilson
WR	Professor *or* Dr. Wilson

Queen

EA	Her Most Gracious Majesty Queen Anne
S	May it please Your Majesty
C	Respectfully
SP	Your Majesty (*initially; thereafter*: Ma'am)
WR	Her Majesty, Queen Anne

Rabbi

EA	Rabbi David L. Fader *or if degreed*: Rabbi David L. Fader, D.D.
S	Dear Rabbi Fader *or* Dear Dr. Fader
C	Respectfully yours *or* Sincerely yours
SP	Rabbi Fader
WR	Rabbi Fader

Representative, Congress (current)

EA   The Honorable Douglas Scrimshaw, United States House of Representatives, Washington, DC 20515

S   Dear Sir/Madam *or* Dear Representative Scrimshaw

C   Very truly yours *or* Sincerely yours

SP   Mr./Mrs./Miss/Ms. Scrimshaw

WR   Douglas Scrimshaw, U.S. Representative from _____ *or* Congressman Douglas Scrimshaw

Representative, Congress (former)

EA   The Honorable Greg Linton (*plus local address*)

S   Dear Mr./Mrs./Miss/Ms. Linton

C   Very truly yours *or* Sincerely yours

SP   Mr./Mrs./Miss/Ms. Linton

WR   Mr./Mrs./Miss/Ms. Linton

Representative, State (including Assemblyperson, Delegate)

EA   The Honorable Nancy Northcutt, The State Assembly *or* The House of Representatives *or* The House of Delegates

S   Dear Mr./Mrs./Miss/Ms. Northcutt

C   Sincerely yours *or* Very truly yours

SP   Mr./Mrs./Miss/Ms. Northcutt

WR   Mr./Mrs./Miss/Ms. Northcutt, the State Representative *or* Assemblyperson *or* Delegate

Secretary of State (of a state)

EA   The Honorable James Cobb *or* The Secretary of State of _____

S   Dear Mr./Madam Secretary

C   Sincerely yours *or* Very truly yours

SP   Mr./Mrs./Miss/Ms. Cobb

WR   Mr./Mrs./Miss/Ms. Cobb

Senator, U.S.

EA   The Honorable Larry Zezula, United States Senate, Washington, DC 20510

S	Dear Senator Zezula
C	Sincerely yours *or* Very truly yours
SP	Senator Zezula *or* Senator
WR	Senator Zezula *or* The Senator from _____ *or* The Senator

Senator (state legislature)

EA	The Honorable Martin Allen, The Senator of _____
S	Dear Senator Allen
C	Sincerely yours *or* Very truly yours
SP	Senator Allen
WR	Senator Allen

Senator-elect

EA	The Honorable Mary Branson, Senator-elect (*plus local address*)
S	Dear Mr./Mrs./Miss/Ms. Branson
C	Sincerely yours *or* Very truly yours
SP	Mr./Mrs./Miss/Ms. Branson
WR	Senator-elect Branson

Sister (member of a religious order)

EA	Sister Mary Martha, S.C.
S	Dear Sister *or* Dear Sister Mary Martha
C	Respectfully yours *or* Sincerely yours
SP	Sister Mary Martha
WR	Sister Mary Martha

Sister (superior of a religious order)

EA	The Reverend Mother Superior, S.C.
S	Reverend Mother *or* Dear Reverend Mother
C	Respectfully yours
SP	Reverend Mother
WR	The Reverend Mother Superior *or* The Reverend Mother

Speaker, U.S. House of Representatives

EA   The Speaker of the House of Representatives *or* The Honorable Allan Carl, Speaker of the House of Representatives

S   Dear Mr./Madam Speaker

C   Sincerely yours *or* Very truly yours

SP   Mr./Madam Speaker *or* Mr./Mrs./Miss/Ms. Carl

WR   The Speaker *or* Mr./Mrs./Miss/Ms. Carl

Supreme Court Justice (United States, Associate Justice)

EA   Mr. Anthony Barrett, The Supreme Court, Washington, DC 20543

S   Dear Mr./Madam Justice *or* Dear Justice Barrett

C   Sincerely yours *or* Very truly yours

SP   Mr./Madam Justice Barrett

WR   Mr./Madam Justice Barrett

Supreme Court Justice (United States, Chief Justice)

EA   The Chief Justice of the United States
(*never*: The Chief Justice of the Supreme Court)

S   Dear Mr./Madam Chief Justice

C   Respectfully *or* Respectfully yours

SP   Mr./Madam Chief Justice

WR   The Chief Justice of the United States *or* The Chief Justice

Supreme Court Justice (State, Associate Justice)

EA   The Honorable Lewis Ritenour, Associate Justice of the Supreme Court of _____

S   Dear Justice Ritenour

C   Sincerely yours *or* Very truly yours

SP   Mr. /Madam Justice

WR   Mr. /Madam Justice Ritenour *or* Judge Ritenour

Supreme Court Justice (State, Chief Justice)

EA   The Honorable Margaret W Smoot, Chief Justice of the Supreme Court of _____

S   Dear Mr./Madam Chief Justice

C   Sincerely yours *or* Very truly yours

SP   Mr. /Madam Chief Justice *or* Chief Justice Smoot

WR   Mr./ Madam Chief Justice

United Nations Delegate (United States)

EA   The Honorable Edwin L. Rutherford, United States Permanent Representative to the United Nations, United Nations, New York, NY 10017

S   Dear Mr./Madam Ambassador

C   Respectfully *or* Sincerely yours

SP   Mr./Madam Ambassador

WR   The United States Representative to the United Nations

United Nations Delegate (foreign)

EA   His Excellency Charles Turner /Her Excellency Allison Turner

S   My dear Mr. /Madam Ambassador

C   Respectfully *or* Sincerely yours

SP   Mr. /Madam Ambassador

WR   The Representative of Canada to the United Nations

United Nations Secretary-General

EA   His Excellency Juan Perez/ Her Excellency Juanita Perez, Secretary General of the United Nations, United Nations, New York, NY 10017

S   Dear Mr. /Madam Secretary-General *or* Your Excellency

C   Respectfully

SP   Sir/Madam *or* Mr./Mrs./Miss/Ms. Perez

WR   The Secretary-General of the United Nations

University Chancellor

EA   Dr. Barbara R. Rodgers, Chancellor (*plus name and address of university*)

S   Dear Dr. Rodgers

C   Sincerely yours *or* Very truly yours

SP   Dr. Rodgers

WR   Dr. Barbara R. Rodgers, Chancellor of (*name of university*)

University or College Dean

EA	Dean Hamilton Smythe *or* Dr. Hamilton Smythe, Dean (*plus name and address of university*)
S	Dear Dr. Smythe *or* Dear Dean Smythe
C	Very truly yours *or* Sincerely yours
SP	Dean Smythe *or* Dr. Smythe
WR	Dr. Smythe, Dean of (*name of university*)

University or College President

EA	Dr. Thomas A. Harmon, President *or* President Thomas A. Harmon (*plus name and address of university*)
S	Dear President Harmon *or* Dear Dr. Harmon
C	Sincerely yours OR Very truly yours
SP	Dr. Harmon
WR	Dr. Harmon

Vice President of the United States

EA	The Vice President, United States Senate, Washington, DC 20510
S	Dear Mr./Madam Vice President
C	Respectfully
SP	Mr./Madam Vice President
WR	The Vice President

Warrant Officer

EA	Warrant Officer John C. Calhoun, Jr. *or* Chief Warrant Officer John Smith
S	Dear Mr./Mrs./Miss/Ms. Calhoun
C	Very truly yours
SP	Mr./Mrs./Miss/Ms. Calhoun
WR	Warrant Officer Calhoun *or* Mr./Mrs./Miss/Ms. Calhoun

◇ **SOME ADDITIONAL GUIDELINES**

The Honorable and The Reverend

"The Honorable" is a title of distinction reserved for appointed or elected government officials such as congressional representatives, judges, justices, and cabinet officers. "The Honorable" is never used before a surname alone—for example, The Honorable Thomas Jones, *not* The Honorable Jones. Also, do not combine "The Honorable" with a common courtesy title, such as "Mr." or "Ms."—for example, *not* The Honorable Mr. Thomas Jones. Never abbreviate "The Honorable" in either forms of address or formal writing.

"The Reverend" should be used in official or formal writing. "The Reverend" is often abbreviated to "The Rev." or just "Rev." in informal and unofficial writing. However, when used in conjunction with a full name, "The Reverend" must be used— for example, The Reverend John Reeves or The Reverend Dr. Louise A. McGinnis. Notice that both titles are used with the full name on the envelope address but not in the salutation of the letter. Also note that "The" always precedes these titles.

Esquire

When the title "Esquire" is used, it is always abbreviated after the full name, and no other title is used before the name—for example, James Rogers, Esq. Although the abbreviation "Esq." is most commonly seen after the surnames of attorneys, it may also be used after the surnames of other professionals—engineers, consuls, architects, court clerks, and justices of the peace. "Esquire" is written in signature lines and addresses but is never used in salutations. It is commonly used regardless of sex, but there are some who object to using "Esquire" as a title for a woman professional.

Women Clergy

The issue of addressing women clergy reflects the problem of our ever changing vocabulary. In many instances, "Reverend" or "Doctor" suffices for both men and women, but some denominations address their ordained male members as " Father." The natural tendency then is to address the female counterpart as "Mother," but there may be strong resistance to this title from both the individual and the group. Whenever possible in such a situation, try to discover the preference of the individual.

Retired Military

When military officers retire from active duty, they retain their highest rank, and this rank is always used when they are addressed.

30

Legal Documents and Terms

◇ GRAMMALOGUES

Business secretaries are not generally called upon to take legal dictation, but it's helpful to have a brief knowledge of legal *grammalogues*. A grammalogue is a shorthand shortcut for full expressions used. When taking dictation, it's useful to be able to write in one stroke the representation for "time is of the essence," "writ of habeas corpus," "denied certiorari," and other phrases. You can have your notes complete before the person dictating has finished a sentence because you know what the dictator means to say and how to record it quickly.

◇ DOCUMENT FORMATS

When you are asked to type or print a legal document, use plain white legal paper, 8½ × 13 or 14 inches, or legal cap paper, which is the same size but has a wide ruled margin at the left and a narrow ruled margin at the right. The text must be kept within these ruled margins. Wills are written on heavy non-correctable paper of legal size without ruled margins.

Always double-space legal papers and reports, with triple spaces between paragraphs. Retain a 2-inch margin at the top and a 1-inch margin at the bottom of the page. If plain paper is used rather than ruled, leave a 1½-inch margin on the left and a ¾-inch margin on the right.

Indent paragraphs ten spaces; for land descriptions or quotations that are single spaced, indent an additional five spaces.

If copies are to be signed (called duplicate originals), they are printed on the same kind of paper as the original.

Number the pages in the center of the bottom of the page (¾ inch from the bottom edge), except for briefs, which are numbered in the upper right corner. The first page number is not marked.

Legal documents are bound with a sheet of heavy backing paper (9 × 15 inches). The backing sheet should be folded to provide four sections of the sheet 9 inches long. On one of these sections, type an endorsement, and label to briefly describe what the document represents. Following is an example of an endorsed mortgage backing:

No. A–31075
RELEASE OF OIL AND GAS LEASE
FROM
WILLIAM P ALLEN
TO
FIRST CITY BANK OF NEW YORK

Printed legal forms of many kinds, referred to as "law blanks," can be obtained at stationery and office supply stores and at legal stationers. They are easily filled in on the typewriter and are quickly read. They may sometimes serve as a guide in drafting a document.

When writing numbers in legal documents, write them in words, and repeat them immediately in numerals inside parentheses, for example, ten thousand five hundred and seventy-five (10,575), ten thousand five hundred and seventy-five dollars ($10,575). Dates may be spelled out, or you may express the day and the year in numerals, with the month always spelled out.

The following words and phrases often used in legal documents are customarily written in full capitals, usually followed by a comma, a colon, or no punctuation:

THIS AGREEMENT, made this second day of . . . .
KNOW ALL MEN BY THESE PRESENT, that . . . .
IN WITNESS WHEREOF, I have this day . . . .
MEMORANDUM OF AGREEMENT made this twenty-fifth day of . . . .

Case titles are always underscored, followed by a comma, the volume and page numbers, and date:

Johnson v. Smith, 201 Okla. 433, 32 Am. Rep. 168 (1901).

◇ NOTARY PUBLIC FORMS

In a small office and even in many larger offices, the administrative assistant is probably also a notary public. Figure 30–1 shows commonly used forms of notary public acknowledgments on legal documents.

◇ CODICILS TO A WILL

Additions to and changes in a will are made by an instrument known as a codicil, sometimes written on the last page of the will. It must be dated, formally executed, signed, witnessed, and probated with the will (Figure 30–2).

For an individual

State of _____ SS
County of _____
On the _____ day of _____, 20___, before me came _____ known
to me to be the individual described in and who executed the foregoing instrument
and acknowledged that he (or she) executed the same.

(S)

_____
Notary Public

[Stamp and Seal]

For a corporation

State of _____ SS
County of _____
On the _____ day of _____, 20___, before me personally appeared
_____ to me known, who, being by me duly sworn, did depose and
say that he (or she) resides at _____; that he (or she) is
_____(title) of _____(Company), the corporation
described in and which executed the foregoing instrument; that he knows the seal
of said corporation; that the seal affixed to said instrument is such corporate seal;
that it was so affixed by order of the (title) of said corporation; and that he (or she)
signed his (or her) name thereto by like order.

(S)_____
Notary Public

[Seal]

For a partnership

State of _____ SS
County of _____
On the _____ day of _____, 20___, before me personally appeared
_____ to me known, and known to me to be a member of
_____ (name of partnership), and the person described in and who executed the foregoing instrument in the firm name of _____, and he (or
she) duly acknowledged to me that he (or she) executed the same as and for the
act and deed of said firm of _____ (repeat name of partnership).

(S)_____
Notary Public

[Seal]

Figure 30–1. Commonly used forms of notary public acknowledgments.

⟡ **AGREEMENTS AND CONTRACTS**

Agreements or contracts should state the obligations of each party (Figure 30–3).

I, JOHN PHILIP MOORE, a resident of the City of Chicago, County of Cook, State of Illinois, do hereby make, publish, and declare the following as and for a codicil to the Will and Testament heretofore by me executed, bearing date of the _____th day of _____, 20_____.

FIRST: [state provisions]

SECOND: [state provisions]

In all other respects and except as hereinbefore set forth, I hereby republish, ratify, and confirm my said Will, dated the _____th day of _____, 20_____.

WITNESS MY HAND AND SEAL this _____ day of _____, 20_____.

(S)_____

[Seal]

Sample of attestation

The foregoing Codicil, consisting of one-half page, containing no interlineations or erasures, was on the date thereof signed by the above-named Testator and at the same time published and declared by him (or her) to be a Codicil to his (or her) Last Will and Testament. The said Testator signed this instrument in the presence of the undersigned, who acted as attesting witnesses at his (or her) request. Each of the undersigned signed as a witness in the presence of the Testator and in the presence of each other. At the time of the execution of this Codicil the said Testator was of sound mind and memory and under no undue influence of restraint.

NAME *_____ ADDRESS: *_____

(S)_____

(S)_____

*The secretary usually types the name and address of each witness beneath these lines.

Figure 30–2. Sample of a codicil to a last will and testament.

◇ PROXY

A proxy is a form of power of attorney given by one person to another, authorizing the second person to vote in lieu of the first person at a meeting of a corporation (Figure 30–4).

◇ GLOSSARY OF LEGAL AND REAL ESTATE TERMS

Here is a partial list of common legal terms that you may have occasion to use:

A

Abstract of title   A brief history of the title to a piece of real estate, including data regarding transfer of the property from the time of the first recorded owner to the present owner.

Acceleration clause   A clause in a note or deed of trust causing the entire balance to become due and payable should a default in one of the provisions therein be triggered.

THIS AGREEMENT, made this _____ day of _____, 20____, between _____ of _____ , First Party (hereinafter called the Seller), and _____ a corporation under the laws of the State of _____, with principal place of business in _____, _____ (city and state), Second Party (hereinafter called the Purchaser),

WITNESSETH:

WHEREAS the Seller has this day agreed to _____; and WHEREAS the Purchaser is willing to _____; and WHERE-AS _____; NOW, THEREFORE, it is agreed that _____. WITNESS the signatures of the parties hereto on the date aforesaid.

(S) _____
Seller

(S) _____
Purchaser

By _____
President

[Corporate Seal]

Figure 30–3. Sample contract.

[Corporate Seal]

I, JOHN WILLIAM SMITH, do hereby constitute and appoint HAROLD JACKSON attorney and agent for me, to vote as my proxy at a meeting of the stockholders of THE JOHN SMITH CORPORATION, according to the number of votes I should be entitled to cast if personally present.
Date: _____ (S) _____

Figure 30–4. Sample proxy.

Accessory after the fact A person who aids one whom he or she knows to be a felon.

Accessory before the fact A person who instigates or contributes to the commission of a crime but does not actually take part in it.

Accrual method An accounting system that records income when earned and expenses as incurred.

Acknowledgment A certification appearing at the end of a legal paper showing that the paper was duly acknowledged and executed.

Ad valorem tax Tax according to the market value of subject property.

Administrator (male), Administratrix (female) A person appointed by a court to administer an estate.

Advocate A person who pleads the cause of another before a tribunal or judicial court.

Affidavit A certification attesting the authenticity of statements made in a legal paper.

Alienation clause A specific clause in a note and/or deed of trust stating that, should the property be sold or transferred in any manner, the entire balance of the note shall be immediately due and payable. To "alienate" is to transfer.

Answer A statement made by the defendant through an attorney stating his or her version of the situation (often called a plea).

Appeal   The act of taking a legal case to a higher court.

Appurtenances   Improvements that pertain to the land. See also *Tenements*.

Arraignment   The calling of an accused person into court, reading the indictment to that person, and asking that person whether he or she is guilty or not guilty.

Assessment   A levy made on property for improvements.

Attachment   A court order authorizing a seizure or a taking into custody of property or monies to satisfy a claim.

Attestation   A certification as to the genuineness of a copy.

Attorney   One who is legally appointed by another to transact business for him or her.

Attorney-in-fact   One who is appointed by another, by means of a letter or a power of attorney, to transact business for him or her out of court.

B

Beneficiary   The person who is benefited by a gift, proceeds of an insurance policy, income from a trust estate, etc.

Bequeath   To make a bequest or to give personal property by will.

Brief   The written argument of an attorney supporting his or her contention as to the correct interpretation of the law and the proper inference from the evidence in a particular case.

Burden of proof   A term meaning that the party making a claim must prove it. Burden of proof rests on the plaintiff.

C

Capital punishment   The death penalty.

Certified copy   A copy of an instrument made from the records in a recorder's office and certified to by the recorder as being an exact copy of the paper on file or of record.

Certiorari   A writ from a superior court to call up for review the records of an inferior court.

Change of venue   A change in the place of trial.

Civil action   An action to enforce a civil right or to remedy a private wrong.

Complaint   A formal allegation against a party.

Conditional binder   A sales agreement that contains certain conditions that must be met before it becomes unconditionally binding on all parties.

Conditional sale   A contract covering goods sold and delivered to a buyer on condition that he or she make periodic payments thereon (or meet other stipulated conditions).

Contingency clause   The clause in an agreement that makes the entire agreement conditional on the happening of a certain event.

Corporal punishment   Punishment applied to the body of the offender.

Corporation   An entity of joint ownership in which all parties have a share (equal and unequal) but that acts in the same capacity as an individual owner. Usually governed by a board of directors elected by the shareholders.

Criminal action   An action in which it is sought to determine the guilt of a person who is accused of a crime specifically prohibited by law.

Cross-complaint   A complaint seeking affirmative relief against a codefendant.

D

Defalcation   A misappropriation of funds by one who has them in trust.

Demographics   The study of population trends and/or buying habits of the public in a certain geographic area.

Demurrer   A plea by the defendant asking the court to dismiss the action because of insufficient cause for complaint.

Deposition   A testimony under oath in writing; often taken orally and signed after it has been recorded.

Due-on-sale clause   The clause in the loan papers that gives the lender the right to call the loan due and payable upon the happening of a certain occurrence, such as sale of the property.

E

Easement   An acquiring privilege or right of use or enjoyment that one person may have in the land of another.

Eminent domain   That superior dominion of the sovereign power over property that authorizes the state to appropriate all or any part of it to a necessary public use, reasonable compensation being awarded.

Encumbrance   A claim or lien upon an estate.

Environmental impact report   Report required in some states that shows the effects a proposed development will have on the environment of the area. Such reports study the effects on the wildlife, traffic, schools, terrain, and so forth.

Escrow   The procedure of placing all papers and money concerning a transaction in the hands of a disinterested third party with instructions on how such items are to be treated in the event all conditions are or are not met.

Exclusionary zoning   Zoning sometimes used to exclude multiple-family dwellings from predominantly single-family neighborhoods.

Exclusive agency listing   In real estate, a listing that contains a termination date in which an owner and broker enter into a written contract for the broker to sell a property. The broker, as agent for the seller, receives a commission if the property is sold during the term of the listing by that broker or by any other, but not if the owner sells the property independent of the broker's efforts.

Exclusive right-to-sell listing   In real estate, similar to an exclusive agency listing, except that even if the owner sells the property before the termination date, the owner must still pay a commission to the broker.

Executed agreement   An agreement that has been signed by all parties to it.

F

Factor times gross income   An investment analysis formula for judging the worth of a piece of income property by multiplying the annual gross income by a factor derived from the ratio of gross income to the selling price of similar properties.

Farmers Home Administration (FMHA)   A branch of the U.S. Department of Agriculture concerned with making home loans in rural areas that lack the usual financing sources.

Federal Housing Administration loans   Loans made by conventional lenders but with a portion insured by the Federal Housing Administration.

Felony   Any of various crimes graver in their penal consequences than those called misdemeanors.

Fiduciary   The person named in a trust or agency agreement to act for another on his or her behalf and in the same manner as if acting for himself or herself.

First deed of trust   A mortgage security instrument that has first priority over any other voluntary financing liens on a property.

Foreclosure   The process in which property used as security for a mortgage is sold to satisfy the debt when a borrower defaults in payment of the mortgage note or on other terms in the mortgage document.

Foreclosure suit   A suit brought to foreclose a mortgage.

Foreclosure under court action   A foreclosure procedure that is handled in a court of law and allows the lender to obtain a deficiency judgment against the borrower. It also allows the borrower a year's right to redeem the property by paying all back monies and costs incurred to and from the date of foreclosure.

Foreclosure under right of sale (deed of trust)   An automatic procedure that allows the lender to foreclose on the property through the power-of-sale provision in the contract. It usually takes about four months. The original borrower is released from responsibility for the debt in exchange for the sale of the property. However, in some cases, the borrower may be held liable for any difference between the loan amount and the sale amount.

Franchise   Right to operate a business under the name and operating procedures of a large, often nationwide parent company.

G

Garnishment   Legal notice to one to appear in court, usually regarding the attachment of property to secure a debt.

General agent   One who performs continuing services for the principal client.

General partnership   An entity of ownership in which all partners in it hold voting rights as to decisions being made and in which all partners share in the profits and liabilities as their interests appear.

Grand jury   An appointed group of citizens to examine accusations against persons charged with a crime and to issue bills of indictment if the evidence warrants.

H

Habeas corpus   A common law writ to bring a party before a court or judge, usually when the party is confined to jail.

Hereditaments   Rights and property inherited or inheritable. See also *Appurtenances, Tenements*.

Holographic will   A will entirely written, dated, and signed in the handwriting of the maker.

I

Impeachment   Arraignment of a public officer for misconduct while in office.

Indictment   The formal written statement charging one or more persons with an offense, as framed by the prosecuting authority of the state and issued by the grand jury.

Inflation   Abnormal increase in the volume of money and credit that results in a substantial, continuing rise in the general price level.

Injunction   A court writ requiring a party to perform or to forbear certain acts.

Interlocutory   Intermediate; not final or definite.

Intestate   A person who dies without having a will.

J

Judgment   The decree or sentence of a court.

Jurisdiction   The legal power, right, or authority to hear and determine a cause or causes.

L

Larceny   The unlawful taking of objects with intent to deprive the rightful owner.

Law of agency   The section of statutes pertaining to the relationship that is created when one entity is authorized to act on legal matters for the benefit of another.

Legatee   One to whom a legacy is bequeathed.

Letters of administration   The instrument by which an administrator or administratrix is authorized to administer the estate of a deceased person.

Letters patent   An instrument covering rights and title to an invention or public lands.

Letters testamentary   An instrument authorizing an executor of a will to act.

Leverage   The process whereby an investment can be burdened with a loan or loans and still provide a higher yield than if an investor had paid all cash for it.

Libel   Written public defamation.

Limited partnership   Syndication in which many parties can participate, except that the limited partners have no voice in the operation of the venture and do not suffer any recourse from potential liabilities beyond their initial investment.

Line of credit   A prearranged commitment from a lending institution to advance up to a specific amount of money to a customer of that bank.

Liquidity   The facility with which an asset can be converted to cash.

M

Malfeasance   The performing of an act that a person ought not to perform.

Mandamus   A writ issued by a superior court directing some inferior court or person in authority to perform some specific duty.

Misdemeanor   A crime less than a felony.

Misfeasance   A trespass or injurious act.

Money supply   A figure issued weekly by the Federal Reserve Bank indicating the amount of money in circulation in the United States during the past week.

Mortgage   A written conveyance of property intended to be a security for the payment of money. There are two parties to a mortgage: the mortgagor (the borrower) and the mortgagee (the lender).

Motion   An application made to a court to obtain an order, ruling, or direction.

N

Net operating income (NOI)   A figure arrived at in completing an investment analysis form that indicates the amount of income to be derived from the property after the vacancy factor and all other operating expenses have been deducted from the gross income but before any loan payments are applied.

NOI   See *Net operating income.*

Notary public   A public officer who attests to or certifies deeds, affidavits, and depositions.

Notice of default   A notice recorded by the trustee under a deed of trust that indicates that the trustor (borrower) is in default on the note and is in danger of foreclosure.

O

One-time capital gain credit   A provision in the Internal Revenue Code that allows a taxpayer who is over fifty-five years of age to sell his or her home once without having to pay income tax on a certain amount of the profits.

P

PACs   See *Political action committees.*

Perjury   False swearing; voluntary violation of an oath.

Petit jury   A body of twelve persons selected impartially to hear cases and render decisions under the direction of a judge.

Plea   An allegation of fact, as distinguished from a demurrer; in common law practice, a defendant's answer to the plaintiff's declaration or, in criminal practice, the accused person's answer to the charge against him or her.

Political action committees (PACs)   Committees allowed by the federal government to collect contributions that are used for the political advancement of candidates or causes favorable to the aims of the organization forming the committee.

Prepaid interest   Interest charged by a lender before it is actually due or earned.

Prepayment privilege   The privilege spelled out in a loan agreement that allows the borrower to pay off a loan ahead of maturity.

Probate   Official proof, especially of an instrument offered as the last will and testament of a person deceased.

Promissory note   The note evidencing a debt and outlining the terms under which the debt is to be repaid.

Proxy   Written power to act for another in a specific instance.

Q

Quasi-franchise   An organization to which a company can belong that does not pose the requirements of a regular franchise.

Quiet title suit   Proceedings brought to settle a property title dispute.

R

Rent control   A practice that rigidly controls the amount of rents that a landlord can charge on his or her units.

Restraining order   A court order temporarily restraining a party from committing a certain act until the court can decide whether an injunction should be issued.

Right of redemption   The right to redeem a property foreclosed on through court action, usually because of default on a mortgage but sometimes on a deed of trust.

S

S corporation   A special kind of corporation allowed by law that provides all of the protective benefits of a regular corporation but also allows income and deductions to pass through to the shareholders, much the same as in a partnership.

Second deed of trust   A deed of trust second in priority to the first deed of trust.

Security device   A device such as a mortgage or deed of trust that is used to secure real property for the repayment of the terms on a note.

Slander   A false report maliciously uttered and tending to injure the reputation of another.

Square footage   The area of a given property (either the land plot or the building alone). Land sales are often computed on a price per square foot, and commercial and industrial buildings are leased by this method.

Statute of limitations   A statute assigning a certain time after which rights cannot be enforced by legal action.

Stay of execution   Court order to withhold execution of a judgment.

Subpoena   A writ commanding the addressee to attend court.

Subpoena duces tecum   A subpoena that orders a witness to bring certain documents into court.

Summons   A warning or citation to appear in court.

T

Tax-deferred exchange   An arrangement under Section 1031 of the Internal Revenue Code that allows an owner to accept another property of like kind in exchange for his or her present holding, thereby eliminating payment of tax on the profit from the one he or she is disposing of.

Tax shelter   An accounting term describing an investment that throws off tax deductions from interest and depreciation allowances.

Tenements   Rights and interests that pertain to the land. See also *Appurtenances, Hereditaments.*

Testator (male), Testatrix (female)   A person who leaves a will in force at death.

Title company   A company that specializes in searching the abstract of titles to a property and then insuring that title for a new buyer for a fee. Some title companies in some areas of the country can also handle escrow for real estate transactions.

Transfer tax   The tax charged by many cities, counties, and states for the privilege of transferring title to property.

Trust   An equitable right or interest in property distinct from the legal ownership.

Trustee under deed of trust   The entity under a deed of trust that holds a form of title to the property to ensure the repayment of a debt (usually a corporation formed by the lender).

Truth-in-Lending laws   A group of laws enforced by the Federal Trade Commission to ensure that consumers are made fully aware of the cost of credit and are protected against false credit claims in advertising.

Two-party exchange   An Internal Revenue Code Section 1031 tax-deferred exchange in which only two parties are involved as distinct from a three-party or multiparty exchange.

U

Usury   Interest in excess of the legal rate charged to a borrower for the use of money.

V

Verdict   The decision of a jury on the matter submitted in trial.

Vested rights   Rights that are permanent and undisputed.

W

Waiver   Act of intentionally abandoning some known right, claim, or privilege; also the instrument evidencing such an act.

Without prejudice   Without effect on any rights that existed previously.

Writ   An order issued by a court commanding the performance or nonperformance of some act.

Z

Zoning   Laws in most cities, counties, and states that stipulate the uses to which any property may be put.

LANGUAGE USAGE

SECTION FOUR

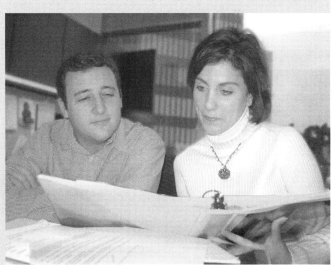

An administrative assistant reviews a report she is preparing for her manager.

Photo by Jennifer Wauson.

CHAPTER 31

Grammar

◇ THE PARTS OF SPEECH

There are nine parts of speech within the English language:

1. Nouns
2. Verbs
3. Adjectives
4. Adverbs
5. Pronouns
6. Prepositions
7. Conjunctions
8. Articles, determiners, and quantifiers
9. Interjections

This chapter examines the correct use of these parts of speech.

◇ NOUNS

A *noun* is the name of a person, place, thing, or idea. A *proper noun*, which names a specific person, place, or thing (Kevin, Atlanta, God, English, Jennifer), is usually capitalized. A proper noun used as someone's name is called a *noun of address*. The remaining nouns for everything else are called *common nouns* and are not usually capitalized.

A group of related words can act like a noun within a sentence. This is called a *noun clause*, and it contains a subject and a verb. Here is an example of a noun clause:

- What he did for the country was unbelievable.

In this example, "What he did for the country" is the noun clause.

A *noun phrase* consists of a noun with several modifiers that act as a single noun. The following are examples of noun phrases:

- Professional football team
- Money market account

- Grossly exaggerated totals
- Abnormally long fingers
- Real estate investment trust

There are also groups of words that can form *compound nouns*. Some examples include:

- Son-in-law
- Stick-in-the-mud

Other Noun Categories

There are additional categories of nouns:

- **Count Nouns**—Used for anything that can be counted, such as five dollars, a dozen, and seven continents
- **Mass Nouns**—Used for naming things that can't be counted, like water, air, energy, and data
- **Collective Nouns**—Used for naming groups of individuals or things, such as team, class, or jury
- **Abstract Nouns**—Used for naming intangible things, such as love, peace, justice, hope, hatred, and friendship

Some words can be a count noun or a non-count noun, depending on how they are used. Whether a noun is a count or non-count noun determines whether it can be used with articles and determiners. For example:

- **Non-count:** The team got into trouble.
- **Count:** The team had many troubles.

Noun Case

Nouns can be in the subjective, possessive, and objective case. The case tells you the role of a noun in a sentence. Here are some examples:

- The football player (*subject*) runs very fast.
- He selected a car (*object*).
- The football player's (*possessive*) jersey was torn.

Nouns in the subjective and objective case are identical. Nouns in the possessive usually require an apostrophe followed by the letter *s* or *es*.

◇ VERBS

Verbs are used in a sentence to describe an action or the idea of being. Consider the following:

- **Idea of being:** I *am* an administrative assistant.
- **Action:** The assistant *worked* late.

There are many different ways to classify verbs. *Transitive* verbs require an object, for example: "Will you *lay* the book on the desk?" In this example, "the book" is the object. *Intransitive* verbs do not require an object, for example: "The dog *lies* down everyday after lunch." Some verbs can be both transitive and intransitive depending on how they are used in a sentence. Others can be used only one way.

Verbs are also classified as either *finite* or *nonfinite*. A finite verb can stand alone as the main verb of a sentence. A nonfinite verb cannot. For example:

- **Finite:** The car *destroyed* the mailbox.
- **Nonfinite:** The *broken* mailbox . . .

Verb Forms

There are four basic forms of verb inflections (endings). They are:

1. Base form
2. Past form
3. Present participle
4. Past participle

These are used to help determine the tense of the verb. Tense tells you whether an action is happening now, is going to happen in the future, or has already happened in the past. Unlike some languages, English verbs do not form their tense just with the endings. Instead, they use auxiliary words. For example:

- **Base form:** I write.
- **Past form:** I wrote.
- **Present participle:** I am writing.
- **Past participle:** I have written.

Linking Verbs

A *linking verb* is used to connect a subject and its complement (a noun or adjective that describes the subject). These are often forms of the verb *to be*, but they sometimes include verbs related to the five senses (sight, sound, smell, feel, taste) and verbs that relate to a state of being (appear, seem, become, grow, turn, prove, remain). Here are some examples of linking verbs:

- These children *are* all students.
- Those clouds *look* dark.
- Rain *seems* likely.

Mood

Mood in verbs refers to the attitude of the speaker or writer. There are three attitudes that can accompany a verb. The first is *indicative mood*, which is used to make a statement or ask a question. These are the most common verb moods. The second attitude is *imperative mood*, which is used to give directions, give orders, or make a strong suggestion. Verbs used in the imperative mood do not need a subject since it is understood to be "you." For example:

- Get out of here.
- Go to the store before you come home.

The third attitude is *subjunctive mood*, which is used (1) with dependent clauses to express a wish, (2) with "if" and a condition, (3) with "as if" or "as though" along with a speculation, or (4) with expressions that begin with "that" and express a demand. For example:

- He wishes she were here.
- We would have won the game if we played harder.
- They acted as if they were hungry.
- The letter demanded that membership dues be paid on time.

One of the most important things about a verb's mood is the ability it gives to distinguish between factual statements and hypothetical statements. Hypothetical statements often use the words *could, would*, or *might*.

Phrasal Verbs

Phrasal verbs consist of a verb along with another word or phrase. Usually phrasal verbs are accompanied by a preposition. They are usually casual conversational phrases that are accepted into mainstream language usage. Here are some examples:

- The old people were *sitting around* doing nothing.
- He *looked up* his old teacher in the phone book.

In each case, the word that is joined with the verb is called a *particle*. The problem with phrasal verbs is that their meaning is often unclear. They can be used in conversation, but it is best to avoid them in formal business writing.

Causative Verbs

Causative verbs are used to describe an action that is necessary to cause another action, for example: "The devil *made* me *do* it." In this example, "made" causes the "do" to happen. There are many other causative verbs, including let, make, help, allow, have, *require, motivate, get, convince, hire, assist, encourage, permit, employ*, and *force*. Most causative verbs are followed by an object (a noun or pronoun) and an infinitive ("to" plus a verb). For example:

- He *allows his dog to sleep* all day.

There are three causative verbs that do not follow this pattern: *have, make,* and *let*. These verbs are usually followed by an object and the base form of the verb. For example:

- She *made her associates read* the entire report.

Factitive Verbs

Verbs like *make, choose, judge, elect, select,* and *name* are called *factitive verbs*. These verbs can take two objects. For example:

- The people elected Mike Jackson president of the homeowners association. ("Mike Jackson" is the object and "president of the homeowners association" is the second complement.)

Verb Tenses

A *tense* shows the time of an action or state of being. There are three tenses that change the endings of verbs. The *present tense* means that something is happening now, for example: "He is an executive. He wears nice suits." The *simple past tense* indicates that something happened in the past: "He was an executive. He wore nice suits." The *past participle* is combined with an auxiliary verb to indicate that something happened in the past prior to another action: "He had been an executive. He had worn nice suits."

Unlike other languages, English does not have a future tense. Instead, future verb forms are created with the use of auxiliaries: "He will be an executive. He will wear nice suits."

Progressive Verbs

Progressive verbs, which indicate something being or happening, are formed by the present participle form (ending in "-ing") along with an auxiliary. Here are some examples:

- She is crying.
- She will be crying.
- She had been crying.
- She was crying.
- She has been crying.
- She will have been crying.

The progressive form occurs only with dynamic verbs (verbs that show the ability to change). *Stative verbs*, on the other hand, are those that describe a quality that is incapable of change. For example, you wouldn't say, "She is being tall."

There are a variety of *dynamic verbs*: activity verbs, process verbs, verbs of bodily sensation, transitional events verbs, and momentary verbs. Following are some examples:

- **Activity verbs**—ask, play, work, write, say, listen, call, eat
- **Process verbs**—change, grow, mature, widen
- **Verbs of bodily sensation**—hurt, itch, ache, feel
- **Transitional events verbs**—arrive, die, land, leave, lose
- **Momentary verbs**—hit, jump, throw, kick

There are two classifications of *stative verbs:* verbs of inert perception and cognition, and relational verbs. Following are some examples:

- **Verbs of inert perception and cognition**—guess, hate, hear, please, satisfy
- **Relational verbs**—equal, possess, own, include, cost, concern, contain

Irregular Verbs

Most verbs form the simple past and past participle by adding "ed" to the base verb, for example: "He walked. He has walked." There are some irregular verbs that do not follow this pattern. For example, common verbs such as "to be" and "to have" have irregular forms.

Sequence of Tenses

There is a relationship between verbs in a main clause and verbs in a dependent clause. The verb tenses do not have to be the same as long as they are accurate about time and order. For example: "My father *will have returned*, before I *leave*."

Verbals

Verbals are words that seem to mean an action or a state of being but do not function as a real verb. They are sometimes called *nonfinite verbs*. Verbals are frequently used with other words in what is called a *verbal phrase*.

Participles

A *participle* is a verb that acts like an adjective, for example: "The *running* dog chased the *speeding* car." A present participle describes a present condition; a past participle describes something that has already happened. For example: "The *burned* tree fell down in the storm."

The Infinitive

An *infinitive* is formed with the root of a verb and the word "to," for example: "To be, or not to be." A *present infinitive* describes a present condition, for example: "I like to dream." The *perfect infinitive* describes a time earlier than that described by the verb, for example: "I would like to have slept until nine."

Gerunds

A *gerund* is a verb form ending in "-ing" that acts as a noun, for example: "Walking in the street after dark can be dangerous." Gerunds are usually accompanied by other words that make up a gerund phrase. In the example given, "walking in the street after dark" is a gerund phrase.

Because gerunds and gerund phrases are nouns, they can be used just like nouns. For example:

- **As a subject**—"*Being president* is a difficult job."

- **As objective of a verb**—"He didn't really like *being poor*."

- **As objective of a preposition**—"He read a book about *being careful*."

Problems with Split Infinitives

One of the most common grammar mistakes is the *split infinitive*. An infinitive is said to be split when a word (usually an adverb) is placed between the "to" of the infinitive and the root of verb, for example: "To boldly go where no man has gone before."

The argument against split infinitives is based on the idea that an infinitive is a single unit and should not be divided. Because it is so easy to spot, many writers try to avoid this construction. However, many word usage books now say that the rule against splitting infinitives can be ignored. To avoid the argument, it is a good rule to avoid split infinitives in business writing.

Infinitives, Gerunds, and Sequence

Although infinitives and gerunds are not really verbs, they describe action. When combined with auxiliary verb forms, infinitives and gerunds can also express concepts of time. (See Table 31–1.)

TABLE 31–1. Infinitives, Gerunds, and Sequence

Simple Forms	■ We had planned *to watch* the Super Bowl.
	■ *Seeing* the Cowboys win is always a great thrill.
Perfect Forms	■ The Cowboys hoped *to have won* the Super Bowl.
	■ I was thrilled about their *having been* in the big game.
Passive Forms	■ *To be chosen* as an NFL player must be the biggest thrill in any football player's life.
	■ *Being chosen*, however, doesn't mean you get to play.
Perfective Passive Forms	■ The men did not seem satisfied simply *to have been selected* as players.
	■ *Having been honored* this way, they went out and earned it by winning the Super Bowl.
Perfective Progressive Infinitive	■ *To have been competing* at this level was quite an accomplishment.

Passive and Active Voices

Verbs can either be *active* ("The assistant *used* the computer") or *passive* ("The computer *was used* by the assistant") in voice. In the active voice, the subject and verb relationship is easy to understand. The subject is the do-er or be-er and the verb describes an action. In the passive voice, the subject is not a do-er or be-er. Instead, the subject is being acted upon by something else.

Computerized grammar checkers, such as the one built into Microsoft Word, can detect passive voice construction and suggest a revision. There is nothing incorrect about using passive voice verbs; however, if you can say the same thing using the active voice, you should do so. Your writing will be easier to understand.

The passive voice does have its uses. When it is more important to draw attention to the person or thing that was acted on, the passive voice can be used, for example: "George *was killed* while riding a bicycle." Another situation where the passive voice is more appropriate is when the subject is not important, for example: "The meteor shower *can be observed* just after dark."

The passive voice is sometimes required for technical writing, where the do-er or be-er can be anyone, and the process being described is more important. Instead of writing, "I developed a computer program that can print checks," you would write, "A computer program was developed that can print checks."

The passive voice is created by combining a form of the "to be" verb with the past participle of the main verb. Other helping verbs are sometimes used.

Only transitive verbs (those that are objects) can be transformed into passive voice. However, some transitive verbs cannot be transformed into passive voice. "To have" is an example. You can say or write, "She has a new computer," but you can't say, "A new computer is had by her." Some other examples of verbs that cannot be used with the passive voice include *resemble, look like, equal, agree with, mean, contain, hold, comprise, lack, suit, fit*, and *become*.

Verbals can also be used in the passive voice. An infinitive phrase in the passive voice can perform a variety of functions in a sentence. The same is true for passive gerunds and passive participles.

◆ ADJECTIVES

Adjectives are words that describe or modify a person, place, or thing. Articles such as *a, an*, and *the* are adjectives. So are words like *tall, solid*, and *cold*.

A group of words containing a subject and verb may act as an adjective. These are called an *adjective clause*, for example: "My brother, *who is much older than I am*, is a psychologist." If the subject and verb are removed from an adjective clause, an *adjective phrase* results, for example: "He is the man *keeping my family fed*."

One thing to keep in mind about adjectives is not to ask too much of them. Use nouns and verbs to describe something. Sometimes adjectives don't add much to a sentence in the first place. For example, what do *interesting, beautiful, lovely*, and *exciting* really do for a sentence?

Adjective Position in a Sentence

Unlike adverbs, which can go almost anywhere in a sentence, adjectives almost always appear immediately before a noun or noun phrase that they modify. Sometimes adjectives appear in a string, and when they do, they must appear in a particular order according to category. When indefinite pronouns—such as *something, someone*, and *anybody*—are modified by an adjective, the adjective comes after the pronoun.

The order in which adjectives are arranged in a sentence is difficult for people learning English. They wonder why we wouldn't say "red big barn" instead of "big red barn." Adjectives are ordered as follows:

- **Determiners**—Articles and other limiters, such as a, an, five, her, our, those, that, several, and some

- **Observation**—Post-determiners and limiter adjectives and adjectives subject to subjective measure, such as beautiful, expensive, gorgeous, dilapidated, and delicious

- **Size and Shape**—Adjectives subject to objective measure, such as big, little, enormous, long, short, and square

- **Age**—Adjectives describing age, such as old, antique, new, and young

- **Color**—Adjectives denoting color, such as red, white, and black

- **Origin**—Adjectives denoting the source of the noun, such as American, French, and Canadian

- **Material**—Adjectives that describe what something is made of, such as silk, wooden, silver, and metallic

- **Qualifier**—Final limiter that is often part of the noun, such as rocking chair, hunting cabin, passenger car, or book cover

Sentences that run two or three adjectives together can be laborious to read. In addition, when adjectives belong to the same class, they are called *coordinated adjectives* and require a comma between them in a sentence. One good rule is to consider whether you could have inserted *and* or *but* between the adjectives. If so, then use a comma between them. For example, you could say "inexpensive but comfortable house." If the *but* is not in the sentence, you would punctuate it as "inexpensive, comfortable house."

Degrees of Adjectives

Adjectives can express degrees of modification: positive, comparative, and superlative. We use the comparative for comparing two things and the superlative for comparing three or more things. Sometimes the word *than* accompanies the comparative adjective and the word *the* precedes the superlative adjective. The inflected suffixes "-er" and "-est" are used to form most comparative and superlatives. Sometimes "-ier" and "-iest" are added when a two-syllable adjective ends in *y*. Table 31–2 gives some examples.

TABLE 31–2. Degrees of Adjectives

Positive	Comparative	Superlative
Rich	Richer	Richest
Lovely	Lovelier	Loveliest
Beautiful	More beautiful	Most beautiful

Some adjectives have irregular forms in the comparative and superlative degree, as shown in Table 31–3.

TABLE 31–3. Irregular Forms in the Comparative and Superlative Degree

Positive	Comparative	Superlative
Good	Better	Best
Bad	Worse	Worst
Little	Less	Least
Much, Many, Some	More	Most
Far	Further	Furthest

You should be careful not to form comparative or superlative adjectives that already describe a unique condition or extreme of comparison. *Perfect* and *pregnant* are good examples; a person cannot be *more* perfect or *more* pregnant.

Also be careful not to use the word *more* along with a comparative adjective formed with the "-er" suffix, or the word *most* along with a superlative adjective formed with the "-est" suffix. You'll end up with phrases such as *more larger* and *most largest*.

Less and Fewer

When making a comparison of quantities, we often have to make a choice between the adjectives *less* and *fewer*. When you are talking about countable things, you should use the word *fewer*. When you are talking about measurable quantities that cannot be counted, you should use the word *less*, for example: "He has fewer assets, but less worries."

Than I or Than Me

When making a comparison between yourself and something else, you often end with a subject form or object form like "taller than I/she." In the sentence "He is taller than I am," or "He is taller than she is," normally we leave out the verb in the second clause (*am* or *is*).

Be careful with comparisons such as "I like him better than she" or "I like him better than her." In the first case, you are saying that you like him better than she likes him. In the second case, you are saying that you like the male person better than you like the female person. To avoid confusion with the word *than*, you should write, "I like him better than she does" or "I like him better than I like her."

Capitalizing Proper Adjectives

When an adjective's origin is a proper noun, it should be capitalized, for example: Christian music, Nixon era, Victorian poet, and Jeffersonian democracy.

Collective Adjectives

When the article *the* is combined with an adjective describing a class or group of people, the resulting phrase can act as a noun: the meek, the rich, the poor. The difference between a collective noun and a collective adjective is that the collective adjective is always plural and requires a plural verb, for example: "The *meek will* inherit the earth."

Adjectival Opposites

The opposite of an adjective can be formed in a number of different ways. One way is to find an adjective antonym. For example, the opposite of cold is hot. A thesaurus can help you find an appropriate antonym. Another way to form a negative adjective is through use of a prefix. Consider the following pairs:

- Fortunate—unfortunate
- Prudent—imprudent
- Considerate—inconsiderate
- Honorable—dishonorable
- Alcoholic—nonalcoholic
- Filed—misfiled

A third way to form an adjectival opposite is to combine the adjective with *less* or *least*. In fact, this method allows for tact and a smoother tone in some cases. For example, "That is the least beautiful girl in the class" is somewhat more tactful than "That is the ugliest girl in the class."

Good Versus Well

Frequently we have to choose between using *well* and *good* in our sentences. *Good* is an adjective and *well* is an adverb. Therefore, when describing an action verb, the only choice is the adverb *well*, for example: "He speaks well."

When using a linking verb or a verb that has to do with the five human senses, you want to use the adjective *good* instead, for example: "You smell good today." Many writers use *well* after linking verbs related to health, since *well* is related to wellness. For example: "How are you doing? I am well, thank you."

Bad Versus Badly

The same rule that applies to *well* and *good* also applies to *bad* and *badly*. *Bad* is an adjective and *badly* is an adverb. Use the adjective *bad* when referring to human feeling: "I felt bad." If you said, "I felt badly," this would imply that there was something wrong with your sense of touch.

A-Adjectives

There are a group of adjectives that follow their own unique rules. These so-called a-adjectives are *ablaze, afloat, afraid, aghast, alert, alike, alive, alone, aloof, ashamed, asleep, averse, awake,* and *aware.* These adjectives are used after a linking verb, for example: "The man was ashamed."

Sometimes you can use an a-adjective before the word it modifies, for example: "the alert driver." A-adjectives are sometimes modified with "very much," for example: "The man was very much ashamed."

✦ ADVERBS

Adverbs are words that modify verbs, adjectives, or another adverb. Adverbs often describe when, where, why, or under what circumstances something happened. Adverbs often end in "-ly"; however, there are many words not ending in "-ly" that serve as adverbs. There are also words ending in "-ly" that are not adverbs. For example, the words *lovely, lonely, motherly,* and *friendly* are adjectives.

When a group of words containing a subject and a verb act as an adverb (modifying another verb in the sentence), it is called an *adverb clause.* Here is an example: "*When this game is over,* we're going home for dinner." When a group of words not containing a subject and a verb act as an adverb, it is called an *adverbial phrase.* Prepositional phrases frequently have the function of an adverb, for example: "She works *on weekends.*"

An infinitive phrase can also act as an adverb, for example: "The assistant ran *to catch the bus.*"

Adjectives cannot modify adverbs, but adverbs can modify adjectives, for example: "The executive showed a *wonderfully* casual attitude." Like adjectives, adverbs can have comparative and superlative forms, for example: "You should walk *faster* if you want to get some exercise. The candidate who types *fastest* gets the job." Sometimes words like *more* and *most, less* and *least* are used to show an amount, for example: "The house was the *most beautifully* decorated home on the tour."

Another construction used to create adverbs is use of *as . . . as,* for example: "He can't read *as* fast *as* his sister."

A small group of adverbs have two forms, one that ends in "-ly" and one that doesn't. In some cases, the two forms have different meanings. For example: "They departed *late.*" "*Lately,* they can't seem to be on time." In most cases, the form without the "-ly" should be reserved for casual conversation and not business writing. for example: "He did her wrong."

Adverbs are often used as *intensifiers* in order to convey a greater or lesser meaning. Intensifiers have three different functions. They can emphasize, amplify, or tone down a verb. The following are some examples of each type:

- **Emphasize**—I *really* don't like him. He *simply* ignores me.

- **Amplify**—He *completely* wrecked his new car. I *absolutely* love fresh fruit.

- **Tone down**—I *kind of* like this restaurant's food. She *mildly* disapproved of his smoking.

Types of Adverbs

There are five main types of adverbs:

1. **Adverbs of manner**—He spoke *slowly* and walked *quietly.*
2. **Adverbs of place**—He lives *there* now.
3. **Adverbs of frequency**—He drives to work *every morning.*
4. **Adverbs of time**—He slept *late.*
5. **Adverbs of purpose**—He drives his car slowly *to avoid getting a ticket.*

Adverbs in a Numbered List

Within normal text, it is usually best not to number items beyond three or four. Anything more than that should be formatted in a vertical numbered list. When you create a numbered list, do not use adverbs with an "-ly" ending (secondly, thirdly, etc). Instead, use first, second, third, and so on.

Adverbs to Avoid

Adverbs like *very, extremely,* and *really* don't intensify anything. They are often too imprecise for business writing. You should avoid using such adverbs.

Positions of Adverbs

Adverbs have a unique ability to be placed in different places within a sentence. Adverbs of manner are unusually flexible in this regard. For example:

- Solemnly, the president returned the salute.
- The president solemnly returned the salute.
- The president returned the salute solemnly.

Adverbs of frequency can appear at the following places within a sentence:

- **Before the main verb**—He *never* gets up before noon.
- **Between the auxiliary verb and the main verb**—I have *rarely* called my sister without a good reason.
- **Before the verb "used to"**—I *always* used to talk to him at the bus stop.

Indefinite adverbs of time can appear either before the verb or between the auxiliary and the main verb:

- He *finally* showed up for the date.
- He has *recently* traveled to France.

Order of Adverbs

There is a basic order in which adverbs can appear in a sentence when there is more than one. (See Table 31–4.)

TABLE 31–4. Order of Adverbs

Verb	Manner	Place	Frequency	Time	Purpose
John jogs	enthusiastically	in the park	every morning	before sunrise	to keep in shape
Mary drives	hurriedly	into town	every afternoon	before dinner	to do her shopping

As a general rule, shorter adverbial phrases precede longer ones, regardless of content. For example: "Mike takes a short swim *before breakfast every morning in the summer*." Among similar adverbial phrases of kind (manner, place, frequency), the more specific adverbial phrase goes first, for example: "He promised to meet her *for coffee sometime next week*." If you move an adverbial modifier to the beginning of a sentence, additional emphasis will be placed on that modifier. This is especially useful with adverbs of manner, for example: "*Slowly, ever so carefully*, the little boy crept into his parents' bedroom."

Inappropriate Adverb Order

Modifiers can sometimes attach themselves to the wrong word, for example: "They reported that Leslie Fiedler, a famous literary critic, had won the lottery *on the evening news*." It would be better to move the modifier immediately after the verb it is modifying (reported) or to the beginning of the sentence: "They reported on the evening news that Leslie Fiedler, a famous literary critic, had won the lottery."

The adverbs *only* and *barely* are often misplaced modifiers, for example: "He *only* grew to be five feet tall." This would be better stated as follows: "He grew to be *only five feet tall*."

Adjuncts, Disjuncts, and Conjuncts

Adverbs are usually neatly integrated into the flow of a sentence. When this is true, the adverb is called an *adjunct*. When an adverb does not fit into the sentence flow, it is called a *disjunct* or *conjunct* and is usually set off by a comma or a series of commas. A disjunct acts as if it is evaluating the rest of the sentence. Rather than modify the verb, it modifies the entire clause, for example: "*Honestly*, Bill, I don't really care." Conjuncts serve as a connector within the flow of the text, signaling a transition, for example: "If they start talking politics, *then* I'm leaving." One variation is the adverbial conjunction. These are words like *however* and *nevertheless*. For example: "I love this job, *however*, I don't think I can afford to stay."

Special Adverbial Clauses

Some adverbs have special rules for their placement. For instance, the adverbs *enough* and *not enough* usually take a post-modifier position, for example: "Is your food *hot enough*? This food is *not hot enough.*" *Enough* can also be an adjective. When it is used as an adjective, it comes before the noun, for example: "The teacher didn't give us *enough time.*" The adverb *enough* is often followed by an infinitive verb, for example: "They didn't play hard *enough to win.*"

The adverb *too* usually comes before adjectives and other adverbs, for example: "He ate *too fast*. He eats *too quickly.*" When *too* appears in a sentence after an adverb, it is a disjunct adverb and is set apart with a comma, for example: "John works hard. He works *quickly, too.*" The adverb *too* is sometimes followed by an infinitive verb, for example: "He talks *too slowly to keep* my attention." The adverb *too* can also be followed by the prepositional phrase *for* + the objective of the preposition + an infinitive. An example is: "This food is *too spicy for grandma to eat.*"

Relative Adverbs

Adjectival clauses can be introduced by *relative adverbs*: *where, when,* and *why.* Although each of these is an adjectival clause and modifies a noun, the relative word itself serves in an adverbial function, modifying the verb within the clause. The relative adverb *where* begins a clause that modifies a noun of place, for example: "My family now lives in the *town where* my grandfather used to be sheriff." The relative pronoun *where* modifies the verb *used to be,* but the entire clause modifies the noun *town.*

A *when* clause modifies nouns of time, for example: "My favorite day of the week is *Friday, when* the weekend is about to begin."

A *why* clause modifies the noun *reason,* for example: "Do you know the *reason why* school is out today?" Sometimes the relative adverb is left out of these clauses and the writer substitutes *that* instead, for example: "Do you know the *reason that* school it out today?"

Viewpoint Adverbs

A *viewpoint adverb* usually comes after a noun and is related to an adjective that precedes the noun, for example: "Investing all our money in technology stocks was probably not a *good idea financially.*"

Focus Adverbs

A *focus adverb* is used to limit a specific aspect of the sentence, for example: "He got a promotion *just* for being there."

Negative Adverbs

Negative adverbs can create a negative meaning in a sentence without the use of words like *no, not, neither, nor,* or *never.* Here are some examples: "He *seldom* smiles. He *hardly* eats anything since he got sick. After losing so many key players, *rarely* did anyone attend the games."

◈ PRONOUNS

Usually, *pronouns* refer to a noun, an individual or a group, or a thing whose identity has been made clear previously. The word a pronoun substitutes for is called its *antecedent*. "Jeanne accepted Carmelo's proposal. She knew *he* was the right guy for *her*." Not all pronouns refer to an antecedent. For example, in the sentence "Everyone on this floor charges over one hundred dollars an hour," the pronoun *everyone* does not have an antecedent.

Types of Pronouns

There are a variety of different kinds of pronouns, which are discussed in the following sections:

- Personal
- Demonstrative
- Relative
- Indefinite
- Intensive
- Reflexive
- Interrogative
- Reciprocal

Personal Pronouns

Personal pronouns change form according to their various uses within a sentence. The pronoun I is used as the subject of a sentence, for example: "I am tall." The pronoun *me* is used as an object in various ways, for example: "He gave me a car." The pronoun *my* is used for the possessive form, for example: "That's my house." The same is true for other personal pronouns: the singular *you* and *he/she/it* and the plurals *we*, *you*, and *they*. These forms are called *cases*. (See Table 31–5.)

TABLE 31–5. Various Cases for Pronouns

	Subjective	Possessive	Objective
Singular first person	I	My, mine	Me
Singular second person	You	Your, yours	You
Singular third person	He, she, it	His, her, hers, its	Him, her, it
Plural first person	We	Our, ours	Us
Plural second person	You	Your, yours	You
Plural third person	They	Their, theirs	Them
Relative and interrogative pronouns	Who, whoever, which, that, what	Whose	Whom, whomever, which, that, what
Indefinite pronouns	Everybody	Everybody's	Everybody

When a personal pronoun is connected by a conjunction to another noun or pronoun, it does not change case, for example: "I am taking a course in Latin. John and I are taking a course in Latin." You'll notice in the second sentence that "John" is listed before "I." The same is true when the object form is used: "The professor gave the Latin books to me. The professor gave the Latin books to John and me."

When a pronoun and a noun are combined, you must choose the case of the pronoun that would be appropriate if the noun were not there, for example: "*We* teachers are demanding a raise." With the second person, there's not as much confusion because the pronoun *you* is the same for both subject and object form: "*You* teachers are demanding too much money."

Among the possessive pronoun forms, there are nominative possessives such as *mine, yours, ours*, and *theirs*. Here are some examples: "This new house is mine. Look at those houses. Theirs needs work. Ours is in good shape. Mine is newer than yours."

Demonstrative Pronouns

The *demonstrative pronouns—this, that, these, those*, and *such*—can be used as either pronouns or as determiners. As pronouns, the demonstrative pronouns identify a noun: "*That* is marvelous! I will never forget *this*. *Such* is life."

As determiners, the demonstrative pronouns adjectivally modify a noun that follows. They are used to convey a sense of time and distance. For example: "*These* (strawberries that are in front of me) look delicious. *Those* (that are further away) look even better."

A sense of emotional distance can also be conveyed through the use of demonstrative pronouns, for example: "You're going to eat *that*?" Pronouns used in this way receive special emphasis in a spoken sentence.

When used as subjects, demonstrative pronouns can be used to refer to objects as well as persons, for example: "This is my mother. This is my book."

Relative Pronouns

The *relative pronouns—who, whoever, which*, and *that*—relate to groups of words, nouns, and other pronouns. The pronoun *who* connects the subject to the verb within a dependent clause. Choosing between *which* and *that* and between *who* and *whom* is difficult for many people. Generally, we use *which* to introduce clauses that are parenthetical in nature. That means they can be removed from the sentence without changing the meaning of the sentence. For that reason, a *which* clause is often set apart with a comma or a pair of commas. We use *that* to introduce clauses that are indispensable for the meaning of the sentence. *That* clauses are not set apart with commas. The pronoun *which* refers to things, *who* refers to people, and *that* usually refers to things but also refers to people in a general way.

The expanded relative pronouns *whoever, whomever*, and *whatever* are known as indefinite relative pronouns. They do not define any thing or person in particular, for example: "The company will hire *whomever* it pleases. She seemed to say *whatever* came to mind. *Whoever* took the money will be punished." *What* can be an indefinite relative pronoun when used like the following: "He will give you *what* you need for the trip."

Indefinite Pronouns

The *indefinite pronouns—everybody, anybody, somebody, all, each, every, some, none,* and *one*—do not substitute for specific nouns but act as nouns themselves.

One of the problems with the indefinite pronoun *everybody* is that is seems to be plural but takes a singular verb, for example: "*Everybody* is coming." The indefinite pronoun *none* can be either singular or plural. It is usually plural except when something else in the sentence forces it to be singular. *Some* can be singular or plural depending on whether it refers to something countable or not countable.

Some indefinite pronouns also double as determiners, such as *enough, few, fewer, less, little, many, much, several, more, most, all, both, every, each, any, either, neither, none,* and *some.*

Intensive Pronouns

The *intensive pronouns—myself, yourself, herself, ourselves,* and *themselves*—consist of a personal pronoun plus the suffix "-self" or "-selves." They are used to emphasize a noun, for example: "I *myself* didn't play baseball."

Reflexive Pronouns

Reflexive pronouns indicate that the subject in a sentence also receives the action of the verb: "People who cheat on their taxes are only hurting *themselves.*" Whenever there is a reflexive pronoun in a sentence, there must be a person to whom the pronoun can reflect. For example, "Please give the food to *myself*" is incorrect because there is no other subject such as "I" in the sentence.

There is a tendency to use reflexive and intensive pronouns (those ending in "-self") when they are not appropriate. For example, "These books will be read by *myself*" should be "These books will be read by *me.*"

The indefinite pronoun *one* has its own reflexive form, for example: "One must trust oneself." Other indefinite pronouns use either *himself* or *themselves* as reflexives.

Interrogative Pronouns

Interrogative pronouns are used to introduce questions, for example: "*What* is that? *Who* is coming? *Which* dog do you like best?" *Which* is used for specific reference rather than *what.* For example, in the sentence "Which dogs do you like best?" you are referring to specific dogs. "What dogs do you like best?" refers to general dog breeds you like best.

Interrogative pronouns can also act as determiners, for example: "It doesn't matter which road you take." In this role, the pronouns are called *interrogative adjectives.*

Interrogative pronouns are used to introduce noun clauses. Like relative pronouns, the interrogative pronouns play a subject role in the clause they introduce, for example: "I already told the salesman *what I thought about it.*"

Reciprocal Pronouns

The *reciprocal pronouns*—*each other* and *one another*—are used for combining ideas, for example: "My brother and I give *each other* a hard time." If more than two people are involved, you would use *one another.*

Reciprocal pronouns can also take the possessive form, for example: "They borrowed *each other's* clothes."

Pronouns and Antecedent Agreement

A pronoun usually refers to its antecedent, and the two must agree in number. Therefore, if the antecedent is plural, the pronoun must be plural. The same is true if the antecedent is singular; the pronoun must then be singular.

Certain pronouns like *anyone, anybody, everyone, everybody, someone, somebody, no one,* and *nobody* are always singular. This is perplexing for some people, because they feel that *everyone* and *everybody* refer to more than one person. The same is also true for *either* and *neither.* Even though they seem to be referring to two things, they are singular.

One of the most frequently asked grammar questions is regarding the pronoun *who* (*who, whose, whom, whoever, and whomever*). The choice of singular or plural is determined by what the pronoun refers to. It can refer to a single person or a group. For example: "*The person who* broke my window should confess. *The people who* have been without power should complain." One good way to understand the uses for *who* is to compare it with the pronouns *he* and *they.* (See Table 31–6.)

TABLE 31–6. The Pronoun *Who* Compared to *He* and *They*

	Subject Form	Possessive Form	Object Form
Singular	He	His	Him
	Who	Whose	Whom
Plural	They	Their	Them
	Who	Whose	Whom

So one good way to choose between the various forms of *who* is to think of the sentence in terms of the choice between *he* and *him.* If *him* feels right, choose *whom.* If *he* sounds better, pick *who.* For example:

- *Who* do you think is coming? (Do you think *he* is coming?)
- *Whom* shall we invite to the movie? (Shall we invite *him* to the movie?)
- Give the money to *whomever* you please. (Give the money to *him.*)
- Give the money to *whoever* wants it most. (*He* seems to want it most.)
- *Whoever* guesses my age will win the prize. (*He* guesses my age.)

Another related problem is confusing *whose* with *who's. Who's* looks like it is possessive; however, it is really a contraction of "who is."

◆ PREPOSITIONS

Prepositions are used to describe relationships between other words in a sentence. Prepositions like *in, on,* or *between* are good examples because they describe the spatial nature of things.

Prepositions are almost always combined with other words to become prepositional phrases. Prepositional phrases consist of a preposition plus a determiner, along with an adjective or two, followed by a pronoun or noun that is called the object of the preposition. The prepositional phrase takes on a modifying role of its own, acting as either an adjective or adverb to locate something in time and space, or explaining when or where, or understanding under what circumstances something occurred.

Types of Prepositions

Prepositions can be divided into types: (1) prepositions of time, (2) prepositions of place, (3) prepositions of location, and (4) prepositions of movement.

Prepositions of Time: **At, On, In, For, *and* Since**

At, on, and *in* often serve as prepositions of time. We use *at* to designate specific times, for example: "Meet me *at* five o'clock." We use *on* to designate days and dates, for example: "I work all day *on* Saturdays." We use *in* for nonspecific times, for example: "He likes to read *in* the evenings."

The preposition *for* is used to measure time, for example: "He worked *for* twenty years." The preposition *since* is used with a specific date or time, for example: "I have known him *since* January 2003."

Prepositions of Place: **At, On, *and* In**

At, on, and *in* can also serve as prepositions of place. We use *at* for specific addresses: "I live *at* 5203 Legendary Lane." We use *on* to designate streets: "I live *on* Legendary Lane." We use *in* for the names of towns, states, and countries: "I live *in* Acworth."

Prepositions of Location: **At, On, *and* In**

At, on, and *in* can also be used as prepositions of location. Their usage is specific to certain places. For example, we say: "in the bed," "in the bedroom," "in the car," "in the class," "in the library," "in the room," and "in the school." We also say "at class," "at home," "at the library," "at the office," "at school," or "at work." Depending on the specific situation, we can say: "on the bed," "on the ceiling," "on the floor," "on the horse," "on the plane," or "on the train."

Prepositions of Movement: **To** *and* **Toward**

The preposition *to* is used to express movement to a place, for example: "I am driving to work."

Toward and *towards* are also used to express movement, for example: "We were working toward a common goal." They are both the same word with a spelling variation; you can use either one.

Preposition Combinations

Some prepositions are so commonly used with particular nouns, adjectives, and verbs that they have almost become one word. The following is a list of nouns and preposition combinations:

- Approval of
- Awareness of
- Belief in
- Concern for
- Confusion about
- Desire for
- Fondness for
- Grasp of
- Hatred of

- Hope for
- Interest in
- Love of
- Need for
- Participation in
- Reason for
- Respect for
- Success in
- Understanding of

The following is a list of adjectives and preposition combinations:

- Afraid of
- Angry at
- Aware of
- Capable of
- Careless about
- Familiar with
- Fond of
- Happy about
- Interested in

- Jealous of
- Made of
- Married to
- Proud of
- Similar to
- Sorry for
- Sure of
- Tired of
- Worried about

A combination of a verb and preposition is called a *phrasal verb*. The word that is joined with the verb is called a *particle*. The following is a list of verb and preposition combinations:

- Apologize for
- Ask about
- Ask for

- Belong to
- Bring up
- Care for

- Find out
- Give up
- Grow up
- Look for
- Look forward to
- Look up
- Make up
- Pay for

- Prepare for
- Study for
- Talk about
- Think about
- Trust in
- Work for
- Worry about

◇ CONJUNCTIONS

Conjunctions are words that connect parts of a sentence. The simplest conjunctions are called *coordinating conjunctions*. They include *and, but, or, yet, for, nor,* and *so.*

When a coordinating conjunction connects two independent clauses, it is often accompanied by a comma, for example: "John wants to play football for Texas, *but* he has had trouble with his grades." It is also correct to use a comma with *and* when used to attach the list item in a list, for example: "John needs to study harder in math, history, physics, *and* economics." When a coordinating conjunction is used to connect all the elements in a series, a comma is not used, for example: "Math *and* history *and* physics are the subjects that give John the most trouble." Commas are also used with *but* when a sentence expresses a contrast, for example: "John is a great player, *but* not very smart."

The most common coordinating conjunctions are *and, but*, and *or*. Each has its own unique uses.

Coordinating Conjunction: *And*

The coordinating conjunction *and* can be used in the following ways:

- To suggest that one idea is sequential to another, for example: "Steve sent in his application *and* waited for the response in the mail."

- To suggest that an idea is the result of another, for example: "Linda heard the thunder *and* quickly took shelter inside the house."

- To suggest that one idea is in contrast to another, for example: "Lori is an artist, *and* her sister is a doctor." Frequently, the conjunction *but* is used for this purpose.

- To suggest an element of surprise, for example: "Atlanta is a beautiful city *and* has symptoms of urban blight." Frequently, the conjunction *yet* is used for this purpose.

- To suggest that one clause is dependent, for example: "Drink too much water before the trip *and* you'll soon find yourself stopping at every rest area."

- To make a comment on the first clause, for example: "Horace became addicted to gambling—*and* that's why he moved to Las Vegas."

Coordinating Conjunction: *But*

The coordinating conjunction *but* can be used in the following ways:

- To suggest an unexpected contrast, for example: "Tom lost money in his investments, *but* he still maintained a comfortable lifestyle."

- To express positively what the first part of the sentence implies negatively, for example: "Tom never invested foolishly *but* listened carefully to the advice of investment newsletters."

- To connect two ideas with the meaning "with the exception of," for example: "Everyone *but* Tom is making money in the stock market."

Coordinating Conjunction: *Or*

The coordinating conjunction *or* can be used in the following ways:

- To suggest that only one possibility is realistic and excludes the other, for example: "You can sell your investment now *or* you can lose all your money."

- To suggest alternatives, for example: "We can go out to eat and to a movie, *or* we can just stay home and see what's on TV."

- To suggest a refinement of the first clause, for example: "The University of Texas is the best school in the state, *or* so it seems to every UT alumni."

- To suggest a correction to the first part of the sentence, for example: "There's no way you can lose money in this investment, *or* so Eric told himself."

- To suggest a negative condition, for example: "You have two choices: pay taxes *or* die."

Other Conjunctions

The conjunction *nor* is used occasionally by itself; however, it is most commonly used in a correlative pair with *neither*, for example: "He is *neither* rich *nor* poor." Nor can also be used with negative expressions, for example: "This is not how I normally dress, *nor* should you get the idea I have no taste in clothes."

The word *yet* sometimes functions as an adverb and has various meanings such as *in addition, even, still*, and *eventually*. It also functions as a coordinating conjunction with a meaning of *nevertheless* or *but*, for example: "Rosemary is an expert in computer programming, *yet* her real passion is poetry."

The word *for* is often used as a preposition, but it does sometimes act as a coordinating conjunction. When it is used as a coordinating conjunction, it has a meaning of *because* or *since*, for example: "For he's a jolly good fellow."

The conjunction *so* can be used to connect two independent clauses along with a comma. It has the meaning of *as well* or *in addition*. Many writers would eliminate the *so* and use a semicolon between the two clauses.

Subordinating Conjunctions

A subordinating conjunction comes at the beginning of a dependent clause and establishes the relationship between the clause and the rest of the sentence, for example: "He spoke Spanish *as if* he had been born in Mexico."

Many subordinating conjunctions also serve as prepositions. When they serve as subordinating conjunctions, they introduce the dependent clause. (See Table 31–7.)

TABLE 31–7. Common Surrounding Conjunctions

After	If	Though
Although	If only	Till
As	In order that	Unless
As if	Now that	Until
As long as	Once	When
As though	Rather than	Whenever
Because	Since	Where
Before	So that	Whereas
Even if	Than	Wherever
Even though	That	While

Correlative Conjunctions

Correlative conjunctions combine with other words to form grammatically equal pairs. The following is a list of correlative conjunctions:

- Both . . . and
- Not . . . but
- Neither . . . nor
- As . . . as

- Not only . . . but also
- Either . . . or
- Whether . . . or

◆ ARTICLES, DETERMINERS, AND QUANTIFIERS

Articles, determiners, and *quantifiers* are little words that precede and modify nouns, for example: "*the* dog, *a* cat, *those* people, *whatever* purpose, *either* way, *your* choice." Sometimes these words tell you whether the subject is something specific or more general. Sometimes they tell you how much or how many.

The choice of the proper article or determiner is usually not a problem for the native English speaker. The following is a list of determiner categories:

- Articles—an, a, the
- Determiners—articles and other limiters such as a, an, five, her, our, those, that, several, and some
- Possessive nouns—Kevin's, the worker's, my mother's

- Possessive pronouns—his, your, their, whose

- Numbers—one, two, three, etc.

- Demonstrative pronouns—this, that, these, those, such

Articles

The three articles *a, an*, and *the* are a type of adjective. *The* is called the *definite article* because it tends to name something specific. *A* and *an* are called *indefinite articles* because they refer to things in a less specific way.

The is used with specific nouns and is required when the noun refers to something that is unique, for example: "*The* earth orbits *the* sun." *The* is also used for abstract nouns, for example: "The city of Atlanta has encouraged *the* use of mass transit."

A is used before singular nouns that begin with consonants, for example: "*A* dog, *a* cat, *a* mountain." *An* is used before singular nouns that begin with vowels or vowel-like sounds, for example: "*An* apple, *an* eagle, *an* invitation."

Predeterminers

Predeterminers occur prior to other determiners and include multipliers (*double, twice, two/three times,* etc.); fractional expressions (*one-half, one-third,* etc.); the words *both, half,* and *all*; and the intensifiers *quite, rather,* and *such.*

Multipliers precede plural count and mass nouns and with singular count nouns denoting numbers or an amount, for example: "This classroom holds *three times* the students as my old room."

Fractional expressions have a similar construction as multipliers and optionally include *of,* for example: "*One-half of* the voters favored lower taxes."

Intensifiers occur primarily in casual speech and are more common in British English than in American English, for example: "This food is *rather* bland, isn't it? The voters made *quite a* fuss over the debate."

Quantifiers

Quantifiers are words that also precede and modify nouns. They are used to communicate how many or how much. Selecting the correct quantifier depends on whether it is used with a count or non-count noun. For example, the following quantifiers can be used with count nouns: *many* people, *a few* people, *several* people, *a couple of* people, *none of the* people. The following quantifiers can be used with non-count nouns: *not much* eating, *a little* eating, *little* eating, *a bit of* eating, *a good deal of* eating, *a great deal of* eating, *no* eating.

INTERJECTIONS

Interjections are words or phrases used to communicate excitement, orders, or protests. Sometimes they can be used by themselves, but often they are contained within more complex sentence structures, for example: "*Wow*, I can't believe it. *Oh*, I didn't realize you were here. *No*, you shouldn't have done that."

Most interjections are treated as parenthetical elements and are set apart from the rest of the sentence by commas or a set of commas. If the interjection is more forceful, it is followed with an exclamation point.

Language Usage and Style

◇ SENTENCE SUBJECT

The *subject* of a sentence is the person, place, or thing that is the main focus of the sentence. To find the subject of a sentence, first locate the verb. Then answer the question: "What or who is being 'verbed'?" For instance, in the sentence "The monkeys in the treetops must be observed," the verb is *must be observed*. So, what must be observed? The answer is *monkeys*. A *simple subject* is the subject without any modifiers. For example, the simple subject of the following sentence is event: "The upcoming *event*, stripped of all the hype, is nothing but a fund-raiser."

Sometimes a simple subject can be more than one word or even an entire clause. Consider the following: "*What he had forgotten about the law* was amazing considering how many years he spent in law school." The simple subject is the entire clause printed in italics.

Usually, when the subject of a sentence is *you* and the sentence is a suggestion, order, or command, the *you* is left out. For example, in the sentence "Get out of the way!" you is understood to be the subject.

For sentence analysis, the person who initiates an action is called the *agent* of a sentence. When the active voice is used, the subject is the agent, for example: "The class failed the test." When the passive voice is used, the agent is not the subject. In fact, some passive sentences don't contain an agent.

◇ SUBJECT–VERB INVERSION

Normally, a sentence contains a subject and then a verb in that order. This pattern is disturbed in only a few instances. Here are a few examples:

- **In questions**—"Have you read that book?"

- **In expletive constructions**—"Here is your book."

- **To put focus on a particular word**—"What's more important is his reluctance to find a job."

- **When a sentence begins with an adverb, adverbial phrase, or clause**—"Rarely have so many been eaten in just one meal."

- **After the word "so"**—"I believe him; so do the people."

◆ SUBJECT-VERB AGREEMENT

The basic rule of subject-verb agreement is that a singular subject needs a singular verb. Likewise, plural subjects need plural verbs. For example: "My *brother is* a psychologist. My *brothers are* psychologists."

Indefinite pronouns like *anyone, everyone, someone, no one*, and *nobody* are singular subjects and, thus, require singular verbs. For example: "Everyone *is* studying hard."

Some indefinite pronouns, such as *all* and *some*, can be singular or plural depending on whether the thing they're referring to is countable or not. For example: "Some of the candy *is* missing. Some of the dogs *are* barking."

There is one indefinite pronoun, *none*, that can be either singular or plural, and it doesn't matter whether you use a singular or plural verb—that is, unless something in the sentence specifies its number. For example: "None of you *write* poetry. None of the cars *are* speeding."

Some indefinite pronouns like *everyone* and *everybody* sound like they are talking about more than one person; however, they are both singular. For example: "Everyone *is* working hard." The pronoun *each* is often followed by a prepositional phrase ending in a plural word: "Each of the monkeys . . . " *Each*, however, is also singular. For example: "Each of the monkeys *is* eating a banana."

Don't confuse the word *and* with the phrases *together with, as well as*, and *along with*. They do not mean the same and do not create compound subjects the same way *and* does. For example: "The boy, as well as his brother, *is* going to school. The boy and his brother *are* going to school."

The pronouns *neither* and *either* are singular even though they appear to be referring to two things, for example: "Neither of the two computers *is* obsolete. Either *is* a good choice for a student." Sometimes *neither* and *either* take a plural verb when they are followed by a prepositional phrase that begins with *of*, for example: "*Have* either of you two kids seen my dog? *Are* either of you listening to me?"

When the conjunctions *or* and *nor* are used, the subject closest to the verb determines whether the verb is singular or plural, for example: "Neither the bear nor the monkeys *were* awake when we visited the zoo." It's also a good idea to put the plural subject closest to the verb since the following version of the same sentence would be incorrect: "Neither the monkeys nor the bear was awake when we visited the zoo."

The words *there* and *here* can never be subjects in a sentence. For example: "Here *are* my two books. There better *be* a good reason you have them." These are called *expletive constructions*, and the subject follows the verb and determines whether the verb is singular or plural.

Verbs for third-person, singular subjects like *he, she*, and *it* have -s endings, for example: "He loves to eat."

Sometimes modifiers slip between a subject and a verb. When this happens, don't let them confuse the subject-verb agreement. For example: "The *workers*, who always seem to be standing around taking a break, gathered around in a circle like a football huddle, *are* being fired."

Sometimes nouns take peculiar forms that make it confusing to tell whether they are singular or plural. Words such as *glasses, gloves, pliers,* and *scissors* are thought of as plural unless they're preceded by the phrase *pair of*—in which case *pair* becomes the subject. For example: "My glasses *are* on the desk. The pair of glasses *is* on the desk."

Some words that end in -s seem to be plural but are really singular and thus require singular verbs. For example: "The evening news *is* full of disasters." There are other words that end in -s that refer to a single thing but are actually plural and require a plural verb. For example: "His assets *were* totally wiped out by the bankruptcy."

Fractional expressions such as *half of* and *a percentage of* can be either singular or plural. The same is true when words like *some, all*, and *any* serve as subjects. For example: "One-half of the population *is* over sixty-five. One-quarter of the students *were* absent. Some of the houses *are* painted white. Some of the money *is* missing."

Finally, when you have a sentence that combines a positive and a negative subject and one is plural and the other singular, the verb should agree with the positive subject. For example: "It's the teacher not the students who *decides* what to teach."

◆ PREDICATES

Predicates are used to complete a sentence. While the subject names the person, place, or thing that is doing something, a simple predicate consists of a verb, verb string, or a compound verb. For example: "The flower *bloomed*. The flowers *have been blooming*. The bulbs *opened, blossomed, and then closed for the night*."

A *compound predicate* consists of two or more predicates connected, for example: "The mountain biker *began to ride down the trail* and *eventually entered one of the most beautiful valleys in the area*."

A *complete predicate* consists of a transitive verb and all modifiers and other words that complete its meaning, for example: "The slowly moving thunderstorm *flashed lightning across the dark foreboding sky*."

A *predicate adjective* follows a linking verb and describes the subject of the sentence, for example: "The minerals in the water taste *bad*."

A *predicate nominative* follows a linking verb and describes what the subject is, for example: "Lucy Edson is *president* of the firm."

◆ OBJECTS

Objects are the part of a sentence that receives actions. In the sentence "He threw *the ball*," "the ball" is a *direct object*.

An *object complement* renames or describes a direct object. Take the sentence "He named his monkey, Meep." In this example, "his monkey" is the direct object; "Meep" is the object complement.

An *indirect object* identifies to what or to whom the action of a verb is directed. Take the sentence "He sold me his car." In this example, "me" is the indirect object; "his car" is the direct object. The word *me*—along with other pronouns such as *him, us*, and *them*—is not always an indirect object; it can also serve as a direct object, for example: "Save me!"

COMPLEMENTS

A *complement* is any word (or phrase) that completes a subject, object, or verb. A *subject complement* follows a linking verb and is used to rename or define the subject, for example: "A tarn is a small glacial *lake*."

An *object complement* follows or modifies a direct object and can be a noun or adjective. In the sentence "The players named Logan *captain* to keep him *happy*," the noun "captain" complements the direct object "Logan"; the adjective "happy" complements the object "him."

A *verb complement* is either a direct or indirect object of a verb, for example: "Mark gave *Terry* (indirect object) all his old *albums* (direct object)."

MODIFIER PLACEMENT

Modifiers are words that limit certain aspects of a sentence. Some modifiers—such as *only, just, nearly*, and *barely*—can easily end up in the wrong place in a sentence. Compare these two sentences: "He only threw the ball ten feet." "He threw the ball only ten feet." The best rule is to place these modifiers immediately before the word they modify. When a modifier improperly modifies something, it is called a *dangling modifier*. One common example is starting a sentence with a prepositional phrase, for example: "Cleaning the windows every six months, the building seemed to look better." Buildings can't clean their own windows. This example could be rewritten as: "Cleaning the windows every six months, the maintenance staff made the building look better."

If you have a sentence where a participial phrase is followed by an expletive construction, you often have a *dangling participle*. For example: "Cleaning the windows every six months, there is a simple way to keep a building looking better." This example could be rewritten as: "If you clean the windows every six months, you can keep a building looking better."

Another situation where dangling participles can occur is when you have a participial phrase followed by a passive verb. This happens because the real subject of the sentence is disguised. For example: "Cleaning the windows every six months, the building was kept in beautiful condition." This example could be rewritten as: "Cleaning the windows every six months, they kept the building in beautiful condition."

Infinitive phrases can also end up as dangling modifiers, for example: "To keep the employees interested in their health, a fitness center was set up in the basement." In this example, the infinitive phrase *To keep the employees interested in their health* should probably modify the person who set up the fitness center. Thus, this example could be rewritten as: "To keep the employees interested in their heath, the manager set up a fitness center in the basement."

Finally, one additional misplaced modifier problem involves adverbs. Adverbs can be placed almost anywhere in a sentence, but their placement can sometimes obscure their meaning, for example: "The people who listen to public radio often like classical music." Does this mean that anyone who listens to public radio even for a few minutes likes classical music? By moving the placement of the adverb *often*, this example could be rewritten as: "The people who often listen to public radio like classical music."

NOUN PHRASES

A *phrase* is a group of related words that does not include a subject and verb. If a subject and verb are present, it is considered to be a *clause*. A noun phrase includes a noun and its modifiers, for example: "The tall dark man." The modifiers that are included in the noun phrase can be any of the following:

- **Adjectives**—"tall dark man"
- **Participial phrase**—"the bushes following the edge of the sidewalk"
- **Infinitive phrase**—"the first woman to fly around the world"
- **Modifying clause**—"the mistakes he had made the day before"
- **Prepositional phrase**—"the trail next to the lake, over by the dam"

Usually. all the words in a noun phrase are together; however, occasionally they can be broken up into what is called a *discontinuous noun phrase*. For example: "*Several burglaries* have been reported *involving people who were gone for the weekend*." There is nothing wrong with a discontinuous noun phrase. They are sometimes useful for balancing a subject and predicate. Otherwise, we end up with a ten-word subject and a three-word verb.

One common problem to avoid involves a long string of compound noun phrases. This often happens when the string also involves a group of compound nouns, such as *student body*, *book cover*, or *meeting place*. If you put together a long string of these phrases, the result can be a very difficult sentence.

An addressed person's name or substitute name is called a *vocative*. These sometimes take the form of a noun phrase. A vocative is treated as a parenthetical element and is set apart from the rest of the sentence by a pair of commas if it appears within the flow of a sentence, for example: "Mike, stop the car." You do not need to add commas every time someone's name is mentioned in a sentence. Commas are used only when the name refers to someone who is being addressed in the sentence. Overall, there are four types of vocatives:

1. Single names, with or without a title
2. The personal pronoun *you*
3. Appellatives of endearment, such as *darling, my dear, sweetheart*, and *sir*
4. Nominal clauses, such as "whoever is singing, stop it now"

PREPOSITIONAL PHRASES

A *prepositional phrase* consists of a preposition, a noun or pronoun that serves as the object of the preposition, and an adjective or two that modifies the object. Prepositional phrases usually tell us when or where something is happening, for example: "in a half hour."

A prepositional phrase used at the beginning of a sentence is called an introductory modifier. You can set apart an *introductory modifier* with a comma; however, it is optional unless the introductory modifier is long.

You have probably heard the rule regarding not ending a sentence with a preposition. Although you can easily revise sentences that do this, sometimes the revision results in a very clumsy sentence.

APPOSITIVE PHRASES

An *appositive phrase* involves renaming or amplifying a word that immediately precedes it, for example: "My favorite professor, *a world famous author*, just won a prestigious literary award."

ABSOLUTE PHRASES

An *absolute phrase* is a group of words consisting of a noun or pronoun, a participle, and any modifiers. Absolute phrases do not connect to or modify any other word in a sentence; instead, they modify the entire sentence. Absolute phrases are often treated as parenthetical elements set off from the rest of the sentence with a comma or pair of commas, for example: "*National champions three out of four years*, the university's football team were treated as gods."

INFINITIVE PHRASES

An *infinitive phrase* consists of a infinitive—the root verb preceded by *to*—along with modifiers or complements. Infinitive phrases can act as adjectives, adverbs, or nouns. Consider the following examples:

- His plan *to eliminate smoking* was widely popular. (*To eliminate smoking* serves as an adjective that modifies *plan*.)

- *To watch him eat ribs* is something you have to see. (*To watch him eat ribs* serves as the noun-subject of the sentence.)

- Eric went to college *to study to be an engineer*. (*To study to be an engineer* tells us why he went, so it's an adverb.)

GERUND PHRASES

Gerund phrases consist of verbals that end in -ing but act as nouns, along with modifiers and complements. These phrases can do anything a noun can do, for example: "*Walking after dark* is not very safe."

PARTICIPIAL PHRASES

Present participles (verbals ending in -ing) and past participles (verbals ending in -ed) or other irregular verbs can be combined with complements and modifiers to create a *participial phrase*. They always act as adjectives. When they begin a sentence, they are set apart by a comma just like an introductory modifier. If they appear within the middle of a sentence, they are set apart with a pair of commas. For example: "*Working around the clock*, the workers repaired the airport runway in less than a week. The concrete, *having been damaged by the crash landing of the airliner*, needed to be replaced."

CLAUSES

A *clause* is a group of words that contains a subject and a verb. As discussed earlier, a clause is different from a phrase because a phrase does not include a subject and a verb.

Independent Clauses

An *independent clause* could stand by itself as a sentence. However, if it did, it would be a sentence and not a clause. When an independent clause is included in a sentence, it is usually separated from the rest of the sentence by a comma. Being able to recognize when a clause is acting as an independent clause is essential to knowing when to use commas in avoiding sentence fragments and run-on sentences.

Two independent clauses can be combined into a single thought, for example: "Charlie didn't mean to run away, but he did it because he was angry." In this example, two independent clauses are separated by a comma and the coordinating conjunction *but*. If the word *but* was missing, this example would be a comma splice.

Clauses can be combined three different ways:

1. With coordination
2. With subordination
3. By using a semicolon

Coordination involves using coordinating conjunctions such as *and, but, or, nor, for, yet*, and sometimes *so*. By using a coordinating conjunction, you avoid monotony and what is often called "primer language"—simple sentence constructions. Your sentences are also balanced.

Subordination involves turning one of the independent clauses into a subordinate element using a subordinating conjunction or a relative pronoun. When the clause begins with a subordinating word, it transforms into a dependent clause, for example: "Linda never liked to fly in airplanes, because she was afraid of heights."

Semicolons can be used to connect two independent clauses with or without the help of a conjunctive adverb. However, semicolons should be used only when the two independent clauses are very closely related and nicely balanced in length and content, for example: "Sheena is a very pretty girl; she looks like an angel."

Dependent Clauses

A *dependent clause* cannot stand by itself like an independent clause. It must be combined with an independent clause in order to become a sentence.

Dependent clauses can perform a variety of different functions within a sentence. They can be noun clauses, adverb clauses, or adjective clauses. Noun clauses can do anything a noun can do in a sentence, for example: "*What he knows about boxing* is not important to me." Adverb clauses tell us about what is going on in the independent clause: where, when, or why. For example: "*When the game is over*, we'll go get some burgers." Adjective clauses function just like multi-word adjectives to modify a noun, for example: "My wife, *who is a video producer*, has just completed an award-winning documentary about music."

◇ SENTENCE FRAGMENTS

A *sentence fragment* fails to be a sentence because it cannot stand by itself. It does not contain at least one independent clause. There are several reasons why a group of words may appear to be a sentence but turn out instead to be a sentence fragment. The sentence fragment may contain a series of prepositional phrases without a proper subject-verb relationship, for example: "In Texas, sometime in early April, just before the bluebonnets appear." The sentence fragment may be a verbal phrase that wants to modify something, but that something is missing, for example: "Working deep into the night in an effort to get his taxes completed." Finally, the sentence fragment may have a subject-verb relationship, but it has been subordinated to another idea or word so it cannot stand by itself, for example: "Although he was taller than his older brother."

◇ SENTENCE VARIETY

A *sentence* is a group of words containing a subject and a predicate. There are many different types of sentences, and the way they are used in your writing, the order they are used in, and the way they are combined and punctuated determines your writing style.

It is relatively easy to write short sentences. However, if you use only short sentences, your writing will appear to be primer style and give your reader a poor impression of your level of professionalism.

To write more complicated sentences, you have to create constructions of clauses and phrases. Long sentences and run-on sentences are not the same thing. Combining too long a series of clauses may cause the reader to get confused. However, many writers are afraid they'll create run-on sentences and tend to lean toward the shorter variety.

By coordinating the use of clauses and punctuation, you can allow the complexity of a sentence to develop after the verb, not before it. The key is to make the subject-verb connection and then allow the sentence to paint a picture of the world surrounding that subject and verb. As you allow a sentence to develop, be careful to keep your structures in the predicate in parallel form.

One issue that is difficult for many business writers is the need to repeat key terms in long sentences. It feels awkward. When properly handled, though, repeated phrases can create a rhythm that helps to emphasize the meaning of the sentence.

Another way to enhance sentence variety and complexity is to avoid clumsy "which clauses" and replace them with dependent clauses. Take the following sentence: "Atlanta continues to grow in every direction, which means that homes are rapidly replacing the fields and forests in outlying areas." An alternative would be: "Atlanta continues to grow in every direction, as homes are rapidly replacing the fields and forests in outlying areas."

When used sparingly, you can create an interesting twist to a sentence by ending it with a set of prepositional phrases, each beginning with a present or past participle. For example: "You'll find working with Videologies to be an excellent experience, one that will develop into a lasting relationship, into a partnership, winning future business for us all."

⟡ RESUMPTIVE AND SUMMATIVE MODIFIERS

By adding modifying phrases to the end of a sentence, you take a sentence in an unexpected direction. A *resumptive modifier* takes a word from a sentence that appears to be ending and adds additional information. For example: "You'll find working with Videologies to be both enlightening and rewarding—enlightening due to the many innovations we'll introduce to your company, rewarding because of the enhancements to productivity your company will experience."

A *summative modifier* renames or summarizes what has been going on earlier in the sentence and adds new information. For example: "The e-mail etiquette seminar promises to show employees how to write effective e-mails, e-mails that get results, and e-mails that result in a positive image for your business—three benefits that can enhance the productivity of any business."

⟡ MODIFIER PLACEMENT

You can add variety to your sentences by the way you place modifiers. This section gives four different strategies for modifier placement.

Using Initial Modifiers

- **Dependent clause:** "Although he was tired, Bob wrote the report."
- **Infinitive phrase:** "To please his boss, Bob wrote the report."
- **Adverb:** "Slowly and laboriously, Bob wrote the report."
- **Participial phrase:** "Hoping to be promoted, Bob wrote the report."

Using Mid-Sentence Modifiers

- **Appositive:** "Bob, an expert on regulations, wrote the report."
- **Participial phrase:** "Bob, hoping to catch up on his work, worked late."

Using Terminal Modifiers

- **Present participial phrase:** "Bob worked on the report, hoping to please his boss."
- **Past participial phrase/Adjectival phrase:** "Bob worked on the report, pushed by ambition."

Combining Modifiers

- "Slowly and laboriously, Bob, an expert on regulations, worked on the report, hoping to please his boss."

OTHER IDEAS ON SENTENCE VARIETY

Remember to throw an occasional question, exclamation, or command into your writing. Questions can be useful at the beginning of a paragraph to summarize the content that follows. Commands provide direction and energy by telling your readers what to do.

Occasionally, try to begin sentences with something other than the normal subject-verb combo. Try starting with a modifying clause or participial phrase. Consider beginning a sentence with a coordinating conjunction (*and, but, nor, for, yet,* or *so*). Many people think they should never begin a sentence with *but*. Instead, it should be linked to the previous sentence into a compound structure. But, a sentence like this calls attention to itself and can be a useful device.

SENTENCE TYPES

There are a variety of basic sentence structures including:

- **Simple**—One independent clause
- **Compound**—More than one independent clause
- **Complex**—One independent clause and at least one dependent clause
- **Compound complex**—More than one independent clause and at least one dependent clause
- **Periodic**—Begin with modifying phrases and clauses and end with an independent clause
- **Cumulative**—Begin with an independent clause and end with a series of modifying constructions

COMPOUND SENTENCES

A *compound sentence* consists of two or more independent clauses. Thus, there are two thoughts within the sentence and either can stand alone. The clauses of a compound sentence are either separated by a semicolon or by a comma and a coordinating conjunction. The most common coordinating conjunction is *and*; it simply links the two ideas. Other coordinating conjunctions, such as *but, or, for, yet,* and *so*, establish a relationship between the two clauses.

Compounding Sentence Elements

You can combine various sentence elements to create compound sentences:

- **Subjects**—Two or more subjects doing parallel things can be combined as a compound subject, for example: "Working together, *IBM and Apple Computer* developed the Power PC processor."

- **Objects**—When the subjects are acting on two or more things in parallel, the objects can be combined, for example: "The company president believed *that* the partnership between the two companies might help them increase sales *and that* he could eventually force a merger."

- **Verbs and Verbals**—When the subjects are doing two things simultaneously, the elements can be combined by compounding verbs and verbals, for example: "He *studied* sentence structure and grammar *and learned* how to speak and write effectively."

- **Modifiers**—When appropriate, modifiers and prepositional phrases can be compounded, for example: "The company recruited their programmers *from universities across the country and various competing companies.*"

◇ TRANSITIONS

As you compound sentences and vary your sentence structures to add variety to your writing, you will want to consider using transitions between ideas. Transitions help guide a reader from one idea to the next.

There are four general ways to add transitions between ideas:

1. Using transitional expressions
2. Repeating key words and phrases
3. Using pronoun reference
4. Using parallel forms

Transitional Expressions

In addition to coordinating conjunctions—*and, but, nor, for, yet, or,* and *so*—you can use conjunctive adverbs and transitional expressions such as *however, moreover*, and *nevertheless* to transition your sentences from one thought to the next. The key is to avoid using the same transitional elements, as it becomes boring. The following is a list of some conjunctive adverbs that can add spice to your transitions.

- **Addition**—again, also, and, and then, besides, equally important, finally, first, further, furthermore, in addition, in the first place, last, moreover, next, second, still, too

- **Comparison**—also, in the same way, likewise, similarly

- **Concession**—granted, naturally, of course

- **Contrast**—although, and yet, at the same time, but at the same time, despite that, even so, even though, for all that, however, in contrast, in spite of, instead, nevertheless, on the contrary, on the other hand, otherwise, regardless, still, though, yet

- **Emphasis**—certainly, indeed, in fact

- **Example**—after all, as an illustration, even, for example, for instance, in conclusion, in short, it is true, namely, specifically, that is, to illustrate, thus

- **Summary**—all in all, altogether, as has been said, finally, in brief, in conclusion, in other words, in particular, in short, in simpler terms, in summary, on the whole, that is, therefore, to put it differently, to summarize

- **Time sequence**—after a while, afterward, again, also, and then, as long as, at last, at length, at that time, before, besides, earlier, eventually, finally, formerly, further, furthermore, in addition, in the first place, in the past, last, lately, meanwhile, moreover, next, now, presently, second, shortly, simultaneously, since, so far, soon, still, subsequently, then, thereafter, too, until, until now, when

Repeating Key Words

By repeating a key word or phrase, you can establish its importance in the mind of the reader.

Pronoun Reference

Pronouns can be used to refer the reader to something earlier in the text. A pronoun such as *this* causes the reader to summarize what has been said so far. For example: "There has been an increase in the number of earthquakes in California in the past ten years. *This* is true because we have geological records that go back almost 150 years and *they* show a clear trend."

Parallelism

Parallel constructions are expressions with similar content and function. Their similarity enables the reader to more easily recognize the content and understand the message.

An article such as *the, a,* and *an* must either be used only before the first term in a group, or it must be repeated before each term. For example: "At the World's Fair, we saw all the latest model automobiles, including the new Hondas, Toyotas, and Nissans. We left on Sunday for vacation with the Wilsons, the Wausons, and the Bruecks."

Correlative expressions (*both, and; not, but; not only, but also; either, or; first, second*) should be followed by the same grammatical construction. For example: "It was not only the blowing wind, but also the freezing temperatures that made travel so treacherous."

When making comparisons, the things compared should be in parallel form.

◆ AVOIDING REDUNDANCIES

While a well-rounded writing style includes compound and complex sentences, it is important to avoid redundancies. Avoid saying the same thing twice. The following is a list of some of the most common redundant phrases:

- 12 midnight
- 12 noon
- 1 a.m. in the morning
- Circle around
- Close proximity
- Completely unanimous
- Cooperate together
- Each and every
- Enclosed herewith
- End result
- Exactly the same
- Final completion
- Free gift
- In spite of the fact that
- In the field of
- In the event of
- New innovations
- One and the same
- Particular interest
- Period of X days
- Personally, I think
- Personal opinion
- Refer back
- Repeat again
- Return again
- Revert back
- Shorter in length
- Small in size
- Summarize briefly
- Surrounded on all sides
- The future to come
- There is no doubt but
- We are in receipt of

◆ PHRASES AND WORDS TO OMIT

The following is a list of words that are usually not necessary in a sentence. They don't add anything and can be omitted without changing the meaning:

- Really
- Quite
- Severely
- As a matter of fact
- At the present time
- By means of
- Due to the fact
- For the most part
- Very
- Extremely
- All things considered
- As far as I'm concerned
- Because of the fact that
- By virtue of the fact
- For all intents and purposes
- For the purpose of

- Have a tendency to
- In a very real sense
- In the case of
- In the event that
- In the process of
- The point I am trying to make
- What I mean to say is

- In a manner of speaking
- In my opinion
- In the final analysis
- In the nature of
- It seems that
- Type of

◇ CLICHÉS

Clichés are overused expressions that have become trite and even annoying. The following is a list of clichés that should be avoided:

- Acid test
- At loose ends
- Babe in the woods
- Better that than never
- Black as night
- Blind as a bat
- Bolt from the blue
- Brought back to reality
- Busy as a bee (or beaver)
- Cat's meow
- Cool as a cucumber
- Cool, calm, and collected
- Crack of dawn
- Crushing blow
- Cry over spilt milk
- Dead as a doornail
- Dog-eat-dog world
- Don't count your chickens
- Dyed in the wool
- Easier said than done
- Easy as pie
- Face the music
- Feathered friends
- Flash in the pan

- Flat as a pancake
- Gentle as a lamb
- Go at it tooth and nail
- Good time was had by all
- Greased lightning
- Happy as a lark
- Head over heels
- Heavy as lead
- Horns of a dilemma
- Hour of need
- Keep a stiff upper lip
- Ladder of success
- Last but not least
- Looking a gift horse in the mouth
- Meaningful dialogue
- Moving experience
- Needle in a haystack
- Open-and-shut case
- Pain in the ass
- Point with pride
- Pretty as a picture
- Put it in a nutshell
- Quick as a flash (or wink)
- Rat race

- Ripe old age
- Ruled the roost
- Sad but true
- Sadder but wiser
- Set the world on fire
- Sick as a dog
- Sigh of relief
- Slow as molasses
- Smart as a whip
- Sneaking suspicion
- Spread like wildfire
- Straight as an arrow
- Straw that broke the camel's back
- Strong as an ox
- Take the bull by the horns
- Thin as a rail
- Through thick and thin
- Tired but happy
- To coin a phrase
- To make a long story short
- Trial and error
- Tried and true
- Under the weather
- White as a sheet
- Wise as an owl
- Work like a dog
- Worth its weight in gold

◇ UNBIASED LANGUAGE

Most gender problems can be avoided without the use of *he/she, he or she, him or her*, or *him/her* constructions. Plural pronouns such as *they* can be very helpful in this regard. An occasional he or she is OK, but after a while it becomes distracting. When a singular pronoun is necessary, use either he or she consistently to avoid confusion.

Sexist Language

There are a variety of words and phrases that make demeaning assumptions about gender role. However, in some cases people go out of their way to be politically correct and try awkward alternatives. Substitutes should be reasonable and appropriate. Try not to highlight the fact you are trying to avoid sexist language.

The following is a list of words to avoid and their alternatives:

- Actress—Use *actor*
- Anchorman—Use *anchor*
- Businessman—Use *businessperson*
- Chairman—Use *chairperson* or *chair*
- Coed—Use *student*
- Forefathers—Use *ancestors*
- Foreman—Use *supervisor*
- Freshman—Use *first-year student*
- Mailman—Use *mail carrier*

- Male nurse—Use *nurse*
- Man (meaning human being)—Use *person, people*
- Managers and their wives—Use *managers and their spouses*
- Mankind—Use *humanity, people*
- Poetess—Use *poet*
- Policeman—Use *police officer*
- Salesman—Use *sales representative*
- Stewardess—Use *flight attendant*
- Waiter/Waitress—Use *server*

Common English Usage Problems

◇ LANGUAGE: KEY TO YOUR SUCCESS

Give careful attention to your use of the English language. The ability to write and speak correctly is so important to a business career that you'll find the following to be almost always true: As you improve your speech, you will also naturally improve your business success.

Words, phrases, and sentences that are outworn should not be used in a business letter. Stock phrases, like slang, give the impression that the writer has not thought the idea through and has not chosen the best language for expressing those ideas. It's necessary first to understand thoroughly what you want to say and then to say it forcefully with words as natural to you as those of a conversation. This will help you accomplish the purpose of communication.

To help yourself write naturally, consider how you would respond to a luncheon invitation from an acquaintance. Would you say, "In accordance with your request that I have lunch with you, I beg to advise that I shall be happy to do so"? No. You would be more likely to say, "Thanks. I'll be glad to have lunch with you."

◇ VERBOSE EXPRESSIONS

You should be alert to everything you write. Beware of words that do not mean exactly what you want to say. Also beware of phrases that are careless, vague, or wordy. Table 33–1 gives examples of such pitfalls. After studying this list, protect yourself from similar mistakes. As a famous company once said in its ads, "The audience is listening!"

TABLE 33–1. Verbose Expressions

Verbose Expressions	What You Really Mean
I beg to be advised	Please tell me
Thank you kindly	Thank you
I feel that you are able to appreciate	You can appreciate
Which you will remember is in connection with	Regarding
I am not at present in a position to	I am unable to
I would, therefore, ask that you kindly write	Please write

Verbose Expressions	What You Really Mean
We would appreciate it if you would investigate the matter and inform us and report	Please check the matter
You have my permission to	You may
I am in receipt of a complaint from John Smith	John Smith complains
You have not, I believe, favored us with a reply	You have not replied
I acknowledge receipt of your letter	I received your letter

◇ CORRECT USAGE

In addition to being verbose, many letter writers frequently misuse parts of speech. The following examples are given to alert you to these errors. Some of the examples are grammatically correct for colloquial use but not for formal speech and writing—which is the only kind you should use in business.

Affect, Effect

Affect is most commonly used as a verb, meaning "to influence." It is used as a noun only as a psychological term, meaning "feeling or emotion." *Effect* is a verb meaning "to bring about." It is also used as a noun, meaning "a result or consequence, or a mental impression."

> **WRONG:** The light effects my vision.
>
> **RIGHT:** The light affects my vision.
>
> **WRONG:** Can you affect a change in the operation?
>
> **RIGHT:** Can you effect a change in the operation?

Already, All Ready

Already denotes time; *all ready* denotes preparation.

> **RIGHT:** She had already arrived.
>
> **RIGHT:** We are all ready to leave.

All Right

Always spell *all right* as two words, never one.

> **WRONG:** It will be alright if you wish to go.
>
> **RIGHT:** It will be all right if you wish to go.

Altogether, All Together

Altogether means "quite" or "in all." All *together* means "in one place."

RIGHT: She is altogether pleasant.

RIGHT: His bills came to fifty-seven dollars altogether.

RIGHT: The books were all together on one shelf.

Any, Either

Any refers to one of several. *Either* refers to one of two.

RIGHT: You may have any of the six books.

RIGHT: Either of those two cars will be acceptable.

Awful, Awfully

Never use *awful* or *awfully* as a synonym for "very."

WRONG: She performed an awful hard task.

RIGHT: She performed a very difficult task.

WRONG: Bill is awfully smart.

RIGHT: Bill is unusually smart.

A While, Awhile

Awhile is an adverb and should never be used as the object of a preposition (which can only be a noun or pronoun).

WRONG: Please come to my home for awhile before you start your journey.

RIGHT: Please come to my home for a while before you start your journey.

RIGHT: Relax awhile before you begin the task.

Badly

Badly is an adverb, but it is often mistakenly used as an adjective.

WRONG: He wanted badly to go with them.

RIGHT: He wanted very much to go with them.

WRONG: She felt badly after her operation.

RIGHT: She did not feel well after her operation.

Because

Because is not to be used in place of *that*.

WRONG: The reason he did not attend the party is because he was in Chicago.

RIGHT: The reason he did not attend the party is that he was in Chicago.

RIGHT: He did not attend the party because he was in Chicago.

Between, Among

Between is used to differentiate two, and only two, objects. *Among* is used to differentiate more than two.

RIGHT: The dog was sitting between John and me.

RIGHT: There were three good books among the many he gave me.

Both, Alike

It's illogical to use the combination *both alike* since two items can't be alike if one is not.

WRONG: The cars are both alike.

RIGHT: The two cars are alike. They are both of the latest model.

Both, Each

Both is used to describe a condition that applies to two entities. *Each* is used to describe a single entity.

WRONG: There is a picture on both sides of the mantel.

RIGHT: There is a picture on each side of the mantel.

Bring, Take

Bring is used to denote movement toward someone or something, while *take* is used to denote movement from someone or something.

RIGHT: Bring me the book.

RIGHT: Take the book to him.

Bushel

Add an *s* when referring to more than one bushel.

WRONG: Eight bushel of oats.

RIGHT: Eight bushels of oats.

Business

Don't use *business* when you really mean *right*.

WRONG: What business is it of theirs to question my action?

RIGHT: What right have they to question my action?

Came By

Came by is a colloquial phrase that you should not use.

WRONG: He came by to see me.

RIGHT: He came to see me.

Can't Seem

Seem is a verb that means "look" or "appear." Using *can't* with *seem* is awkward.

WRONG: I can't seem to make the journey in an hour.

RIGHT: It seems impossible for me to make the journey in one hour.

Combination

Don't confuse *combine*—normally a verb unless referring to farm equipment—with *combination*, which is a noun referring to a group of entities.

WRONG: That combine will be a large one.

RIGHT: That combination will be a large one.

Cooperate

Cooperate is a verb that means "to work together." Therefore, *cooperate together* is redundant.

WRONG: If they cooperate together, their purpose will be accomplished.

RIGHT: If they cooperate, their purpose will be accomplished.

Council, Counsel, Consul

A *council* is a group of persons convened for advisory purposes. *Counsel* is advice; the word sometimes means "attorney." A *consul* is an official appointed by a government to report on matters that the official observes while residing in a foreign land.

Credible, Credulous

Credible means "believable" or "worthy of being believed." *Credulous* means "inclined to believe too readily."

RIGHT: He related the incident in a credible manner.

RIGHT: She is too credulous for her own good.

Data

Data is always plural. *Datum* is the singular form.

WRONG: This data proves that our business is growing.

RIGHT: These data prove that our business is growing.

Deal

Deal should not be used informally to refer to a business agreement.

WRONG: She made a deal to buy the house.

RIGHT: She made an agreement to buy the house.

Different From, Different Than

Different from takes an object; *different than* is used to introduce a clause.

WRONG: That coat is different than mine.

RIGHT: That coat is different from mine.

RIGHT: He was different than I remembered.

Don't, Doesn't

Don't means "do not"; *doesn't* means "does not."

WRONG: He don't care to go with us.

RIGHT: He doesn't care to go with us.

Each, Their

Pronouns must agree in number and person with the words to which they refer.

WRONG: Each drives their own car.

RIGHT: Each drives his own car.

RIGHT: Each of the women listed her needs. (The singular pronoun *each* is the subject.)

Either, Neither

Either and *neither* refer to two.

WRONG: Neither of the four books suited him.

RIGHT: None of the four books suited him.

WRONG: Either of the three books is the one I want.

RIGHT: Either of the two books will do.

RIGHT: Any of the three books will suit me.

Enthuse, Enthusiastic

Enthuse is used only as a colloquialism. For the formal language needed for business writing, use *to be enthusiastic*.

WRONG: He was enthused over winning the award.

RIGHT: He was enthusiastic about winning the award.

Except, Unless

Except is a preposition used to introduce a prepositional phrase. *Unless* is an adverbial conjunction used to introduce a subordinate clause. They are not interchangeable. *Except* may be used as a conjunction only when it's followed by the word *that*; however, that construction, although correct, is often awkward, and *unless* is preferable.

WRONG: The horse cannot be entered in the race except the judges permit.

RIGHT: The horse cannot be entered in the race unless the judges permit.

Expect

Don't use *expect* to mean *think* or *suppose*.

WRONG: I expect she was well received.

RIGHT: I suppose she was well received.

RIGHT: I expect you to be there at 8 a.m.

Farther, Further

Farther shows a specific, quantifiable distance. *Further* shows degree or extent.

RIGHT: I walked farther than he did.

RIGHT: He will go further with your help than without it.

Fix

Fix means to repair. Don't use it to mean a bad situation.

WRONG: She is in a desperate fix.

RIGHT: She is desperate because of her present situation.

Foot, Feet

Foot is singular, *feet* is plural.

WRONG: The room is twelve foot long.

RIGHT: The room is twelve feet long.

Got

Don't use *got* when you could use *have*, *has*, or *must*.

WRONG: I have got a new car.

RIGHT: I have a new car.

RIGHT: He has a new job.

WRONG: I've got to stop at his house. (colloquial)

RIGHT: I must stop at his house *or* I have to stop at his house.

Gotten

This is an obsolete term. Do not use; replace with *got*.

Guess

Don't use *guess* when you really mean *think*.

WRONG: I guess you are right.

RIGHT: I think you are right.

RIGHT: In the word game, Marcus was the first to guess correctly.

Inaugurate

Don't use *inaugurate* in place of *started* or *began*.

WRONG: The program was inaugurated on August 1.

RIGHT: The program was begun on August 1.

RIGHT: The president of the United States was inaugurated on January 4.

Inside Of, Within

Don't use *inside of* where you could use *within*.

WRONG: He will visit us inside of a week.

RIGHT: He will visit us within a week.

Invite

Don't confuse *invite* (a verb) with *invitation* (a noun).

WRONG: I have an invite to the party.

RIGHT: I have an invitation to the party.

Its, It's

Its (without an apostrophe) is a possessive pronoun. *It's* (with an apostrophe) is a contraction meaning "it is."

RIGHT: It's getting dark (meaning "it is getting dark").

RIGHT: The ship was flying its flag at half-mast.

Kind

Kind is singular; *kinds* is plural.

WRONG: She asked for those kind of flowers.

RIGHT: She asked for those kinds of flowers.

RIGHT: She asked for that kind of flower.

Kind Of, Sort Of

Kind of and *sort of* are unclear. Be definite when speaking or writing.

WRONG: He appeared to be kind of ill.

RIGHT: He appeared to be rather ill.

WRONG: She was sort of ill at ease.

RIGHT: She was somewhat ill at ease.

Learn, Teach

Before you can *learn*, someone must first *teach* you.

WRONG: She learned me how to type.

RIGHT: She taught me how to type.

RIGHT: If I teach him correctly, he will learn quickly.

33 ▪ COMMON ENGLISH USAGE PROBLEMS

Less, Fewer

Less refers to a smaller amount, degree, or value. *Fewer* refers to a quantifiable number.

RIGHT: This mine contains less gold than the Jackass Mine.

RIGHT: This city has fewer people today than it had a year ago.

Let, Leave

Let means "to permit." *Leave* means "to depart," "to bequeath," or "to allow, to remain."

RIGHT: Leave her alone.

RIGHT: Let her go with us.

Liable, Likely

Liable should be used when referring to legal responsibility.

RIGHT: The landlord is liable for damages.

RIGHT: That horse is likely to win the race.

Lie, Lay

Many people confuse these two words because the word *lay* is both the present tense of *lay* (*lay, lay, laid*) and the past tense of *lie* (*lie, lay, lain*). *Lie* means "to remain in position" or "to rest." It is intransitive, meaning no object ever accompanies it. *Lay* means "to place something somewhere." It is transitive, meaning an object always accompanies it.

WRONG: He lays down after lunch every day.

RIGHT: He lies down after lunch every day.

RIGHT: Yesterday he lay on the couch for two hours.

RIGHT: Will you please lay the book on the table?

RIGHT: The pen lay on the desk all day.

Like, As

Like is a preposition always followed by a noun or pronoun in the objective case. *As* is an adverbial conjunction used to introduce a subordinate clause.

WRONG: It appears like he isn't coming.

RIGHT: It appears as if he isn't coming.

RIGHT: Though he was such a little boy, he marched like a major.

Line

Line should not be used in place *of business*.

WRONG: He is in the jewelry line.

RIGHT: He is in the jewelry business.

Loan

A *loan* should be used as a noun to refer to an agreement to borrow. To allow someone to borrow is *to lend*.

WRONG: Loan me your pen.

RIGHT: Lend me your pen.

RIGHT: He went to the bank to receive a loan.

Lost

Don't use extra words—like *out*—that are not necessary for meaning.

WRONG: He lost out.

RIGHT: He lost.

Lots

Don't use *lots* when referring to an amount of something.

WRONG: She receives lots of fan mail.

RIGHT: She receives a great deal of fan mail.

Mad, Angry

Use *angry* rather than *mad*. Remember, dogs go mad, people get angry.

WRONG: Mary was mad at Jane.

RIGHT: Mary was angry with Jane.

May, Can

May refers to permission. *Can* refers to ability.

WRONG: Can I help you?

RIGHT: May I help you?

RIGHT: Can he drive a car?

Might Of, Would Of, Could Of

This construction is the result of poor pronunciation. The correct phrases are *might have*, *would have*, and *could have*.

WRONG: If you could of arranged it, I would of gone.

RIGHT: If you could have arranged it, I would have gone.

Most, Almost

Most of all is a colloquial expression. Use *most of* or *almost* instead.

WRONG: We walked most of all the way.

RIGHT: We walked most of the way.

RIGHT: We walked almost all the way.

Never

Never means never; it does not refer to a limited period of time.

WRONG: We never saw your dog since yesterday.

RIGHT: We have not seen your dog since yesterday.

RIGHT: We never saw your dog. What breed was he?

Off

Off is always used alone and not with *of*.

WRONG: The ribbon was taken off of the package.

RIGHT: The ribbon was taken off the package.

Only

Be careful of where you place this adverb; position determines which word you modify.

WRONG: I could only get him to play one piece.

RIGHT: I could get him to play only one piece.

Open

Open should be used without *up*.

WRONG: We open up the doors promptly at noon.

RIGHT: We open the doors promptly at noon.

Party

Party can be used to refer to a person in legal documents, but it is too formal for common use. A *party* can also be a celebration.

WRONG: The party I called was disturbed.

RIGHT: The person I called was disturbed.

RIGHT: (In legal documents): The party of the second part hereby agrees . . .

RIGHT: He celebrated his birthday with a party.

People

People refers to a large group of individuals. When referring to people of a particular organization or place, it's better to use *people* before the name.

WRONG: The General Motors people

RIGHT: The people of General Motors; the people of Massachusetts

Percent

This is one word following an amount, never *per cent*.

RIGHT: Six percent interest was charged.

Percentage

Use when no amount is given.

RIGHT: What percentage of interest was charged?

Posted, Informed

Don't use *posted* in place of *informed*.

WRONG: You are well posted on the subject.

RIGHT: You are well informed about Australia.

Raise, Rise

Raise is a transitive verb and must always take an object. *Rise* is a transitive verb and never takes an object.

RIGHT: They raise the question at every meeting.

RIGHT: I rise to make a motion.

Real

Don't use *real* when you really mean *very*.

WRONG: He is real handsome.

RIGHT: He is very handsome.

Run

When referring to a business or organization, don't use *run* in place of *manage*.

WRONG: He runs the bakery.

RIGHT: He manages the bakery.

Same

Don't use *same* to refer to the subject of a sentence.

WRONG: Your letter arrived and I acknowledge same with thanks.

RIGHT: Your letter arrived and I acknowledge it with thanks.

Shape (meaning tangible form)

Don't use *shape* to refer to the status of something.

WRONG: The transaction was completed in good shape.

RIGHT: The transaction was completed to everyone's satisfaction.

Shall, Will

Use *shall* to express a simple expected action with the first person. Use *will* with second and third persons. However, to express determination or command, reverse the order; use *will* for the first person and *shall* for the second and third.

RIGHT: I shall go tomorrow.

RIGHT: He will go, too.

RIGHT: You will be at school by the time we arrive.

RIGHT: I will go tomorrow, and no one can stop me.

RIGHT: He shall go with me even if I must force him.

RIGHT: You shall never do that again.

Should, Would

Use *should* with the first person and *would* with the second and third persons to express expected action. However, using *should* and *would* instead of *shall* and *will* implies a doubt that the action will take place. *Should* and *would* may also be used with all persons, but in these instances, the meaning of the verbs is different. *Should* may be used with all persons to show obligation. *Would* may be used with all persons to show habit or determination.

RIGHT: A child should love his parents.

RIGHT: If I had enough money, I would buy a car.

Sit, Set

Sit is an intransitive verb. *Set* is a transitive verb.

RIGHT: She sits near her husband at every meeting.

RIGHT: He sets the plates on the table in an orderly manner.

So

Avoid overuse of this adverbial conjunction. *Consequently, therefore*, and *inasmuch as* are good substitutes when you want to vary the style.

AVOID: It had snowed over a foot that day, so we drove the jeep into town.

RIGHT: It had snowed over a foot that day; consequently, we drove the jeep into town.

Sometime, Some Time

Sometime means occasional. *Some time* means an amount of time.

WRONG: I will go sometime this morning.

RIGHT: If I have some time this morning, I shall do the job for you.

To, At

Do not use either of these words with *where*.

WRONG: Where are you at?

RIGHT: Where are you?

WRONG: Where did he go to?

RIGHT: Where did he go?

Try And, Come And, Be Sure And

Don't use a word if it is not necessary to convey your meaning.

WRONG: Try and be here at noon.

RIGHT: Try to be here at noon.

WRONG: Come and see me tomorrow.

RIGHT: Come to see me tomorrow.

WRONG: Be sure and watch out as you cross the street.

RIGHT: Be sure to watch out as you cross the street.

Wait On

When *wait* refers to time, *on* is not needed. When it refers to the actions of a waiter or waitress, *wait on* is acceptable.

WRONG: Please do not wait on me if I am not at the station when you arrive.

RIGHT: Please do not wait for me if I am not there when you arrive.

RIGHT: The headwaiter assigned the red-haired woman to wait on me.

Where

Whether used as an adverb or a conjunction, *where* denotes position or place. It should never be used as a substitute for *that* when introducing a clause.

WRONG: Did you read in the paper where our mayor was honored at a banquet?

RIGHT: Did you read in the paper that our mayor was honored at a banquet?

Which

When used to introduce a clause, *which* must refer to a specific noun or pronoun and not to a whole situation.

WRONG: He did not arrive in time for the meeting, which caused the president embarrassment.

RIGHT: His failure to arrive in time for the meeting caused the president embarrassment.

RIGHT: His failure to arrive, which caused the president embarrassment, was the reason for his dismissal.

Who, Which, That

Who is used to refer to people. *Which* and *that* refer to objects.

RIGHT: She is the woman who smiled at him.

RIGHT: She is the kind of person whom everyone likes.

RIGHT: I read the book on bridges, which I found fascinating.

◇ PROBLEM PRONOUNS

I, We, He, She, They

Pronouns in the nominative case—*I, we, he, she, they*—serve as subjects of verbs but never objects of verbs or prepositions. You can often tell that the wrong case is being used because the sentence sounds odd. However, when compound subjects or compound objects are used, it may be difficult to hear the correct case.

To test such an instance, drop the other subject or object and repeat the sentence with only the pronoun in question.

I—nominative case, never an object

WRONG: This is just between you and I.

RIGHT: This is just between you and me.

WRONG: He asked that the money be given to you and I.

TEST: He asked that the money be given to I.

RIGHT: He asked that the money be given to you and me.

TEST: He asked that the money be given to me.

She, He—nominative case, never an object

WRONG: If you stay there, the ball will hit you and she.

TEST: If you stay there, the ball will hit she.

RIGHT: If you stay there, the ball will hit you and her.

TEST: If you stay there, the ball will hit her.

They—nominative case, never an object

WRONG: I will give the money to you and they.

TEST: I will give the money to they.

RIGHT: I will give the money to you and them.

TEST: I will give the money to them.

WRONG: You and them are welcome to come.

TEST: Them are welcome to come.

RIGHT: You and they are welcome to come.

TEST: They are welcome to come.

We—nominative case, never an object

WRONG: Us boys are ready to play the game.

TEST: Us are ready to play the game.

RIGHT: We boys are ready to play the game.

TEST: We are ready to play the game.

Me, Us, Her, Him, Them

Similarly, pronouns in the subjective case—*me, us, her, him, them*—are always used as objects, of either verbs or prepositions, and never as subjects. With a compound subject, use the same way of testing as above, changing the number of the verb as needed.

Me, Us—objective case, never a subject

WRONG: Jim and me went to the movies.

TEST: Me went to the movies.

RIGHT: Jim and I went to the movies.

RIGHT: Jim went to the movies with me.

TEST: I went to the movies.

WRONG: Julie and us sat on the top bleacher.

TEST: Us sat on the top bleacher.

RIGHT: Julie and we sat on the top bleacher.

TEST: We sat on the top bleacher.

RIGHT: Julie sat on the top bleacher with us.

Her, Him, Them

Her, him, and *them* are used as objects. *She, he*, and *they* are the subjective case.

WRONG: Tommy and her [him, them] argued every day.

TEST: Her [him, them] argued every day.

RIGHT: Tommy and she [he, they] argued every day.

◇ DANGLING PARTICIPLES

A dangling participle modifies the noun or pronoun to which it refers. Since position determines the referent, how you construct the sentence determines the meaning.

WRONG: Walking down Main Street, the art museum is visible. (This implies the art museum is walking down Main Street.)

RIGHT: Walking down Main Street, you can see the art museum.

Spelling

With easy access to spelling checkers in word-processing programs, is there really a need for an administrative assistant to be concerned with spelling? For some people, running spell-check on their word-processing document takes the place of a good proofread. Computerized spell-checkers are indeed useful to any writer. However, there are many words that may appear to be correctly spelled according to the word processor's spell-checker when in reality they are incorrectly spelled for the particular context, or the wrong word has been used entirely. For example, a spelling checker cannot tell the usage differences between *there, their,* and *they're*.

Thus, there is a need for basic spelling skills. This chapter focuses on the most common spelling rules that any good administrative assistant should know.

◇ DICTIONARY USES

The constant study of spelling and the exact meaning of words are an important aspect of every administrative assistant's career. Always keep a dictionary close at hand. Besides providing spelling and definitions, this invaluable aid also sets out such information as the following:

- Syllabication (useful when you want to split a word at the end of a typewritten line)
- Variant spellings, with the preferred spelling listed first
- Pronunciations, with the preferred form shown first
- Capitalization
- Hyphenation
- Italicization
- Part of speech
- Plural of nouns
- Cases of pronouns
- Verb tenses
- Comparative and superlative forms of irregular adverbs and adjectives
- Derivations of the word
- Synonyms and antonyms
- Status label (if a word is colloquial, obsolete, etc.)

Some words whose spelling frequently puzzles many of us are discussed in this chapter in order to sharpen your awareness of spelling in general.

◆ PLURALS

1. The general rule is to form the plural of a noun by adding *s*:

   - book—books
   - clock—clocks
   - pen—pens

2. A noun ending in *o* preceded by a vowel takes an *s* for the plural:

   - curio—curios
   - folio—folios
   - radio—radios
   - ratio—ratios
   - studio—studios

   Some nouns ending in *o*, preceded by a consonant, take *es* to form the plural, while others take *s*:

   - banjo—banjos
   - buffalo—buffaloes
   - cargo—cargoes
   - Eskimo—Eskimoes
   - hero—heroes
   - mosquito—mosquitoes
   - motto—mottoes
   - piano—pianos
   - potato—potatoes
   - soprano—sopranos
   - tomato—tomatoes

3. A singular noun ending in *ch, sh, s, x,* or *z* takes *es* for the plural:

   - bush—bushes
   - chintz—chintzes
   - dress—dresses
   - inch—inches
   - wax—waxes

4. A noun ending in *y* preceded by a consonant changes the *y* to *i* and adds *es* for the plural:

   - ability—abilities
   - auxiliary—auxiliaries
   - discrepancy—discrepancies
   - facility—facilities
   - industry—industries
   - lady—ladies
   - society—societies

5. A noun ending in *y* preceded by a vowel takes only an *s* for the plural:

   - attorney—attorneys
   - galley—galleys
   - kidney—kidneys
   - monkey—monkeys
   - turkey—turkeys

6. Some plurals end in *en*:

- child—children
- man—men
- ox—oxen

7. Some nouns ending in *f* or *fe* change the *f* or *fe* to *v* and add *es* for the plural:

- calf—calves
- knife—knives
- leaf—leaves
- life—lives
- loaf—loaves
- shelf—shelves

But there are some exceptions:

- bailiff—bailiffs
- belief—beliefs
- chief—chiefs
- gulf—gulfs
- roof—roofs

8. Some nouns require a vowel change for the plural:

- foot—feet
- goose—geese
- mouse—mice
- tooth—teeth

9. The plural of numerals, signs, and letters is shown by adding an *s* (or an apostrophe and an *s* to avoid confusion):

- COD—CODs
- one B—four B's

10. To proper names ending in *s* or in an *s* sound, add *es* for the plural:

- Brooks—the Brookses
- Burns—the Burnses
- Jones—the Joneses

11. A compound noun, when hyphenated or when consisting of two separate words, shows the plural form in the most important element:

- attorney-in-fact—attorneys-in-fact
- brigadier general—brigadier generals
- brother-in-law—brothers-in-law
- notary public—notaries public
- passer-by—passersby

12. The plural of solid compounds (a compound noun written as one word) is formed at the end of the solid compound:

- bookshelf—bookshelves
- cupful—cupfuls

- lumberman—lumbermen
- stepchild—stepchildren
- stepdaughter—stepdaughters

13. Some nouns have the same form for singular and plural:

- Chinese
- corps
- deer
- salmon
- sheep
- vermin
- wheat

14. Some nouns are always treated as singular:

- civics
- mathematics
- measles
- milk
- molasses
- music
- news
- statistics

15. Some nouns are always treated as plural:

- pants
- proceeds
- remains
- riches
- scissors
- thanks
- trousers
- tweezers

◇ THE SUFFIX

1. Words whose roots end with *ge* or *ce* generally retain the *e* when a suffix is added:

- change—changeable
- damage—damageable
- disadvantage—disadvantageous
- outrage—outrageous

2. A final silent *e* is usually dropped before a suffix that begins with a vowel:

- argue—arguing
- change—changing
- conceive—conceivable

3. A final silent *e* is usually retained before a suffix that begins with a consonant:

- achieve—achievement
- definite—definitely

4. In words ending in *c*, add *k* before a suffix beginning with *e, i,* or *y*, so that the hard sound of the original *c* is retained:

- frolic—frolicked—frolicking
- mimic—mimicked—mimicking
- picnic—picnicked—picnicking

5. A word ending in *ie* changes the *ie* to *y* when adding a suffix:

- die—dying
- tie—tying
- lie—lying
- vie—vying

6. Words that end in *y* preceded by a vowel retain the *y* when adding the suffix:

- survey—surveying—surveyor

7. Words that end with *y* preceded by a consonant change *y* to *i* when adding a suffix, except when the suffix is *ing*:

- embody—embodying—embodied
- rely—relying—relied
- satisfy—satisfying—satisfied

8. A final consonant is usually doubled when it is preceded by a single vowel and takes a suffix:

- mop—mopping

9. A final consonant is doubled when it is followed by a suffix, and the last syllable is accented when the suffix is added:

- acquit—acquitted

10. The final consonant is not doubled when the accent is shifted to a preceding syllable when the suffix is added:

- refer—referring—reference

or when the final consonant is preceded by two vowels:

- fooled—fooling

◇ IRREGULAR SPELLING

1. Irregular spellings to watch closely:

- acknowledgment
- awful
- judgment
- ninth
- truly
- wholly

2. While they may sound the same, there are three ways to spell words ending in *ceed, cede,* and *sede*:

- exceed
- intercede
- precede
- proceed

- recede
- secede
- succeed
- supersede

Memorize: The only English word that ends in *sede* is *supersede*. The only English words that end in *ceed* are *exceed, proceed,* and *succeed*.

3. Watch for *ant* and *ent* endings:

- relevant
- correspondent
- eminent

4. Watch for *ance* and *ence* endings:

- occurrence
- perseverance

5. Watch for *able* and *ible* endings:

- accessible
- compatible
- deductible

- affordable
- comfortable

5. Don't omit silent letters:

- silhouette
- acquisition
- abscess

- hemorrhage
- diaphragm

6. Don't be confused over double consonants:

- accommodate
- necessary

- commitment
- occurrence

7. Some words are not spelled the way they are pronounced:

- asterisk
- auxiliary
- prerogative

- separate
- boundary

◇ CAPITALIZATION

Proper nouns that denote the names of specific persons or places are capitalized, though names that are common to a group are not. Following are examples of words that are capitalized:

Acts of Congress

- Civil Rights Act
- Child Labor Amendment
- Taft-Hartley Act
- Eighteenth Amendment

Associations

- Society of Professional Engineers
- American Business Association
- Young Women's Christian Association
- American Heart Association

Cars of Railroads and Automobile Models

- Car 54, Train 93
- Plymouth
- Cadillac

Churches and Church Dignitaries

- Fifth Avenue Presbyterian Church
- the Archbishop of New York
- Bishop John Barnes

Cities

- Jefferson City, Missouri
- Los Angeles
- *BUT*—the city of Los Angeles

Clubs

- Possum Kingdom Club
- the Do-Gooders

- the Union League Club
- *BUT*—many Toastmasters clubs in the West

Codes

- the Code of Building Maintenance
- *BUT*—the building code
- Code VI

Compass Points Designating a Specific Region

- the Northeast (*section of the country*), the Pacific Northwest
- *BUT*—just drive north
- the West
- *BUT*—west of town

Constitutions

- the Constitution of Texas
- the Constitution of the United States
- *BUT*—the constitution of any nation

Corporations

- American Brake Corporation
- Container Corporation of America
- *BUT*—The corporation was dissolved.

Courts

- the Criminal Court of Appeals
- *BUT*—a court of appeals
- the Supreme Court
- the Magistrate's Court
- *BUT*—a county court

Decorations

- Purple Heart
- Good Conduct Medal

- Croix de Guerre
- *BUT*—Soldiers are given decorations to signal their acts of heroism.

Degrees (academic)

- B.A.
- M.D.
- D.D.S.
- Ph.D.

Districts

- First Congressional District
- *BUT*—a congressional district

Educational Courses

- English 101
- Spanish Grammar
- Mathematics Made Easy
- *BUT*—He is studying physics and chemistry.

Epithets

- First Lady of the State
- Alexander the Great

Fleets

- the Third Fleet
- *BUT*—The ship was part of the fleet.

Foundations

- Carnegie Foundation
- Ford Foundation
- *BUT*—He established a foundation.

Geographic Divisions and Designations

- Lone Star State
- Sooner State

- *BUT*—There are fifty states in our country.
- Northern Hemisphere
- South Pole
- Old World, Near East

Government Divisions

- Federal Reserve Board
- the Boston Fire Department
- *BUT*—The department was headed by Mr. Charles Bleeker.

Historical Terms

- Dark Ages
- Christian Era
- Battle of the Bulge
- Magna Carta
- Renaissance
- World War II
- Declaration of Independence

Holidays

- Thanksgiving Day
- Easter Sunday
- Passover
- New Year's Eve

Libraries

- Carnegie Library
- Albany Public Library
- *BUT*—The library is a source of information.

Localities

- Western Europe
- Wheat Belt
- Mississippi Delta
- East Africa
- West Side

Military Services

- United States Navy
- Second Battalion
- Squadron 28
- Signal Corps
- Company B

Nobility and Royalty

- Queen of Belgium
- *BUT*—Many queens were honored here.
- Duke of Windsor
- *BUT*—She was proud to have met a duke.

Oceans and Continents

- Pacific Ocean
- *BUT*—He was glad to be crossing the ocean.

Parks

- Greenleaf Park
- Lake Texoma State Park
- Yellowstone National Park
- *BUT*—The park was in a southern state.

People and Tribes

- Jews
- Malay
- Christians
- Chickasaw

Personification

- He sang about Summer in all its glory.
- *BUT*—In summer the days are longer.

Planets and Other Heavenly Bodies

- Mars
- Venus
- Big Dipper
- *EXCEPTIONS:* moon, sun, stars

Publication Titles and Their Subdivisions

- **The American Way,** Chapter VI
- **Remembrance of Things Past,** Volume II

- **Forest Flower Magazine**
- **Wall Street Journal**

Rivers

- Mississippi River
- Wabash River
- *BUT*—The Mississippi and Wabash rivers were flooding after the torrential rains.

Sports Stadiums and Teams

- Dallas Cowboys
- Super Bowl
- Madison Square Garden
- Dodgers

◇ CONFUSING HOMONYMS

Homonyms are words that are pronounced the same but have different meanings, for example: *brake* for *break* or *there* for *their*. The following is a list of commonly confused homonyms:

- advise—advice
- altar—alter
- born—bourn
- breach—breech
- caret—carrot
- compliment—complement
- council—counsel
- cubicle—cubical
- deserts—desserts
- discrete—discreet
- dual—duel
- foreword—forward
- led—lead
- loath—loathe
- mettle—metal
- peace—piece
- piqued—peaked
- principal—principle
- rein—reign—rain
- ringer—wringer
- role—roll
- stationary—stationery
- tick—tic
- tow—toe
- vice—vise
- waved—waived
- yoke—yolk

◇ AMERICAN ENGLISH AND BRITISH ENGLISH DIFFERENCES

There are differences between the way certain words are spelled in American English and the way they are spelled in British English. Table 34–1 provides a list of words that have this peculiar treatment.

TABLE 34–1. Words Spelled Differently in American English and British English

American English	British English
Acknowledgment	Acknowledgement
Aging	Ageing
Analyze	Analyse
Anesthetic	Anaesthetic
Burned	Burnt
Canceled	Cancelled
Catalog	Catalogue
Center	Centre
Check	Cheque
Dialog	Dialogue
Draft	Draught
Dreamed	Dreamt
Encyclopedia	Encyclopaedia
Endeavor	Endeavour
Fetus	Foetus
Fiber	Fibre
Honor	Honour
Humor	Humour
Maneuver	Manoeuvre
Paralyze	Paralyse
Plow	Plough
Program	Programme
Spoiled	Spoilt
Theater	Theatre
Usable	Useable
Worshiping	Worshipping

◇ COMPOUND WORDS AND HYPHENATION

Compound words are two or more words that are used to mean a single concept. Some compound words are written as two separate words with a space between them. These are called *open compounds*. Some compound words are combined into a single word, called *closed compounds*. Another variation are compound words that are separated by a hyphen. These are called *hyphenated compounds*.

Open Compounds

The following is a list of commonly used open compounds:

- drop in
- time frame
- side effects

- life cycle
- stick up
- half brother

- bed wetter
- more or less
- V neck
- bona fide

- under way
- T square
- ad hoc
- vice versa

Closed Compounds

The following is a list of commonly used closed compounds:

- backslide
- deadpan
- lifeline
- standstill
- waterlogged
- sidecar
- coldcock
- makeup
- shortlist
- ongoing

- clearheaded
- handwrite
- longtime
- twofold
- stickhandle
- crossbreed
- layoffs
- sendoff
- carryover

Hyphenated Compounds

The following is a list of commonly used hyphenated compounds:

- bed-wetting
- cross-fertilize
- back-check
- off-color
- time-out
- anti-inflammatory
- pre-engineered
- de-emphasize
- all-knowing
- ex-employee
- president-elect
- self-doubts
- do-able

- cold-shoulder
- time-out
- dead-on
- stand-in
- water-resistant
- non-native
- multi-item
- all-encompassing
- ex-husband
- self-esteem
- nuclear-free
- co-worker
- community-wide

Hyphenation with Numbers

You should include a hyphen when spelling out any two-word number or fraction:

- twenty-nine
- ninety-nine

When a fraction includes more than two numbers, you should hyphenate only the two-word number:

- twenty-nine
- thirty-six
- one twenty-fifth
- one hundred seventy-five
- two and three-quarters

◇ **NEGATIVE FORMATIONS**

Just as not all plurals are made by adding *s* to a word, not all negatives are made by adding *un* as a prefix. There are many other methods for creating negatives. The following is a list of common negative formation techniques.

A or An

A or *An* is often used before a vowel or words beginning with *h*:

- amoral
- asexual

Anti

Anti is added to a word to mean "the opposite of":

- antichrist
- antifreeze
- antimatter
- antibiotic

Counter

Counter is added to a word to mean "the opposite of or contrary to":

- counterculture
- counterclockwise

De

De is added to a word to mean "the reverse of":

- de-emphasize
- demagnetize
- decompose
- deforestation

Dis

Dis is added to a word to mean "the reverse of":

- disrespectful
- disarm
- discontented

Dys

Dys is added to a word to mean "abnormal or impaired":

- dysfunctional
- dyspeptic

Mal

Mal is added to mean "bad or incorrect":

- malformed
- malfunctioning

Mis

Mis is added to mean "bad or incorrect":

- misuse
- misinterpret
- misfortune

Non

Non is added to a word to reverse the meaning:

- nonexistent
- nonfattening
- nonintoxicating

Un, In, Il, Im, Ir

These are added to a word to reverse the meaning:

- undressed
- incapable
- imbalance
- irrefutable

- undrinkable
- illegitimate
- implausible
- irrevocable

Less

Less is added to the end of a word to mean "without":

- shoeless
- motionless
- helpless

Free

Free is added to a word to mean "without":

- caffeine-free
- sugar-free
- crime-free

◇ COMMONLY MISSPELLED WORDS

A

absence   abundance   accessible   accidentally   acclaim   accommodate
accomplish   accordion   accumulate   achievement   acquaintance   acquire
acquitted   across   address   advertisement   advice   advise   affect
alleged   amateur   analysis   analyze   annual   apartment   apparatus
apparent   appearance   arctic   argument   ascend   atheist   athletic
attendance   auxiliary

B

balloon   barbecue   bargain   basically   beggar   beginning   belief
believe   beneficial   benefit   biscuit   boundaries   business

C

calendar   camouflage   candidate   Caribbean   category   cemetery
challenge   changeable   changing   characteristic   chief   choose   chose
cigarette   climbed   cloth   clothes   clothing   collectible   colonel
column   coming   commission   committee   commitment   comparative
competent   completely   concede   conceivable   conceive   condemn
condescend   conscience   conscientious   conscious   consistent   continuous
controlled   controversial   controversy   convenient   correlate   correspondence
counselor   courteous   courtesy   criticism   criticize

D

deceive   defendant   deferred   definitely   definition   dependent
descend   describe   description   desirable   despair   desperate   develop
dictionary   difference   dilemma   dining   disappearance   disappoint
disastrous   discipline   disease   dispensable   dissatisfied   dominant
drunkenness

E

easily   ecstasy   effect   efficiency   eighth   either   eligible   eliminate
embarrass   emperor   encouragement   encouraging   enemy   entirely
environment   equipped   equivalent   especially   exaggerate   exceed
excellence   exhaust   existence   existent   expense   experience   experiment
explanation   extremely   exuberance

F

facsimile   fallacious   fallacy   familiar   fascinating   feasible   February
fictitious   fiery   finally   financially   fluorescent   forcibly   foreign
forfeit   foresee   formerly   forty   fourth   fueling   fulfill   fundamentally

G

gauge   generally   genius   government   governor   grammar   grievous
guarantee   guardian   guerrilla   guidance

H

handkerchief   happily   harass   height   heinous   hemorrhage   heroes
hesitancy   hindrance   hoarse   hoping   humorous   hygiene   hypocrisy
hypocrite

I

ideally   idiosyncrasy   ignorance   imaginary   immediately   implement
incidentally   incredible   independence   independent   indicted   indispensable
inevitable   influential   information   inoculate   insurance   intelligence
interference   interrupt   introduce   irrelevant   irresistible   island

J

jealousy   judicial

K

knowledge

L

laboratory   laid   later   latter   legitimate   leisure   length   license
lieutenant   lightning   likelihood   likely   loneliness   loose   lose   losing
lovely   luxury

M

magazine   maintain   maintenance   manageable   maneuver   manufacture
marriage   mathematics   medicine   millennium   millionaire   miniature
minuscule   minutes   miscellaneous   mischievous   missile   misspelled
mortgage   mosquito   mosquitoes   murmur   muscle   mysterious

N

narrative   naturally   necessary   necessity   neighbor   neutron   ninety
ninth   noticeable   nowadays   nuisance

O

obedience   obstacle   occasion   occasionally   occurred   occurrence
official   omission   omit   omitted   opinion   opponent   opportunity
oppression   optimism   optimistic   orchestra   ordinarily   origin   outrageous
overrun

P

pamphlets parallel particular pavilion peaceable peculiar penetrate perceive performance permanent permissible permitted perseverance persistence personal personnel perspiration physical physician piece pilgrimage pitiful planning pleasant portray possess possession possessive possibility possible potato potatoes practically prairie precede precedence preceding preference preferred prejudice preparation prescription prevalent primitive principal principle privilege probably procedure proceed profession professor prominent pronounce pronunciation propaganda psychology publicly pursue

Q

quantity quarantine questionnaire quizzes

R

realistically realize really recede receipt receive recognize recommend reference referring relevant relieving religious remembrance reminiscence repetition representative resemblance reservoir resistance restaurant rheumatism rhythm rhythmical ridiculous roommate

S

sacrifice sacrilegious safety salary satellite scary scenery schedule secede secretary seize sense sentence separate separation sergeant several severely shepherd shining siege similar simile simply simultaneous sincerely skiing sophomore souvenir specifically specimen sponsor spontaneous statistics stopped strategy strength strenuous stubbornness studying subordinate subtle succeed success succession sufficient supersede suppress surprise surround susceptible suspicious syllable symmetrical synonymous

T

tangible technical technique temperamental temperature tendency themselves theories therefore thorough though through tomorrow tournament toward tragedy transferring tries truly twelfth tyranny

U

unanimous   undoubtedly   unforgettable   unique   unnecessary   until
usable   usage   usually   utilization

V

vacuum   valuable   vengeance   vigilant   village   villain   violence
visible   vision   virtue   volume

W

warrant   warriors   weather   Wednesday   weird   wherever   whether
which   wholly   withdrawal   woman   women   worthwhile   writing

Y

yacht   yield   young

35

Pronunciation

How you pronounce the words you choose to say can dramatically support—or undercut—the substance of what you're saying. Incorrect pronunciation or slurred enunciation reflects poorly on one's intelligence and ability. While this judgment may be unfair, it's reality: First impressions count. To make a favorable impression, try to perfect your speech.

Begin by carefully listening to the speech of others and comparing it with your own. What are the differences, especially between your speech and that of the people you most admire? Consult the dictionary when you hear differences to see whether you or the other person has made a mistake. This moment of truth will quickly improve your pronunciation and help you enlarge your vocabulary. It is one of the finest steps toward cultivation of improved speech patterns.

Following is a partial list of words often mispronounced; perhaps a vowel or a consonant sound is mispronounced, or a syllable is commonly dropped, added, or slurred. Sometimes letters that should be silent are sounded, or vice versa. Study the correct pronunciation carefully. You may be accustomed to pronouncing several of these words differently, but remember: Colloquial pronunciation is not preferable for business standards. Words followed by a double asterisk (**) denote that the word is among the most mispronounced in the English language.

◇ WORD LIST

abject (ab' jekt)

absolutely (ab' so lute lee)

abstemious (ab stee' mee us)

absurd (ab serd')

accede (ak seed')

accept (ak sept')

accession (ak sesh' un))

accessories (ak sess' o reez)

accidentally (ak si den' tal e)

acclimate (a kly' mut)**

address (a dress'; both noun and verb)**

admirable (ad' ma ra bl)**

adult (a dult'; NOT add' ult

aerial (air' ree al)

ally (verb: al ly'; noun: al' ly)

applicable (ap' pli ka bl)**

architect (ar' ki tekt)

arctic (ark' tik)

area (air' ee a)

attacked (a takt')

attitude (at' i tyud)

attorney (a ter' nee)**

autopsy (aw' top see)**

avenue (av' a nyu)

aviation (ay vi ay' shun)

battery (bat' er e; *NOT* bat' tree)

being (pronounce the *g*)

beneficent (be neff' i sent)

bicycle (by' sik l)

biography (by og' ra fee)

breadth (bredth; pronounce the *d*)

casualty (cazh' ul tee)x

champion (cham' pee un)

chastisement (chass tyze' ment)

chauffeur (show' ferr)**

chestnut (chess' nut)

chocolate (chock' o lut)

clique (klik)**

comment (com' ment)

compromise (com' pro myze)

concave (con cayv')

concentrate (con' sen trayt)

concierge (con se arzh')**

condolence (con doe' lens)

conversant (con ver' sunt)**

convex (con vex')

corps (kor)

creek (kreek; *NOT* krik)

cruel (kroo' el)

data (day' tah)**

deaf (def)

decade (deck' ayd)

decisive (dee sy' siv)

defect (de fekt)

deficit (def' i sit)

demonstrable (de mon' stra bl)

depot (dee' po)

depths (pronounce the *th*)

dessert (de zert')

detour (dee' toor)

diamond (dy' a mund)**

distribute (dis trib' yute)

divide (di vyd')

doing (doo' ing; pronounce the *g*)

drowned (drownd; one syllable,
    NOT drownded)

duly (dyu' lee)

duty (dyu' tee)

edition (eh dish' un)

educate (edd' yu kate)

elm (as written; *NOT* elum)

envelop (verb: en vell' up)

envelope (noun: en' va lowp)

epitome (ee pitt' o mee)

equitable (ek' wi ta bl)**

era (ihr' a)

err (urr; rhymes with *fur*)**

etiquette (ett' i kett)

every (ev' a ree)

exigency (eks' i jen see)

exponent (eks po' nent)

exquisite (eks' kwi zit)**

extant (eks' tent)

extraordinary (eks tror' di ner ee)

fact (pronounce the *t*)

family (fam' a lee)

fasten (fass'en)

favorite (fay' vo ritt)

figure (fig' yur)

film (as written; *NOT* fill um)

finance (verb: fi nans'; noun: fi' nans)**

financial (fin nan' shul)

financier (fin nan seer')

forehead (for' id)

forte (for' tay)

formidable (for' mi da bl)**

fragmentary (frag' men ter ee)

friendship (frend' ship; pronounce the *d*)

genuine (jenn' yu inn)

gingham (ghing' um)

glisten (gliss' en)

gondola (gonn' do la)

government (guv' ern ment;
    pronounce both *n*'s)

grievous (gree' vuss)

guardian (gar' dee un)

hasten (hayss' en)

height (hyt; does *NOT* end in *th*)

heinous (hay' nuss)**

herculean (herk yu lee' un)

heroism (her' o izm)

homeopathy (ho mee opp' a thee)

horizon (ho ryz' un)

hostile (hoss' til)**

hundred (as written; *NOT* hunnerd)

idea (eye dee' a)

ignoramus (ig no ray' muss)

immediate (im mee' dee ut)

impious (im' pee uss)

incognito (in cog nee' toe)

incomparable (in com' pa ra bl)

indictment (in dyt' ment)

industry (in' dus tree)**

inexorable (in eks' o ra bl)

inexplicable (in eks' pli ka bl)

infamous (in' fa muss)

inquiry (in kwy' ree)**

Iowa (i' o wah)

irrevocable (ir rev' o ka bl)**

Italian (itt al' yun)

italics (ih tal' iks)

judiciary (joo dish' a ree)

just (as written; *NOT* jest)

knew (nyu)

lapel (la pel')

large (larg; no *d* sound)

latent (lay' tent)

length (pronounce the *g*; *NOT* lenth)

library (as written; *NOT* ly' bay ree)

lieu (lyu)

lightning (lyt' ning; *NOT* lyt' en ning)

long-lived (long' lyvd')**

longevity (lon jev' i tee)

luxury (luk' shu ree; *NOT* lug'
    shu ree)**

lyceum (ly see' um)

manufacture (manvu fakt' yur)

maturity (ma tyu' rit tee)

memorable (mem' uh ra bl)

mischievous (miss' cha vuss)**

municipal (myu niss' i pul)

museum (myu zee' um)

new (nyu)

oblique (o bleek')

office (off' fiss; *NOT* aw' fuss)

often (off' en)

on (as written; *NOT* awn)

ordeal (or deel')

osteopath (oss' tee o path)

osteopathy (oss tee opp' a thee)

overalls (as written; *NOT* over halls)

parade (pa rayd'; *NOT* prayd)

partner (as written; *NOT* pard' ner)

patron (pay' trun)

pecan (pe kon')

pecuniary (pee kyu' nee er ee)**

peremptory (per emp' te ree)

piano (pee an' o)

picture (pik' tyur)

pique (peek)

plumber (plum' er)

positively (poz' it tiv lee)

possess (po zess')

precedence (pre see' dens)**

preface (pref' iss)

preferable (pref' er a bl)

prescription (pre scrip' shun)

presentation (prez en tay' shun)

radiator (ray' dee ay tor)

radio (ray' dee o)

rambling (as written; *NOT* ram' bol ing)

realm (relm; *NOT* rellum)

recognize (rek' og nyz)

recourse (ree' cors)

refutable (re fyut' a bl)

reputable (rep' yut a bl)

research (re serch')

resources (ree sors' ez)

respite (res' pit)**

revocable (rev' o ka bl)**

robust (ro bust')**

romance (ro mans')

Roosevelt (ro' za velt; *NEVER*
    roose' a velt)**

route (root)

sagacious (sa gay' shuss)

schism (si' zem)

simultaneous (sy mul tay' nee uss)

short-lived (short' lyvde')**

slippery (as written; *NOT* slip' ree)

solace (sol' uss)**

solder (sod' er)

sphere (sfeer)**

status (stay' tuss)**

strictly (as written; *NOT* strick' li)

subpoena (sup pee' na)

subtle (sut' tl)

suit (sute)

superfluous (soo per' floo uss)

surprise (ser pryz')

telegrapher (tell egg' ra fer)

temperament (as written;
    NOT tem' per ment)**

tenet (ten' ett)

theater (thee' a ter)**

tract (as written; *NOT* track)**

trembling (as written;
    NOT trem' bol ing)

tremendous (tre men' dus)

tribune (trib' yun)

tube (tyub)

Tuesday (tyuz' day)**

tumult (tyu' mult)

umbrella (as written;
    NOT um ba rel' lah)**

usurp (yu serp')

Utica (yu' tik a)

vagary (va gair' ee)**

vehement (vee' a ment)**

vehicle (vee' ih kel)**

verbose (ver bowss')

was (wahz)

461

water (wa' ter)**

what (hwot; *NOT* wot)**

wheel (hweel; *NOT* weel)**

whether (hweth' er)**

white (hwyt)**

wrestle (res' l)

36

Punctuation

◇ PURPOSE OF PUNCTUATION

The sole purpose of punctuation is to make the text clear. If a mark of punctuation does not clarify the text, it should be omitted. Of course, you'll follow your boss's preference if he or she instructs you, for example, to insert more commas or semicolons than today's magazines and newspapers typically use. When public changes occur, not every person immediately approves. But if a matter is left to your discretion, remember that the old tried-and-true comma rule also applies for many other marks of punctuation: "When in doubt, leave it out."

Nevertheless, there are still standards and formalities in punctuation that you must fully grasp, not only to satisfy your boss but also to help promote your own career. Once it leaves the office, your work speaks for itself. You want it to be a source of pride for both your employer and you.

Following is a list of punctuation marks with usage rules and examples for each.

◇ THE PERIOD

A period is used at the end of a declarative sentence to denote a full pause:

- I am going to town.
- You may go with me if you wish.

Use a period, not a question mark, when the sentence contains an indirect question:

- He could not understand why she was leaving.

Also use a period for a request phrased as a question:

- Will you please return the diskette when you are finished.

The period is used in decimals to separate a whole number from a decimal fraction:

- 5.6 percent
- $19.50

It is also used in abbreviations:

- Mrs.
- Ph.D.
- etc.

◆ THE COMMA

The presence of a comma, or its absence, can cause different interpretations of a written sentence. It is thus of vast importance, particularly in legal documents. The comma tells the reader to pause. Some writers can tell where commas belong by reading their sentences aloud and inserting commas where there seems to be a natural pause. This works, however, only if you read a sentence carefully and accurately.

Series

Commas are used to separate nouns in a series or adjectives in a series of the same rank modifying the same noun:

- The workers picked cherries, peaches, and plums.
- We swam in cool, clear, fresh water.

Some bosses may prefer to omit the comma before the *and* in such sentences unless it's needed for clarity. The same applies to commas before *but* and *or*. Many writers believe these words take the place of the final comma in a series.

Sometimes a term consisting of years, months, and days is considered not a series but a single unit of time. No commas are used:

- Interest will be computed for 6 years 3 months and 2 days.

Compound and Complex Sentences

Two sentences are often connected with a comma and conjunction, such as *and* or *but*. A comma is used between the clauses of a compound sentence:

- John went to the theater, but he left before the play ended.

Do not confuse this with a compound predicate, which takes no comma:

- John went to the theater but left before the play ended.

An adverbial clause usually follows the independent clause, and no comma is used. But for emphasis, the order of the clauses is sometimes transposed. Then a comma is used.

- **USUAL ORDER:** John was met by a large delegation when he came home.
- **TRANSPOSED ORDER:** When John came home, he was met by a large delegation.

Introductory Expressions

Introductory expressions, such as transitional words and phrases, mild exclamations, and other independent expressions, are set off by a comma when they occur alone at the beginning of a sentence:

- Yes, I will go.
- Well, perhaps she is right.
- Nevertheless, I wish he had waited for me.
- To tell the truth, I think you should go.
- As a rule, he arrives very early.

A few introductory expressions are more emphatic without punctuation, however, and need not be followed by a comma:

- Doubtless she just couldn't be here.
- At least you tried.
- Undoubtedly the plane's engines both failed.
- Indeed you may bring your friends with you.

To distinguish between the two, ask whether you naturally pause after the word or words in question. A comma is used to signal the natural pause.

Other Transitional Words

A comma is used to set off the transitional words *however, therefore*, and *moreover* when used within the sentence or as the first or last word of the sentence:

- Jean may not arrive until noon, however.
- Her problem, therefore, must be solved at once.
- I will be there, moreover, as soon as I can.

Sometimes *though* is used to mean *however* and should be set off with commas:

- I will be there, though, if at all possible.

Prepositional Phrases

No comma is used for prepositional phrases within a sentence unless the phrase comes between the subject and the predicate of the clause:

- I am sure that because of your generosity we will be able to build the new dormitory.
- The bag, in addition to a hatbox, will be sent to you today.

Contrasting Phrases

Contrasting expressions within a sentence are set off by commas:

- The lion, not the tiger, growled.
- We walk slowly, never quickly, to the garage.
- This letter was meant for you, not for me.
- *BUT*—This letter was meant for you but not for me.

Nonrestrictive Modifiers

Nonrestrictive modifiers are phrases or clauses that could be omitted without affecting the meaning of the main clause. These should be set off from the rest of the sentence by a comma or by parenthetical commas:

- John, my favorite friend, is visiting me.
- That car is, I believe, a new model.
- Mary Brown, who lives next door, is in the third grade.
- *BUT*—That is the girl who lives next door.

Infinitive Phrases

An infinitive phrase used independently is set off by commas:

- The color is too dark, to list one fault.

If the phrase is used as a modifier, it is not punctuated:

- The piano is too large to fit in the room.

Dialogue

A comma is used to separate a dialogue quotation from the main sentence:

- "Please go with me," the boy said.
- "What do you think," Mr. Bleeker asked, "the mayor will do next?"

Commas also separate the name of the person addressed in dialogue from the remainder of the sentence:

- "Will you come with me, John?"
- "But, Jane, how do you know that the plane is late?"

A confirming question within a sentence is set off by commas:

- "He left, did he not, on the noon plane?"

Repeated Words

A comma is used for clarity and to avoid confusion when the same word is repeated:

- Whoever goes, goes without my consent.

Omission

When words are omitted in one part of a sentence because they were used in a previous part, a comma is used to show where the words were omitted:

- Sam's first car was a Cadillac, and mine, a Ford.

Transposed Adjective Order

An adjective normally precedes the noun it modifies. When an adjective follows a noun, the adjective is set off by commas; when an adjective precedes a noun but also precedes the article before the noun, a comma follows the adjective:

- The physician, dignified and competent, told them the bad news.
- Dignified and competent, the physician told them the bad news.

Numbers

A comma is used in writing large numbers, separating the thousands digits from the hundreds, the millions digits from the thousands, and so forth:

- 249,586
- 1,345,000

A comma is used to separate two or more unrelated numbers:

- On August 1, 1992, 437 people visited the museum.
- Out of eighty, twenty were discarded.

Do not forget the second comma when the date occurs in the middle of the sentence:

- She left for England on June 22, 2007, and returned a month later.

However, it is acceptable if your boss prefers no commas at all:

- She left for England on June 22 2007 and returned a month later.

Addresses

Elements of an address are set off by commas:

- He lives at 410 Hawthorne Street, Chicago, Illinois, near the University of Chicago campus.

On an envelope address, there is no comma between the state and the zip code.

Titles

A comma is used to separate a name and a title:

- The letter was from Mrs. Masterson, our president, and contained a list of instructions.

Set off Jr. and Sr. from a proper name by a comma. A Roman numeral is not set off by a comma:

- Philip W. Thompson, Sr.
- Philip W. Thompson III

Degrees are also set off by a comma:

- Jennifer Galt, M.D.

But descriptive titles are not:

- Attila the Hun

Company Names

Company names consisting of a series of names omit the last comma in the series:

- Pate, Tate and Waite

When *and Company* completes a series of names, the last comma is also omitted:

- Pate, Tate, Waite and Company

Set off *Incorporated* from the name of a company by a comma:

- Johnson Brothers, Incorporated

◇ THE QUESTION MARK

A question mark closes a question:

- What time is it?

A question mark is used to express a doubt:

- He is older (?) than she.

If the question is indirect, no question mark is used:

- I wonder whether he will be here.

When a question is asked in the middle of a sentence, the question is enclosed by commas and the sentence ends with a question mark:

- They are arriving, aren't they, on the noon train?

When the question is enclosed in parentheses, the question mark is inside the parentheses, not at the end of the sentence:

- The magazine (did you see it?) describes the city in great detail.

If the question mark is part of a quotation, it is placed inside the closing quotation mark; if it is not a part of the quotation, it is placed outside the closing quotation mark:

- The statement ended, "And is that all?"
- What did she mean by "jobless years"?

If the last word in a question is an abbreviation and thus contains a period, the question mark is also used:

- Do you think he will arrive by 4 p.m.?

When it is desired to make a question of a statement, the question mark is used:

- He is arriving today?
- Really?

◇ THE EXCLAMATION POINT

An exclamation point is used when making extravagant claims or to express deep feeling:

- Here is the finest car on the market!
- The announcement was unbelievable!

An exclamation point is used after a word or phrase charged with emotion:

- Quick! We don't want to be late.

It is also used for double emphasis:

- Did you catch that innuendo!

CAUTION: Some people get into the habit of using exclamation points far too often to express strong emotion, and they end up blunting the very purpose of the punctuation. For effective writing, show emotion through the choice of words instead, and reserve exclamation points for only the strongest of feelings.

◇ THE SEMICOLON

A semicolon is used when the conjunction is omitted between parts of a compound sentence:

■ I went with them; I should have stayed at home.

A semicolon precedes words such as *however, moreover,* or *otherwise* when they introduce the second of two connected full sentences:

■ She is arriving at noon; however, she will not stay long.

If parts of a series contain inner punctuation such as a comma, the parts are separated by a semicolon:

■ He came to see his mother, who was ill; his sister, who lived in the next town; and his old schoolmate.

◇ THE COLON

The colon generally follows a sentence introducing a tabulation or a long quotation:

■ The following quotation is from the *Detroit Free Press*: "Regardless of what may be accomplished, the company will still be involved."

■ During your first year, you will study such subjects as these: algebra, physics, chemistry, and psychology.

EXCEPTION: When the tabulated list is the object of a verb or a preposition, a colon is never used:

■ During your first year, you will study algebra, physics, chemistry, and psychology.

Emphasis or Anticipation

The colon is also used to stress a word, phrase, or clause that follows it or when a sentence creates anticipation for what immediately follows:

■ The newspaper published a startling statement: the city had been completely destroyed by fire.

Time

The colon is used to separate hours and minutes in expressions of time:

■ 4:15 a.m. CST

Titles

The colon is used to separate a title from a subtitle:

- *Gone With the Wind: A Story of the Old South*

◇ QUOTATION MARKS

Double quotation marks are used to set off any material quoted within a sentence or paragraph. If the quoted material consists of several paragraphs, the opening quotation mark is used at the beginning of the quotation and at the beginning of each paragraph within the quotation; a closing quotation mark, however, is used only at the conclusion of the quotation. It is not used at the end of each paragraph within the quotation, as many people mistakenly think. For example:

> The passage he read aloud was from the first chapter: "The discovery of this energy brings us to the problem of how to allow it to be used. The use of atomic power throws us back to the Greek legend of Prometheus and the age-old question of whether force should be exerted against law.
>
> "The man of today must decide whether he will use this power for destruction or for peaceful purposes." When he had finished the reading, there was loud applause.

Quotations Within Quotations

Single quotation marks indicate a quotation within the quotation:

- He said, "Did you hear John make the statement, 'I will not go with her,' or were you not present at the time he spoke?"

Titles

In printed text, the titles of essays, articles, poems, stories, or chapters are set off within quotation marks; titles of plays, books, and periodical publications are italicized:

- The name of the article is "I Believe."
- The *Eternal Echos* CD contains the poem "Tread Gently."
- The title of the book is *Journey Into Night*.
- It was first published in *Harper's Magazine*.

Quotation Marks and Punctuation

Place quotation marks outside the comma and the period:

- "Don't stop now," he said, "when you have so little left to finish."

Place quotation marks inside the colon and the semicolon:

- He called her a "little witch"; that was right after she broke his model plane.

Place quotation marks outside an exclamation point or a question mark when the quoted material alone is an exclamation or a question:

- "I passed my test!"

Place quotation marks inside an exclamation point or a question mark when the quoted material alone is not an exclamation or a question:

- Didn't he claim to be "too tired"?

◇ ITALICS

Italics are sometimes used for emphasis:

- Notice where you are, not where you *have been*.

But the best writing avoids italics for this purpose, depending on choice of language to bring out the emphasis. As mentioned earlier, italics are used for the names of books, pamphlets, and periodicals:

- *Saturday Evening Post*
- *Black Beauty*
- *Washington Daily News*

The names of ships are italicized but not abbreviations in front of them.

- *Sea Witch*
- USS *Heinz*

NOTE: When using a typewriter and not a word processor or computer, indicate italics by underlining:

- <u>Sea Witch</u>
- USS <u>Heinz</u>
- <u>Washington Daily News</u>

◇ THE APOSTROPHE

As a mark of omission, the apostrophe may denote that a word has been contracted intentionally:

- It's time to go.
- Haven't you finished the task?

Possession

To show possession, use an apostrophe followed by an s after a singular noun:

- the city's founder

Use it alone after plural nouns ending in s:

- the books' titles

Plural nouns not ending in s form the possessive by adding an apostrophe and an *s*:

- men's clubs
- sheep's clothing

The plural of compound nouns and joint possessive nouns is formed by adding an apostrophe followed by an s to the second word only:

- the Secretary-Treasurer's decision
- Mary and John's cassette player

But if the items are separately owned, the compound nouns each add an apostrophe followed by an *s*:

- Mary's and John's coats

No apostrophe is used with possessive pronouns:

- his
- its
- ours
- hers
- yours
- theirs

The apostrophe is used to express duration of time:

- a day's traveling time
- twelve months' duration

For a proper name ending in *s*, use an apostrophe followed by an *s*:

- Lewis's hat
- Miss Bliss's book

Two proper names are traditionally observed as exceptions:

- Moses' robe
- Jesus' parable

For proper names ending in *s*, use an apostrophe only:

- The Joneses' boots were left in the hall.

◇ THE DASH

The dash (in typing, indicated by two hyphens) is used to introduce an added thought:

- I shall go with you—you don't mind, do you?

The dash also breaks the continuity of a thought as a digression:

- "The Scherzo Sonata" by Tolstoy is a sad story—but the writing is magnificent.

It is sometimes used before and after a parenthetical expression in place of commas:

- Henry Higgins—bareheaded and without a coat—left the house and ran down the road.

Sometimes you can think of a dash as a super comma. When a sentence already contains a series separated by commas, a dash is a good tool for separating a clause that might otherwise look like it was part of the series. Consider the following:

- The Mississippi River weaves between Tennessee, Arkansas, and Louisiana—a state famous for its French culture—before emptying into the Gulf of Mexico.

◇ ELLIPSES

To show omission of words in quoted material, three spaced dots (ellipses) are used if material is deleted within the sentence. When the last part of a quoted sentence is omitted, it is followed by three spaced dots plus its punctuation. At the end of the quotation, only the punctuation is used:

- "Five hundred firemen . . . attended the ball . . . . "
- Mr. Brown went on to say: "The shoe department functions smoothly . . . many salespeople have won prizes for efficiency."

Ellipsis dots may also be used to mark a thought expressed hesitantly:

- He said, "If . . . if I do go with you, will you return early?"

◇ PARENTHESES

Parentheses are used to enclose matter that is introduced by way of explanation:

- If the lessor (the person owning the property) agrees, the lessee (the person renting the property) may have a dog on the premises.

Parentheses are used to enclose figures that enumerate items:

- The book contained chapters on (1) capitalization, (2) spelling rules, (3) troublesome verbs, and (4) punctuation.

They are also used to enclose citations of authority:

- The definition of action is "the process or state of being active (*American College Dictionary*)."

And they are used to enclose figures repeated for clarity, as in legal documents:

- He was willed five thousand dollars ($5,000) by his uncle.
- You will be paid twenty (20) percent interest.

◆ BRACKETS

Brackets and parentheses are sometimes used interchangeably; however, brackets have two common uses: (1) they identify changes to quoted material, and (2) they enclose digressions within parentheses.

Changes to Quoted Material

If you are quoting someone but make a change to the quote in order to clarify something, you should put your change within brackets. Consider the following:

- Original Quote—"Everyone knew it was about to break any day now."
- Revised Quote—"Everyone knew it [the dam] was about to break any day now."

Digressions Within Parentheses

Sometimes you find situations where you need an extra set of parentheses nested within a previous pair. Consider the following:

- The computer's memory (Random Access Memory [RAM] and Read Only Memory [ROM]) is where software is loaded.

◆ THE HYPHEN

Hyphens are used both in spelling and in punctuation. When it is used as punctuation, it is not part of a word or phrase. There are four general ways the hyphen can be used as punctuation:

1. Breaking a word at the end of a line
2. Combining words that form a compound adjective
3. Acting as a substitute for a repeated word
4. Indicating special pronunciations

Line Breaks

Most word-processing programs, such as Microsoft Word, have a built-in hyphenation feature that you can turn on and off. This feature automatically adds hyphens to long words that won't fit on the end of a line. Sometimes the computer's idea of where to put a hyphen can cause the hyphenated word to look ridiculous. Therefore, it's important for you to know the general rules regarding line break hyphenation. Here are some of those rules:

- Don't break one-syllable words.
- Don't break a word if just one letter is left on a line.
- Break hyphenated compound words at the hyphen.
- Break closed compound words between the words.

Compound Adjectives

Compound adjectives are groups of words or phrases used in a sentence to describe a noun. Consider the following:

- It was a once-in-a-lifetime opportunity.
- I wouldn't touch that line with a ten-foot pole.
- The computer's processor has a 512 single-byte bus.
- Eight-month-old kittens were given away.
- Eight month-old kittens were given away.

Do not use hyphens when the first word of a compound adjective ends in -ly. The following examples are *INCORRECT*:

- It was a highly-motivated student body.
- It was a beautifully-made sweater.

Hyphens as Substitute Words

If a word repeats with a different modifier in a sentence, it can make the sentence sound long and difficult. One way to solve this problem is to use a hyphen. Consider the following examples:

- We both over- and underestimated the amount of driving time for the trip.
- The Dallas Cowboys used a three-, four-, and five-man line.
- Most computers today have either a 32- or 64-bit processor.

Hyphens for Pronunciation

You can use hyphens when writing dialogue in order to achieve a particular pronunciation in the reader's mind:

- "S-s-s-s," said the snake.
- "Mr. S-s-smith," he stuttered, "May I p-p-please have some w-w-water?"

◇ THE SLASH

The slash is often used as shorthand or when the choice between outcomes is nebulous. Since the slash is often ambiguous, it should be used with caution.

The slash is used: (1) with and/or combinations, and (2) to indicate other relationships between words.

And/Or Combinations

The slash can be used to indicate options that are available, to indicate equal possibilities, or to show that something has more than one function. For example:

- The potter worked alone in the cold garage/studio.
- Dear Sir/Madam:
- The ingredients of the drink are: ice, rum, lime/lemon, and cola.

Indicating Other Relationships

The slash can be used to separate elements that are being compared, to separate origins and destinations, to separate the numerals in a date, to indicate a period that spans two or more calendar years, in place of the word "per," and to write fractions.

- The Redskins/Cowboys rivalry has a long history.
- The Dallas/Atlanta flight was canceled.
- 12/31/2008
- For the 2008/09 school year, the eighth graders will be taking technology education for the first time.
- 1000 km/hour
- $1/2 = 1/4 + 1/4$

CHAPTER 37

Numerals

◆ **WORDS OR FIGURES?**

Your main concern with numbers is whether to spell them out in words or to express them in figures. As so often happens with matters of English usage, there are many times when both forms are correct, and you will regularly come across variations not covered in a book of rules, so use your discretion. Clarity is always your strongest guideline.

Printed Text and Prose Text

Generally, in prose text, numbers under 101 are spelled out, and numbers over 101 are shown in figures. The more formal the text is, the greater is the tendency to express the number in words.

In printed text, a number used for comparison with other numbers in the same section should be in numerical form:

- An excavation of 500 feet can be finished as rapidly as 200 feet if the right equipment is used.

At the Beginning of a Sentence

A number appearing at the beginning of a sentence, if it can be expressed in one or two words, should be spelled out:

- Sixteen new cars were delivered.
- Thirty or forty bushels were needed.
- *NOT:* 2,746,892 copies were purchased.

The last example should be rewritten so that the figure appears later in the sentence:

- The company purchased 2,746,892 copies.

Legal Documents

In legal documents, numbers are written in both words and figures to prevent misunder-standing, and the same is true in papers that transfer land title:

- The west thirty (30) feet of Lot Nine (9) in Block Four (4) . . .

Round Numbers

Approximate round numbers are spelled out:

- The station is about fifty blocks away.
- He found nearly two thousand dollars.

Sets of Numbers

To differentiate two sets of numbers occurring in the same sentence, use words for one and figures for the other:

- Three of the men drove 2,000 miles each; four drove 3,000 miles each; and only one drove the complete 3,000 miles.

If the sentence cannot be rewritten, use a comma or dash to separate the numbers:

- During the year 1992, twenty million people visited the park.
- We received 1,213—113 of which . . .

Large Numbers

As a general rule, write out numbers up to and including one hundred, and use figures for numbers over one hundred. But for large numbers, if a number can be written as one or two words, do so:

- four hundred
- five million
- two billion

Use the short form for writing numbers over a thousand not pertaining to money:

- fourteen hundred
- *NOT:* one thousand four hundred

Large, even amounts may combine figures and words:

- Production of 37 million paper clips and a budget of $146 billion . . .

If a figure or the word *several* precedes *hundred, thousand, million, billion,* and so on, the singular form is used. After *many,* the plural form is used:

- six hundred pages
- several million years
- many hundreds of pages

Separating Digits

All numbers above 999 are written with commas to separate every group of three digits, counting from the units place:

- 1,001
- 123,000
- 1,436,936

EXCEPTIONS: Commas are omitted in long decimal fractions, page numbers, addresses, telephone numbers, room numbers, and form numbers:

- 10356
- Page 3487
- 1467 Wilshire Boulevard
- 201-555-9088
- Room 2630
- Form 2317-A

Commas are also omitted in four-digit year numbers, but they are added for years with five or more digits:

- The company began in 1992.
- The pottery shards were dated at about 14,000 B.C.
- This science fiction novel takes place in the year 27,345 A.D.

Patent numbers are written with commas:

- Patent No. 3,436,987

Serial numbers are written without commas:

- Motor Number 245889954
- Policy Number 894566

◇ DOLLARS AND CENTS

Use figures for money:

- 1 cent
- 20 cents

- $20,000

However, as with other numbers, amounts of money are always written out when beginning a sentence:

- One cent was contributed by each child.
- *NOT:* 1 cent was contributed by each child.

A series of prices is written in figures only:

- These shoes were priced at $50, $60, and $85.

Dollar and Cent Signs

Use the dollar sign before the number, not the word *dollar* or *dollars* after the number.

- The duplex rents for $700 per month.

If a large number combines figures and words, use the dollar sign before the figure:

- The budget calls for $850 billion.
- *NOT:* The budget calls for 850 billion dollars.

Repeat the dollar sign with successive numbers:

- The bonds could be purchased in denominations of $10,000, $12,000, $15,000, and $20,000.

EXCEPTION: Omit all but the first dollar sign when numbers are in tabulated form:

- The bonds could be purchased in denominations of the following amounts:
- $10,000
- 12,000
- 15,000
- 20,000

The dollar sign is not used when the figure given is in cents alone. Use the cent sign ¢ after amounts less than one dollar, but never use the cent sign with a decimal point:

- 25¢
- *NOT:* .25¢, for that would mean one-fourth of a cent

EXCEPTION: The only time the dollar sign is used when the figure is in cents alone is in statistical work when the part of the dollar is carried out to more than two decimal places:

- $0.3564

Decimal Points

Decimal points are another way of writing fractions, especially large fractions. When a decimal occurs with no unit before it, use a cipher (a zero) for quick interpretation:

- a 0.75-yard measurement
- rainfall of 0.356 inch

Sometimes the fraction is part of a dollar. When the amount of dollars given is not followed by cents, omit the decimal point and the ciphers:

- $3
- $1,200
- *BUT:* $17.75

The decimal point and ciphers are not used with even amounts of money unless in tabulated form. If tabulated, and some amounts contain cents and some do not, the even amounts should contain ciphers:

- $19.36
-   5.00
-   2.14
- 37.00
-   1.23
-   .19
-   .02

◆ TIME

When a figure and a word come together as an adjective to express time, connect the two with a hyphen:

- a 24-hour day
- *BUT:* a day of 24 hours
- two 2-year 12-percent notes
- *BUT:* two notes for two years at 12 percent

Hours, minutes, and seconds are separated by a colon:

- 10:05:02 a.m.

Never use "this a.m." instead of "this morning." With *a.m.* or *p.m.*, the word *o'clock* should not be used:

- I will meet you at 4 p.m.
- I will meet you at four o'clock this afternoon.

Ciphers after the number of the hour are unnecessary. For exact noon and midnight, it is correct to use the words:

- I will meet you at noon.
- The horn blew at midnight.

◇ DATES

The day is written in numerals, without *th, st,* or *d,* unless the day is written before the name of the month:

- May 1, 2008
- *NOT:* May 1st, 2008
- *BUT:* On the 2d of June 2008
- In the August 21 and September 3 editions (*NOT* 21st or 3d)

In legal documents, dates are spelled out:

- the twelfth day of May, A.D. Two Thousand and Eight

◇ THE HYPHEN

Written-out numbers below one hundred are hyphenated:

- thirty-three
- ninety-nine
- twenty-seven

Hundreds and thousands are not hyphenated:

- six hundred thousand
- three hundred million

When modifying a noun, numbers are hyphenated, as are any compound adjectives:

- five-thousand-foot mountain
- three-foot rule

Fractions of less than one are hyphenated:

- one-third
- three-quarters
- *BUT:* one twenty-third

Mixed numbers are not hyphenated between the whole number and the fraction, both when written as words and figures:

- one and one-half
- 1 1/2

Do not write one part of the fraction as a numeral and the other as a word:

- one-fourth-inch bolt
- *NOT:* 1 fourth-inch bolt

When a mixed number is the subject of a sentence, the noun is plural. However, the verb is singular because the quantity is considered as a single unit:

- 1 5/8 inches is needed
- 2 1/4 miles is the length of the track

◇ AGES

Use the general rule in giving the age of a person or a period of time (write out up to and including one hundred; use figures over one hundred):

- She is twelve years old.
- He has held the same position for twenty-six years.
- She is now 105 years of age.
- The company has been in this city for 102 years.

In compound adjectives denoting age, the words designating time may be used before *old*, but in that event the words *year* and *day* must appear in the singular:

- 12-day-old baby elephant
- 6-month-old pony
- 200-year-old building
- 3-day-old kitten

◇ DIMENSIONS

The signs reserved for technical writing are ' for feet, " for inches, and × for by.

- 9' × 12' (9 feet by 12 feet)
- 8" × 10" (8 inches by 10 inches)

In regular prose text, write out the word "by" for "×."
  Ciphers can be used to indicate exact measurement if they improve clarity:

- 9'0" × 12'0" × 20'6"

◇ WEIGHTS AND MEASURES

Abbreviations are used without capitalization:

- 6 lb. 3 oz.   ■ *OR* 6 pounds 3 ounces
- 192 lbs   ■ *OR* 192 pounds

In a compound adjective showing a weight or a measure, the numeral is hyphenated to a singular noun:

- 600-mile-an-hour speed
- *BUT:* speed of 600 miles an hour
- a 40-hour workweek
- *BUT:* a workweek of 40 hours

◇ PERCENTAGES

The numeral is retained whether or not a percentage sign is used:

- 5% price reduction
- loss of 10 percent
- almost 30 percent of the population

For percentages in succession, use the sign after each numeral:

- 30% to 50%
- 6%, 8%, and 10%

◇ PAGE NUMBERING

For all page numbering, use figures to show the numbers. Commas are not used in page numbers greater than 999.

Page Number Formats

On legal documents, a page number is centered at the bottom of each page; on other papers, it is usually shown at the top. Manuscripts and briefs are numbered in the upper right corner; papers that are to be bound at the left are numbered in the lower right corner. In each case, all numbers should appear at exactly the same place on all pages. Title pages are not numbered. A first page of a work or of a chapter is not marked with a number, although the numbering of the following pages takes into consideration the number of the first page.

It is acceptable to use a short dash before and after the page number, -3-, without a period. Never use quotation marks and never type the word *page* before the number. Frequently, the number stands alone, 3, without a period.

◇ THE ABBREVIATION FOR *NUMBER*

The abbreviation for *number*—no.—or the number sign—#—is usually omitted:

- Building 38
- Invoice 3457
- Page 92

- *NOT:* Building No. 38
- *NOT:* Invoice #3457
- *NOT:* page no. 92

In text, however, it may be convenient to use the abbreviation:

- When he came to No. 16, he halted.
- The only houses to be painted this year are No. 16, 17, and 18.

◇ PLURALS OF NUMBERS

Form the plural of a numeral or other character by adding *s* or *es* to the word. If the number is a figure, use *s* or *es* as your boss prefers:

- 5s and 6s *OR* 5's and 6's *OR* fives and sixes
- the 1890s *OR* the 1890's
- MD88s OR MD88's

◇ ROMAN NUMERALS

Roman numerals are often used in outlines and some dates. Table 37–1 lists the most commonly used Roman numerals. Use the forms listed in Table 37–2 for dates.

TABLE 37–1. Most Commonly Used Roman Numerals

Arabic	Roman	Arabic	Roman	Arabic	Roman
1	I	15	XV	150	CL
2	II	16	XVI	200	CC
3	III	17	XVII	300	CCC
4	IV	18	XVIII	400	CD
5	V	19	XIX	500	D
6	VI	20	XX	600	DC
7	VII	30	XXX	700	DCC
8	VIII	40	XL	800	DCCC
9	IX	50	L	900	CM
10	X	60	LX	1,000	M
11	XI	70	LXX	1,500	MD
12	XII	80	LXXX	2,000	MM
13	XIII	90	XC	3,000	MMM
14	XIV	100	C		

TABLE 37–2. Roman Numeral Dates

1900	MCM	1960	MCMLX	2020	MMMXX
1910	MCMX	1970	MCMLXX	2030	MMMXXX
1920	MCMXX	1980	MCMLXXX	2040	MMMXL
1930	MCMXXX	1990	MCMXC	2050	MMML
1940	MCMXL	2000	MM		
1950	MCML	2010	MMMX		

FINANCIAL ACTIVITIES

SECTION FIVE

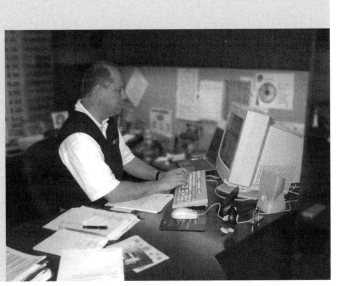

An administrative assistant uses a PC to store financial records.

Photo by Jennifer Wauson.

38

Bookkeeping and Accounting

FINANCIAL RECORD KEEPING

Bookkeeping and accounting are fields requiring special training. Smaller companies may assign these duties to the administrative assistant, especially with today's new computerized accounting programs. Larger companies typically have an in-house accounting department or contract for the services of an accountant to prepare tax statements and other important records. Even so, it's useful to familiarize yourself with the simple mechanics of bookkeeping and accounting no matter what size company you work for. The more informed you are, the more valuable you are to the company.

ASSETS

Property owned by a business organization and used in its operation is known as *assets*. The proprietor or owner of the business may be one person, two persons (in a partnership), half a dozen persons, or numerous persons operating a corporation. The interest of the owner or proprietor in the assets of the business is called proprietorship, net worth, or capital. If the business is free of claims against these assets, except for those of the proprietor, then assets equals proprietorship. For example, if John King purchased a stationery store for $10,000, his financial condition would be expressed in this way: Assets $10,000 equal proprietorship $10,000.

LIABILITIES

A business owner may obtain additional property by borrowing money to purchase the property needed or by purchasing the property with a promise to pay for that property at some future date. Those from whom business owners borrow are known as creditors. The creditor has a claim on the property until the proprietor pays in accordance with an agreement. This claim is known as the *liabilities* of the business.

For example, Mary Brown borrows $5,000 from a bank to enlarge the building used for her dry cleaning establishment. The bank thus becomes her creditor. This $5,000 increase in Brown's assets is accompanied by the bank's corresponding claim on her assets until the borrowed $5,000 is repaid. To fill the newly enlarged building, Brown purchases additional equipment and merchandise from the American Dry Cleaning Equipment Company amounting to $5,000; the American Dry Cleaning Company thus becomes another creditor. If Brown fails to pay this $5,000, the company can enforce its claim by legal action; this potential claim of the company on Brown's assets is another liability.

Assets of a business are, therefore, subject to two kinds of claims: (1) those arising from the rights of creditors, and (2) those arising from the rights of the proprietor. The sum of these rights is equal to the value of the assets. Thus, assets equal liabilities plus proprietorship.

EFFECT OF BUSINESS TRANSACTIONS

The proprietor must know the effect of all business transactions on his or her assets, liabilities, and proprietorship in order to make decisions regarding future operations. Accounts furnish the proprietor with a record for this purpose, which is why it's critical that accounts be concrete, precise, and accurate.

For example, if the proprietor is considering hiring additional sales associates, he or she should know the results of the existing sales force to be able to estimate the probable results of hiring additional personnel. If the proprietor is considering purchasing additional merchandise, equipment, or space, attention should be given to the results from existing facilities.

The efficient proprietor is always seeking information concerning the effect of past operations in order to plan future operations. Such plans are known as *budgets*. Therefore, the primary purpose of accounting records is to give the proprietor information concerning the nature of his or her liabilities and proprietorship, as well as to furnish a concrete record of the effect of the business operation on these.

The purposes of accounting are to (1) record, (2) analyze and classify, and (3) summarize the activities of the business and their effects on each enterprise. Accounting simply reduces to writing the activities of a business.

ACCOUNTING STATEMENTS

Accounting statements (1) list a description of and amounts of property, together with ownership rights, and (2) report the effects of the operations on the owner's equity.

The first statement is known as the *balance sheet* (Figure 38–1). The balance sheet shows the assets, together with the rights of the creditors and the rights of the proprietor. The second statement is known as the *income statement* or *profit and loss statement* (Figure 38–2). It shows income and costs of operation, with the resulting increase or decrease in proprietorship. The balance sheet shows the financial condition of the business at a given time; the income statement covers the periods between any two balance sheets.

These summaries are interesting to persons other than the proprietor. When the owner of the business wishes to borrow money from a bank, the bank officers, in order to judge the owner's ability to repay the loan, ask for information concerning the assets and liabilities and the profits earned in previous periods. Creditors request the same

```
┌──────────────────────────────────────────────────────────────┐
│                       BALANCE SHEET                            │
│                     November 30, 2008                          │
│                                                                │
│  Current Assets                                                │
│  Cash on hand and in the bank          $ 4,000                 │
│  Merchandise inventory                  90,000                 │
│  Accounts receivable                     6,000                 │
│  Total Current Asset                              $100,000     │
│                                                                │
│  Fixed Assets                                                  │
│                                                                │
│  Real Estate—Land                                   18,000     │
│  Real Estate—Building Original Cost    $64,000                 │
│  Less Depreciation                       3,000      61,000     │
│  Furniture, fixtures and equipment—    $12,000                 │
│  original cost                                                 │
│  Less Depreciation                         600      11,400     │
│                                                                │
│  Total Assets                                     $190,400     │
│                                                                │
│                                                                │
│  Current Liabilities                                           │
│                                                                │
│  Accounts Payable                      $32,000                 │
│  Notes Payable                          16,000                 │
│                                                                │
│  Total Current Liabilities                        $ 48,000     │
│  Long-term Debt                                     22,000     │
│  Capital                                           120,400     │
│  Total Liabilities & Capital                      $190,400     │
└──────────────────────────────────────────────────────────────┘
```

Figure 38–1. A balance sheet.

information before selling merchandise on account. The Internal Revenue Service (IRS) also requires a similar statement to be assured that the income tax for the coming year is being estimated properly.

A large business has hundreds and even thousands of assets to list; these are classified as current assets, fixed assets, and deferred charges to expenses.

Current assets appear in the form of cash or items that may reasonably be expected to be converted into cash in the near future by the regular operation of the business. This includes stocks, bonds, mutual funds, and other negotiable financial instruments. When listed on the balance sheet, these assets are arranged in the order in which they will be converted. Columns are also provided to show the quantity, description, price, and extensions. When all these sheets are extended and totaled, their sum is entered on the balance sheet as merchandise inventory.

Fixed assets are those of a permanent (or fixed) nature that will not be converted into cash as long as they serve the needs of the business. They are not intended for resale but are expected to wear out in the course of the business. They include store equipment, office equipment, delivery equipment, building, and land.

Deferred charges to expenses are assets purchased for use in the business that will

PROFIT AND LOSS STATEMENT November 30, 2008		
Sales		$200,000
Cost of Sales		140,000
Gross Income		60,000
Selling Expenses	$25,000	
General Expenses	10,000	
Operating Expenses		35,000
Operating Income		25,000
Interest Expense		1,200
Net Income Before Taxes		23,800
Income Taxes		6,600
Net Income		$17,200

Figure 38–2. Profit and loss statement.

be consumed in the near future—for example, store supplies, office supplies, and prepaid insurance.

The classification commonly used for liabilities is similar to that for assets: current liabilities, fixed liabilities, and deferred credits to income.

Current liabilities are those that will be due within a short time. For example, if John King purchases equipment on account with the agreement that he will pay for it within thirty days, this transaction results in a current liability. A liability is considered to be a current one if it comes due within one year after the balance sheet date. Under this heading are notes payable, accounts payable, and accrued liabilities.

Notes payable are promises given by the proprietor to someone to whom he or she owes money. The proprietor may give these to a creditor from whom he or she has purchased equipment or merchandise, or to a bank when borrowing money. *Accounts payable* are the financial obligations of a business, usually arising from a purchase on account, when the buyer has given his or her promise to pay at some future time for the goods received. *Accrued liabilities* are amounts owed to the government on taxes, to employees on wages, or to creditors on interest. If one of these is unusually high, it may be set up singly under some designation such as "taxes payable," "wages payable," and so forth.

Fixed liabilities are those that will not be due for a comparatively long time after they are contracted. They usually arise in the purchase of fixed assets and include liabilities that will not be liquidated within one year from the date of the balance sheet—for example, mortgages payable or bonds payable.

A *mortgage payable* represents a debt owed by a business for which the creditor possesses a mortgage on a particular asset. *Bonds payable* are long-term obligations of corporations commonly evidenced by bonds without referencing a particular asset.

Deferred credits to income are the unearned portion of a payment when a business is paid in advance for a service. For example, an insurance company receives in one fiscal period a payment for insurance that extends over a future fiscal period. The unearned portion of the premium is a deferred credit to income and would usually be listed as unearned premium income.

The Balance Sheet

Usually the purpose of any business is to increase its proprietorship—that is, to make money. The amount of profit or loss incurred during a given period is the most important single fact.

A *balance sheet* (see Figure 38–1) shows the proprietor the amount of his or her proprietorship to help determine whether the proprietorship is increasing or decreasing; it does not, however, show the cause of the increase or decrease.

The Income Statement

At various intervals, the proprietor has to plan to increase profit and eliminate future losses. For this, a report is needed to show the amount of sales, the cost of procuring and selling the goods that are sold, and the difference between the two, which is the profit or loss. The *income statement* (see Figure 38–2) gives such information, as well as the gross profit on sales, operating expenses, and depreciation. The period it covers is known as the *fiscal period.*

Income Statement Terms

There are a variety of important terms included on an income statement that need some explanation.

- **Sales**—The gross return from operations. Different businesses use different terms for their sales, depending on whether the business sells commodities or services. For example, sales in a mercantile business are the total amount of money customers have paid or agreed to pay for merchandise sold to them. Airlines have passenger revenue or freight revenue, whereas professional men and women have fees. Investment trusts have interest income and dividend income.

- **Cost of goods sold**—The purchase price paid by a business for the goods it has sold, as distinguished from the sales price. Cost of goods sold is made up of (1) the price charged by the seller as shown on the invoice of sale, and (2) the shipping and handling charged for the delivery of the goods.

- **Gross profit on sales**—Derived by subtracting the cost of merchandise sold from the total sales, representing the profit that would be made if no expenses were incurred in conducting the business. Because expenses are always incurred, they must be considered in determining profit. The expenses of operating the business must be deducted to obtain the net profit.

- **Operating expenses**—Includes all commodities and services expended in the operation of a business: services of personnel, paper, electricity, fuel, postage, and so forth.

- **Depreciation**—The cost arising from the decrease in value of the fixed assets. Not only are supplies and services used to operate a business, but fixed assets, such as office equipment and store equipment, are gradually worn out through use.

The income statement shows the result of the operations of a specific business during a particular period of time. It lists the income from sales and subtracts from this the expenses of the business in making such sales. The last figure is the net profit from operations.

◇ THE ACCOUNT

Each time a business performs a transaction, a change is made in one or more elements of the equation "assets equal liabilities plus proprietorship." Regardless of the number of transactions, the results of all changes must be ascertained in order to prepare an accurate balance sheet and an accurate income statement at the end of the fiscal period. To accomplish this, each transaction must be recorded as it occurs. The *account* is the method used to record these individual transactions, and it is from this word that the subject of accounting receives its name.

The Account Record

The account is the record of each item entered on the balance sheet and on the income statement—that is, the increases and decreases that occur. In its simplest form, the account provides (1) the name of the customer, (2) transactions decreasing the amount of proprietorship, and (3) transactions increasing the amount of the same item.

The Ledger

The *ledger* is a book containing a group of accounts. It contains a page for each account, or several pages if the account is large. A separate account is maintained for each entry on the balance sheet and the income statement. Accounts are arranged in the ledger in the same order in which they are listed on the accounting statements. Current asset accounts precede fixed asset accounts, and all asset accounts come before liability accounts. Proprietorship accounts are listed last. Looseleaf ledgers should be used, so that new accounts may be inserted alphabetically.

Trial Balance

If the bookkeeper has correctly recorded each transaction, the total of all the debits in all the accounts equals the total of the credits in all the accounts. A test is made at intervals, usually at the end of the month, to check whether the debits do equal the credits; this test, known as a *trial balance*, summarizes the ledger information. If the sum of the debits does not equal the sum of the credits, an error has been made, and then the bookkeeper has the job of reconciling.

Mixed Accounts

If all transactions recorded in the accounts coincide with the accounting period as shown on the balance sheet and the income statement, the trial balance is a satisfactory check. But it is impossible to arrange transactions so that there will be no carry-overs between accounting periods. A means must therefore be provided to meet this condition; this is called a mixed account: an account with a balance that is partly a balance sheet amount and partly an income statement amount.

For example, the trial balance amount for the account called Office Supplies summarizes all office supplies purchased plus those on hand at the beginning of the period covered. To find out how many office supplies have been used during the accounting period, an inventory of office supplies is taken. The office supplies on hand are a balance sheet entry; the office supplies used are an income statement entry. Therefore, the account Office Supplies is a mixed account.

The adjustment of mixed accounts must determine the correct balance sheet amount and the correct income statement amount for any trial balance entry that is mixed. For example, a typewriter is recorded as an asset at the time of purchase and appears in the trial balance. The depreciation of the typewriter is not recorded each day and must, instead, be recorded by an adjustment at the end of the accounting period.

Other types of business operations continually affect accounts, for example, as insurance expires and wages and salaries accrue. It's necessary to record all such mixed accounts. A purchase of office supplies is debited to the asset account Office Supplies, or it can be debited to the expense account Office Supplies Used. By means of an account for Office Supplies Used or Expired Insurance, the adjustment can be made. This is an asset adjustment. A liability adjustment is made similarly.

Adjusted Trial Balance

The *trial balance* summarizes only transactions during the accounting period. Insurance has expired, supplies have been used in operating the business, office and other salaries are incomplete, and equipment has depreciated. The adjustments must be combined with trial balance amounts by means of an adjusted trial balance.

◆ PAYROLL

A good bookkeeping system must provide accurate information concerning the *payroll* (Figure 38–3). Because of Social Security laws, income-tax–withholding laws, and other state and federal regulations, any and all of this information must be instantly available. Therefore, an individual payroll record book should be maintained. The following information is needed for accurate and complete payroll accounting:

- Name of employee, with address and personal data
- Social Security number
- Company number (if any)

- Department number (if any)
- Date employment began and ended (and reason for separation)
- Dates worked, rate of pay, hours per day worked, regular and overtime status
- Regular salaries paid if not on hourly basis
- Deductions (federal withholding tax, Social Security taxes, state and local taxes, medical insurance premiums, union dues, retirement plan contributions, etc.)
- Totals by month, quarter, and year

◆ TRAVEL AND ENTERTAINMENT AND AUTO-EXPENSE RECORDS

If your boss travels as part of the job, he or she may ask your help in maintaining a record of travel and entertainment expenses. If the boss uses his or her personal vehicle for business travel, you need to maintain a vehicle expense record as well. The IRS requires detailed records with documentary evidence for each, especially for expenses over the "standard amounts" it specifies. Such records should be accurate.

Travel and Entertainment Expenses

Records for all travel and entertainment expenses should show:

- Expenditure amount
- Date of departure and date of return for every trip
- Number of days spent on business versus days spent on pleasure
- Business purpose of the expenditure
- Place of travel or place of entertainment (if clients were entertained)

Monthly Payroll Summary

Company Name: *Videologies, Inc.*   Month: *June 2008*

Employee Name: *Kevin Wilson*

Social Security Number: *123-12-1234*   Address: *2200 Main Street*

City: *Atlanta*   State: *Georgia 30234*

WK	Date Paid	Regular Wages	O.T. TIPS	Total Wages	S.S.	Med	FED TAX	ST. TAX	OTHER	NET WAGES
1	6-15	2500	0	2500	155	36.25	298.10	143.75	0	1867
2										
3										
4										
5										
Total	6-15	2500	0	2500	155	36.25	298.10	143.75	0	1867

Figure 38–3. Sample payroll form.

■ Relationship to the business of the person or persons being entertained by the taxpayer

Evidence for these expenses is required, such as credit card charge copies and receipts of all bills paid for lodging and meals while traveling. In addition, travel expense report forms are useful to keep track of out-of-pocket expenses, such as tolls, taxies, tips, and telephone calls. These forms are obtainable from any office supply store.

Figures 38–4 and 38–5 show samples of expense report forms that can be created using the Task Wizard in Microsoft Works.

Automobile Expenses

Anyone who uses a personal automobile for business purposes (other than commuting) is entitled by the IRS to deduct such expenses on his or her income tax return. If the personal vehicle is used entirely for business, all expenses can be deducted; if the vehicle has both business and personal use, its expenses may be deducted in part. A printed form, Record of Automobile Expenses, is obtainable in most office supply stores. So is a pocket-size booklet that can be handily kept in a briefcase or automobile glove compartment.

You can also use a PDA (personal digital assistant) to record automobile mileage and expenses. A sample of an automobile expense record that can be created using one of the Task Wizards available in Microsoft Works is shown in Figure 38–6.

Figure 38–4. Sample travel expense record.

Screen shot reprinted by permission from Microsoft Corporation.

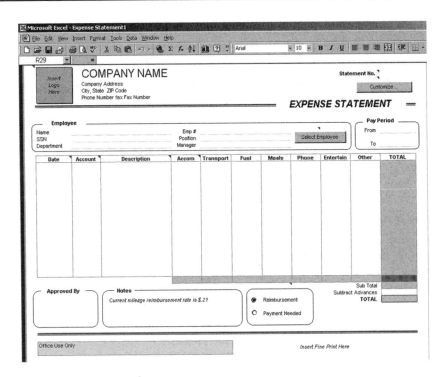

Figure 38–5. Sample expense report.

Screen shot reprinted by permission from Microsoft Corporation.

If the boss does not want to keep detailed records of automobile expenses, an optional deduction method is allowed. Instead of deducting a vehicle's actual fixed and operating expenses with a separate deduction for depreciation (for an individual), the boss could deduct a standard mileage rate for annual business miles traveled. State and local taxes (not including gasoline tax) and interest payments on loans to purchase business vehicles are deductible as well.

These laws change frequently, and it would be wise for you or your employer to secure up-to-date IRS booklets for rules on required record maintenance and reporting to make sure you're keeping adequate records. But even with these booklets, your employer should also utilize the services of a competent accountant.

◇ CASH BUDGETS

A *cash budget* is an estimate of expected cash receipts and expenditures. It is necessary for any business, especially a small business where every dime counts. Cash budgets should be prepared six months ahead or, if possible, twelve months ahead with revision as needed.

When you help your boss develop a cash budget, it must be a realistic estimate. A cash budget is completely useless unless it is based on realistic, sober judgment springing entirely from experience.

Figure 38–6. Sample automobile expense record in Microsoft Works.

Screen shot reprinted by permission from Microsoft Corporation.

Figure 38–7 shows a cash flow statement that can be created using one of the many Task Wizards available in Microsoft Works software.

RECORDS FOR LENDERS

If your employer is just starting a business, a lender is likely to request a specific list and total estimate of the business's startup costs. Table 38–1 shows a sample. You might help your employer gather the necessary information.

TABLE 38–1. An Estimate of Startup Costs for a Retail Shop

Description	Cost
Inventory	$50,000
Fixtures and Equipment	7,000
Decoration	9,000
Legal and Professional Fees	2,000
Utility Deposits	100
Pre-opening Promotions	1,800
Cash Contingency Fund	2,000
Insurance	500
Supplies and Equipment	1,500
Description	**Cost**
Security	2,000
Miscellaneous	500
Total	$76,400

As with a startup estimate, a lender is likely also to request an estimate of probable monthly expenses, which when multiplied by twelve will be an estimate of first-year expenses. Table 38–2 shows a suggested form to use.

TABLE 38–2. An Estimate of Monthly Expenses for a Retail Shop

Description	Cost
Salaries	$2,000
Rental	800
Description	**Cost**
Utilities and Telephone	200
Inventory Replenishment	4,000
Advertising	100
Supplies and Postage	200
Insurance	125
Maintenance	70
Professional Fees	100
Delivery Expense	250
Interest on Loan	80
Subscriptions and Dues	40
Miscellaneous	250
Monthly Total	$8,215

Figure 38–7. Cash flow statement.

Screen shot reprinted by permission from Microsoft Corporation.

Business Taxes

◇ THE SECRETARY'S ROLE

Although your duties may not include filling out tax forms, it can be important to know what taxes are payable when and what forms are required. If you work for a small business, your chance is greater of being asked to help in this area. But if in no way else, you can help by keeping a list of tax forms and due dates and by reminding your employer a few weeks in advance of each deadline.

◇ BUSINESS TAXES

If the business that employs you is a corporation, a corporate tax form is due each year. This is Form 1120, and it's due March 15 of each calendar year, one month prior to the due date for personal returns. Throughout the year, estimated tax payments are also due; these are payable January 15, April 15, June 15, and September 15. To pay estimated taxes, a tax coupon book must be obtained from the Internal Revenue Service (IRS). This coupon book is used to make payments for a variety of different taxes. When filled out correctly, the coupon shows the type of tax (in this case, 1120), along with the particular quarter of the year for which the payment is being made. Rather than send these payments directly to the IRS, you may pay them at the bank where the company maintains its checking account.

◇ EFTPS

The Electronic Federal Tax Payment System (EFTPS) is one of the most successful federal government programs undertaken in recent years. Millions of businesses are already enrolled in this system. It saves time and money, since there are no more last-minute trips to the bank or post office, lost checks, or missed deadlines.

Here's how it works. By 8:00 p.m. Eastern Time—at least one calendar day prior to your tax due date—you log on to the EFTPS website, enter your tax payment report, review the information, and click submit to initiate the payment. Per your instructions, EFTPS automatically debits your indicated bank or credit union account and transfers the funds to the U.S. Treasury on the date you indicate. Your tax records are updated with the IRS.

In order to use EFTPS, you must enroll online at www.EFTPS.com. After enrolling, you receive a PIN and password.

STATE TAXES

If your state charges an income tax (and most do), the corporation must also pay estimated state taxes. You must obtain a state coupon book and make quarterly payments. In most cases these payments are made directly to the state by sending them in the mail.

FRANCHISE TAX

The franchise tax is an annual state tax on corporations payable to the secretary of state's office in order to keep the corporation's status current. Usually the state sends the company a bill.

SALES TAX

If your employer is involved in the sale of goods or provides certain services, he or she may be liable to collect and pay sales tax. Sales tax amounts vary across the country, and forms sent by the state and county explain how much to collect. Periodically, usually once each month, sales tax reports are sent to each business. These must be filled out and returned with a check for the sales tax collected.

EMPLOYMENT TAXES

A variety of employment taxes must be filed and paid. For example, the federal and state taxes, Social Security tax, and Medicare fees that are withheld from employee paychecks must be paid periodically to the IRS and the state taxing authority. Federal and state guides for employers are available to explain how much to withhold from an employee's check and when payments are due. These withholding tax payments must be made promptly. In some cases, the deadline is as fast as three days following the pay date. Form 941 must be filled out each quarter for federal tax reporting. Payments are made by using the tax coupon books at your local bank.

Another withholding tax is the unemployment tax, levied against businesses by your local state government throughout the year. If the company files with the state department of labor and the U.S. Department of Labor, it receives reporting forms a few weeks before the filing deadlines. State taxes and report forms are sent to the state through the mail along with the payment. On the federal level, this tax requires filling out Form 940 once each year and using the coupon book to make the payment at the company's local bank.

◆ SELF-EMPLOYMENT TAX

If your boss does business as a partnership or a sole proprietor, he or she receives profits directly from the company. No Social Security tax is withheld from these profits. Therefore, when it comes time to file annual tax returns, your employer must pay a self-employment tax and file a Schedule SE. At the same time, any non-incorporated business owner must also file a Schedule C to report his or her business income. Just as employees on a payroll must pay their taxes throughout the year through withholding, so anyone owing self-employment tax must make estimated tax payments throughout the year. This can be done using 1040ES forms available from the IRS and sending payments to the IRS office for the particular IRS estimated tax region.

◆ EMPLOYEE OR INDEPENDENT CONTRACTOR?

What about you? Are you self-employed? If you are a part-time secretary and do not have "employee" status, your employer may consider you an *independent contractor*. This means that the employer does not withhold taxes from your check, and like a business owner, you are then liable for paying your own taxes. Depending on how much you earn, you may be required to make estimated tax payments throughout the year.

Determining Your Status

Whether you are an employee or a contractor is a difficult question to answer. The Department of Labor and IRS usually state that if you work at the company's place of business, use its tools, and work specific hours set by the company, then you are an employee. If you work at home, use your own computer, and come and go when you please, then you might be considered a contractor.

Effects of Status

The difference in your status can determine whether your employer is liable to pay half of your Social Security taxes (rather than you being solely responsible for self-employment taxes). In addition, an employer may pay unemployment tax and workers compensation.

Workers compensation, sometimes called *workers comp*, is a state-funded insurance policy for employees who become injured or disabled while on the job. If you are injured, the insurance policy pays for some of your medical bills as well as a portion of your wages while you are off the job. Workers compensation is required in many states but varies depending on the size of the business.

◆ PROPERTY AND NET WORTH TAXES

In most states, businesses pay local county and state governments a tax on inventory and on real property such as land or buildings. This tax is filed once each year. Land property tax bills are usually mailed each year, just like those that are sent to you if you own a home.

Net worth taxes are usually reported and paid at the same time the annual tax return is filled out. Taxes must be paid on business assets as well as cash and investments.

◇ BUSINESS LICENSES

All partnerships and sole proprietors along with some corporations are required to obtain a business license from the city and sometimes from the county where they are located and conduct business. To obtain a business license, the business owner must fill out paperwork and pay an annual fee. Business licenses can be renewed each year by paying an annual fee.

◇ TAX ASSISTANCE

Many tax-planning aids are available from the IRS and your state department of revenue. Check your telephone book for the correct numbers, and call to ask for employers' guides and needed forms. Keep these on hand so your boss always has them available in order to meet a deadline.

Banking

One important relationship every business must establish is with a bank. Many of the resulting financial details—whether from a checking account, business loan, or credit card—will be handled by the company's administrative assistant. The smaller the company is, the greater will be your involvement with your company's banking.

What if the bank gave away money and you did not get in line? That's essentially what can happen if you don't understand a bank's full spectrum of financial products and services and use the correct ones when available. To save your company the most in fees while helping it nail down the most in interest, you need to know exactly what a bank can do for you.

A checking account is the most basic account that every business needs. There are several different types available, ranging from the basic checking account with a monthly fee to the money market account. Knowing which account the business qualifies for can help you reduce its monthly fees and even earn interest on its deposit. This is important information to pass on to your employer.

Basic Checking Account

A basic checking account is a convenient way to spend money without making frequent trips to the bank. It also allows you to pay bills through the mail without sending cash; cash should never be sent through the mail. In addition, a basic checking account provides you with a monthly record of the company's transactions, which helps you track income and expenses more easily. Most financial institutions do not pay interest on the money a business keeps in a basic checking account; instead, the banks usually charge a monthly fee. However, there is usually no minimum balance required to maintain this account.

NOW Account

A variation of the basic checking account is the NOW account, as it is known in the banking industry. This checking account has all the features of the basic checking account and also pays interest on money in the account. NOW accounts require that a minimum balance be maintained. If the company's balance falls below that minimum, the account is charged a monthly fee just like a basic checking account.

Super NOW Account

Like the NOW account, the Super NOW is a checking account that bears interest. However, it pays a higher rate of interest than a NOW, a rate that can fluctuate from month to month. The minimum balance required to maintain this account is usually $2,500.

Money Market Account

A money market account is similar to a Super NOW since it pays interest at the market rate, but the number of monthly transactions is limited by law. Like the Super NOW, a minimum balance is required to earn market interest rates, but only up to six transfers of funds such as checks, withdrawals, or wire transfers may be made each month. A money market account may substitute for a regular savings account for businesses that wish to invest on a short-term basis and still have quick access to their money.

◇ PETTY CASH

Most businesses keep a small amount of cash on hand to pay for cash items and to make change for customers. This cash must be accounted for with receipts for each expenditure. You can obtain petty cash by writing a check payable to "cash" or to a particular employee. In either case, whoever cashes the check is responsible for making sure that accurate records are kept of expenditures.

◇ SAVINGS ACCOUNTS

If your employer's business has excess cash available, a variety of accounts can help save those funds for the future: a regular savings account, certificates of deposit (CDs), jumbo CDs, individual retirement accounts, savings bonds, automatic savings plans, and other retirement accounts.

A savings account is an ideal place to deposit cash or checks, providing a safe way to save for any purpose. In addition, excess funds earn interest while in the account. Unlimited withdrawals are permitted, but no checks may be written against the account. Interest rates may vary from one period to the next; the compounding of interest also varies among financial institutions.

Certificates of Deposit

Certificates of deposit (CDs) provide an investment option that pays a higher rate of interest than a savings account. A CD's interest rate and minimum deposit vary depending on the term, such as six months or one year; however, once a CD is purchased, the interest rate is fixed. There are substantial penalties if the company needs to withdraw its funds before the term of the CD expires.

Another type of CD is the jumbo CD, so-called because it requires a minimum of $100,000 to open. The rate of interest is higher than that of a regular CD and varies depending on the term. Usually the longer the term is, the higher the interest rate. Like a regular CD, there is a substantial penalty for early withdrawal.

Savings Bonds

The purchase of government-backed U.S. savings bonds is another safe way to invest and save money. Series EE government bonds are available in denominations from $50 to $10,000 and carry a competitive interest rate. Earned interest is not subject to state or local taxes, and federal tax may be deferred until the bonds are redeemed and the interest is received.

◆ TRUST SERVICES

A retirement plan is one benefit offered by many large corporations. Even small businesses may have retirement plans for some or all employees. Some retirement plans are offered by banks, and others can be set up through a mutual fund. The basic choices are a profit-sharing pension plan, a money-purchase pension plan, a 401(k) plan, a Keogh, and an individual retirement account.

Simplified Pension Plans

A simplified employee pension plan can be adopted by small corporations. It usually consists of a profit-sharing pension plan, a money-purchase pension plan, or both. These plans can be set up by using fill-in-the-blank forms to determine the specifics for your business. With a simplified employee pension plan (SEP), the business contributes a percentage of the employee's annual salary into a pension account. This account is tax deferred and cannot be withdrawn by the employee until retirement age. With a profit-sharing plan, the contribution percentage is determined each year; the percentage can vary from year to year. It is not necessarily based on profits, and the business may have to contribute to the retirement fund even if there is a loss. With a money-purchase plan, the business must make a predetermined percentage contribution each year regardless of the business performance.

401(k) Plans

With a 401(k) plan, funds are deducted from the employee's salary and are deposited into the retirement account. The funds are tax deferred, and the interest earned on the account is also tax deferred. Sometimes the business may match the contribution of the employee up to a predetermined percentage and dollar amount limit determined by law.

Keogh Plans

If your boss is a self-employed individual in a small business, he or she may be interested in a special retirement plan called a Keogh, which provides a basic qualifying self-employment retirement plan for unincorporated business owners and their employees. Keogh participants may contribute up to 25 percent of their salaries and earned income into the retirement account, up to a certain dollar limit. Both the yearly contribution and interest earned on the account are tax deferred.

Individual Retirement Accounts

If the company does not offer its employees a retirement plan and your individual income falls within certain limits, you may qualify for an Individual Retirement Account (IRA). The money that you deposit into an IRA can be deducted from your income before paying taxes. The interest earned by the account is tax deferred until you reach retirement age.

◇ OTHER BANKING SERVICES

Your boss and the company may be able to benefit from some of the other miscellaneous convenience services offered by financial institutions.

ATM Cards

ATM stands for "automated teller machine," a convenient way to get cash twenty-four hours a day. Besides providing you with petty cash for the office, an ATM allows you to check account balances, make deposits, and perform many other routine banking activities at your convenience. To use an ATM, the customer must be issued an ATM card, which is sometimes called a debit card. By using a secret password, the customer is protected and every transaction is conducted in private.

Safe Deposit Boxes

Many financial institutions have spaces within their vaults that are available for rental. These safe deposit boxes are a safe and fireproof way to store valuable documents and other small items of value. Only the owner of the box can access it using a special two-key system. Usually safe deposit boxes are available in several different sizes for a nominal annual rental fee.

Bill Paying by Telephone

Many banks allow you to pay routine bills such as utilities with just a telephone call, a boon for overworked secretaries. The organizations that your company must pay have prearranged code numbers. Use a touchtone telephone to arrange payment from your company's account, and the financial institution makes sure your bill is paid immediately. A monthly statement of each transaction may be available to record expenditures.

Online Banking

With online or Web-based banking services, you can check balances, move funds between accounts, and automate your bill-paying process. Web banking services can be accessed using a standard Web browser such as Microsoft Internet Explorer or Netscape Navigator. You must register to use your bank's Web-based banking services. A user name and password are required to access the bank's secure website.

To automate the bill-paying process, you must first enter information about each payee. This includes the payee's name, address, phone number, and account number. Afterward, the payees appear in a list. You can then enter a payment amount to schedule an electronic payment. You can also automate certain recurring bills such as rent and mortgage payments. Onetime payees can also be entered. If the payee does not accept electronic payments, the bank sends them a bank check.

Online banking services are usually provided for a nominal monthly service fee. Depending on the type of account you have at the bank and the balance you keep, your bank may waive the fee.

Banking by Mail

If you do not want to or cannot visit a financial institution in person, you can use a bank-by-mail service. This service is primarily for making deposits. Users are provided with preaddressed envelopes and deposit tickets to mail checks for deposit into their accounts.

Wire Transfers

If you need to send money quickly from one account to another, a wire transfer is the fastest way. It moves funds by telephone and electronic bookkeeping into another bank account in any part of the country or world.

It's important that you have some type of written authorization between the two parties involved, since once the funds have been transferred, they cannot be returned. To complete the transaction, you need to know the names of the two account holders, the financial institutions involved, the American Banking Association numbers (a reference number that designates a particular bank), and the account numbers. You should get a receipt when the transaction is completed. A small transaction fee is required for the transfer, but the method is a safe and convenient way to transfer funds in a flash.

Foreign Currency Exchange

Foreign currency exchange can be a big help to a business in the import/export trade. The user of this service can convert money from one country to that of another at the current exchange rate. For businesspeople going abroad, changing currency in advance is much more convenient than waiting until they arrive at their destination. Later, after the business trip, the leftover foreign currency can be exchanged back into U.S. funds. Since the financial institution can adjust the exchange rate, there is usually a built-in fee for this service.

Bank Checks

When a business check or cash is not appropriate—such as transactions involving large dollar amounts—there are a variety of bank checks available, widely accepted as safe, guaranteed substitutes for cash. Cashier's checks are issued by the bank and guarantee that funds are available. Money orders serve the same purpose but are usually issued in smaller amounts. Traveler's checks are sold in denominations such as $10, $20, $50, or $100 and can be refunded if lost or stolen.

Notary Service

Another useful business service offered by many banks is a notary service. Notaries verify the identity of individuals who need to sign certain official and legal documents. A notary can witness the signature and seal the signatures with a special stamp. Sometimes there is a small fee for this service, but many banks provide it free to customers who have an active account.

◆ CHECKS

One of the most fundamental activities of any small business is the exchange of products and services for something else of value, normally money. This is called a *transaction*. Selling a product to a customer who pays cash is a typical transaction. But what about customers who pay by check? There are many transactions that do not involve cash, such as writing a check, accepting a check, making deposits or withdrawals at the bank, or transferring funds. It's important to understand the details of these transactions to protect your boss and the company from fraud and theft.

The most common transaction you will be involved in concerns checks, either personal or business. There are many different types and styles of checks, from the plain to the colorful. Yet all checks have some common basic elements such as numbers and

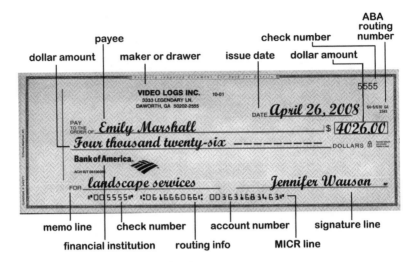

Figure 40–1. Parts of a check.

names, and there is a specific set of requirements necessary before a check can be negotiable or cashable.

The first step in learning to negotiate a check is knowing the significance of each of its parts. There are two general areas to focus on: the preprinted information, and the information filled in by the check writer. (See Figure 40–1.)

Looking at the preprinted information first, you will find the following:

- In the upper left corner is the *name of the maker*—the person or persons who own the account. The maker is also sometimes called the *drawer*.

- The *name and location of the financial institution* should also be printed on the check, usually just below the name of the maker. Often the bank includes its logo here.

- The *sequential number of the check* is printed in the upper right corner.

- Below the check number to the right of the date line is a fraction. This is called the American Bankers Association routing number and is referred to as the *ABA routing number*. When decoded, this number tells where the bank is located, the specific bank branch, and the Federal Reserve Bank serving this financial institution.

- The *MICR line*, printed along the bottom of the check, contains the account number and the check number. MICR means "magnetic ink character recognition"; it is a number that can be read by a computer.

The parts of a check that most concern you are those filled in by the maker:

- The *date line* provides space for the date the check was written.

- The *pay-to-the-order-of* line indicates whom the maker intends to pay. This person or business is called the *payee*.

- A line for the *dollar amount* to be written in figures is next to the payee line.

- Underneath the payee line is a line for the maker to write the *dollar amount in words*.

- A *for* or *memo line* is provided on the bottom left corner for the maker to note what the check is for.

- The maker's signature goes on the *signature line* along the bottom right edge of the check.

Just as a bank examines a check you want to cash, you too should learn what to look for to make sure the checks you accept are legally negotiable:

- There must be a date written on the date line of the check.
- The *pay-to-the-order-of* line must be filled in. Checks written to the company cannot be cashed; they can only be deposited.
- The dollar amount must be filled in, both in numbers and in words, and the two amounts must match.
- The check must be signed by the maker, that is, the person listed on the printed part of the check. Look to see if two or more people must sign the check to make it legal. You'll know because there will be two signature lines on it and often the printed words "two signatures required" as well.
- The name and location of the financial institution must be printed on the check.

Examine the check for alterations. Scratch-throughs, white-outs, or any other indication that the check has been altered may make it unacceptable by the bank.

◇ DEPOSITS

One of the goals of most financial institutions is to receive and retain deposits. Money taken into customer accounts through deposits provides the primary source of funds for the institution to loan and invest. If the company you work for is successful, you may make many routine deposits. There are two different types you can make: demand deposits and time deposits.

Demand deposits are made into checking and regular savings accounts where the money is readily available. The company can make a withdrawal at any time. On the other hand, with a *time deposit* such as a certificate of deposit, the company's money may be tied up for a period of time.

Making Deposits

You cannot walk into any bank on the street and deposit a check someone has given you or the company. Checks received by a business and made payable to the business name can be deposited only at a bank where the business has an established account. You cannot, for instance, go to the bank of the person who wrote the check and try to cash it there.

Another area of making deposits that confuses many people is something the banks classify as "on-us" and "not-on-us" checks. An *on-us* check is one that is written and then deposited or cashed at the same bank. A *not-on-us* check is just what the name says: a check deposited at a bank that does not hold the account from which funds will be drawn. In most cases, there is a longer delay in getting funds transferred when a transaction involves a not-on-us check. The delay can be even longer if the transaction involves an out-of-state or a foreign bank. When there is a delay, most often a hold is placed on the deposit for a specified period of days. This means that the funds are not available as actual cash until the hold has expired and the funds have been transferred into the company's bank account.

When you make a deposit, you are giving the bank access to company funds. The deposit slip gives the bank permission to put money into the company's account or to collect funds from checks the company has received. It's your responsibility to make sure you have followed the correct procedures making the deposit and that you get a receipt to ensure the company receives proper credit for the transaction. Therefore it is important that you understand what is involved in making a deposit.

The Deposit Transaction

Generally, a deposit transaction requires a deposit slip, items to be deposited, processing of the deposit by the bank teller, and the bank teller's issuing a receipt and/or cash back from the deposit. The transaction begins with the deposit slip. This key instrument of negotiation tells who is making the deposit, into what account the deposit is being made, and what amount is being deposited from what items.

Deposit Slip

A deposit slip must have the name and address of the account owner, either preprinted on the slip or written by hand. There must also be a date. In addition, there must be an MICR-encoded account number to ensure proper crediting to your account. Most important, there should be a list of the items being deposited. These items must be listed in the form of currency, coins, and checks. Each check must be listed separately by amount. Additional space is usually provided on the back of the slip when depositing numerous checks. The subtotal of any checks deposited must be listed on the back and must also be filled in on the front part of the slip. Then all of the amounts for currency, coins, and checks should be totaled.

All checks deposited must be endorsed on the back. You must include the name of the company, its account number, and the words "for deposit only."

Processing by the Bank Teller

Bank tellers are trained to check and double-check every transaction. Therefore, you should expect the teller to add up your deposit and to double-check your totals on the deposit slip. The teller should also verify the company's account number and make sure that all checks have been endorsed.

One important area to note concerns depositing cash items. Cash items are not just cash but any items that are accepted for deposit and credited to the company's account. They include all currency, coins, and many types of checks. Non-cash or collection items are accepted for handling but are not immediately credited to the account. These include checks that are not MICR-encoded, foreign checks, promissory notes, and other items with documents or special instructions attached.

The important thing to remember is that, depending on whether you deposit cash or non-cash items, the company may not have instant access to the funds in its account for a specified period of time. If these banking details are your responsibility, it's up to you to find out when funds will be available. In this way, the boss will not accidentally write a check with insufficient funds.

Making Withdrawals

Along with writing checks and making deposits, there may be times when you are asked to make a withdrawal of cash from the company's checking or savings account. Withdrawing money from a checking account requires that you write a check on the company's account payable to yourself or to "cash." Some savings accounts also have checks that may be written to make a withdrawal. However, in some cases, when you do not have checks available, you can use a withdrawal slip.

A withdrawal slip must include the following information: the date, the amount of the withdrawal, the account number, and the signature of someone who has been approved to make withdrawals. If anything is missing or incorrect, the bank teller will ask you to correct your mistake or submit a new withdrawal slip.

If the withdrawal slip is correct, the teller verifies the signature with the one on file with the account. You should also be asked for proper identification. The teller must then check to make sure the company has funds available to cover the withdrawal. If it does, you are given the cash and a receipt.

When withdrawing money from a business account, it's important to keep a few accounting and tax procedures in mind. All transactions must be accounted for. When you take cash from a business account, you must note the purpose. Usually the purpose is to fund a petty cash account so you can pay for business supplies, stamps, or other incidentals. You must account for all cash you spend by getting receipts for your purchases. And before taking additional cash out of the business account, you should account for any previous withdrawals.

◆ SPECIAL SITUATIONS

In addition to understanding normal business banking transactions, it's important that you understand what to do in some special circumstances. For instance, what if the boss accidentally writes or receives in payment an insufficient or "hot" check? Or what if you're asked to withdraw $10,000 or more in cash from the business account?

Returned Checks

A check may be returned to the company for any number of reasons such as a missing signature, closed account, or insufficient funds. If you receive a returned check, your best bet is to contact the person who gave the company the check and try to collect cash instead. If the person is not cooperative, you or the boss should contact local law enforcement authorities since theft of goods or services by check is against the law. If the company inadvertently gives someone a check that is subsequently returned, be prepared to pay cash and possibly to pay a special fee. You should make every effort to settle this matter amicably and at once. The company can be held legally responsible for the returned check; at the least, it could suffer a damaging blow to its reputation.

Large Transactions

Transactions involving $10,000 or more in cash require special attention. The U.S. Treasury Department requires all financial institutions to provide the Internal Revenue Service (IRS) with information on large currency transactions. This information helps the IRS's criminal tax and regulatory investigations by discouraging the use of cash in illegal transactions. Some customers, such as retail businesses, may be exempted from this reporting. However, unless the company has been previously exempted, you must fill out the large currency transaction form. This can usually be done with the help of a teller or bank customer service representative.

Since carrying large amounts of cash is unsafe, what can you do instead if you are involved with withdrawals exceeding $10,000? Let's say the boss is purchasing a car for the business. Many car dealers will not accept a check from the company account and allow the boss to drive away in the new car. Instead, he or she must provide the seller with something that is as good as cash. Alternatives include a cashier's or certified check, a money order, or traveler's checks.

Cashier's or Certified Checks

A cashier's check or a certified check could be used to pay for the car since they verify that funds are available. A cashier's check is issued by a financial institution and is paid for at the time it is issued. A certified check is from the company account, and it has been officially certified by the bank that funds are available and have been set aside to pay this particular check. Both checks are as good as cash and allow the boss to complete the purchase.

Money Orders

Money orders are often used by people who don't have checking accounts. They are sold for specific amounts by financial institutions, post offices, and retail stores. They are made payable to the order of a particular business or individual when they are purchased; therefore, they are as good as cash if you receive one from someone else. They also provide a receipt that can be used to prove payment or to get a refund in the case of theft or loss.

Traveler's Checks

Traveler's checks are also commonly used in many business transactions instead of cash. These special checks are issued by a financial institution in common denominations just like currency. When you purchase a traveler's check, you must endorse the check once before you leave the bank. When you get ready to pay for a transaction with a traveler's check, you then endorse the check a second time. If you accept a traveler's check as payment for goods or services, you should make sure both signatures are the same. This double-signature feature protects the purchaser of the checks in case they are lost or stolen. Receipts are also provided for this same purpose. Usually, some form of identification is required when using traveler's checks.

Credit Cards

Depending on what type of business you work for, you may also be involved in transactions involving credit cards. Credit cards are often used as payment in transactions and are widely accepted all over the world for purchases of goods and services.

Credit cards are issued by a financial institution just like a loan. Each card has a unique account number, which can be verified electronically or by checking the list of accounts published by the card company.

◇ RECONCILING BANK STATEMENTS

Each month the bank provides a statement for the previous month that lists company checks that have cleared and deposits that have been made. The statement also lists any special fees or charges for items such as printing new checks, covering returned checks, renting safe deposit boxes, and so forth. Along with the statement, the bank provides copies of the canceled checks written against the account. Some banks return the physical checks you wrote, while others send a sheet containing small copies of each check.

As soon as bank statements come in, they should be double-checked against the company's checkbook records for mistakes and possible fraud. This process is called *reconciling* or *balancing the checkbook*. If the duty falls to you, follow these guidelines:

- If the bank returns the physical checks, put the checks returned with the statement into numerical order.
- Make sure each canceled check is for the same amount that is listed in the company checkbook, and note in the checkbook that it has cleared.
- Look at the bank statement to make sure each check is listed correctly there.
- Follow the same procedures to verify deposits. Make sure the bank has credited the account for the same amount that you have listed in the company checkbook.

Usually, checks that were written or deposits that were made at the end of a reporting period do not appear on the statement, and sometimes recipients of checks fail to deposit them promptly; all of these checks will be missing from the bank statement. Because of this, there is usually a difference between the bank balance shown on the statement and the balance shown in the checkbook. Follow the simple guidelines for reconciling usually printed on the back of the statement. These guidelines take into account missing checks and deposits made after the cut-off date, items that won't show up until next month's statement.

Although you're busy with many other duties, it's usually a good idea to reconcile the company's bank records as soon as they come in each month. Allowing them to pile up may result in account balance errors and eventual bank charges for returned checks. Also, there are time limits for correcting a mistake if you believe the bank is at fault. To protect your company's rights, its financial security, and its reputation, reconcile the statements as quickly as possible.

Once you've reconciled the statements, keep them in a safe place, where they are available only to people authorized by the business owners. These statements are often needed in the event of tax audits and when applying for business loans. Duplicates of missing statements may be obtained by writing or calling the company's bank.

Special Business and Financial Information for the Small Business Administrative Assistant

Many administrative assistants work in what are considered to be "small businesses" (though under certain definitions, companies with as many as 1,500 employees are considered to be small!). If you're such an assistant, you may perform different roles from those of an administrative assistant in a larger office. In a small business, there's often no payroll department, no accounting department, no purchasing department, no human resources—there's only you. Because of this, you may find yourself with enormous responsibility, privy to the boss's most private concerns about the business.

As the boss's right hand, you are the first person he or she turns to with questions. Here, in a brief format, are answers to some of the most frequently asked questions your boss may have about the company.

- **How does the boss go about registering the company's name?** Contact the county clerk in the county where the business is or will be located.

- **How can the boss incorporate the business?** In most states, this can be done either with or without an attorney. Write to your state's secretary of state in the state's capital city for information, or check the state government's website for instructions.

- **How can the boss obtain a copyright?** For information, write or call the following office or check the website:

U.S. Copyright Office
101 Independence Avenue, S.E.
Washington, DC 20559
202-707-3000
www.copyright.gov

- **How can the boss obtain a patent or a trademark?** For information, write or call the following office or check the website:

    Commissioner of Patents and Trademarks
    Washington, DC 20231
    703-557-3158 or 703-557-3881

    United States Patent and Trademark Office
    www.uspto.gov

- **How can the boss receive patent, trademark, search, and technology assistance?** Technical Applications Centers or Technology and Transfer Centers are located throughout the nation. Write to the Commissioner of Patents and Trademarks at the address above or check the website for the location nearest the company.

- **Where can the boss receive business tax information?** To obtain a State Resale Tax Permit, write to the Comptroller of Public Accounts, State Capitol Building, in your state's capital city or check the state government's website for instructions..To obtain a Federal Employer Identification Number for the boss, write the Internal Revenue Service (IRS) at a district office near you or in Washington, D.C. Alternatively, your boss can attend a workshop conducted by the IRS in your area. Call the nearest office of the IRS for details and dates. The IRS website at www.irs.gov has information and forms you can download for obtaining a Federal Employer Identification Number.

- **Where can the boss receive import and export information?** For importing information, contact your nearest U.S. Customs Department District Office. For information about exporting the company's products, contact an International Assistance Center; these are located throughout the nation and can supply you with an abundance of information concerning exports. A local Small Business Association office can give you the location of a center near you.

◇ TRADING WITH OTHER COUNTRIES

Most small businesses strive to become large businesses and in doing so may seek world markets for their products and services. If your employer is among that group, he or she should ask the International Trade Administration (ITA) of the U.S. Department of Commerce for assistance. The ITA functions to help citizens benefit from foreign trade. The agency explains how to begin exporting the company's products and how to locate buyers and distributors for those products and services. The ITA publishes *A Basic Guide to Exporting*. For information on ordering a copy, write to:

41 ■ BUSINESS INFORMATION

Superintendent of Documents
U.S. Government Printing Office
Washington, DC 20401

This excellent publication is invaluable to business owners who wish to enter international markets. Also of assistance is the U.S. State Department. Using Country Desk Officers, the State Department advises representatives of U.S. companies about the economic climate and political situation of the country each officer represents. For further information, call or write directly to:

Office of Commercial and Business Affairs (CBA)
U.S. Department of State
2201 C Street, N.W.
Room 2318
Washington, DC 20520
202-647-1625

Because of language barriers, it might be wise for the small business owner just beginning to enter foreign markets to start with countries where English is the spoken language. Chapter 5 contains a list of the languages spoken in nations around the world. There are many countries where English is the spoken language. But regardless of language, the boss might consider such questions as these:

- What is the standard of living in each country?
- What is the level of education prevailing in each country?
- What is the anticipated market for the company's product or service? What information can be discovered about competitive products or services now offered in that country?
- What is the price structure prevailing for similar products or services?

Another important agency is the Export-Import Bank of the United States. This organization of the U.S. government helps finance U.S. exports by offering loans to foreign purchasers of U.S. goods and services. The agency works with commercial banks in the United States and overseas to provide financial arrangements, which helps U.S. exporters offer credit assistance to their foreign buyers. For details and assistance, write to:

Export-Import Bank of the United States
811 Vermont Avenue, NW
Washington, DC 20571
202-565-3946

◆ SOURCES OF FINANCING

Some of the following sources provide money for all kinds of businesses, small and large. As you can see by their titles, certain sources concern themselves with groups singled out by Congress for special financial aid. Others supply money to get certain kinds of things done by businesses.

- Area Development Administration
- Bureau of Commercial Fisheries
- Bureau of Indian Affairs
- Commodity Credit Corporation
- Environmental Protection Agency
- Federal Housing Authority
- Federal Reserve System
- Small-business investment companies
- State and local development companies
- Treasury Department
- Department of Veterans Affairs

◆ THE SMALL BUSINESS ADMINISTRATION

What is the U.S. Small Business Administration? How can that agency be of assistance to your boss if he or she is a small business owner? The answers to these questions are so lengthy the rest of the chapter has been devoted to it.

The Small Business Administration (SBA) helps build the future of the United States by being at the forefront of developing this vital sector of the economy. Following is some general information about the SBA. This fundamental knowledge will be useful if your boss asks you to find out what the SBA can do for the company or, later, if the boss asks that agency for information, advice, and assistance, or applies for an SBA loan.

What Is a Small Business?

There's nothing small about small business! The estimated 20 million small businesses in the United States today account for more than 40 percent of the gross national product, provide half of the U.S. workforce, and generate 53.5 percent of all U.S. sales.

Since it was established in 1953, the SBA has delivered approximately 20 million loans, contracts, counseling sessions, and other forms of assistance—an average of 400,000 in every state—to businesses across the nation. The agency has 1,100 service centers covering every state, the District of Columbia, Guam, Puerto Rico, and the Virgin Islands. With loan authorization of $4 billion, it is the government's most flexible and innovative economic development agency.

All SBA programs and services are extended on a nondiscriminatory basis. These programs and services stimulate capital formation, economic growth, and job creation. They address finance, marketing, production, procurement, and human resources management. Credit programs boost the availability of capital and build the confidence of both lenders and borrowers. Credit programs rely on guarantees of loans made by private lenders, so the cost to taxpayers is minimal.

SBA's General Loan Program

The SBA's prime financial assistance activity is the bank guarantee loan program. The SBA generally does not make loans itself, nor does it have a grant program for starting a small business. Rather, it assists small businesses by guaranteeing commercial loans made by local lenders, generally banks, up to $750,000. There is no theoretical minimum; however, most lenders are reluctant to process commercial loans of less than $25,000.

To obtain an SBA loan, each applicant first obtains a participating lender (bank, savings and loan, or regulated non-bank lender). The SBA loan application is then sent in by this lender. The SBA's guarantee is designed for long-term financial needs (five to twenty-five years, depending on use). Eligible small businesses must be independently owned and operated and engaged in non-investment, non-speculative, legal activities. Loans generally can be used for equipment, fixtures, construction, leasehold improvements, inventory, and working capital.

This general loan program represents 90 percent of the agency's total loan effort. It promotes small business formation and growth by guaranteeing up to 90 percent of the amount provided by commercial lenders. A study by Price Waterhouse reports that businesses that get these loan guarantees show higher growth than comparable businesses.

How Does the Loan Program Work?

The prospective borrower is required to provide a capital contribution, normally 30 percent to 50 percent of the total capitalization of the business.

An existing business is required to provide financial statements showing the business is a profit-making concern, does not have delinquent taxes and, after the loan is made, will have a debt-to-worth ratio not to exceed 3:1 or the industry average.

The SBA charges the tender (usually a bank) a 2 percent guarantee fee on the guaranteed portion of the loan. SBA policy allows the lender (the bank) to pass this guarantee fee on to the borrower (the business owner).

The SBA guaranteed loan maturity (length of loan) is based on the following schedule:

- Working capital loans: five to seven years
- Fixed asset loans: seven to ten years
- Real estate and building: up to a maximum of twenty-five years

The general size standards for SBA-guaranteed business loans are based on the average number of employees for the preceding twelve months or on the sales volume averaged over a three-year period according to the following schedule:

- **Manufacturing:** Varies from five hundred to 1,500 employees
- **Wholesaling:** No more than one hundred employees
- **Services:** From $3.5 million to $14.5 million
- **Retailing:** From $3.5 million to $13.5 million
- **Construction:** From $9.5 million to $17 million
- **Special trade construction:** Not to exceed $7 million
- **Agriculture**: From $0.5 million to $3.5 million

Your boss should prepare for an appointment with a lender by having ready answers for the lender's questions. An even better way to prepare is to put all the information into a formal business plan; you can help by gathering and assembling the data. Be sure to include the items listed below:

- Projected profit-and-loss statement
- Cash flow projections
- Market analysis
- Marketing strategy
- Description of the business
- Product or services advantage
- Management ability (resumés of the key staff)
- Financial information (both personal and business)
- Cash requirements

Not all business proposals are eligible for the SBA's guaranteed loan programs. The following are ineligible:

- Partial purchase of a business
- Lending institutions
- Real estate held for speculation, investment, or rental
- Opinion molders (magazines, newspapers, trade journals, TV, radio, live entertainment, schools, etc.)
- Religious organizations and their affiliates

The Application Process

After a formal business plan that includes the information suggested above is developed, schedule an appointment for your boss with a local banker to discuss the plan and loan request. (The SBA can furnish a listing of your area's most active SBA lenders.) If the boss's plan is acceptable, the bank will provide a loan application package for completion. If professional assistance is needed to complete the application, the lender may be able to refer the boss to several qualified loan packagers.

After the loan application package is complete, return it to the lender. If it's acceptable, the lender will forward the loan application along with the lender's credit analysis to the SBA. After SBA approval, the lender closes the loan and disburses the funds.

Other SBA Loan Programs

Following is a description of other SBA loan programs:

- **Development Company Loan Program.** Uses public/private partnerships to finance fixed assets. It has produced more than $5 billion in investments and more than 300,000 jobs since its beginning in 1980.

- **Basic 7(a) Loan Program.** Made up of privately owned and operated investment companies licensed by the SBA to provide equity or venture capital and long-term loans to small companies to help them operate, grow, and modernize. Investment companies normally take an actual or potential ownership position in the small business company to which they provide financing. These investment companies have invested nearly $11 billion in more than seventy thousand small businesses.

- **Microloan Program.** Helps entrepreneurs in inner city and rural areas form small, often home-based enterprises.

- **Export Finance.** Offers normal and specialized loan guarantees of working capital and longer-term financing to promote exporting.

- **Disaster Loans.** Provides low-interest loans to help individuals, homeowners, and businesses rebuild after a disaster.

- **8(a) Program.** Targets socially and economically disadvantaged individuals interested in government contracting. An applicant must be a 51 percent owner and manager of an existing business that has been viable for the past two years. For more information, interested individuals should attend monthly seminars conducted by their nearest SBA office.

- **Surety Bond Guarantee Program.** Has provided more than 236,000 surety guarantees for billions in contracts since 1976, helping businesses win government construction contracts. If the boss needs bid or performance bonds for his or her contracting business, the SBA Surety Bond Guarantee Program is administered by your regional Office of the SBA. Contact it by telephone for information.

SBA Business Development Programs

Separate from the loan programs are other programs that provide marketing and training information, serving as a catalyst for small business development and growth. Programs focus on management training, international trade, veterans' affairs, women's initiatives, and resource partnerships. Here are the basic programs.

Business Initiatives, Education and Training Program

This produces a broad range of management and technical assistance publications and audiovisual materials. Online training is available.

International Trade

Information, advice, and export financing help prepare businesses to take advantage of the new world market, particularly in Mexico, the Pacific Rim, Canada, and Europe.

Veterans' Affairs

This program provides business management, technical training, and counseling. Every year, training conferences are held for prospective and established business owners who were veterans.

Women's Business Ownership Assistance

This program was developed by the SBA for emerging and expanding women businesses through the Women's Business Ownership Act of 1988, to provide long-term training and counseling for women, mentoring programs, and training/counseling centers for women nationwide.

Small Business Innovation Research (SBIR) Program

The SBA is the focal point in helping small businesses gain access to federally funded research and development activities. Any for-profit small business concern may apply directly for competitive research contracts and grants from eleven federal agencies. To obtain a quarterly Pre-Solicitation Announcement containing information on the SBIR solicitations of participating federal agencies, call your nearest SBA office.

Service Corps of Retired Executives (SCORE)

SCORE counselors are experienced former business owners and executives who, free of charge, provide counseling and direction to assist prospective owners and small businesses who are experiencing problems. If your boss would like to talk to someone who can and will help his or her business with related questions, you might contact SCORE. There may be SCORE volunteers in your community. Major service activities are located throughout the nation.

SCORE volunteers sponsor and present monthly "Going into Business" seminars at a minimal cost to attendees. From time to time, they also present a workshop on "How to Start and Manage a Small Business." For a listing of SCORE chapters near you, visit SCORE online at www.score.org.

Small Business Development Center (SBDC)

If your boss needs assistance in preparing a business plan, evaluating business prospects, seeking capital, obtaining specific information on international trade, solving technical problems, or finding opportunities in selling to the government, your local SBDC may be the answer. SBDCs are located in many areas, not necessarily only in the city where an SBA regional office is located. The SBDC program provides in-depth training and counseling assistance to small businesses. Call your nearest SBA office for details and locations of a Small Business Development Center near you.

◆ SELLING TO THE FEDERAL GOVERNMENT

If your employer would like to sell the company's services or products to the federal government, the Small Business Development Center can help through its Center for Government Contracting. A fee may be charged for this help.

You should also contact government contracting agencies such as the Department of Defense in a regional office near you or in Washington, D.C.; the General Services Administration (GSA) in a regional office or in Washington, D.C.; the Regional SBA Procurement Division in a regional office; or the Procurement Automated Source System (PASS) program, which is a computer directory describing the profile of a company interested in competing for federal procurement. Call your SBA office for complete details.

Weights and Measures

The following tables (42–1 through 42–7) list standard U.S. weights and measurements.

TABLE 42–1. Linear Measure

1 inch = .0083 foot
12 inches (in) = 1 foot (ft)
3 feet = 1 yard (yd)
5½ yards = 1 rod (rd), pole, or perch =16½ ft
40 rods = 1 furlong (fur) = 220 yds = 660 ft
8 furlongs = 1 statute mile (mi.) = 1,760 yds = 5,280 ft
3 land miles = 1 league
5,280 feet = 1 statute or land mile
6,076.11549 feet = 1 international nautical mile

TABLE 42–2. Area Measure

144 square inches = 1 sq ft
9 square feet = 1 sq yd = 1,296 sq in
30¼ square yards = 1 sq rd = 272¼ sq ft
160 square rods = 1 acre = 4,840 sq yds = 43,560 sq ft
640 acres = 1 square mile
1 mile square = 1 section (of land)
6 miles square = 1 township = 36 sections = 36 square miles

TABLE 42–3. Cubic Measure

1,728 cubic inches (cu in) = 1 cu ft
27 cubic feet = 1 cu yd

TABLE 42–4. Liquid Measure

1 gill (gi) = 4 ounces (oz)
4 gills = 1 pint (pt) = 28.875 cu in
2 pints = 1 quart (qt) = 57.75 cu in
4 quarts = 1 gallon (gal) = 231 cu in = 8 pts = 32 gills

TABLE 42–5. Dry Measure

2 pints = 1 qt = 67.2006 cu in.
8 quarts = 1 peck (pk) = 537.605 cu in. = 16 pts
4 pecks = 1 bushel (bu) = 2,150.42 cu in. = 32 qts

TABLE 42–6. Units of Circular Measure

Second (") = —
Minute (') = 60 seconds
Degree (°) = 60 minutes
Right angle = 90 degrees
Straight angle = 180 degrees
Circle = 360 degrees

TABLE 42–7. Troy Weight

24 grains = 1 pennyweight (pwt)
20 pennyweights = 1 ounce troy (oz t) = 480 grains
12 ounces troy = 1 pound troy (lb t) = 240 pennyweights =
5,760 grains

◆ THE INTERNATIONAL SYSTEM (METRIC)

The following tables (42–8 through 42–12) list various metric measurements.

TABLE 42–8. Linear Measure (Metric)

10 millimeters (mm) = 1 centimeter (cm)
10 centimeters = 1 decimeter (dm) = 100 millimeters
10 decimeters = 1 meter (m) = 1,000 millimeters
10 meters = 1 dekameter (dam)
10 dekameters = 1 hectometer (hm) = 100 meters
10 hectometers = 1 kilometer (km) = 1,000 meters

TABLE 42–9. Area Measure (Metric)

100 square millimeters (mm²) = 1 sq centimeter (cm²)
10,000 square centimeters = 1 sq meter (m²) = 1,000,000 sq millimeters
100 square meters = 1 are (a)
100 ares = 1 hectare (ha) = 10,000 sq meters
100 hectares = 1 sq kilometer (km²) = 1,000,000 sq meters

TABLE 42–10. Volume Measure (Metric)

10 milliliters (ml) = 1 centiliter (cl)
10 centiliters = 1 deciliter (dl) = 100 milliliters
10 deciliters = 1 liter (l) = 1,000 milliliters
10 liters = 1 dekaliter (dal)
10 dekaliters = 1 hectoliter (hl) = 100 liters
10 hectoliters = 1 kiloliter (kl) = 1,000 liters

TABLE 42–11. Cubic Measure (Metric)

1,000 cubic millimeters (mm³) = 1 cu centimeter (cm³)
1,000 cubic centimeters = 1 cu decimeter (dm³) = 1,000,000
cu millimeters
1,000 cubic decimeters = 1 cu meter (m³) = 1 stere = 1,000,000 cu
centimeters = 1,000,000,000 cu millimeters

TABLE 42–12. Weight Measure (Metric)

10 milligrams (mg) = 1 centigram (cg)
10 centigrams = 1 decigram (dg) = 100 milligrams
10 decigrams = 1 gram (g) = 1,000 milligrams
10 grams = 1 dekagram (dag)
10 dekagrams = 1 hectogram (hg) = 100 grams
10 hectograms = 1 kilogram (kg) = 1,000 grams
1,000 kilograms = 1 metric ton (t)

Conversion Table

The following table (42–13) can be used to convert various U.S. measurements into metric. In the table, × means multiply, / means divide, and # means the value is exact. All other values are approximate.

TABLE 42–13. Conversion Table

From	To	Formula
acres	hectares	× 0.4047
acres	sq. kilometers	/ 247
acres	sq. meters	× 4047
acres	sq. miles	/ 640
barrels (oil)	cu.meters	/ 6.29
barrels (oil)	gallons (UK)	× 34.97
barrels (oil)	gallons (US)	× 42
barrels (oil)	litrers	× 159
centimeters	feet	/ 30.48
centimeters	inches	/ 2.54
centimeters	meters	/ 100
centimeters	millimeters	× 10
cubic cm	cubic inches	× 0.06102
cubic cm	liters	/ 1000
cubic cm	milliliters	× 1
cubic feet	cubic inches	× 1728
cubic feet	cubic meters	× 0.0283
cubic feet	cubic yards	/ 27
cubic feet	gallons (UK)	× 6.229
cubic feet	gallons (US)	× 7.481
cubic feet	liters	× 28.32
cubic inches	cubic cm	× 16.39
cubic inches	liters	× 0.01639
feet	centimeters	× 30.48
feet	meters	× 0.3048
feet	yards	/ 3
fl.ounces (UK)	fl.ounces (US)	× 0.961
fl.ounces (UK)	milliliters	× 28.41
fl.ounces (US)	fl.ounces (UK)	× 1.041
fl.ounces (US)	milliliters	× 29.57
gallons	pints	× 8 #
gallons (UK)	cubic feet	× 0.1605
gallons (UK)	gallons (US)	× 1.2009
gallons (UK)	liters	× 4.54609
gallons (US)	cubic feet	× 0.1337
gallons (US)	gallons (UK)	× 0.8327
gallons (US)	liters	× 3.785
grams	kilograms	/ 1000
grams	ounces	/ 28.35
hectares	acres	× 2.471
hectares	square km	/ 100
hectares	square meters	× 10000
hectares	square miles	/ 259

From	To	Formula
hectares	square yards	× 11 960
inches	centimeters	× 2.54
inches	feet	/ 12
kilograms	ounces	× 35.3
kilograms	pounds	× 2.2046
kilograms	tonnes	/ 1000
kilograms	tons (UK/long)	/ 1016
kilograms	tons (US/short)	/ 907
kilometers	meters	× 1000
kilometers	miles	× 0.6214
liters	cu.inches	× 61.02
liters	gallons (UK)	× 0.2200
liters	gallons (US)	× 0.2642
liters	pints (UK)	× 1.760
liters	pints (US liquid)	× 2.113
meters	yards	/ 0.9144
meters	centimeters	× 100
miles	kilometers	× 1.609
millimeters	inches	/ 25.4
ounces	grams	× 28.35
pints (UK)	liters	× 0.5683
pints (UK)	pints (US liquid)	× 1.201
pints (US liquid)	liters	× 0.4732
pints (US liquid)	pints (UK)	× 0.8327
pounds	kilograms	× 0.4536
pounds	ounces	× 16
square feet	sq. inches	× 144
square feet	sq. meters	× 0.0929
square inches	square cm	× 6.4516
square inches	square feet	/ 144
square km	acres	× 247
square km	hectares	× 100
square km	square miles	× 0.3861
square meters	acres	/ 4047
square meters	hectares	/ 10 000
square meters	square feet	× 10.76
square meters	square yards	× 1.196
square miles	acres	× 640
square miles	hectares	× 259
square miles	square km	× 2.590
square yards	square meters	/ 1.196
tonnes	kilograms	× 1000
tonnes	tons (UK/long)	× 0.9842
tonnes	tons (US/short)	× 1.1023
tons (UK/long)	kilograms	× 1016

From	To	Formula
tons (UK/long)	tonnes	× 1.016
tons (US/short)	kilograms	× 907.2
tons (US/short)	tonnes	× 0.9072
yards	meters	× 0.9144

CAREER ADVANCEMENT

SECTION SIX

There are many opportu-
nities for advancement for
dedicated administrative
assistants who care about
the quality of their work.
Photo by Jennifer Wauson.

43

Your Future

◇ GROWING AS THE COMPANY GROWS

As you begin or continue your career, you have numerous choices regarding type and size of companies. Which is better to work for: a large or a small one? You'll find as many answers as there are administrative assistants. A large company often offers the best available salary and benefits, as well as steady advancement within its corporate structure. Yet small companies, too, offer growth potential. They may not always be able to afford as generous a salary or benefit package but often provide a wider range of experience that would otherwise be impossible to get. And when a small company successfully expands, the administrative assistant has the excitement of getting in on the ground floor and growing with the business. In many instances, the small business administrative assistant can inherit as much responsibility as he or she wants.

◇ LEARN ABOUT THE BUSINESS

It's important that no matter what type of business you work for, what size it is, or where it's located, you should do your best to learn as much about it as possible. This learning process should never stop. Even if your duties are strictly defined and fairly routine, you should do your best to discover how the business is managed, how customers or clients are obtained, and how the products or services provided are produced. Although you may see no immediate need for this knowledge, it can be invaluable in a later emergency, as you advance, or if you seek work with a different company.

◇ UPGRADE YOUR SKILLS

No matter what type or size of company you work for, focus on acquiring essential business skills, whether or not you need any one of them now. Make sure your skills are top-notch in such office-related areas as keyboarding, maintaining a filing system, handling incoming and outgoing mail, setting appointments, answering telephones, taking dictation, and using office machines. Try to acquire proficiency in correspondence, research, customer service, purchasing, budgeting, bookkeeping, invoicing, training new employees, and supervising an office staff. You should learn how to write and speak effectively and be able to plan and organize your work. And finally, you must be computer literate. Having all these skills gives you the most flexible preparation to meet any challenge you face—either an on-the-job crisis or a career opportunity.

As proof of the level of quality of your skills, you may want to investigate being certified by the International Association of Administrative Professionals (formerly the National Secretaries Association) as a Certified Professional Secretary (CPS) or Certified Administrative Professional (CAP). This certification is granted only upon the successful completion of examinations in various aspects of secretarial/administrative procedures and skills. Serious secretaries and administrative assistants may find it worthwhile to inquire about the activities of this outstanding association. Being certified can be a tremendous boost to your career.

◇ RECOGNIZING A TIME FOR CHANGE

One of the trends in modern business is the changing nature of administrative work. Today in businesses of all sizes, more managers are doing work on their own desktop computer systems that in the past would have been handled by a secretary. As these trends continue, there will be fewer and fewer secretaries and more office and information specialists. It's up to you to create a place for yourself in this changing world.

Learning new skills and improving your old ones is the best professional insurance you can acquire, and it can put you in the position of being a better secretary than your current position demands. If you cannot expand your current role but are capable of much more than you're doing, your dissatisfaction may lead you to want to change your direction in life and seek out a new job. Your new skills will help you get the best possible situation.

These skills will also prove invaluable if change is forced upon you. Gone are the days when a secretary might work forty-five years for the same company, many of those years for the same boss. This is true of both large and small companies. A large company used to provide stability, but no longer. Corporate restructurings, which have affected hundreds of thousands of people over the past years, have been a mixed blessing for administrative assistants. In the wake of restructuring, some assistants have to leave their position when their boss leaves, but others are asked to take on greater responsibility, to "take up the slack" as middle managers are phased out. Either situation could be professionally devastating if it was not what the administrative assistant would have chosen himself or herself.

On the other hand, small businesses have their own dangers, particularly in the first eighteen months of operation, though knowing that doesn't make it easier for the secretary who faces possible job loss. Rather than restructure, a small business may just fold completely, perhaps without giving you adequate notice, perhaps even without giving you a final paycheck.

Always be alert to conditions or changes that could affect your job, no matter what size company you work for. In a large company, be wary if your boss is excluded from meetings he or she used to attend, is dropped from routing lists, or is told to cut back on budget and staff. Do people who used to lunch or chat with your boss no longer do so? These warning signs can also signal that your own position might be in jeopardy.

In a small business where you work directly for the owner, pay attention to details. Has business been slipping lately? Is it just a temporary slump or something more serious? Has the boss paid vendors and other creditors, or are you starting to receive dunning letters and telephone calls? Of critical importance to you is whether the boss has paid payroll taxes and health insurance premiums. If your boss has not and the business folds, the Internal Revenue Service will look to the individual worker to pay the overdue taxes even though the money was already withheld from earlier paychecks. The individual may have no healthcare coverage even though deductions for premiums may have been taken. And the individual might not even be able to collect unemployment benefits though taxes for that were deducted too.

What should you do if something like this should happen to you? Your best bet is to consult an attorney; however, be advised that though you might file and win a lawsuit against your former employer, collecting your judgment may prove to be difficult and costly.

The better advice is to be aware of the financial health of your employer so you can take action before it's forced on you. These events are the exception, but it's better to be employed and equipped with this knowledge than to experience it naively when you can least afford it.

◇ FINDING A NEW JOB

When, for whatever reason, you feel the need to find a new job, explore all possible ways. Don't simply look in the paper or sign up at an employment agency for a position as a secretary, administrative assistant, or office manager. A more aggressive search can find you a more satisfying position.

Start by researching companies you might want to work for or areas where you might like to work. With newspapers and trade journals in hand, read about companies that were voted "family friendly," instituted company-wide training programs in computers or second languages, or have a strong policy of promoting from within. One company might be known for its laid-back atmosphere and flexible hours. Another might be known for its hard-driving excellence. Which interests you more? Which do you need more? These are the companies to target.

Locally, drive around office or industrial parks or anywhere else businesses are located. Stop in and talk and ask questions. Find out what the business does and if there are any job openings. These cold-call in-person visits are not as difficult as they might sound. If you are friendly and don't take up too much time, you can gain much valuable information.

You can also conduct research by looking through directories available in larger public libraries. The Better Business Bureau and the Chamber of Commerce of the town or city you're interested in can give you lists of local businesses. Both organizations are also good sources for checking the reputation of a particular business you may be interested in.

Tap your network of relatives, friends, neighbors, and professional associates for information. That insurance agent who calls, that vendor you talk to so frequently, that secretary you met at an office skills conference—these are just some of the people to tell when you're looking for a new position.

Also check job postings on Internet job sites such as Monster.com and HotJobs.com.

You can conduct searches by key word, city, or date. These websites also allow you to post your resumé for perspective employers.

Finally, don't overlook temporary placement services. One benefit is that many agencies provide free training on new equipment and software packages, which can make you more desirable to a prospective employer. A second benefit is that temporary work allows you to experience different companies as an insider; once you find a company you like, apply for full-time work. Yet another benefit is that temporary work allows you maximum flexibility in scheduling your personal time.

◇ Your Resumé

No matter which path you take to look for a new job, you need a professional-looking resumé, the document describing your work history and skills to a potential employer. There are two basic formats to follow. One focuses on a history of where you've worked (Figure 43–1) and the other on particular skills you have (Figure 43–2). All resumés should include:

- Your name, address, and telephone number
- Your educational background: schools attended; degrees, diplomas, or certificates awarded; special training received or courses attended
- A listing of all previous employment
- Your current job

One mistake many people make on a resumé is attempting to explain why they left one job and moved on to another. This is not the place to discuss it. You may be asked this question in an interview, so be prepared with an answer, but don't volunteer it in your resumé.

It can be very useful to prepare several versions of a resumé, adapting the basic facts to emphasize the different skills required for different jobs. Suppose the administrative assistant were applying for a position in a sales department. She might want to rewrite the skills-format version of her resumé, putting her sales experience as the first item and enlarging upon it wherever possible. Did she work with sales representatives? Did she handle objections or close calls herself? Did she find new prospects for the salespeople? Emphasizing this side of her experience could make her more attractive to the interviewer.

This in no way means you should make up qualifications. If you do, it could prove disastrous if you are called on to perform a task you claim to be experienced at doing.

The Cover Letter

Along with your resumé, you should also include an application or cover letter that states your interest in a particular job, briefly lists your qualifications, and explains why you might like to work for this particular employer (Figure 43–3).

Evelyn Flo Boyd
12345 Heartside Drive
Western Branch, GA 31234
404-555-1234

Experience

2007–Present   Lyon's Still Photography
Acworth, Georgia

Office manager and assistant to business owner
Maintained files and records, accounts receivable, and customer database.
Assisted photographer with photo subjects, as well as sales of proofs and prints.
Handled scheduling of business activities, all correspondence, and travel arrangements.

1997–2007   Third Coast Video, Inc.
Austin, Texas

Office assistant
Scheduled clients and facilities for video production and postproduction facility.
Scheduled freelance crews and equipment rentals. Arranged for shipping of equipment and travel for crews. Also handled invoicing and correspondence.

Education
1993–1997   B.A.–English
University of Texas
Austin, Texas

References furnished upon request.

Figure 43–1. Sample resumé in a chronological format.

✦ THE INTERVIEW

If your resumé and letter are successful, your next step will be an interview with the prospective employer. There are several ways you can prepare and techniques you can use for conducting yourself during it:

- Examine your image. How do you look to the outside world? Consider the way you dress, the way you talk, even the way you stand. Can you talk to someone and look that person in the eye, rather than glance around or stare at your feet?

- How about your skills? Can you do anything that someone would want to hire you to do?

- What about experience? Have you ever practiced these skills in an employment situation?

- How much money do you want? What are employers in your area willing to pay for your skills? Find this out before you go to the interview by asking people and checking resources at the library, Chamber of Commerce, or Better Business Bureau.

- What do you know about the company where you're going to interview? How does it make money? What does its success depend on?

Evelyn Flo Boyd
12345 Heartside Drive
Western Branch, GA 31234
404-555-1234

Experience

ADMINISTRATION — Maintained files and records, accounts receivable, and customer database. Handled scheduling of business activities, all correspondence, and travel arrangements.

SALES — Worked with customers to set appointments and to sell photography services.

VIDEO PRODUCTION — Coordinated scheduling of crews and facilities. Hired freelance crews and outline equipment rentals.

TECHNICAL SKILLS — Complete understanding of IBM-compatible software including: Windows, Word for Windows, Excel, and WordPerfect. Also, some understanding of Apple Macintosh computers including Microsoft Word and Excel. Good typing skills (50 wpm). Working knowledge of most office equipment, copiers, fax machines, and typewriters.

Work History
2007–Present
Office Manager and Assistant to Business Owner
Lyon's Still Photography
Acworth, Georgia

1997–2007
Office Assistant
Third Coast Video, Inc.
Austin, Texas

Education
1993–1997 B.A.–English
University of Texas
Austin, Texas

References furnished upon request.

Figure 43–2. Sample resumé in a skills format.

If you can find out this information, you'll be prepared to show how you can help make the business better. And that's what an employer wants to hear.

12345 Heartside Drive
Western Branch, GA 31234
December 2, 2008

Mr. Kevin Wilson
President
Videologies, Inc.
10 North Main St.
Atlanta, GA 30303

Dear Mr. Wilson,

I am very interested in applying for the job of office assistant listed in the *Atlanta Constitution* on December 1.

As you can see from my enclosed resumé, I have worked for both a still photographer and a small video production company. I enjoyed working at both of these companies, and I feel this past experience qualifies me for the position described in your advertisement.

I have a good understanding of the visual medium and the many details you must handle in your work. I believe I can help take responsibility for some of these details with little additional training.

I would appreciate the opportunity for a personal interview. You can reach me at 555-1234.

Thank you for your consideration.

Sincerely yours,

Evelyn Boyd

Figure 43–3. Job application cover letter.

Presentation Skills

◆ WHY MAKE PRESENTATIONS?

As you grow in your career, one way to demonstrate your knowledge and abilities is by making presentations. Perhaps you won't be making presentations at a board of directors meeting, but there will be opportunities to make presentations to your co-workers. For example, your boss may ask you to present a new company policy, or you volunteer to host a lunch-and-learn where you share some of your knowledge in the form of a presentation. You might make presentations on behalf of your boss at regular company meetings.

A formal presentation is a planned event where one or more people speak, visual aids such as PowerPoint or handouts are used, and the purpose is to pass along information that will be useful to the audience.

One key aspect in making a presentation is that it involves public speaking. Many people rate public speaking as their number one fear. Essentially, they are afraid the audience won't accept them; however, this is not true. The audience wants the speaker to succeed. They're glad you are the one speaking and not them. All you need to do in order to be a successful presenter is be prepared, confident, and relaxed. Good preparation will calm your nerves and help you avoid making mistakes.

◆ PREPARING YOUR PRESENTATION

Whenever you are faced with giving a presentation, you should start by focusing on the purpose. Ask yourself: Why am I speaking? What do I want to achieve? What should the audience get from the presentation? What are their needs and expectations? What will be their attitude toward my ideas? What do they already know? Do they need to hear the presentation in a particular order?

Good presenting is about entertaining as well as conveying information. Your audience will remember more if they enjoy themselves.

You'll have approximately ten to fifteen seconds at the start of your presentation to make a positive first impression, so make sure your opening is strong and well rehearsed. Don't start with a joke, since jokes are risky. And, if something goes wrong, don't apologize for anything.

The average attention span of your audience is only about five to eight minutes, so you need to spice up your material to help keep your audience interested. For example, you might include stories, questions, pictures, cartoons, video clips, sound clips, graphs, audience participation, quotes, and props.

Structure

No matter how interesting your material is, your audience will have a difficult time following your presentation if it is carelessly assembled. The structure of your presentation should be simple, clear, and logical.

Start by breaking your main topic into three to five ideas. Then, present each idea along with supporting materials and evidence. Make sure you cite any sources for your data. Some common presentation structures include:

- Problem and solution
- Comparisons
- Chronological order
- Theory and practice
- Desire and action

If your presentation will be longer than forty-five minutes, you need to plan on giving your audience a break. You need to let everyone get up and stretch their legs, otherwise they'll fade out on you regardless of how engaging your presentation. After ninety minutes, you need to schedule a break to allow your audience to use the restrooms.

One thing you can do to take the pressure off yourself is to not talk the entire time. Plan your presentation to include audience participation. Have the audience work together to communicate and solve problems.

Starting and Ending Your Presentation

Before you begin your presentation, you will have gathered some ideas about who your audience is and how they will receive your message. As you begin speaking, your audience will be deciding whether you are worth listen to. Are you interesting? Are you energetic, enthusiastic, and sincere?

The first words out of your mouth must get your audience's attention. You must entice them to listen to you. Here are several suggestions for how to start your presentation:

- Ask the audience a question.
- Quote from someone famous.
- Tell a story.
- Provide some historical background.
- Talk about a current issue in the news.
- Shock your audience with statistics, announcements, and warnings.

Whatever you decide to do, the opening must naturally lead into the body of your presentation. In addition to getting your audience's attention, your introduction should also provide a statement about the purpose of your presentation. You should include an agenda of topics that will be covered.

To conclude your presentation, you should give your audience something they can take with them by summarizing key points, calling for action, asking a question, telling another story, or using a prop or visual aid.

Visual Aids

Visual aids improve the retention of the spoken word by up to 70 percent. Therefore, if you can include printed visual aids (such as handouts) or a projected PowerPoint presentation, you will improve your audience's memory.

When creating PowerPoint presentations, follow these guidelines:

- Keep your slides uncluttered and simple.
- Don't have more than five words to a line.
- Don't have more than seven lines per slide.
- Don't overuse PowerPoint animations and sound effects.
- Use a readable serif font, such as Times, for your headlines.
- Use 14- to 16-point fonts for headlines.
- Use sans serif fonts for your body text. Arial is a popular sans serif font.
- Use no more than two different fonts on each slide.
- Use no more than size/bold/italic combinations.
- Use 12- to 14-point fonts for body text.
- Avoid all uppercase (capital letters) for the body text.
- Use uppercase for headings if you wish.

In addition to PowerPoint presentations, your visual aids can include overhead transparencies, flip charts, photographs, illustrations, maps, graphs, and diagrams.

Handouts

Handouts can also be useful in reinforcing the concepts of your presentation. You can use handouts to provide background material or additional reading material. You can distribute handouts before your presentation or make them available afterward. Handouts should be simple and directly related to the presentation.

For many business presentations that use PowerPoint slides, a copy of the slides is printed in handouts view, with two or three slides per printed page. This gives the audience a place to take notes. One key thing to watch for with handouts is distracting your audience. If you want the audience to pay attention to you rather than having their noses buried in your handouts, distribute the handouts when you are finished.

◇ DELIVERING YOUR PRESENTATION

There are several ways you can deliver your presentation. For example, you can read your notes, memorize your speech, or speak extemporaneously. Free flowing or extemporaneous speaking is usually the most effective style of delivery, since you are able to connect with your audience, make eye contact, and be sincere. While it is unnecessary to write out the entire script of your presentation, many presenters prefer this step. The process of writing helps them remember the presentation later. If you must, you can use cue cards to help jog your memory with key bullet points.

Always rehearse your presentation. Never go into an important presentation without giving yourself time to practice. Some people practice while driving to work. Others practice at home in front of a mirror. The more you practice, the more effective you'll be. As you refine your delivery, you can focus on body language, movement, use of hands, and eye contact. You'll also be more comfortable using your visual aids.

Always check the room where you'll be delivering your presentation. Give yourself enough time to rearrange the room if necessary. Try to get comfortable in the room before anyone else arrives.

While it is natural to feel nervous before a presentation, your job as a presenter is to harness that anxiety and use it to energize your presentation. Without this energy, your presentation can be lifeless.

You can control your nervousness by rehearsing, visualizing a successful presentation, and using positive thinking. Yogic breathing techniques are also helpful. By exhaling completely and holding your diaphragm tightly, you can squeeze out the nervousness. Deep breathing also helps.

As you begin delivering your presentation, speak naturally and loudly enough so you can be heard. Enunciate clearly and vary the pitch and the pace.

Pausing between thoughts is sometimes as important as the thoughts themselves. It gives the audience time to digest what you've just said.

Be aware of your body language, since the way you use your body enhances or weakens your message. Use your hands, your posture, and facial expressions to emphasize your message. Audiences are generally impressed by enthusiasm, energy, and sincerity. Your audience will see you this way if you stand tall, smile, act confident, keep eye contact, gesture when appropriate, and look as if you are enjoying yourself.

For most presentations, people want to ask questions; therefore, it is important that you anticipate the kind of questions you'll get and be prepared to answer them. One good way to manage your presentation is to hold audience questions until the end of the presentation. In many cases, a question someone asks at the beginning is covered later in the presentation itself.

As your audience asks questions, listen carefully and make sure you understand the question. It's a good idea to rephrase the question in your own words, so that everyone can hear it and to confirm that you understood the question correctly. Your answer should be concise and refer to any visuals or slides in your presentation.

If a person asks a long and rambling question, paraphrase only part of it and give it a short answer. Usually, this satisfies the person.

If people in your audience begin to talk among themselves, stop and look at them. You don't have to say anything, just look at them. They'll soon get the point. This technique can work with an entire unsettled audience too.

Don't be defensive when answering questions. Keep your body language open and be as pleasant as possible. Don't make up an answer. If you don't know the answer, be honest and tell your questioner you'll follow up with an answer later. Don't get into arguments with an individual in the audience. And, if you need time to think about a question, take your time and pause.

Don't end your presentation with a "thank you." Your audience should be thanking you; you shouldn't be thanking them. The same goes for "any questions" or "that's it." If you plan time for taking questions, always have a final presentation summary ready that truly concludes your presentation. Inspire your audience. Energize them to follow your ideas and take action. End with a statement or a question that summarizes your presentation in one sentence. If there's only one thing your audience should do or remember when you are finished, now is the time to make sure you communicate it.

◇ GROUP PRESENTATIONS

Sometimes business presentations are made by teams. The same principles apply whether you are delivering a presentation alone or in a group; however, you need to pay attention to the roles of the team members, plan the transitions between individual team member speeches, and provide each other with support and feedback.

Make an assessment of the team's strengths and weaknesses with regard to speaking skills. The strongest speakers should introduce and close the presentation.

The first speaker should introduce the group and try to capture the attention of the audience, motivate them, and give them a preview of the main ideas that will be covered in the presentation. The last speaker needs to summarize the presentation so that the key concepts are reinforced from a different perspective.

The transitions between speakers that occur in group presentations can sometimes be problems, because each individual is working on his or her speech by him or herself. Some attention needs to be given to the entire presentation as a whole and how each person contributes to the common purpose. Therefore, each person adds value to the group. So, rather than just announcing the next person to talk, you can introduce the important concepts the next speaker will cover.

While various members of the team are speaking, make sure you support the speaker. Don't fiddle with your notes or look off into space. Keep your attention on the speaker. If anyone in the audience looks at you, he or she should see that all your attention is focused intently on what the current speaker is saying.

After you finish your group presentation, spend some time reviewing what happened and learn how to make improvements in the future. Did you achieve your objective? Were your visual aids effective? Did the schedule and transitions work out OK? Did anything unexpected happen? What could you do differently next time?

The team members in a group presentation should coach each other throughout the process, from researching and writing to rehearsing and refinement. Then, when you've completed your presentation, you work together as a team of coaches, providing positive and constructive feedback as well as congratulations. By having everyone involved and contributing, a successful group presentation can be a very rewarding work experience.

CHAPTER 45

Communications Skills

Good communications skills are critical to your success in business. You have to be able to communicate your ideas as well as respond to ideas from others. You have to be able to respond to questions, handle conflict, and listen.

Communication starts when two or more people need to exchange information. Perhaps one of your co-workers wants to ask you a question. Perhaps you want to ask your boss something. Perhaps you want someone to do something for you. Each of these situations involves communication.

Talking is not the same thing as communication. Communication is more complicated: it often involves listening and speaking skillfully as you interact with people who are fearful, angry, or frustrated. Miscommunication occurs when we fail to communicate clearly. Many times it is the cause of the conflict in the first place.

◇ GIVING FEEDBACK

Feedback means giving information back to someone. When we think about feedback, most of us think of an opportunity to give someone your opinion about something he or she did. The purpose of the feedback is to make the situation better next time.

When you offer feedback in business, think about the following:

- Be clear about what you want to say to the person.

- Focus on the positive rather than the negative aspects of the performance.

- Be specific and use people's names and project names rather than pronouns like him, her, it, that, and them.

- Focus on the behavior, not the person.

- Explain what should be changed about the behavior.

- Be descriptive about the change you desire, rather than evaluating the behavior as good or bad.

- Give your own feedback, not someone else's.

- Avoid generalizations like always, never, or all.

◇ LISTENING

Only about 25 percent of listeners grasp the ideas being communicated. To be a more effective listener, mentally summarize what a speaker is saying. Listen between the lines to the tone of the person's voice. Weigh any evidence the person provides in stating his or her position. As you listen, think about what's in the message for you. How can you benefit from what the speaker is saying? Fight distractions and concentrate on the person and the message. Avoid judging a speaker until he or she has finished offering all the evidence that supports his or her position.

Don't get distracted by a speaker's poor communications habits. Skip over the delivery errors and focus on the message. Look for central ideas that are the main point of the conversation. Try to keep eye contact with the speaker and help the speaker along by showing an active body posture. Good listeners listen with their faces as well as their ears.

To help remember what was said, take notes during the talk or immediately after the speaker has finished.

◇ NONVERBAL COMMUNICATIONS

Nonverbal communications includes facial expressions, tone of voice, speaking style, gestures, eye contact, posture, touch, and movement. In the case of nonverbal communications, it's not what you say—it's how you say it. Nonverbal messages are an essential part of the communications process.

Your awareness of nonverbal behavior allows you to better understand what a speaker really means. You'll become a better communicator yourself if you learn how to use nonverbal signals that reinforce your point.

Some of the major nonverbal communication behaviors are:

- Eye contact
- Facial expressions
- Gestures made by the arms and hands
- Posture
- Body position in relationship to the listener
- Closeness between the speaker and listener
- Paralinguistics

Eye contact is an important aspect of interpersonal communication because it helps regulate communication. It's like the "uh-huh" of the telephone, which acknowledges that the listener is still there and tuned in. Eye contact shows you are interested in the speaker. Eye contact by a speaker helps increase the speaker's credibility and shows interest, concern, warmth, and credibility.

Perhaps the most powerful facial expression is the smile. Smiling shows happiness, friendliness, and warmth. If you want to come across as likeable and approachable, smile when you speak or listen.

If you don't use your hands while speaking, you come across as boring and stiff. The use of gestures animates your communication as a speaker, capturing your listener's attention and making the material more interesting. As a listener, your head nods to indicate that you are listening.

The way you walk, stand, or sit also communicates information about yourself. Standing tall and leaning slightly forward indicates that you are approachable, receptive, and friendly.

Cultural norms dictate maintaining a certain distance between communicators. You should look for signs of discomfort from others including rocking, leg swimming, finger tapping, and averting one's gaze. Typically, in a group meeting, being too close is not an issue. In fact, there is usually too much distance. To counteract this, arrange your meeting rooms so presenters can interact with their audience and make eye contact with everyone in the group.

Paralinguistics is an aspect of nonverbal communication that involves the tone, pitch, and rhythm of your voice. The idea is to avoid being monotone and boring. Good communicators learn to modulate their voices, use pauses, vary the pitch, raise and lower the loudness, and use inflection as additional communications tools.

INTERVIEWS

One form of communication that is very common in business is the interview. Whether you are interviewing for a job or interviewing someone else, it's important to understand the proper way to conduct an interview. As your business grows and as your role in the business changes, you will likely be involved in conducting interviews of prospective candidates for new positions.

Interviews are a form of communication used for getting the story behind someone's resumé. The interviewer can pursue in-depth information around a topic. An interview might be useful as a follow-up to certain answers on an application. Usually, open-ended questions are asked during interviews.

Before you design your interview questions, make sure you have a clear purpose for the information that will be gathered. This helps you focus on the answers and help you skillfully select follow-up questions.

Getting Started

In preparing for an interview, select a setting that won't be distracting. Try to find a quiet, private place where the interviewee will feel comfortable.

When you meet the interviewee, explain the purpose of the interview. Explain any issues surrounding confidentiality. Let the person know who will get access to information and how answers will be analyzed.

Explain the format of the interview and how it will be conducted. If you want the person to ask questions, let him or her know questions are welcome, or ask the person to wait until the end of the interview. You can also invite questions at the start of the interview.

Types of Interviews

There are several different styles of interviews. The informal, conversational interview has no predetermined questions. The interview remains as open and adaptable as possible depending on the interviewee.

The guided approach to interviewing ensures that the same general information is collected from each interviewee. There's still a degree of freedom for the interviewer, but there's more focus on obtaining specific information in each interview.

The open-ended interview uses a set of open-ended questions that are asked of all interviewees. With an open-ended interview, the respondent is free to decide how he or she wants to answer. This approach results in faster interviews that are easier to analyze and compare.

The closed fixed-response interview is where all interviewees are asked the same questions from a questionnaire with the same set of multiple choice answers.

Types of Interview Questions

There are six categories of interview questions that are commonly asked by interviewers during interviews. Any of these questions can focus on the past, the future, or present. The categories are the following:

1. **Behavior**—What a person has done in his or her life or what he/she is currently doing

2. **Opinions and Values**—What a person thinks about a particular topic

3. **Feelings**—How someone feels about a particular topic or situation

4. **Knowledge**—What a person knows about work-related topics

5. **Sensory**—What a person has experienced in life

6. **Background**—Standard questions such as education, work history, and hobbies

Question Sequence

You should try to get the interviewee involved in the interview as soon as possible. The interview shouldn't start out with a long speech by the interviewer. Before asking about things such as feelings and opinions, start by asking about some facts. Using this approach, the person can get involved in the interview before having to talk about personal matters.

Avoid long lists of fact-based questions. Instead, sprinkle them throughout the interview. Ask questions about the present before you explore the past or future. It is usually easier to talk about what is happening right now than to recall past events or project themselves into an imaginary future. Your last question should allow the interviewee a chance to provide any other information that he or she would like to add, as well as provide his/her impressions of how the interview went.

Question Wording

Your questions should be open-ended. A person should be able to answer in his or her own unique way, rather than just answering yes or no. Your questions should be neutral, so that they avoid expressing an opinion that might sway a person's answers. For example, "You wouldn't want to work in a loud, crowded office, would you?" is a question that already assumes the questioner would be seeking a "no" response.

Questions should be asked one at a time, and each question should be worded clearly. For example, avoid using any company- or industry-specific terms or acronyms in your questions that outsiders wouldn't recognize. Finally, avoid asking, "Why?" Questions that ask why infer a cause-effect relationship that may be much more complex than a single question can explain. Why questions also put interviewees on the defensive, as they feel they have to justify their response.

Conducting the Interview

You can't remember everything that is covered during an interview, so you either need to take notes or use a recording device. Make sure you discuss the use of a recorder with the interviewee and explain its purpose. Check the status of the recorder from time to time to make sure it is still functioning.

As you move through the interview focusing on one question at a time, don't show strong emotional reactions to the person's responses. You should act as if you've heard these same answers before. Be matter-of-fact about it.

Provide encouragement by nodding your head and providing "uh-huhs" verbally. If you don't use a recorder and instead are taking notes, be careful when you break away from the person to write something down. This signals that you were surprised or pleased with an answer, which may influence the answers for future questions.

When you move from one topic to another, provide transitions. For example, say something like "We've been talking about your past work history. Now let's talk about where you want to go in your career."

Keep control of the interview. If the interviewee strays over into another topic and takes a long time to answer a question, time may run out before you've completed everything on your list. Refocus the person back on the topic with additional targeted questions.

After the Interview

When the interview is complete, thank the person for attending the interview and say your good-byes. Then you should check the recorder and turn it off. If it is a digital recorder, transfer the file to your computer.

If you've written notes during the interview, check the notes and make sure they make sense to you. If you need to clarify something or rewrite something that may be difficult to read later, do it now. Then, write down any observations you made during the interview. How did the person come across? Was the person confident or nervous? Were there any surprises?

In many cases, a job candidate interviews with a variety of different people in a business or department before being hired. The interview you conduct may thus be one of many. Be prepared to share your observations in the form of a report or as part of a future meeting with other members of the hiring team.

Office Management and Supervision

As your career evolves over time, it may naturally lead to a role as an office manager or supervisor. In a small office, you may run the overall operations of the office while your boss focuses on business relationships. You may be responsible for interviewing new employees and filtering out the best for your boss to meet in follow-up interviews.

◇ THE ROLE OF THE OFFICE MANAGER

Office managers often hold one of two jobs in a company. They may supervise people, or they may be involved in getting a product or service out the door in order to generate revenue for the business. In a small business, you are likely to be involved in both.

In a small business, the office manager may also provide the services of human resources. You may be responsible for coordinating employee benefits, creating personnel polices, furnishing training and development, conducting performance appraisals, and providing career development. You may also have to handle personnel and performance problems.

Regardless of whether you are running the office in a small business or supervising a department in a large business, the supervisor is usually responsible for making sure the employees follow the organization's policies and procedures for things like vacation time, sick time, leaves, and overtime. You may also have responsibilities of hiring, firing, and promotions.

Supervisors must review the career needs of the employees and the staffing needs of the organization. Supervisors are often the first to recognize the need for a new position, and they may open a new role by getting authorization from management. This likely requires communication in order to justify the new role. The supervisor could then be involved in advertising for job candidates, reviewing resumés, and conducting interviews. You may recommend candidates for a job, then handle all the new hire paperwork if the candidate is hired, including benefits, payroll, and tax forms. Finally, your job may involve making sure the new employee has the necessary workspace, office equipment, and supplies.

A supervisor likely makes sure that new employees get an orientation about the business, including the personnel polices, facilities, and work schedule. You may develop a training plan with the employees to make sure they have the skills needed for the job. At various times throughout the year, you may provide ongoing guidance in the form of coaching and counseling. The goal here is to help the employees take responsibility for their own development but to assist them when they need company approval to take classes or take time away from work for training.

Employee performance management may be a responsibility for an office manager or supervisor. The supervisor maintains job descriptions with responsibilities and qualifications for each position. The supervisor sets the performance standards for each job role and ensures that employees have appropriate and realistic goals. Throughout the year, they give the employees feedback on their performance. Performance reviews are then conducted throughout the year to assess how the employees have performed and what they can do to make improvement.

A good supervisor is also a good coach. Coaching involves working with employees to create realistic goals, action plans, and time lines. The supervisor provides ongoing guidance as the employees work toward their goals. There are five aspects of goal setting that can best be remembered by using the acronym SMART:

1. **S**—Specific

2. **M**—Measurable

3. **A**—Attainable

4. **R**—Realistic

5. **T**—Timely

A good coach also acts like a mentor to the employee. Since a supervisor likely understands the organization better than the employee, the supervisor can serve as a mentor offering advice about the job and career. The employee can look to the supervisor as a role model.

Since the supervisor is the first person to share news about new policies and programs, the supervisor must be an advocate for the organization. Employees get confused and fearful whenever change is involved; however, in the rapidly changing business world, change is evitable. The supervisor must be a supporter of the organization's change initiatives to help reduce the anxiety. You must be authentic in how your present your feelings about new programs and organization change, yet tactful in how you present it.

At the same time, a supervisor must also be an advocate for employees and represent employee requests to management. For example, if an employee deserves a promotion, the supervisor must often justify the reason to management.

It's not unusual for a supervisor to be seen by employees as being one of them and a part of management at the same time. It's a unique combination that has both pluses and negatives.

BUILDING TRUST WITH YOUR TEAM

Trust is important to the relationship between a supervisor and an employee. Teams that trust each other are more productive and have fewer personnel issues. With trust, you learn to depend on each other. There's really no substitute for trust; your team either has it or it doesn't.

Trusting the people on your team means that your employees are willing to take your word for it when you tell them they need to do something they don't really want to do. Trust means you're willing to be influenced. Trust elevates performance because team members are willing to do things without debate.

A conversation is a relationship. Each person influences the other. A supervisor can't build trust with employees without being able to listen. In addition, you must share important information about yourself. You must be vulnerable in order to build trust. There must be a certain amount of interdependence in order to build trust. We must depend on others and they must depend on us. Fulfilling your promises and being fair helps build trust.

Acceptance is the key to trust, so avoid office humor that belittles people. Avoid put-downs or conversations that show disrespect. Trust is built over time as it is used. Disrespect erodes the trust that has been established.

Some people are more likely to trust than others. It depends on their history of experience. It also depends on their character in general. If they've learned not to trust people in the past, or they can't even trust themselves, then they will not trust you either.

Key aspects of trust include the following:

- **Ability**—Has knowledge skills and competencies, so that the person performs in a way that meets your expectations

- **Integrity**—Maintains accepted behavior based on past actions, credibility of communications, and fairness

- **Benevolence**—Is concerned about the welfare of others; would like to advance others or not impede them

- **Open communication**—Shares control and delegates decisions

CONFLICT MANAGEMENT

Another aspect of being an office manager or supervisor is conflict management. Conflict occurs when two or more values, perspectives, or opinions are opposite in nature. You may experience personal conflict when you don't live up to your own values. You experience conflict with someone else when your values or points of view are threatened. You may experience conflict because of fear of the unknown or a lack of fulfillment. Conflict is inevitable and is a natural phase in the team-building process. When you have a diversity of ideas, it often leads to contradictory opinions.

Conflict often helps raise important issues to the forefront. It causes us to work on the most important issues and motivates people to participate in solving problems. Conflict management helps people learn to recognize differences in opinion and learn from those differences. Therefore, conflict isn't the problem. The problem is when conflict is managed poorly. When this happens, conflict hampers productivity, lowers employee morale, mushrooms into larger conflicts, and causes people to react inappropriately.

A supervisor can cause workplace conflict by communicating poorly with employees. If employees are constantly surprised by new programs and policies without having their supervisor explain the situation, the employees don't understand the reasons for the decisions and feel left out of the process and disrespected. As a result, people will resort to getting information from the rumor-mill.

Conflict can be caused by poor leadership, when a manager or supervisor passes the buck rather than dealing with issues head on. If decisions are inconsistent, uniformed, or completely missing, conflict is evitable.

Workplace conflict can also occur when there are not enough resources to go around or there is a disagreement about who does what. Conflict can occur because of personal chemistry between co-workers or between managers and employees. Strong personalities may clash. Opposite opinions may collide.

Minimizing Conflicts

There are several things you can do to minimize conflict at work. Start by reviewing the job descriptions of your team. Set up meetings with your employees and discuss the job descriptions together. Are they still accurate? Do they need to be revised? Make sure that the job roles for your team don't conflict with one another.

Take time to build relationships with each of your employees. Meet with them one-on-one at least once a month. Talk about accomplishments and any issues. You should also hold regular management meetings with your entire team to discuss initiatives and the status of major projects.

Ask your team to provide regular status reports and include accomplishments, current issues, needs from management, and plans for the upcoming period.

You can minimize conflict by training your team on conflict management, delegation skills, and interpersonal communications.

Document the procedures and processes in your department so employees have job aids that describe how to perform routine tasks. Have the employees write the procedures when possible. Distribute the procedures to your team and train the team, so that team members can back each other up for business continuity purposes.

Difficult People

One unpleasant part of being an office manager or supervisor is that from time to time you have to work with difficult people. Difficult people are unhappy people. They are working for the negative side of their personality. They don't intentionally wake up each morning and decide to be difficult. They are often unaware of themselves and how their attitude affects others. They don't realize how their attitude is harmful to the team and to their own careers.

As a supervisor, you are constantly faced with situations where people challenge your decisions and make it difficult to get things done. It's important to be able to understand other people's viewpoints and why they act a certain way.

One well-recognized trait, especially with technical people, is the know-it-all. This trait is often seen with computer programmers, software developers, engineers, doctors, and attorneys. You might ask a know-it-all a simple question and get the response, "How dare you question me." Or, you might make a suggestion for how to do a task and get a multitude of reasons why your idea won't work. Eventually, you give up trying to work with the know-it-all.

This trait is a manifestation of arrogance. People act arrogantly to avoid feeling vulnerable or insecure. They are afraid of being seen as unworthy or incompetent, so they throw up a defensive shield of arrogance. The result of this behavior is that people refuse to work with them, no one believes what they say, people don't think they really know what they're doing, and they lose credibility and respect.

Another common trait of difficult people is the my-way-or-the-highway attitude. This trait seems prevalent in management positions. No matter what anyone else thinks, these people force their ideas on everyone. There is no open discussion about issues. Things must be done the way these people want or else. As an example, if you were in a meeting with this type of person and offered a suggestion, the my-way-or-the-highway person would make it clear your suggestions were not wanted. Eventually, no one wants to contribute, and the added value that comes from having a diversity of ideas is lost.

This trait is an aspect of dominance. Working with this type of person is like living under a dictatorship. When you combine dominance with power, this person becomes king of the planet. The positive side of dominance is leadership. When such people focus on the positive side of their personality, they can be effective and charming. But if these people come under stress, they quickly jump to the dark side.

The result of becoming domineering is that the team refuses to interact with these individuals. People won't tell them the truth or provide them with enough information that might help them make better decisions. People try to ignore the domineering characters and avoid implementing their ideas.

How to Handle Difficult People

When you are working with people who go into attack mode or become extremely defensive, don't try to argue with them. These people are very insecure and the more you push, the worse it gets. Since these people are probably under stress, wait until another time to pursue the discussion. If they are always this way, the only alternative is to find someone else with whom to work. Keep your self-confidence and don't allow yourself to be attacked verbally. If your boss is one of these difficult people, it's probably time to find another job.

When supervising difficult people, try to help them see how their behavior is damaging their career. Set goals that help them learn to work better with others, and monitor their behavior closely to see if it improves. If their attitude doesn't improve, you'll have to terminate their employment.

If you find that you are becoming a difficult person yourself, learn to recognize the signs. Try not to react so quickly, and realize that you are not being attacked personally. Learn to listen when someone else asks a question or makes a suggestion. Repeat what someone has said to confirm that you understand. Ask the person to restate the question or comment if you are still unclear about what was intended. Take some time before you respond. This helps reduce the stress, so you can make a decision without feeling under pressure.

Realize that other people have good ideas that are just as valid as your own. Look for courses or workshops that teach listening skills or team building. Look for someone in the organization who can help you work on the situation. Ask him or her to let you know when you're being a jerk, to call your attention to your behavior. You have to realize that this learned behavior may take years to overcome, but don't give up on yourself.

As you prepare to work with difficult people on the job, you should do the following:

- Confront difficult people face-to-face and by yourself.

- Write down the issue that needs to be handled and your goal for the outcome of your conversation.

- Write down a list of points you need to make to support your goal.

- Write down the objections or reactions the other person may have to your view.

- Organize your notes and gather supportive documents and evidence.

- Arrange a meeting in a private place where you will not be disturbed.

- Hold the meeting and share your view.

- Stay on target by describing your points.

- Listen to the other person's side.

- Communicate and be persistent.

The more frequently you confront and deal directly with difficult people, the easier it becomes. The amount of time it takes to prepare for these types of meetings will decrease. The result is that you will become stronger and tougher.

When you confront and handle these types of situations, people will respect you for your courage and control. Taking positive action in the face of fear is an important trait shared by successful people.

Index

46 ■ OFFICE MANAGEMENT

46 ■ OFFICE MANAGEMENT